COOK SMARTER WITH CHATGPT

A PRACTICAL GUIDE TO USING CHATGPT FOR RECIPES, PLANNING, AND KITCHEN CONFIDENCE

MARC CHAMPAGNE

ANDY FORBES

Roadmap Press
Hillsboro, Virginia, United States

This book is intended for informational purposes only. The authors are not medical professionals or nutritionists, and the guidance in this book is not a substitute for medical advice, diagnosis, or treatment. Readers should use their own judgment and consult qualified professionals when appropriate. Any actions taken based on the material presented are solely at the reader's discretion and risk.

This is a work of nonfiction. Any examples, scenarios, or dialogues generated with or about AI tools are illustrative and may not reflect current capabilities at the time of reading.

First edition

ISBN: 978-1-969489-09-9 (paperback)
ISBN: 978-1-969489-06-8 (ebook)

To the cooks across the ages whose creativity, patience, and passion turned raw ingredients into nourishment, comfort, and art, and built the foundations every home cook stands on today.

To the researchers, engineers, and dreamers who spent decades advancing artificial intelligence, bringing us to a moment where machines can help us become a little braver, a little more curious, and a little more capable in the kitchen.

And to the growing community working at the intersection of cooking and AI.

To eat is a necessity, but to eat intelligently is an art.

La Rochefoucauld

CONTENTS

ACKNOWLEDGMENTS

We are grateful to the many cooks, technologists, and practitioners who continue to explore what happens when centuries of culinary tradition meet modern artificial intelligence. Your experimentation, generosity, and enthusiasm shape this field in ways that no single book ever could, and we are thankful to be learning alongside you.

This book reflects patterns, decisions, and approaches we have encountered through ongoing conversations with people working at the intersection of cooking and AI. While no publication can anticipate every real-world constraint or nuance, the insights shared by this community continually sharpen our thinking and inform the work presented here.

We also appreciate the thoughtful dialogue and professional exchange that has helped refine these ideas over time. Engaging with practitioners who are actively navigating these challenges has been both humbling and energizing, and those conversations continue to influence how we think about the role of AI in the kitchen.

A special thank you to Dave Middleton for introducing us to one another and helping set this collaboration in motion.

AUTHOR'S NOTE

This book is intended to be both practical and flexible.

It can be read on its own as a guide to cooking with greater confidence, curiosity, and intention. It can also be used alongside modern AI tools, treating the ideas, examples, and patterns presented here as starting points rather than fixed instructions. Many readers will likely move between these approaches, reading a section, experimenting in the kitchen, and returning with new questions or insights.

Cooking is always shaped by context. Ingredients vary by season and location. Equipment differs from kitchen to kitchen. Dietary needs, cultural traditions, and personal taste matter. While AI can help surface options, suggest variations, and reduce friction, it does not replace judgment. We encourage readers to treat both this book and any AI tools they use as collaborators that support decision-making, not authorities that replace it.

The perspectives in this book are informed by ongoing conversations with cooks, technologists, and practitioners exploring the intersection of food and artificial intelligence. Those real-world experiences have influenced how the material is organized and where emphasis is placed, even as the underlying technologies continue to evolve.

We see this work as part of an ongoing conversation. Reader feedback and thoughtful, professional discussion continue to shape how we think about future editions and related projects. Information on how to reach the authors appears later in the book.

PROLOGUE

Cooking has always been a mix of instinct, practice, and a willingness to improvise. Now, we are adding something new to that mix: artificial intelligence.

Tools like ChatGPT can help you plan meals, adapt recipes, build shopping lists, explore unfamiliar cuisines, and turn odds and ends in the refrigerator into something genuinely good. Used well, AI can make cooking feel more approachable, more flexible, and more fun. But as powerful as these tools can be, one principle should guide everything you read in this book and everything you try in your kitchen: use common sense.

AI can suggest flavor combinations, substitutions, techniques, ingredients, and timing. It can help adjust recipes for dietary needs, scale meals for a group, and walk you step by step through unfamiliar dishes. What it cannot do is see your ingredients, smell your food, taste your dish, or know exactly how your stove behaves. It cannot tell whether a forgotten chicken breast in the freezer is past its prime or whether that leftover soup is still safe to eat. You are still the cook. You are still in charge.

Think of AI as a helpful sous-chef: one who occasionally has great ideas, but who still relies on you to check the details, trust your senses, and make the final call. When a suggested recipe does not quite match the ingredients you have, adjust it. When cooking times seem off, rely on experience. When in doubt, be cautious, especially when food safety is involved.

This book exists because we found that AI made our own cooking more enjoyable, more adventurous, and more satisfying. We hope it does the same for you. Use these tools to spark ideas, build confidence, simplify decisions, and remove friction from the kitchen. Just remember to pair their suggestions with your judgment, your preferences, and your good sense.

Cooking has always been personal. AI does not change that. If anything, it makes the journey even more interesting.

Welcome to your smarter kitchen.

1

MEET YOUR AI SOUS CHEF

Ever wished you could have a friendly sous-chef by your side, guiding you through every step of cooking at home? Maybe you've imagined how nice it would be to ask a quick question in the middle of a recipe – *"Is there a substitute for buttermilk?"* or *"What does it mean to sauté, exactly?"* – and get an immediate, helpful answer. In today's kitchens, that wish can be a reality. Thanks to advances in artificial intelligence, you *can* have a virtual helper ready to assist 24/7. This chapter will introduce you to ChatGPT, the AI that's poised to become your new kitchen companion. By the end of this chapter, you'll understand what ChatGPT is (in plain language), how it works, and why it's very different from just Googling a recipe. You'll see the many ways it can help with cooking – from finding recipes and substitutions to rescuing a meal gone wrong. We'll also talk about the art of "prompting" (i.e. how to talk to this AI to get the best answers), and how to personalize its advice to *your* needs and tastes. Finally, we'll walk through real examples that you can try out right away. It's going to feel like having an experienced sous-chef who never gets tired of your questions. So, let's dive in and meet your AI sous chef!

Cooking at home can be fun and rewarding, but it also comes

with its share of little challenges. How many times have you stood in the kitchen, staring at a couple of ingredients, wondering what you can whip up with them? Or maybe you've flipped through recipe books and websites, only to feel overwhelmed by choices. We've all been there. The great news is that you no longer have to figure it all out alone. ChatGPT is here to help. Think of it as the friendliest know-it-all cook you've ever met – one who has read *every* cookbook, knows *every* cuisine, and is endlessly patient. Throughout this chapter, you'll learn how to tap into that vast well of knowledge in a way that's actually useful for **you** as a home cook.

In the pages ahead, we'll start with the basics: what *is* ChatGPT, really, and how does it work? (Don't worry, we'll keep it non-technical and easy to understand.) Then we'll explore all the cool things this AI assistant can do for you in the kitchen. By looking at everyday scenarios – like planning a quick dinner, dealing with missing ingredients, or trying something new – you'll get a clear picture of how ChatGPT can make cooking easier and more enjoyable. We'll also cover some essential tips on how to "talk" to ChatGPT. Just like with a human helper, the way you ask questions matters. You'll discover how to ask clear, specific questions that yield the most helpful answers, and we'll discuss what makes a good cooking prompt versus a not-so-good one.

Crucially, this chapter will also show you how to make ChatGPT's advice *personal*. After all, every kitchen and every cook is different. Maybe you're cooking for a family of four on a budget, or you're a vegan home chef working with limited ingredients – ChatGPT can adapt to *your* situation. You'll learn how to tell the AI about your dietary needs, flavor preferences, and even the gadgets you have (or don't have) so that its suggestions fit you like a glove. We'll go beyond recipes, too. Need to convert ounces to grams? Want to know how to save a too-salty soup? ChatGPT has you covered, and we'll show you how to ask.

By the end of this chapter, you'll have a solid understanding of your new "AI sous chef" and how to use it effectively. The tone here is warm and practical because we want you to feel confident – and even excited – to try things out for yourself. Whether you're a kitchen newbie or an experienced cook, ChatGPT has something to offer you, and using it is like having a conversation with a helpful kitchen buddy. So let's get started on this journey to cook smarter. First up, let's pull back the curtain and see what ChatGPT really is and why it's not your average Google search or recipe website.

WHAT IS CHATGPT, REALLY?

Imagine you're meeting a new kitchen helper for the first time. Before you start cooking together, you'd probably want to know a bit about them – who they are, what they know, and how they operate. So, what *is* ChatGPT, really? In simple terms, ChatGPT is an artificial intelligence program designed to communicate with you through text, almost like a very knowledgeable (and very talkative) pen pal. It's often described as a "large language model," which is a fancy way of saying it's a computer program trained to understand and generate human-like language. But you don't need to worry about the complex science behind it. Here's the gist in plain language: ChatGPT learned by reading millions upon millions of words – from books, articles, recipes, you name it – and from that learning, it gained the ability to respond with its own words when you ask it something. It doesn't have a physical form (no robot arms or magical whisk), and it doesn't "think" or "feel" the way humans do. Instead, it works a bit like a super-advanced prediction engine: when you ask a question, it predicts a useful answer based on all the information it has been trained on.

Now, you might be wondering how this is different from just typing a question into Google. The difference is actually huge. Google (or any search engine) is like a librarian: you ask it a question, and it points you to books or websites where you might find your answer. For example, if you search for "chicken soup recipe," Google will give you a list of links to various chicken soup recipes on different cooking sites. It's then up to you to click those links, read through recipes, and decide which one to follow. ChatGPT, on the other hand, is more like sitting down with a knowledgeable chef and asking them directly, "How do I make chicken soup with what I have on hand?" Instead of giving you a list of links, ChatGPT will *generate an answer for you right then and there*. It might say: "Sure! Let's make a chicken soup. What ingredients do you have?" or if you already listed your ingredients, it might go ahead and outline a personalized recipe. In short, **ChatGPT is conversational and generative** – it creates responses on the fly, tailored to your question, rather than directing you elsewhere.

Another big difference is that ChatGPT remembers context (at least within a single conversation). If you ask it, "How do I make chicken soup?" and then follow up with, "I only have one onion, is that okay?" it understands you're still talking about the chicken soup. Google, in contrast, treats each search separately; it doesn't remember that you were looking at chicken soup a moment ago. This contextual understanding is what makes ChatGPT feel a bit like a human conversation partner. You can have a back-and-forth dialogue, refining your questions and getting more detailed answers. For a home cook, that's a game changer. It means you can ask a broad question, get an answer, then ask a more specific question to clarify – just like you might with a real sous chef or a friend who's guiding you in the kitchen.

So, where does ChatGPT get all this knowledge? As mentioned, it was trained on a vast amount of text, which likely included recipes, cooking tips, culinary articles, and general food knowledge from many parts of the world. It's as if someone had read every cookbook and every food blog and could recall the information when needed. However – and this is important – **ChatGPT isn't infallible or all-knowing.** It doesn't actually **verify** the information like a cookbook author or a chef might. It just generates what seems plausible based on what it "learned." Most of the time for common cooking questions, that's perfectly fine. It can tell you the boiling point of water or suggest that basil goes well with tomatoes because those are well-established facts it picked up. But sometimes ChatGPT might sound confident and still give an incorrect answer (for example, if it got some cooking times or rare recipes mixed up in its training data). Think of it this way: it's book-smart, not necessarily experienced in a kitchen. Unlike a seasoned chef who has cooked a recipe hundreds of times, ChatGPT is pulling from written knowledge. This means that while it's *extremely* useful, you should still use your own judgment on things like whether a cooking time seems too short or if an ingredient substitution makes sense. We'll touch more on how to handle those situations later on, but it's good to keep in mind.

Another point to clarify is that ChatGPT is not a traditional recipe site. A recipe site might give you one specific way to make a dish, usually tested by cooks. ChatGPT can give you a recipe too, but it's more flexible. It can combine ideas from multiple recipes, adjust on the fly to fit your needs, and even explain the reasoning behind steps if you ask. It's more of a generalist: instead of specializing in, say, *only Italian cuisine* or *only baking*, it has information about all sorts of cooking. This wide knowledge is great because you can literally ask it *anything*, from "How do I steam broccoli?" to "What's a traditional Thai dessert I could try?" and it will attempt an answer. However, unlike your favorite food blogger, ChatGPT doesn't have personal experiences or original recipes of its own – it creates answers based on patterns in the data it was trained on. If that data had great recipes and advice (and a lot of it did), then it will produce great recipes and advice for you.

Let's also talk about *how* you access ChatGPT, because that's part of understanding what it is. Typically, you interact with ChatGPT through a chat interface on a computer or smartphone. You type in your question or prompt, hit send, and within a few seconds ChatGPT types back a response for you. There's no voice (unless you're using a special app to dictate or speak with it), and it doesn't see or taste things – it relies entirely on text. So, for example, you can't yet show ChatGPT a photo of what's in your fridge (unless you have a version that allows image input) and expect it to identify the ingredients visually. You'd have to list them out in text. Similarly, it can't smell if your milk has gone bad or physically check your oven temperature. You still handle the *physical* side of cooking; ChatGPT handles the *informational* side. It's a tool you wield, like a really sharp knife for knowledge and ideas.

In summary, ChatGPT is a powerful new kind of assistant in the kitchen: one that communicates by conversation, has vast knowledge at its disposal, and can tailor that knowledge to your questions. It's not a search engine handing you links, and it's not a human with actual cooking experience, but it bridges a lot of that gap by giving you quick, context-aware answers. Many home cooks describe using ChatGPT for cooking help as *fun* and even a bit magical – it's like having a conversation with someone who knows an awful lot about food and cooking. Now that we've demystified what ChatGPT is and how it works at a high level, let's get into the exciting part: all the ways you can use it as your **kitchen partner**. After all, even the smartest sous chef is only helpful if you know what to ask of them. In the next section, we'll explore the many things ChatGPT can do for you, from suggesting dinner ideas to solving those last-minute "uh-oh" moments when you run out of an ingredient.

YOUR NEW KITCHEN PARTNER

Alright, so you have this clever conversational AI at your fingertips – how can it actually help you when you're standing in your kitchen wondering what to do? Think of ChatGPT as your new **kitchen partner**, always on call. It won't stir the soup for you, but it can assist with just about everything else that involves knowledge, planning, or creativity. Let's paint a picture of the kinds of kitchen tasks ChatGPT can help with:

- **Recipe Ideas Based on What You Have:** Perhaps the most popular use is asking *"What can I cook with [X, Y, and Z]?"* Imagine it's a Tuesday night and you peek into your fridge to find some eggs, a wilting bunch of spinach, and a bit of cheese. Instead of despairing or randomly searching the internet, you can simply tell ChatGPT what you have and ask for ideas. **You:** "I have eggs, spinach, and cheddar cheese. Any ideas for dinner?" **ChatGPT:** "How about a quick spinach and cheddar frittata? Here's how you can do it: ..." In seconds, you get a suggestion (often multiple) that uses what you have. It's like the AI is scanning an infinite cookbook in its brain to find recipes that match your ingredients. This is fantastic for reducing food waste and saving those last bits of produce or leftovers from ending up in the trash.

- **Last-Minute Dinner Planning:** Similar to using what you have, you can ask for meal ideas even if you haven't settled on specific ingredients. For example, **You:** "I need a quick dinner idea for two people. We're pretty hungry and don't want to spend more than 30 minutes cooking." **ChatGPT:** "Sure! How about making some garlic shrimp pasta? You'll need shrimp, pasta, garlic, and a few pantry staples. It can be ready in 20 minutes. Let me give you a quick recipe..." ChatGPT can tailor suggestions to time constraints ("quick," "ready in 30 minutes"), cuisine preferences ("something Mexican-inspired"), or even diet ("low-carb dinner idea"). It's like brainstorming with a creative partner who has endless suggestions. No more staring blankly at the pantry — just ask and get instant inspiration.
- **Substitutions and Ingredient Swaps:** We've all been in the middle of cooking when we realize an ingredient is missing. Maybe you poured your heart into baking a cake and then discovered you're out of eggs. Instead of running to the store or panicking, you can ask ChatGPT: **You:** "I'm baking brownies but I have no eggs. What can I use instead?" **ChatGPT:** "No eggs? No problem. You can substitute each missing egg with 1/4 cup of unsweetened applesauce, or a mashed half banana, or even a flaxseed 'egg' (mix 1 tablespoon ground flaxseed with 3 tablespoons water and let it gel). Any of those should help bind your brownies in place of eggs." How handy is that! Rather than

combing through a dozen different blogs for "egg substitute in brownies" and getting a bunch of ads and varying answers, you get a clear set of options right away. This applies to all kinds of substitutions – buttermilk, butter, specific spices, gluten-free swaps, etc. ChatGPT's broad knowledge really shines here.

- **Cooking Techniques and "How-To" Guidance:** ChatGPT can act as a teacher or coach for kitchen techniques. If you're unsure how to dice an onion or fillet a fish, you can ask and get step-by-step instructions. For example: **You:** "How do I julienne carrots?" **ChatGPT:** "To julienne carrots (cut them into thin matchsticks), first peel the carrot and cut it into 2-3 inch sections. Then, slice a section lengthwise into thin planks. Stack a few planks and slice them again lengthwise into thin strips. These strips are julienned carrots. Take your time and watch your fingers. Once you get the hang of it, it's easy!" It's patiently explaining just like a cooking instructor might. While videos are great for visual learning, having a quick textual explanation is surprisingly effective when you just need a reminder of the steps or a quick tip mid-recipe. This means ChatGPT isn't just for *what* to cook, but also *how* to cook.
- **Adapting and Adjusting Recipes:** Do you have a great recipe in mind but need to tweak it? ChatGPT can help modify recipes for you. Maybe you have a recipe that serves 4 but you need it for 2 people – you can ask it to adjust ingredient quantities. Or you love a recipe but it's too spicy for your kids; you can ask how to tone it down. For example: **You:** "I have a chili recipe that's too spicy. How can I make it milder for next time?" **ChatGPT:** "To make your chili milder, you have a few options. You can reduce or omit the hot peppers and chili powder, add a bit of sugar or a sweet ingredient like corn to balance the heat, or even stir in something creamy at the end (like sour

cream or peanut butter) to mellow the spice. Also, serving it with rice or bread can help diffuse the heat." That kind of on-the-spot advice can save a meal (and some taste buds). It's like having an experienced cook to consult whenever you want to tweak something.

- **Meal Planning and Dietary Needs:** Your AI kitchen partner can even help with broader planning. Suppose you want to plan meals for the week, or you need to accommodate a special diet (say you or a family member just went dairy-free). ChatGPT can assist: **You:** "Can you help me plan a week's worth of dinners that are vegetarian and kid-friendly?" **ChatGPT:** "Absolutely! Here's a simple 5-day dinner plan: Monday: Veggie stir-fry with tofu and rice (mild flavors for the kids). Tuesday: Homemade cheese-free pizza with lots of veggies. Wednesday: Creamy tomato pasta using cashew cream instead of dairy. Thursday: Black bean tacos with corn and avocado. Friday: Baked macaroni with vegetables and a crunchy breadcrumb topping. Let me know if you want recipes for any of these!" It not only lists ideas, but can dive deeper into each suggestion if you want details. It's like an endless well of meal plans, tailored to whatever constraints or themes you throw at it.
- **Grocery Lists and Shopping Help:** Along with planning meals, ChatGPT can help generate a grocery list. If you ask for a list of ingredients needed for a recipe or even a whole week of the above meal plan, it can list them out for you. For example: **You:** "What groceries do I need for the vegetarian meal plan you suggested?" **ChatGPT:** "You'll need: 1 block of firm tofu, a variety of fresh veggies (broccoli, bell peppers, carrots, spinach, tomatoes, etc.), garlic, onions, rice, pasta, cashews (for cashew cream), black beans, tortillas, avocados, pasta, bread crumbs... [and so on]." It will enumerate what you should buy, which you can then check against what you already have.

> It's not connected to an online store (at least not by default), so it won't know what things cost or if they're in stock near you, but it does know what ingredients typically go into certain dishes. Consider it a smart assistant for planning that saves you the step of writing everything down yourself.

As you can see, ChatGPT is incredibly versatile in the kitchen. It's basically the helper who has answers for *everything* – whether it's coming up with an idea, finding a workaround, or explaining a concept. The beauty of using it as a partner is that it's **interactive.** It's not just a static one-way source of information. You can have a conversation: "Not that, something else," or "What if I don't have oven?" and it will adapt. For instance, if it gives you a recipe that requires baking but you don't have an oven, you can say, "I don't have an oven – can I cook this on the stovetop instead?" and it might suggest a different method or a different recipe altogether. Try doing that with a cookbook!

Before we move on, it's worth noting that while ChatGPT is super helpful, the human is still the boss in the kitchen. You'll make the final calls, and you provide the physical action. In a way, you can think of ChatGPT as an assistant chef who preps the *mental mise-en-place* (the plan, the ideas, the know-how) so you can carry out the actual cooking with more confidence and less stress.

Now that we've explored what ChatGPT can do, you might be eager to start asking it questions. But how you ask *really* matters. Just as you'd phrase a request differently to a person to get a better response (imagine asking a grocery store clerk "Where's the milk?" versus "Hi, could you point me to the milk section?" – small differences, but they help), asking questions the right way will help ChatGPT give you better answers. In the next section, we'll explain the art of communicating with your AI sous chef: how to talk to ChatGPT so that you get exactly the kind of help you need.

HOW TO TALK TO AN AI

Using ChatGPT is as simple as typing out a question and hitting enter – but getting *great* results can depend on how you phrase your question or request. Don't worry, you don't need to learn any complex commands or technical jargon. In fact, the best way to talk to ChatGPT is often the same way you'd talk to a knowledgeable friend. Still, there are some tips and tricks to make your "prompts" (that's the term for the questions or instructions you give to an AI) as effective as possible, especially when it comes to cooking. Let's explore how to chat with this AI in a way that yields delicious results.

Be Clear and Specific (when you can): The more clearly you tell ChatGPT what you want, the better it can tailor its answer. Suppose you ask, *"What should I cook tonight?"* That's a very broad question. ChatGPT has to guess your context – it doesn't know what ingredients you have, what you like, how much effort you want to put in, or if there are any dietary restrictions. You might still get a useful answer (it may suggest a popular dish or ask you follow-up questions), but you can usually save time by being a bit more specific upfront. For example: *"What should I cook tonight? I have some chicken breasts, and I'm in the mood for Italian flavors, but I want it to be fairly quick."* Now you've given context (chicken, Italian, quick) and ChatGPT can work with that to give a relevant suggestion, like an easy chicken pasta or a one-pan chicken with tomatoes and herbs. Think of it like giving the AI a few key ingredients for your answer – literally and figuratively!

To illustrate, let's see a prompt evolve:

You (vague): "I want a dinner idea."

ChatGPT: "Sure! How about trying a stir-fry or a pasta? Those are easy dinner ideas." *(Not bad, but very general.)*

You (more specific): "I want a quick dinner idea with chicken and pasta."

ChatGPT: "How about a simple chicken alfredo pasta? You can cook the pasta, sauté bite-sized chicken pieces with garlic, then toss everything with cream, parmesan, and a bit of pasta water to make a quick sauce. It's ready in 20 minutes." *(Much better – now it's giving you a concrete recipe idea.)*

See how adding a bit more detail – *quick, with chicken and pasta* – guided the AI to a more useful answer? As a rule of thumb, include any details that matter to you: ingredients you want to use (or avoid), the time you have, the style of cuisine, dietary preferences, etc.

Ask One Thing at a Time (when possible): ChatGPT is pretty good at handling multi-part questions, but sometimes it helps to break things down. If you ask, *"Can you give me a recipe for chicken curry and also tell me how to store leftovers?"* it will likely answer both, but one request might get more attention than the other. You could instead ask about the recipe first, then follow up with the leftovers question. The conversation memory means ChatGPT will remember you're talking about chicken curry, making the follow-up easy: *"Thanks! And how should I store the leftovers?"* This step-by-step approach can yield more thorough answers for each part. However, if you're in a hurry, bundling related questions is okay – just be aware the answer might be more brief for each part.

Use Natural Language – No Need for Fancy Words: You don't have to phrase things in a robotic or overly formal way. **You:** "What can I use instead of butter when baking cookies?" is just as fine as saying, "List butter substitutes for cookies." In fact, adding a bit of context or a casual tone can help. The AI doesn't require "please" and "thank you" (though it's nice to be polite out of habit!), but it does appreciate context. For example, "I'm baking cookies and ran out of butter. What can I substitute?" provides a scenario, which can sometimes help it give a more tailored answer (like it might consider common cookie ingredients in its suggestion).

Prompt Format Can Guide the Response: ChatGPT will try to format its answer based on what it thinks is best, but you can steer it. If you'd like a list, you can prompt with "List five ideas for...". If you want a step-by-step recipe, you can say "Give me step-by-step instructions for...". For example: **You:** "Give me step-by-step instructions for making a basic omelette." **ChatGPT:** "1. Crack 2 eggs into a bowl and whisk with a pinch of salt and pepper. 2. Heat a pan with a bit of butter... (and so on)." It will likely do that anyway for a recipe, but stating it ensures you get that clear format. If you prefer a brief answer, you can say "in one paragraph" or if you want more detail, "explain like I'm a beginner," etc. You have some control over the style of the response by the way you ask.

What Makes a Good Cooking Prompt?: In cooking scenarios, a good prompt often includes:

- **The Goal or Problem:** e.g. "I want to bake a cake without sugar" or "I need a side dish for grilled fish."
- **Relevant Details:** e.g. "I have almond flour and honey available" or "it should be something light and quick."
- **Any Constraints:** e.g. "gluten-free," "only using one pot," "something my kids will eat.
- **Desired Output Format (optional):** e.g. "Can you give me a simple recipe with bullet points for each step?" or "Just list a few ideas, not full recipes."

Here's a concrete example of a well-crafted prompt vs. a weaker one:

- ***Weaker:*** "Give me a cake recipe." (You'll get a generic cake recipe, which might be fine, but it might not suit your needs or ingredient availability.)
- ***Stronger:*** "I want to bake a chocolate cake, but I only have almond flour and honey (no regular sugar). I'm also new to baking, so make it simple. Can you give me a recipe?"

Now ChatGPT knows the flavor you want, the ingredient substitution needed (honey instead of sugar, almond flour instead of regular flour), and that you're a beginner so it should keep it simple. The recipe you get will be far more customized – perhaps it'll suggest a specific honey-sweetened almond flour chocolate cake with straightforward steps.

Don't Fear Trial and Error: Sometimes you might not even know what to ask – you just know you need *something*. It's perfectly fine to start with a vague or broad prompt and then refine. ChatGPT might throw a broad answer back at you, or ask a clarifying question like, "Do you have any specific ingredients in mind?" This is its way of saying it's ready to help, just give it a bit more to work with. You can then follow up with more info. Think of the first prompt as starting the conversation. You might start with, "I have no idea what to cook for a special dinner," and ChatGPT could reply with, "No worries! Can you tell me if you have something in mind like a cuisine or a main ingredient? Any dietary preferences?" That's your cue to continue the dialogue, e.g., "Well, maybe something Italian, and I have some good tomatoes on hand." Now the AI has direction.

Examples of Good Prompts for Cooking:

- "I have chicken thighs, potatoes, and green beans. Can you suggest a one-pan dinner recipe? I'd like it to be garlicky."
- "Give me three ideas for a vegan dessert that doesn't require baking. I have cocoa powder and peanut butter available."
- "How do I know when my steak is done cooking? I prefer medium-rare."
- "What's a quick appetizer I can make for a party with minimal ingredients? Something finger-food style."
- "Explain the technique of tempering chocolate in simple terms. I've never done it before."
- "I want to meal prep lunches for the week. Can you suggest a plan using chicken, rice, and vegetables, with different flavors each day?"

Each of these prompts sets a clear task or question and gives the AI some context or criteria to work with. They're likely to get very targeted answers.

Tone and Language: You might wonder if you need to phrase things as commands or questions, or if the AI understands casual language. The answer is: it's very flexible. You can say "I need..." or

"Could you..." or just state "List me..." and it'll all work. If anything, adding a bit of a friendly tone ("please," "thank you," or explaining why you need something) might inadvertently give the AI more context which can improve the answer. For instance, "I'm really tired today, so I need a super easy dinner recipe with ground beef" might prompt it to prioritize simplicity in its answer, more than if you just said "easy dinner with ground beef." It's not necessary to chat with it like a person, but since it responds in a conversational way, many people find themselves naturally typing as if to a human. That's fine! Do what feels comfortable – the AI doesn't get *truly* offended or anything if you're brief, and it doesn't actually feel flattered if you're polite, but a conversational tone can make the whole experience feel more pleasant and human for *you*.

Before leaving this section, a quick note on misunderstandings: Sometimes ChatGPT might misinterpret your question. If you get an answer that seems off-base or not what you meant, don't be discouraged. Just try rephrasing or adding more detail. For example, if you ask "Can I make pasta in a rice cooker?" and it gives you a pasta recipe for a stove instead (maybe it missed the "rice cooker" part), you could clarify: "I want to *cook the pasta* in a rice cooker because I don't have a stove available. Is that possible?" This gentle nudge will help refocus the AI on your actual need. Remember, it's not *trying* to be difficult – it might just need that clarification.

Great, so now you know how to ask questions and give prompts effectively. Think of it as learning the right way to ask your sous chef for help so they can give you exactly what you need. But our journey doesn't stop at asking questions. Next, we'll look at how to make sure the answers you get from ChatGPT are tailored to you personally. Because every cook is unique, and ideally, your AI helper should adapt to *your* personal tastes, needs, and kitchen situation. Let's explore that.

MAKING IT PERSONAL

One of the coolest things about ChatGPT is that it doesn't give one-size-fits-all answers – at least not when you provide a bit of personal context. You can (and should!) let your AI sous chef know about your own preferences and needs, so its responses can be as useful and relevant as possible. Think of it like briefing a human assistant on your quirks: "I'm allergic to peanuts, I *hate* cilantro, I only have a microwave to cook with, and by the way, I'm cooking for a picky toddler." ChatGPT will take whatever personal details you give and try to incorporate them into its answers. Let's go over how you can tailor ChatGPT's responses to fit *you* and your kitchen.

Dietary Restrictions and Preferences: Always feel free to mention any diet info upfront in your prompt. For example, if you're vegetarian, you can include that: *"I'm vegetarian. Can you suggest a dinner recipe with eggplant?"* Then you won't get a suggestion that includes meat. If you or someone you cook for has an allergy, definitely mention it when relevant: *"Find me a dessert recipe without nuts (peanut allergy in the family)."* ChatGPT will then avoid nuts or clearly suggest substitutes. The AI has knowledge of lots of dietary patterns – vegetarian, vegan, gluten-free, dairy-free, low-carb, you name it – and it will adapt a recipe or idea to those needs if you tell it to. **You:** "I want to make enchiladas but I need them to be gluten-free." **ChatGPT:** "No problem! Use corn tortillas (they're naturally gluten-free) instead of flour tortillas, and ensure your enchilada sauce is gluten-free. You can fill them with... [continues with recipe]." The key is, *let it know.* It won't automatically assume any restrictions unless you say so. The more you share your eating style, the more it will shape the answers around it.

Flavor and Ingredient Likes/Dislikes: We all have our flavor loves and hates. Some people can't stand cilantro (to them it tastes like soap!), others might love spicy food and want every dish to have a kick. When asking for a recipe or dish idea, mention these preferences. *"Make it spicy," "I love sour flavors," "please no cilantro," "I prefer mild foods," "use lots of garlic,"* etc. These kind of notes will be taken into account. **Example: You:** "Can I have a Thai noodle recipe that's not too spicy? I'm okay with a little heat, but not too much." **ChatGPT:** "Sure. Let's make a mild Pad Thai. We'll use just a pinch of chili flakes for a hint of heat, and we'll focus more on tangy tamarind and a bit of sweetness. Here's a recipe...". The AI will actively dial ingredients up or down based on what you say. If you say you love something (like garlic or chocolate or a certain herb), it might emphasize that in the suggestions. If you say you dislike something, it will omit it or find an alternative. Essentially, you are training ChatGPT on *your* taste profile with each prompt that includes those details.

Kitchen Equipment and Skills: Every kitchen is different. You might have an Instant Pot, an air fryer, a high-power blender – or conversely, you might be working with just a microwave and a hot plate in a small apartment. Let ChatGPT know what tools you have or don't have, especially if it might affect the recipe. For example: *"I only have a microwave and a toaster, no oven. What desserts can I make?"* will prompt the AI to skip any oven-baking ideas and stick to fridge-set desserts or microwave mug cakes, etc. Or if you specifically want to use a gadget: *"I have an Instant Pot – suggest a beef stew recipe using it."* and it will tailor the method to pressure cooking. Also, be open about your skill level. If you're a beginner, you can say so: *"I'm a beginner cook, so please keep the recipe simple."* ChatGPT will then avoid assuming you know terms like "deglaze" or techniques like trussing a chicken, unless it explains them. If you're more advanced and want a challenge, you can say: *"I love to cook and don't mind a challenge. How about a complex Italian dish to try?"* and it might give you something more involved.

Number of Servings or People: If you're cooking just for yourself or for a crowd, mention it. *"I'm cooking for one – can you adjust this recipe?"* or *"I need to feed 6 people."* ChatGPT can scale recipes up or down. It's pretty good at basic math for ingredient scaling (though always double-check if something seems off, just like you would if you were scaling a recipe yourself). For instance, **You:** "That pasta recipe looks great, but it's for 2 servings and I need it for 4." **ChatGPT:** "Got it. To serve 4, just double all the ingredients: if it called for 1 cup of tomatoes, use 2 cups; 2 cloves of garlic become 4, and so on. Cooking times remain about the same." It may explicitly list the new amounts too, which is handy.

Budget and Availability: If you're on a tight budget or only have access to certain ingredients (maybe you live in a place where some items are hard to find), you can include that info. *"Give me a budget-friendly meal with rice and beans,"* or *"I live in a small town, so exotic ingredients might be hard to find – keep it basic."* ChatGPT doesn't know prices in real-time, but it understands generally that beans, rice, and in-season veggies are budget-friendly, whereas saffron or pine nuts are pricey. It will adjust suggestions to be cost-conscious if you ask. Similarly, *seasonal and local* hints help: *"It's winter and I have a lot of root vegetables available,"* could lead it to suggest hearty stews or roasts with carrots, potatoes, etc., since it knows those are wintery produce.

Combination of Factors: You can combine several of these personal details in one prompt to really tailor the response. For example: *"I need a quick, dairy-free dinner recipe for two people. We have tofu, broccoli, and noodles on hand. Also, I love spicy food, but my partner prefers mild – maybe a way to adjust at the end?"* Look at all the personal touches there: quick (time), dairy-free (dietary), two people (servings), ingredients on hand, spice level differences. A tall order for a human perhaps, but ChatGPT will do its best to accommodate all of it. It might come back with: "How about a quick tofu stir-fry with broccoli and noodles? Use soy sauce, ginger, and garlic for flavor. You can add chili oil or sriracha to your own bowl for heat, and leave your partner's portion mild. No dairy needed. Here's how to make it...".

Teach it Your Favorites: Over a long conversation, you might even build up a profile with ChatGPT. For instance, early on you could mention, "By the way, I really enjoy Italian and Mexican flavors, and I'm not a big fan of seafood." Later in the chat, even if you don't restate those, it might remember and slant suggestions toward, say, pasta or tacos rather than fish dishes. Each session (conversation) will remember details you give, but note that if you start a new chat session, you might have to mention important personal notes again since it doesn't carry memory across separate sessions. For the scope of a single chapter or a single cooking session, once you tell it something, you can just refer back to it casually: *"Can you give me another idea like that chicken recipe, but maybe vegetarian this time? (Remember, I can't have dairy.)"* It will remember you can't have dairy from earlier and follow those rules.

Examples of Personalization in Prompts:

- "I'm cooking for my kids who are picky and don't like vegetables. Can you hide some veggies in a dinner recipe?"
- "I only have a basic kitchen setup in my dorm (just a microwave). What meals can I make?"
- "I absolutely love Thai food. Suggest a Thai-inspired dish I can make at home, but I don't eat shrimp."
- "I have a cast iron skillet and I love using it. Maybe a one-skillet meal? I eat keto (low-carb) by the way."
- "I hate waste. Can you help me use up a bunch of leftover roasted vegetables in a new recipe?"
- "I have celiac disease, so everything needs to be gluten-free. I'm craving pizza – any ideas for a gluten-free pizza or flatbread?"

In each case, see how the cook is giving the AI a little window into their life and kitchen. That's exactly what you should do. The more you "chat" about your needs, the more it will shape the output appropriately.

One amazing aspect of ChatGPT is how it can adjust tone too. If you say, *"Explain it to me like I'm five years old,"* it will simplify the language. If you say, *"I want to cook together with my kids, so make the recipe fun and easy to follow,"* it might even add a playful tone or simple steps that kids could do (like "Have your little helper wash the veggies"). It can be very adaptable not just in *what* it suggests, but *how* it presents it.

Remember, though, ChatGPT doesn't *truly* know you. It only knows what you tell it in that conversation. So don't assume it's aware of anything you haven't mentioned. For example, if in one conversation you spent a long time talking about being vegetarian, and then you start a fresh conversation the next day without mentioning it, it won't automatically know you're vegetarian in the new chat. Always mention the key personal details if they're relevant to the request at hand.

By making your prompts personal, you transform ChatGPT from a generic recipe generator into a customized kitchen assistant attuned to *your* life. It's the difference between browsing a generic cookbook versus having a cookbook written just for you. Now, up to now we've focused a lot on recipes and food suggestions – essentially the content of cooking. But cooking is more than just the recipes; it's also about techniques, timing, and sometimes troubleshooting when things go sideways. ChatGPT can help with those aspects too, because it's not just about giving you recipes. In the next section, we'll see how this AI sous chef can assist with all sorts of cooking queries beyond "what should I make?" – from converting measurements to rescuing a dish that's on the brink of disaster. After all, a true sous chef isn't just there for prep; they're there for the tough moments too. Let's check out these other uses for ChatGPT in the kitchen.

IT'S NOT JUST RECIPES

By now, it's clear that ChatGPT can dish out recipes and meal ideas like a pro. But what if you're not looking for a new recipe? What if you're halfway through cooking and *something goes wrong*, or you stumble on a term you don't understand? Good news: your AI kitchen companion isn't just a recipe generator – it's also a coach, a teacher, and a problem-solver. Let's explore some of the many **non-recipe tasks** ChatGPT can help with in the kitchen, turning it into a versatile tool for all your cooking questions and conundrums.

Explaining Cooking Techniques: Ever read a recipe instruction and thought, "What does that even mean?" Perhaps a phrase like "blanch the green beans" or "deglaze the pan" has left you scratching your head. Instead of googling and sifting through long articles, you can ask ChatGPT directly: *"What does it mean to blanch vegetables?"*

You'll get a straight-forward answer: **ChatGPT:** "Blanching is a cooking process where you briefly boil vegetables and then quickly cool them in ice water. For example, to blanch green beans, you'd drop them in boiling water for a minute or two, then transfer them to a bowl of ice water. This keeps them crisp and bright in color." Short, sweet, and now you know what to do. You can ask about any technique – julienne, fold (in baking context), braise, proof yeast, sear vs. sauté, etc. The AI will give you an explanation and often a quick how-to. It's like having a cooking encyclopedia that actually *talks* to you.

Conversions and Measurements: Kitchen math can get tricky, especially if you're working with a recipe that uses different units than you're used to. ChatGPT can convert measurements for you on the fly. For instance: *"How many tablespoons are in 1/4 cup?"* will get the answer **"There are 4 tablespoons in 1/4 cup."** Or if you have 500 grams of flour in a European recipe and need to know what that is in cups: *"Convert 500g of flour to cups."* It might respond, *_"500 grams of flour is roughly 4 cups (assuming all-purpose flour)."_ (Note: Conversions for ingredients like flour and sugar are often approximations because of density, but ChatGPT generally gives a reasonable estimate or mentions the assumption.) You can also scale recipes: *"If a soup recipe calls for 2 liters of water, how many cups is that?"* – **"That's about 8 1/2 cups of water."** Or temperature: *"Bake at 180°C – what is that in Fahrenheit?"* – **"180°C is about 356°F (often rounded to 350°F for baking)."** Essentially, any little conversion that might normally have you pulling out a phone calculator, you can just ask ChatGPT.

Timing and Doneness: Perhaps you want to know how long to cook something or how to tell when it's done. ChatGPT can offer general guidelines: *"How long should I boil an egg for a soft center?"* – **"For a soft-boiled egg with a runny yolk, boil for about 6 minutes."** Or *"What internal temperature should chicken reach to be safe?"* – **"Chicken should reach an internal temperature of 165°F (75°C) at the thickest part to be safe to eat."** It can guide you on how to check doneness too: *"How do I know when my brownies are done?"* – **"Insert a toothpick near the center; if it comes out with a few moist crumbs (not wet batter), they're done. If it's totally clean, the brownies**

might be on the cakey side." These little tips are often gleaned from its extensive knowledge of cooking lore.

Troubleshooting and Rescuing Mistakes: This is a big one. Every cook, no matter how experienced, has kitchen mishaps. Salt spills, soup scorches, sauce separates – it happens. When you're in panic mode ("Oh no, I added sugar instead of salt!" or "The stew is way too salty now!"), ChatGPT can be a lifesaver. Ask it how to fix things:

- *"Help! My soup is too salty. What can I do?"*
- **ChatGPT:** "Don't worry. You have a few options: You can add more water or unsalted broth to dilute the saltiness (you might need to add a bit more seasoning of other kinds to balance the flavor). You could also throw in a peeled potato and simmer for a while – the potato will absorb some salt (just remember to take it out later). Another trick is to add a bit of something acidic like lemon juice or vinegar; sometimes acidity can balance perceived saltiness. Lastly, serving the soup with something bland like rice or bread can help balance out the salt when eating."
- *"I accidentally burned the bottom of my stew. How do I save it?"*
- **ChatGPT:** "First, don't stir the pot – carefully pour or ladle the unburned stew into a new pot, leaving the burnt bottom behind (you don't want the burnt bits mixing in). Then taste the stew. If it has a slight burnt taste, you can try adding a teaspoon of peanut butter or a bit of sugar to counteract the bitterness. Spices or smoked paprika might mask the flavor too. In the future, remember to keep the heat low and stir more frequently to avoid burning."
- *"My sauce broke (it's all curdled/oily). Can I fix it?"*
- **ChatGPT:** "Yes, you can often rescue a broken sauce. One method is to take a fresh pan, add a small amount of the broken sauce and a splash of warm water (or cream if

> appropriate), and whisk vigorously to create a new emulsion, then slowly whisk in the rest of the broken sauce. Another method: remove from heat, let it cool slightly, then whisk in a little liquid (water, stock, or cream depending on the sauce) gradually. If it's something like a hollandaise or mayo, you can sometimes fix it by whisking a new egg yolk in a bowl and slowly pouring the broken sauce into it while whisking."

These are the kinds of tips you might find buried in online forums or hear from grandma. ChatGPT has a lot of them at the ready. It's great for on-the-spot advice when you're thinking "how do I salvage this?"

General Food Knowledge and Questions: Maybe you're just curious about something food-related. *"What's the difference between baking soda and baking powder?"* or *"Why do recipes call for unsalted butter instead of salted?"* or *"What exactly is umami flavor?"* ChatGPT can explain these concepts. This can deepen your understanding of cooking as you go. It's like having a foodie friend who also happens to be a scientist and historian, ready to give you context. For example: **You:** "Why do you sear meat before braising?" **ChatGPT:** "Searing meat (browning it at a high temperature) before braising helps develop a richer flavor and color. The browning creates what's called the Maillard reaction, which adds depth and a savory taste to the dish. It also gives the meat a nice color. While searing doesn't 'seal in juices' as the old myth goes, it does make the final dish more flavorful."

Planning and Strategies: You can ask ChatGPT for strategies like *"How can I cook efficiently for a dinner party of 10?"* or *"What can I make ahead of time for Thanksgiving to save time on the day?"* and it will provide suggestions such as prepping ingredients, choosing dishes that hold well, etc. It's like a consultant for kitchen project management!

Cooking Ethics and Choices: Perhaps you wonder about sustainable choices: *"Which fish are sustainable to eat?"* or *"How can I reduce* *food waste while cooking?"* ChatGPT can provide general guidelines and tips based on what it has learned from reputable sources. It might say to use vegetable scraps for stock, or suggest commonly recommended sustainable fish like Pacific halibut or farmed mussels, for example.

Fun and Creativity: Not every query has to be serious. You can use ChatGPT to add some fun to your cooking. *"Tell me a fun fact about tomatoes,"* might yield something interesting about how tomatoes were once feared as poisonous by Europeans. Or *"Give me a cooking challenge to try this weekend,"* could prompt a suggestion like making homemade pasta from scratch or trying a dish from a different culture. If you have kids, *"Can you write a silly song about making pancakes that I can sing with my kids while cooking?"* – you might get a cute little rhyme you can actually use to engage them. These might not be *essential* cooking tasks, but they add to the joy and learning aspect of cooking, and ChatGPT can certainly play along.

Kitchen Safety and Food Storage: You can ask things like *"How long can I keep cooked rice in the fridge?"* (Answer might be: ~4-6 days, but ideally 4 to be safe). Or *"What's the safe way to defrost chicken?"* (Likely: "in the fridge overnight, or using a cold water bath, but not on the counter at room temp"). Or *"Can I refreeze meat after defrosting?"* (Answer: It's generally not recommended unless it was defrosted in the fridge and still cold; quality may suffer). These are important bits of knowledge to keep your cooking safe, and the AI often provides the standard food-safety guidelines if asked.

What's remarkable is having all these different kinds of knowledge accessible in one place – no toggling between a recipe site, a cooking forum, a conversion app, and a YouTube tutorial. You just ask questions in one chat thread, and you get answers in the same place, tuned to your situation if you've given context. It really underscores the idea that ChatGPT is more of an all-around kitchen assistant than just a recipe source.

At this point, we've covered understanding ChatGPT, using it for recipes, personalizing it, and leveraging it for every other cooking need from emergencies to education. But there's one more skill to really master: the back-and-forth refinement process. In a live kitchen setting with a human sous chef, you'd naturally say, "Hmm, that's not exactly what I meant, can we try doing it this way instead?" and they'd adjust. You can (and should) do the same with ChatGPT. In the next section, we'll focus on the iterative process – how to improve the results you get by refining your prompts or asking follow-ups. It's the final piece of the puzzle in making ChatGPT truly work for you in the kitchen. Let's dive into that interactive process of iterating and improving, which will turn you from a casual user into a power user of your AI sous chef.

ITERATE, IMPROVE, REPEAT

One of the greatest strengths of ChatGPT – something we've hinted at throughout this chapter – is that it's not a one-shot deal. You don't just ask a question, get an answer, and call it a day (though you certainly can for simple needs). The real magic happens when you treat the interaction as a **conversation.** Think of the first answer you get as a draft or a starting point. From there, you can refine, adjust, and ask follow-ups to zero in on exactly what you need. This iterative loop of asking, receiving, tweaking, and asking again is where ChatGPT transforms from a static tool into a dynamic kitchen partner.

Let's walk through an example of an iterative interaction with ChatGPT to see how it works in practice:

Scenario: You want to make a nice dinner using salmon, and you're in the mood for something a little fancy, maybe even fit for a small dinner party, but you're not sure what. You also have some dietary considerations: suppose one of your guests doesn't eat dairy.

First Prompt (Starting Point): *"Give me a gourmet dinner recipe using salmon."*

ChatGPT's First Answer: It might respond with something like, "How about a pan-seared salmon with a creamy dill sauce, served with roasted asparagus and garlic mashed potatoes? Here's how to make it..." and it will list the recipe steps and ingredients, possibly including butter and cream for the sauce and butter in the mashed potatoes.

Now, that sounds delicious, but you realize: (a) it has dairy, which you need to avoid for your guest, and (b) maybe you were thinking of something more unique than the classic creamy dill sauce.

Iteration 1 (Refine Dietary Needs): You follow up: *"That sounds great, but one guest is lactose intolerant. Can we do it dairy-free?"*

ChatGPT Adjusts: "Sure. We can modify the dish to be dairy-free. For the sauce, instead of a traditional cream dill sauce, let's make a dill vinaigrette or a dairy-free dill yogurt sauce using coconut yogurt. And for the mashed potatoes, use olive oil or a dairy-free margarine and some chicken stock to make them creamy instead of butter and milk. Here's the adjusted recipe..." and it provides the alternations in the steps accordingly.

Now you have a dairy-free version. But you're still thinking it's a bit standard. Perhaps you want something more creative.

Iteration 2 (Change Style): *"Actually, can we try a different style? Maybe something with an Asian flair, still using salmon?"*

ChatGPT New Idea: "Absolutely. How about miso-glazed salmon with sesame garlic greens and jasmine rice? It's elegant and full of flavor. You'd marinate the salmon in a mixture of miso paste, soy sauce, ginger, and a touch of honey (we can keep it dairy-free easily). Then roast or broil the salmon so it caramelizes. Serve it on a bed of garlicky sautéed greens (like bok choy or spinach) with sesame oil, and a side of fluffy jasmine rice. If you want a sauce, a simple drizzle of soy and rice vinegar would do. Here's a recipe breakdown..." and it goes on to list that recipe.

This sounds more interesting to you. It suits the fancy vibe (miso glaze is always impressive), and it's naturally dairy-free except maybe the honey (which is fine for lactose intolerance). You review the answer and like it.

Iteration 3 (Clarify or Add Details): Maybe the recipe mentions "broil the salmon for 5-7 minutes until done." You might ask, *"How do I know when the salmon is done cooking under the broiler?"*

ChatGPT Clarifies: "You'll know the salmon is done when it flakes easily with a fork and has turned opaque all the way through. Under a broiler, the top might get a little browned and caramelized due to the miso glaze – that's good. If you have a food thermometer, you can check for an internal temperature of about 145°F in the thickest part. Be careful not to overcook; salmon goes from perfect to dry if left too long. So keep an eye on it around the 5-minute mark."

That follow-up answer gives you confidence in executing the cooking correctly.

Iteration 4 (Presenting/Other Ideas): Feeling satisfied, you might wrap up. Or you might think, "What about an appetizer or dessert to go with this dinner?" You could ask: *"What would be a good appetizer to serve before this miso-glazed salmon?"*

ChatGPT Suggests: "Since the main has Asian flair, you could do a light appetizer like cucumber avocado sushi rolls (no raw fish, just veggies) or a small bowl of miso soup to set the theme. Even some edamame sprinkled with sea salt and chili flakes could be a simple snack. If you want something fancier, maybe mini shrimp spring rolls with a sweet chili dip." You pick one of those suggestions and now have a full menu idea.

Iteration 5 (Final Touches): Perhaps you want to double-check timing: *"In what order should I cook these so everything is ready together?"*

ChatGPT Guides: "You can prepare the miso marinade earlier in the day and let the salmon marinate for an hour (not too long because miso is salty). Wash and trim the greens ahead of time. If you're making jasmine rice, start that first since it can stay warm. While rice is cooking (about 15 minutes), preheat your broiler and place the salmon in. While salmon is broiling (5-7 minutes), quickly sauté your greens with garlic and sesame oil – that takes about 5 minutes. The salmon and greens should finish around the same time. Keep an eye on the salmon so it doesn't burn. Serve the salmon hot from the oven on the rice, greens on the side. If doing an appetizer like edamame, you can have that boiled and seasoned beforehand, and just set it out for guests to nibble as you finish the main."

Now you're really set – you have not just a recipe, but a game plan.

This iterative process might seem like a lot of steps, but it's very natural in conversation, and you can do as many or as few rounds as you need. Sometimes one follow-up is enough to fine-tune an answer; sometimes you might go back-and-forth for a while if it's a complex project. The key is: **don't be shy about asking follow-up questions or saying exactly what you need.**

Here are some common ways to iterate with ChatGPT in cooking scenarios:

- **Ask for Clarification:** "What do you mean by simmer until 'reduced'? How much should it reduce?"
- **Ask for Alternatives:** "That recipe uses wine but I don't have any. What can I use instead?" (Maybe the answer will be grape juice + vinegar, or just broth, etc.)
- **Adjust Quantity or Size:** "Can I double this recipe? Do I need to adjust cooking time?"
- **Simplify or Elaborate:** "That method seems too complicated. Is there an easier way?" or vice versa, "Can you give me more details on how to do this part?"
- **Troubleshoot Outcome:** "I tried this and it came out too bland. What can I add to improve the flavor?" (Yes, you can even come back *after* trying and get advice for next time!)
- **Explore Variations:** "How could I turn this soup recipe vegetarian?" or "What if I added cinnamon to this bread recipe?" (The AI might weigh in on whether that's a good idea.)
- **Get a Second Opinion:** "Thanks for the recipe. Can you suggest one more idea for salmon, so I can choose?" (It's okay to ask for multiple different answers; ChatGPT can generate another distinct suggestion if you ask.)

Think of each interaction as iterative refinement. ChatGPT doesn't get annoyed or tired of questions – it's literally what it's here for. So take advantage of that patience and depth. When you ask a follow-up, you can reference what it already said without repeating everything. For example, "Could you make that dairy-free?" works because it knows what "that" refers to from context. Or "I'd like a second option" it knows you mean a second recipe idea for the scenario you described. This context retention is powerful.

There might be times when ChatGPT's answer isn't what you expected or seems off track. That's where iterating is crucial. If it misunderstood you, try rephrasing. If it gave an answer that's not quite right (like a recipe with an ingredient you don't have, even though you forgot to mention that), just tell it and it will likely correct course. It doesn't take offense – it's collaborative. You can even say, "No, that's not what I meant. I was thinking of something more like..." and it will try again. This iterative process is a two-way street: you refine your request, and it refines its answer.

A tip: Sometimes, *how* you ask a follow-up can direct the change. For instance, saying "Can you give me other options?" might yield a completely different recipe. Whereas "Can you tweak this to use chicken instead of salmon?" keeps most of it same but changes the protein. So be clear if you want a small tweak vs a totally new idea.

By embracing an iterative mindset, you'll get the most out of ChatGPT. Instead of settling for the first answer if it's not perfect, you'll naturally engage in a dialogue that improves the output. This is something that no cookbook or static website can offer – that give-and-take until it's just right for you.

Now that we've covered the art of iteration, let's do something fun and practical: try out some real prompts end-to-end and see what ChatGPT's full answers look like. In the final section of this chapter, we'll walk through sample scenarios – as if you were chatting with ChatGPT – demonstrating everything we've discussed: asking clear questions, adding personal context, and refining the answers. These examples will give you a taste of real conversations you can have with your AI sous chef. Ready to see it in action? Let's jump into some real-world prompt examples that you can even try yourself right after reading.

TRY IT NOW: REAL-WORLD PROMPT EXAMPLES

Enough talk about ChatGPT – let's actually *use* it! In this section, we're going to walk through a series of sample prompts and conversations, just like ones you might have with ChatGPT in your own kitchen. These examples will cover common real-life situations and show how ChatGPT's responses might look. Feel free to take inspiration from these and try similar prompts with your own ingredients and ideas. The best way to learn is by doing, so consider this an invitation to interact with your new AI sous chef. Let's see ChatGPT in action:

Example 1: The Fridge Forage Dinner

Scenario: It's evening, you're hungry, and you haven't planned dinner. You open the fridge and find some ingredients: say you have a package of **chicken thighs**, a bunch of **broccoli**, and a jar of **teriyaki sauce.** You're not sure what to make, but you want it to be quick and tasty.

You: "I have chicken thighs, fresh broccoli, and a bottle of teriyaki sauce. What can I make for dinner that's quick and tasty?"

ChatGPT: "How about a simple Teriyaki Chicken Stir-Fry with Broccoli? Here's a quick recipe:

- **Prep:** Cut the chicken thighs into bite-sized pieces and chop the broccoli into florets. Mince a clove of garlic and a bit of ginger if you have it (optional, for extra flavor).
- **Cook Chicken:** Heat a tablespoon of oil in a pan on medium-high. Add the chicken pieces and cook until they're browned and mostly cooked through (about 5-7 minutes).
- **Add Broccoli:** Toss the broccoli florets into the pan with the chicken. Cook for another 3-4 minutes, stirring occasionally, until the broccoli turns bright green and starts to tenderize. If the pan seems dry, splash in a little water to help steam the broccoli.

- **Add Sauce:** Pour in about 1/4 cup (or to taste) of teriyaki sauce over the chicken and broccoli. Stir to coat everything. Let it simmer for 2-3 minutes so the sauce thickens and glazes the chicken and veggies. (Make sure the chicken is fully cooked at this point).
- **Serve:** Enjoy it as-is for a low-carb meal, or serve it over rice if you have some (even quick microwavable rice works).
- **Optional:** Sprinkle some sesame seeds or chopped green onions on top for a nice finish. Dinner will be ready in about 15 minutes and it's going to be delicious!"

You (follow-up): "I only have instant ramen noodles, no rice. Can I serve this with ramen?"

ChatGPT: "Sure! You can cook the instant ramen noodles (just the noodles, skip the seasoning packet if it has one) and use them as the base for your stir-fry. Once the noodles are cooked and drained, you could even toss them in the pan for a minute with the chicken, broccoli, and teriyaki sauce to coat them in the sauce. Teriyaki chicken & broccoli over ramen noodles sounds great – kind of like a makeshift noodle bowl!"

What we saw: The initial answer provided a step-by-step recipe using exactly what you had, and the follow-up question about ramen was easily handled. This is how ChatGPT can help turn a random fridge gathering into a concrete meal.

Example 2: The Substitution Emergency

Scenario: You're baking **pancakes** on a Saturday morning, and you suddenly realize the recipe calls for 2 eggs but you only have **one egg** left. You need a substitute for that second egg.

You: "I'm making pancakes but I only have one egg, and the recipe calls for two. What can I use instead of an egg in pancake batter?"

ChatGPT: "No worries! Pancakes are pretty forgiving. To replace one egg in pancake batter, you have a few options:

- **Option 1: Flax Egg** – Mix 1 tablespoon of ground flaxseed with 3 tablespoons of water, let it sit for 5 minutes until it gels. This mixture can act as an egg substitute.
- **Option 2: Mashed Banana or Applesauce** – Use about 1/4 cup of mashed banana or applesauce. This will add a slight flavor (banana flavor or apple sweetness), but in pancakes that can be yummy.
- **Option 3: Yogurt** – 1/4 cup of plain yogurt can replace an egg. If you have Greek yogurt, maybe thin it with a tablespoon of milk.
- **Option 4: Just Increase Baking Powder** – Sometimes you can get away with just using one egg and adding an extra 1/2 teaspoon of baking powder to help with fluffiness, especially since pancakes don't rely on eggs for structure as much as, say, a custard would.

Any of these should work for pancakes. If I had to pick: if you have yogurt, I'd use that; if not, applesauce or banana works well for a breakfast pancake. Happy cooking!"

You (follow-up): "I do have yogurt, yes. Should I add a bit more milk if I use yogurt so the batter isn't too thick?"

ChatGPT: "Good thinking. If the recipe already uses milk, you might not need extra, but check the batter consistency after you mix in the 1/4 cup yogurt. Pancake batter should be a bit pourable (like thick paint). If it looks too thick, you can splash in an extra tablespoon or two of milk to loosen it up. The yogurt will add moisture and tenderness, so your pancakes should turn out nice and fluffy."

Outcome: You managed to save breakfast by substituting an egg, and ChatGPT gave you multiple options, with a bit of extra advice on adjusting consistency. It's like having a baking expert on call.

Example 3: Technique Tutor

Scenario: You're following a recipe that says "simmer the sauce until it reduces by half" but you're not entirely sure how to judge reduction or why it's needed. You want a quick explanation.

You: "Hi! My recipe says: 'simmer until the sauce reduces by half.'

Can you explain what that means and how to know when it's reduced by half?"

ChatGPT: "Sure! 'Reduce by half' means you want to gently cook the sauce so that some of the water evaporates, making the sauce thicker and more concentrated. When they say by half, they literally mean the volume should be about 50% of what you started with.

How to do it: Keep the sauce on a simmer (a low, gentle boil) – you'll see small bubbles, not a vigorous boil. Stir occasionally to prevent sticking.

ow to know it's half: You can eyeball the level of the sauce in the pan. A neat trick: if your sauce started at, say, a line on the pot, once it's about half that height, it's reduced by half. Some people stick a wooden spoon in at the start, note where the sauce comes up to on the spoon, then check later. Or if it started as 2 cups in the pan (if you happened to know the volume), you'd stop when it looks like about 1 cup."

The consistency will also change – it will be thicker and coat the back of a spoon more heavily. Reducing intensifies flavor (and thickens texture), which is likely why the recipe suggests it. Just keep an eye on it because you don't want it to reduce too much and burn. Once it's roughly half the original amount and nicely thickened, you're good to go."

You: "Great, thanks! And roughly how long does that take?"

ChatGPT: "It depends on the sauce quantity and your stove's heat, but as a rough ballpark, reducing by half could take anywhere from 5-10 minutes for a small amount (like a cup or two of sauce) to 15-30 minutes for a larger pot. Since you're likely making a single recipe's worth, I'd start checking after 5-7 minutes of simmering. If it's not there yet, keep simmering and check every few minutes. You'll notice the change in volume over time."

This mini conversation cleared up a potentially confusing recipe instruction, and you learned a bit about why to reduce sauce. ChatGPT acted as your on-demand cooking teacher.

Example 4: Meal Plan Mode

Scenario: You want to plan a week of **healthy dinners**, and you have some ingredients in mind. Let's say you want to use **chicken breast, salmon, ground turkey, and tofu** across different nights, and you'd like all meals to include veggies and be relatively low-carb.

You: "Can you help me plan 4 healthy dinner menus for this week? I have chicken breasts, salmon fillets, ground turkey, and tofu that I'd like to use (one for each dinner). I prefer low-carb meals with lots of veggies."

ChatGPT: "Absolutely! Let's create a 4-night dinner plan:

1. Monday – Lemon Herb Chicken & Roasted Veggies: Grill or bake the chicken breasts with a marinade of lemon, garlic, and herbs. Serve with a big side of roasted vegetables (broccoli, bell peppers, zucchini, etc.) tossed in olive oil, salt, pepper, and maybe some rosemary. This is high-protein and low-carb.

2. Tuesday – Teriyaki Salmon Bowl (Low-carb style): Marinate the salmon in a sugar-free teriyaki (or just soy sauce, ginger, garlic, and a touch of honey for a little sweetness). Bake or pan-sear the salmon. Serve it over cauliflower "rice" (to keep it low carb) sautéed with peas and carrots. Add a side of steamed bok choy or broccoli. Drizzle extra teriyaki sauce on everything.

3. Wednesday – Turkey & Veggie Stir-fry Lettuce Wraps: Brown the ground turkey with ginger and garlic. Add lots of veggies like shredded cabbage, carrots, and mushrooms. Season with soy sauce or a stir-fry sauce that's not too sweet. Spoon the savory turkey-veggie mix into large lettuce leaves (like romaine or butter lettuce) and eat as wraps. You can serve with a side of cucumber salad. All protein and veggies!

4. Thursday – Tofu and Vegetable Curry: Use firm tofu, cubed, and loads of vegetables (cauliflower, spinach, bell peppers – whatever you have). Simmer them in a coconut milk-based curry sauce (you can use a ready curry paste like Thai green or red curry, or make your own spice blend). Serve it in bowls as a stew, or over cauliflower rice if you want it extra filling. It's hearty, but still low on carbs especially if you go easy on starchy veggies or skip rice.

These four dinners use your main proteins and pack in the veggies. They're all low in carbs but high in flavor. You can swap the order as you like. Also, feel free to add a side salad to any of these for even more greens. Enjoy your week of healthy eating!"

You (follow-up): "That looks great! Could you give me a quick grocery list for these meals?"

ChatGPT: "Sure. Here's a basic grocery list based on those menus (excluding the proteins you already have):

- **Produce:** Lemons, garlic, fresh herbs (like rosemary or thyme for chicken), broccoli, bell peppers, zucchini, bok choy (or extra broccoli), cauliflower (especially if doing cauli-rice for two meals), carrots, mushrooms, cabbage (or bag of coleslaw mix for ease), cucumber, lettuce (large leaf for wraps, plus maybe salad greens if you want salad sides), spinach (for the curry).
- **Others:** Olive oil, soy sauce (or tamari for gluten-free/low carb), ginger (fresh or ground), a low-sugar teriyaki sauce or ingredients to make one (soy sauce, ginger, garlic, a little honey or sweetener), coconut milk (1-2 cans for curry), Thai curry paste (green or red, 1 small jar) or curry spices, sesame oil (optional, for stir-fry flavor).
- **Staples:** Salt, pepper, any sweetener substitute you like if keeping things low-carb (like stevia or erythritol if needed for sauces), nuts or sesame seeds (optional garnish on various dishes).

Double-check what you already have (like spices, oil, etc.) and adjust accordingly. This list covers the basics for those recipes."

This turned into a mini meal-planning session: ChatGPT provided a diverse set of dinners and even helped compile a shopping list. You can see how it kept track of the requirements of each meal to make the list.

Example 5: Cooking Conversation with Iteration

Scenario: Let's simulate a somewhat longer back-and-forth where you start with a vague idea and refine it. Suppose you say: "I want to bake something fun this weekend, maybe with apples, but I'm not sure what. Any suggestions?" and then iterate based on the AI's answer.

You: "I want to bake something fun this weekend, maybe with apples, but I'm not sure what. Any suggestions?"

ChatGPT: "If you're in the mood for apples, there are lots of delicious options! How about making an **Apple Crisp**? It's simpler than a pie but gives you that warm, cozy spiced apple goodness with a crunchy oat topping. Or, if you want more of a challenge, you could try an **apple galette** (which is like a rustic free-form pie). There's also apple muffins or an apple cake if you prefer something more cake-like. For fun and weekend vibes, I'd vote for the Apple Crisp – it makes the house smell amazing and it's great with a scoop of ice cream on top. What do you think?"

You: "Apple Crisp sounds great. I've never made one from scratch before. What's the recipe?"

ChatGPT: "Awesome, let's do Apple Crisp. Here's a straightforward recipe:

Ingredients:

- 4 apples (if you have Granny Smith or Honeycrisp, those are great, but any firm apples work)
- 2 tablespoons of sugar (you can use brown sugar for richer flavor)
- 1 teaspoon cinnamon (plus a pinch of nutmeg if you have it)
- 1 teaspoon lemon juice (optional, helps prevent apples from browning and adds brightness)
- 1 cup rolled oats
- 1 cup all-purpose flour
- 1/2 cup brown sugar (for the topping)
- 1/2 teaspoon cinnamon (for the topping as well)
- 1/2 cup butter, cold (one stick, cut into small pieces) – this is for that crumbly topping.

Steps:

Preheat & Prep Apples: Preheat your oven to 350°F (175°C). Peel and core the apples, then slice them or chop into bite-sized pieces. In a bowl, toss the apple pieces with 2 tbsp sugar, 1 tsp cinnamon, and the lemon juice. Pour these spiced apples into a baking dish (an 8x8 inch pan works well).

Make Topping: In another bowl, mix the oats, flour, brown sugar, and 1/2 tsp cinnamon. Add the cold butter pieces to this mixture. Using your fingers or a pastry cutter, mix the butter into the oat-flour mixture until it looks like coarse crumbs (it's okay if some bits of butter are larger – that makes for a nice crumbly top).

Top & Bake: Spread the crumbly topping evenly over the apples in the dish. Bake in the preheated oven for about 40-45 minutes, until the topping is golden brown and the apples are bubbly and soft.

Enjoy: Let it cool for a few minutes (it will be very hot!). Serve warm, ideally with a scoop of vanilla ice cream or a dollop of whipped cream. Enjoy your homemade apple crisp!

Let me know if you have any questions or need variations!"

You: "I only have quick oats, not rolled oats. Will that be okay?"

ChatGPT: "Yes, quick oats will work in a pinch! The texture of the topping might be a bit softer (quick oats are cut smaller than rolled oats), but it'll still be tasty. If you have any nuts (like almonds or walnuts) you could toss a handful into the topping to add extra crunch to make up for the softer oats, but that's optional. Overall, go ahead and use the quick oats."

You: "Also, I have a mix of apples, some are sweet (like Fuji) and some tart (Granny Smith). Is that okay?"

ChatGPT: "That's actually great! Combining sweet and tart apples can make the flavor more interesting. The sweet ones (Fuji) will hold shape and add natural sweetness, and the Granny Smith will add tang and break down a bit more into a jammy texture. Just what you want in a crisp. So yes, use a mix – it'll likely make the crisp even better."

You: "Perfect. I'll try this tomorrow. Thank you!"

ChatGPT: "You're welcome! Happy baking, and enjoy your apple crisp. Your kitchen is going to smell heavenly. Let me know how it turns out!"

This example showed a dialog from idea to specific recipe, with some real-time troubleshooting (oats substitution, using mixed apples). It demonstrates how you can lean on ChatGPT from start to finish of a cooking project.

These real-world examples hopefully give you confidence that interacting with ChatGPT is easy and practical. You can ask it pretty much anything cooking-related, and it will do its best to help. The prompts we tried covered ingredient-based suggestions, emergency fixes, technique explanations, meal planning, and iterative recipe creation. You can mix and match these approaches depending on what you need at any moment.

Now it's your turn: think of something you might want to cook or a kitchen question that's been on your mind. Try phrasing it as a prompt and see what ChatGPT says. Don't forget, you can always refine your question or ask another if the first answer isn't quite right. Your AI sous chef is ready 24/7 to brainstorm, advise, and inspire.

As we wrap up this chapter, let's reflect on what we've covered and look ahead to where we'll go next in our journey to cook smarter with ChatGPT.

In this first chapter, you met your AI sous chef and learned how to make it an ally in your kitchen adventures. We started by understanding **what ChatGPT is** – not just a search engine, but a conversational assistant with a wealth of culinary knowledge, capable of generating custom answers (and even full recipes) to suit your needs. We saw **all the ways it can partner with you** in cooking, from suggesting creative recipes with whatever you have on hand, to handling substitutions, to planning meals. You picked up tips on **how to talk to this AI**, discovering that clear, specific prompts lead to better results, and that you can guide the response format by how you ask. We emphasized **making it personal**: you can (and should) tell ChatGPT about your dietary needs, taste preferences, and kitchen setup so that its help is tailored just for you. We explored how ChatGPT isn't limited to recipes – it's also there to **teach and**

troubleshoot, whether you need a measurement converted or a fallen cake rescued. Crucially, you learned the skill of **iterative prompting** – treating the interaction like a dialogue where you can refine and improve the answers continuously. Finally, we walked through tangible examples showing these principles in action, turning theory into practice.

By now, you should feel more comfortable with the idea of having ChatGPT as a companion while you cook. It's like having a knowledgeable friend who never judges your questions, no matter how basic or advanced, and who is always ready with helpful advice or a new idea. Cooking with an AI sous chef is a new experience for many, but as you try it out, you'll likely find yourself wondering how you managed without that instant second opinion or creative spark on demand.

As we move on to the next chapter, we'll build on this foundation. With the basics under your belt, you're ready to dive deeper into advanced tips and use cases, turning you into an even more adept **AI-empowered home cook.** We'll explore topics like refining the tone and complexity of ChatGPT's answers, using it for culinary education, and integrating it into your routine. But for now, take a moment to reflect on what you've learned here and, importantly, give yourself permission to experiment in the kitchen with your new digital assistant. The more you practice, the more natural it will become to cook smarter with ChatGPT by your side.

Happy cooking, and see you in the next chapter – our journey with ChatGPT in the kitchen is just getting started!

2

FROM PANTRY TO PLATE: INVENTORY-BASED COOKING

Picture this: It's a weeknight, you're staring into your pantry and fridge, and all you see are a few mismatched ingredients. Maybe there's a can of beans, a couple of eggs, half an onion, and some wilting spinach. What on earth can you make for dinner out of that? We've all been there – the *"there's nothing to eat"* moment of despair. But in an AI-first kitchen, that moment turns into an opportunity. Instead of giving up or ordering takeout, you can turn to ChatGPT, your virtual sous-chef, and ask it to transform those odds and ends into a satisfying meal. In this chapter, we'll show you how to go from pantry to plate with confidence, using ChatGPT as your guide every step of the way.

Inventory-based cooking means crafting meals using only what you already have on hand. It's cooking *from the pantry forward*, rather than starting with a recipe that might send you grocery shopping. This approach not only saves time and money, but also reduces food waste and encourages creativity. With ChatGPT, inventory-based cooking becomes easier and more fun. You can simply list the ingredients you have, and ask for recipe ideas tailored to those items. The AI's vast knowledge of culinary possibilities can spark ideas you might never have considered. Suddenly, that lonely can of beans and those eggs could become a hearty bean skillet or a flavorful frittata. The magic lies in how you prompt the AI and how it responds with delightful suggestions.

In this chapter, you'll learn the full power of ingredient-based prompts – essentially how to tell ChatGPT what's in your kitchen and get tasty recipes in return. We'll start by exploring the basics: how to ask ChatGPT to generate recipes using only what you have on hand. From there, we dive into creativity: you'll see techniques for stretching a sparse pantry into interesting meals with AI's help. As you get comfortable, we'll discuss *smart prompting* – tips on phrasing your requests to get diverse, well-balanced, and appealing meal ideas. You'll also find out how to refine and filter the AI's suggestions, whether you need a simpler version of a dish or have to work around dietary needs and time constraints.

Beyond single meals, this chapter covers how ChatGPT can assist with bigger cooking strategies. We'll look at *batch cooking and reuse* – using the AI to craft meal sequences that let you cook once and eat multiple times without getting bored. And of course, we all face those "emergency" situations when it feels like there's nothing for dinner. You'll discover prompts for those last-minute pantry rescues: quick, filling, fuss-free ideas that ChatGPT can provide when you're out of options.

Throughout the chapter, we'll pepper in plenty of real-world examples. You'll see actual ChatGPT prompts and responses based on common fridge and pantry scenarios, so you know exactly how to apply these ideas at home. By the end of this chapter, you'll feel comfortable treating ChatGPT like a friendly kitchen companion who can brainstorm recipes with you based on whatever ingredients you have. *From pantry to plate*, you'll be able to turn even random ingredients into a delicious meal, all while building confidence and having fun in the kitchen. Let's get started!

THE POWER OF INGREDIENT-BASED PROMPTS

The beauty of using ChatGPT in the kitchen is that you don't need a specific recipe in mind – you just need to know what ingredients you have. With a simple prompt, you can tap into a world of recipes tailored to *your* pantry. Instead of searching the web for "recipes with chicken and rice," you can literally type into ChatGPT: *"I have chicken, rice, a can of tomatoes, and some garlic. What can I make for dinner?"* In seconds, you'll get a response that uses exactly those ingredients in a coherent dish. This is the power of ingredient-based prompts: they allow you to generate meal ideas starting from what's on hand, no extra shopping required.

When you ask ChatGPT to create a recipe from your ingredients, it acts like a knowledgeable friend who knows thousands of recipes. It will often suggest a dish that uses most or all of the items you listed. For example, if you told ChatGPT *"I have a can of chickpeas, a tomato, and some rice – what can I cook?"*, it might come back with a creative suggestion like a quick chickpea tomato curry over rice. It could respond with something along these lines:

Prompt: "I have a can of chickpeas, a tomato, and some rice. What can I cook with these ingredients?"

ChatGPT: "How about a simple chickpea tomato stew served over rice? Sauté the chopped tomato with spices (if you have any like garlic or cumin), add the can of chickpeas (drained) to simmer together, and season with salt and pepper. Meanwhile, cook the rice. In about 20 minutes you'll have a hearty chickpea-tomato curry to spoon over the rice for a satisfying meal."

In this example, the AI took a handful of humble ingredients and immediately turned them into a comforting dish – no cookbook or Google search needed. Ingredient-based prompts are liberating because they flip the usual cooking process. Traditionally, you might find a recipe first and then check if you have everything required. Here, you start with what you *do* have and let the recipe idea emerge from that. It makes cooking more spontaneous and less wasteful – you're using up items you already bought.

In fact, using ChatGPT this way can help rescue ingredients that might otherwise go to waste. If you notice a zucchini starting to wilt or a half carton of mushrooms with no dinner plans, toss them into your prompt along with whatever else you have. ChatGPT might propose a soup, stir-fry, or pasta that incorporates those soon-to-expire items, ensuring they get used in a tasty dish instead of ending up in the trash. By embracing inventory-based cooking, you save money and avoid the guilt of throwing food out.

Another benefit is avoiding decision fatigue. How many times have you looked at a nearly empty fridge and felt too tired to figure out a meal? ChatGPT removes that mental strain by doing the brainstorming for you. You can throw it even a bizarre assortment of ingredients and often get back a surprisingly workable idea. For instance, say it's the end of the week and you have only eggs, a bit of cheese, and a couple of potatoes left. If you ask, *"Can I make a decent dinner with eggs, cheese, and potatoes?"*, ChatGPT might suggest something like a simple cheese and potato frittata. It could outline how to whisk the eggs, grate the cheese, slice and sauté the potatoes, then combine everything in a pan to cook into a hearty omelet. Suddenly, what looked like a meager dinner becomes comforting and delicious.

The key to harnessing this power is just to be clear about what you have. List the main ingredients you want to use, and don't worry if they seem like a random mix. ChatGPT excels at finding connections between ingredients. It knows, for example, that tomatoes and garlic are a classic base for many sauces, or that chickpeas pair well with cumin and turmeric for a curry vibe, or that eggs and cheese can anchor a rich, filling dish. By stating your inventory up front, you give the AI the pieces to puzzle together a meal. And because it has been trained on countless recipes and culinary texts, it often recognizes an actual dish that fits your ingredients (or invents a new twist on one).

One great aspect of ingredient-based prompts is that you can specify *only* what you have on hand. If you make it clear you're sticking to those items, ChatGPT will usually honor that. It might assume you have basic staples like salt, pepper, or water for boiling – which most kitchens do. But it won't suddenly tell you to add an exotic spice or a fresh herb unless you hinted you have it or it's truly essential (and even then, you can always say you don't have it, and it will adapt). In other words, ChatGPT is very content to work within the boundaries you set, which means the recipe suggestions are practical and immediately achievable.

By using ingredient-based prompts, cooking becomes more about possibilities than limitations. Each item in your pantry is no longer just a lone soldier – it's a potential meal waiting to happen when combined with the right partners. ChatGPT helps you see those possibilities. The next time you're faced with a pantry challenge, try listing out everything that's available and let ChatGPT surprise you. You'll quickly gain confidence that no matter what ingredients you have, a good meal is just a prompt away. Even if your list is very short or seemingly incompatible, ChatGPT can often find a creative angle to turn it into something tasty.

As we'll explore next, even a sparse pantry can spark delicious ideas with a little AI creativity.

GETTING CREATIVE WITH LIMITED INGREDIENTS

One of the joys of using ChatGPT for cooking is seeing how it can conjure up ideas from a very short or unexciting list of ingredients. When your pantry is almost bare, the AI's creativity truly shines. Instead of resigning yourself to plain toast or yet another bowl of cereal, you can challenge ChatGPT with whatever bits and bobs you do have. Often, it will respond with a suggestion that transforms those few items into a satisfying dish. The key here is *stretching* ingredients – finding ways to make a little into enough, and something simple into something special.

ChatGPT has been trained on recipes from all over the world, which means it knows many traditional dishes that use minimal ingredients. It can tap into this knowledge to help you. For example, suppose you only have *flour, water, and a pinch of salt* in your kitchen – hardly a feast. If you tell ChatGPT *"I just have flour, water, and salt.*

What can I make?", you might get an answer like: "*You can whip up a quick flatbread. Mix the flour, water, and salt into a dough, press it flat, and cook it in a hot pan. It won't need yeast or baking powder – it'll be like a rustic tortilla. Once it's done, you could drizzle a bit of olive oil or butter on top if available, or use it as a wrap for any leftovers.*" In one stroke, the AI turned the most basic staples into a simple bread – something many of us wouldn't think to do offhand. That flatbread could then be the base for a more filling meal if you find just one or two more items to put on it.

The AI is also great at making unexpected connections between ingredients. Let's say you peek in your fridge and see only a *tomato and an egg*. It sounds like breakfast-for-dinner might be your only route (and indeed, ChatGPT could suggest a basic fried egg with sliced tomato). But it might also come up with a more interesting idea: tomato-poached eggs, a twist on shakshuka or a simple tomato and scrambled egg stir-fry (a popular Chinese home-style dish). With just those two ingredients, plus a bit of seasoning, you suddenly have a dish that's more than the sum of its parts. ChatGPT's breadth of culinary knowledge means it might recall that tomatoes and eggs are a known good pair in certain cuisines, and present you with that solution.

Another scenario: you have a lone *banana, some oats, and a spoonful of peanut butter*. Individually, none of these are a meal. But if you ask ChatGPT for a creative use of banana, oats, and peanut butter, it could give you a quick recipe for chewy banana-oat cookies or energy balls. For instance, it might say, "*Mash the banana and mix it with the oats and peanut butter to form a batter, then bake spoonfuls of it in the oven to make simple cookies.*" Suddenly, a sweet treat emerges from ingredients you thought were only good for a boring snack. This demonstrates how AI can combine ingredients in ways you might not realize work well together.

When the cupboard is nearly bare, *technique* becomes just as important as ingredients. ChatGPT might suggest using water or broth (if you have bouillon cubes, for example) to turn a small handful of vegetables into a filling soup. Or it might recommend a stir-fry or fried rice as a way to make a meal out of scraps, because stir-frying can bring together tiny portions of meat, veggies, and rice into one cohesive dish. If you mention even a few spices or condiments in your prompt – like soy sauce, garlic powder, or cinnamon – the AI will leverage those to add flavor and interest. A sparse pantry with the right spice can turn "rice and beans" into a nicely seasoned Mexican-style rice bowl, or turn "plain lentils" into a curried lentil stew. Don't hesitate to list your seasonings; ChatGPT will creatively incorporate them.

ChatGPT can also think of substitutions or ingredient "hacks" when you're missing something. Perhaps you're craving pancakes but you've run out of eggs. If you tell ChatGPT what you *do* have (say flour, milk, baking powder, but no eggs), it might recall an egg-free pancake recipe that uses a little extra baking powder and milk to compensate. Or maybe you have some spaghetti but no sauce – ChatGPT could suggest a simple aglio e olio (garlic and oil pasta) if you have garlic or even a butter-and-herb pasta if you have just butter and dried herbs. These ideas show how AI can adjust to limitations: by using a cooking technique or an alternate ingredient to fill in the gaps.

The suggestions you get might occasionally surprise you. You could learn a new cooking trick from ChatGPT's answer. For instance, you might not know that the liquid from a can of chickpeas (aquafaba) can whip up like egg whites to make a mousse or a vegan meringue – but if you asked what to do with chickpea liquid and sugar, the AI could point that out. Or if you only have a can of tuna and some pasta, ChatGPT might remind you that you can make a quick tuna pasta salad or tuna casserole with minimal other ingredients. In effect, using ChatGPT is like brainstorming with a very inventive chef: no combination is too odd to at least consider.

To get the most creative answers, be sure to tell ChatGPT about **everything** you have, even if it's just a spoonful of something. Those little details can spark big ideas. And if its first suggestion still seems too plain, you can always prompt it further: *"That's nice, but do you have a more interesting idea using these same ingredients?"* Often, it will come back with a more offbeat or gourmet take once you ask it to dig deeper. You'll find that even with a sparse pantry, there are layers of possibility – from the obvious quick fix to the surprisingly clever recipe – all accessible through a bit of prompting.

Ultimately, this section is about hope and ingenuity. Limited ingredients don't have to mean limited meals. With ChatGPT's creative input, you can approach those nearly-empty fridge days with a sense of curiosity rather than dread. You might even have fun seeing what unconventional dish you can whip up next. And as you experiment with these suggestions, you'll start learning new ways to stretch ingredients on your own. Next time you confront a barren pantry, remember that ChatGPT can help you cook up something out of almost nothing, sparking creativity in even the simplest of kitchens.

Now that we've seen how AI can inspire creativity when supplies are low, it's time to consider how the way you ask ChatGPT for help influences the suggestions you get.

SMART PROMPTING FOR BETTER SUGGESTIONS

How you frame your request to ChatGPT can make a big difference in the kind of answer you get. By now, you've seen that simply listing ingredients works – but adding a bit more detail or direction can take the suggestions from good to great. Smart prompting is all about telling the AI exactly what you're looking for in a meal idea. Do you need dinner in under 30 minutes? Are you cooking for kids or aiming for something healthy? Is there a cuisine you're craving, or a cooking method you'd prefer (like a stir-fry versus a casserole)? Including those details in your question will help ChatGPT tailor its response to your needs and give you more relevant, appealing options.

For example, imagine you have chicken, broccoli, and cheddar cheese on hand. If you just ask, *"What can I make with chicken, broccoli, and cheddar?"*, you might get a perfectly decent suggestion such as a chicken and broccoli cheese casserole. But maybe that wasn't what you had in mind. Suppose you really wanted something quick and kid-friendly. If you instead prompt, *"I have chicken, broccoli, and cheddar, and I need a quick kid-friendly dinner. Any ideas?"*, you'll likely get a different answer. ChatGPT might propose a cheesy chicken and broccoli pasta that comes together in 20 minutes – a simpler, stovetop dish that kids might gobble up. In this way, by specifying *what kind* of meal you want, you guide the AI toward a suggestion that fits your situation better.

In general, when asking ChatGPT for cooking ideas, try to paint a picture of your needs. The more context you provide, the more the AI can fine-tune its response. Here are some tips for phrasing prompts to get the best results:

- ***Mention any dietary preferences or restrictions:*** If you're vegetarian, halal, gluten-free, on a low-carb diet, or cooking for someone with allergies, include that. For instance, *"I have zucchini and tomatoes. What can I make that's vegan?"* will yield a different idea than just *"What can I make with zucchini and tomatoes?"*.
- ***Specify the type of dish or cuisine if you have a leaning:*** You could say, *"I'm in the mood for Italian. I have mushrooms, garlic, and pasta – what could I make?"* This might prompt an answer like a garlic mushroom pasta, whereas without mentioning Italian, you might have gotten a generic pasta or even a stir-fry suggestion.
- ***Include time or effort constraints:*** Let ChatGPT know if you need something quick, or if you're up for a slow-cooked meal. For example: *"I only have 30 minutes to cook and I have shrimp, rice, and bell peppers."* The AI will likely stick to fast cooking methods (like a quick stir-fry or sauté) in its answer.
- ***State the number of ideas you want for variety:*** Instead of one answer, you can ask for multiple suggestions. *"Can you give me three different dinner ideas using chickpeas and spinach?"* might return, say, a curry, a salad, and a soup –

offering you a range of choices. This is great when you want to explore options or have picky eaters to please.

- ***Describe the style or mood of the meal:*** If you want comfort food, or something light, or maybe a "fancy" dish to impress guests, let ChatGPT know. *"Using lentils and carrots, suggest a light, healthy meal."* or *"I have beef and potatoes; give me a fancy dinner idea for a date night."* You'd get very different recipes (a salad or stew in the first case, perhaps a bistro-style steak and potatoes in the second).
- ***Indicate if you need specific details in the answer:*** For instance, you can ask for just dish names and a short description if you're in brainstorming mode, or request a full recipe with steps if you're ready to cook. Saying *"please list a few ideas, without detailed recipes yet"* versus *"give me the recipe with instructions for..."* will shape the kind of output you get.

By following these prompting strategies, you essentially teach ChatGPT what's important to you before it formulates an answer. You'll notice that a well-crafted prompt often yields an answer that feels custom-made. It's the difference between a generic "here's something to cook" and a suggestion that truly fits your evening's needs.

There's also the element of *balance*. If you ask very generally, you might get a very general answer. If you ask with a huge list of requirements, you might constrain the AI too much and the idea could become overly simplistic or forced. For example, *"Give me a gluten-free, low-fat, high-protein, vegan dessert using only these two ingredients..."* is a lot to juggle at once. ChatGPT will try its best, but the result might not be as satisfying as a prompt that's slightly more flexible. Try to prioritize what matters most and leave a bit of creative room for the AI to work with.

One handy approach is to have ChatGPT help you iterate. You can start with a moderate prompt – include a couple of key details – and see what it suggests. If the idea isn't quite right, you can then refine it (which we'll cover in the next section). But often, that first answer will be on target if your prompt was specific enough about the things that matter to you.

Let's say you have some tofu and you want something *really different*. You could prompt: *"I have tofu, but I'm bored of stir-fries. Can you suggest a unique way to cook tofu for dinner?"* A smart prompt like this tells the AI not only what ingredient you have but also what you want to avoid (the usual preparations). In response, you might get a suggestion for tofu tacos with spicy seasoning, or a baked tofu 'steak' with a marinade – something a bit outside the ordinary.

In summary, don't be afraid to talk to ChatGPT as if it's a chef who needs your guidance. The more you tell it about your vision for the meal, the better its recommendations will align. Whether it's specifying "a hearty soup" or saying "no oven, please" because yours is broken, putting those details in the prompt sets you up for success. Once you receive some suggestions, you can then choose the one that appeals most – and if needed, you can always ask ChatGPT to elaborate or adjust. Speaking of which, after getting an initial answer, how do you refine it or tweak it? That's where the next step comes in: learning to refine and filter ChatGPT's results to perfectly suit your needs.

REFINING AND FILTERING RESULTS

Getting a recipe idea from ChatGPT is just the beginning. One of the best features of this AI assistant is that you can have a back-and-forth conversation to fine-tune the suggestions. After you receive an initial answer, you don't have to take it as-is – you can ask ChatGPT to modify the recipe or offer alternatives until it fits your exact needs. This process of refining the results is like collaborating with a chef: you say "hmm, what if we change this or that?", and ChatGPT will adjust accordingly.

Let's say ChatGPT suggests a dish that sounds tasty but includes an ingredient you don't have or don't like. You can simply tell it that and ask for a change. For example, maybe it proposed a *spicy chili* but your family can't handle much heat. You could reply: *"That chili idea sounds good, but can we make it mild? I don't want it spicy."* ChatGPT will then reinterpret the recipe, perhaps suggesting to omit the chili powder and use flavorful herbs instead, or recommending a completely different mild dish using the same main ingredients (like a savory bean and turkey stew with herbs). The key is that you're not starting from scratch – you're building on the previous answer.

Refinement can also mean simplifying a complex suggestion. Imagine the AI gives you a gourmet recipe with many steps, and you're just not up for that level of effort tonight. It's perfectly fine to say something like: *"This recipe seems a bit complicated. Can you simplify it or give me an easier version?"* ChatGPT might then trim down the steps or suggest shortcuts. For instance, if it initially suggested a scratch-made pie for dessert, a simplification might be to make a crisp or crumble instead, using the same fruits but less fuss. Or if the recipe had a long list of ingredients, you can ask, *"What are the essential ingredients here? I'd like to use as few as possible."* The AI can then pare it down to the basics.

Another common refinement is adjusting for dietary needs or missing items. Perhaps the first suggestion wasn't vegetarian, but you want it to be. You can ask, *"How could I make this recipe vegetarian?"* and ChatGPT will offer substitutions (maybe swapping chicken for chickpeas, or suggesting mushrooms instead of ground beef). If the recipe calls for butter and you're dairy-free, you could ask for a substitute – and you'll probably get options like olive oil or coconut oil in place of butter. The model is quite good at knowing classic ingredient swaps, like using applesauce instead of eggs in baking or yogurt instead of cream in a sauce. So don't hesitate to ask for adjustments to meet your dietary requirements.

Time and equipment are other factors you can filter by. If the dish sounds great but takes too long, you might say, *"I only have 30 minutes – how can I make this faster?"* ChatGPT could then suggest precooking something in the microwave, or cutting the food into smaller pieces to reduce cook time, or even using a pressure cooker if you have one. If the recipe requires an oven but you don't have access to one (or it's a hot day and you'd rather not bake), you can ask, *"Can I cook this on the stovetop instead?"* Often, the AI will have an alternative method ready, like pan-searing a protein instead of roasting it, or making a stovetop stew instead of an oven braise.

Sometimes ChatGPT gives you a list of multiple dish ideas and you need to pick one. You can use follow-up questions to help make that decision. For example, after getting three suggestions, you might ask, *"Which of these would be simplest for a beginner?"* or *"Which one is the healthiest option?"* ChatGPT can then provide a bit more analysis or detail about each choice, helping you narrow it down. You could even say, *"I like the sound of the second idea – can you give me more details on how to make that?"* and the AI will happily dive deeper into that specific recipe.

The refining step is also a chance to inject your own creativity or cravings into the mix. Maybe the suggestion was for a tomato-based soup, but you wonder if it could be turned into a creamy version. Ask ChatGPT: *"What if I wanted this soup to be creamy? What would I add?"* You'll get advice perhaps to add some milk or blended beans, etc. Or you might combine ideas: *"Could I add the spice mix from the first idea to the second recipe?"* Because ChatGPT remembers the context of your chat, it can cross-reference and merge ideas from earlier in the conversation.

Through refining and filtering, you're steering ChatGPT's guidance closer and closer to your perfect meal. It's an iterative process that feels a bit like recipe development, but without the hard work on your part – you're just chatting and the AI is doing the heavy lifting of figuring out the details. This flexible dialogue turns ChatGPT from just a recipe finder into a true kitchen assistant who adapts to you.

By now, you've learned how to come up with meal ideas and refine them to fit your needs. But cooking smarter isn't just about one meal at a time – it's also about planning ahead. How can ChatGPT help you cook once and eat twice (or more)? Let's explore using AI for batch cooking and clever reuse of ingredients so nothing goes to waste.

BATCH COOKING AND REUSE STRATEGIES

Cooking with an eye toward leftovers or multiple meals is a smart way to save time and reduce waste. ChatGPT can be a great ally in this kind of strategic meal planning. Instead of thinking of each dinner in isolation, you can ask the AI to help you plan a sequence of meals that build on each other. This means that what you cook today could intentionally become part of tomorrow's dish. The idea is to "cook once, eat twice" – or even thrice – and ChatGPT can come up with creative ways to make that happen.

One way to use ChatGPT for batch cooking is to start with a base ingredient that you want to use in multiple meals. For example, suppose you have a whole chicken or a big pot of chili. You can prompt: *"Help me plan three different meals using a roasted chicken over the next few days."* The AI might then output a mini meal plan, for instance:

ChatGPT: "Sure! Here's a 3-day meal plan using your roasted chicken:

Day 1: Enjoy the roasted chicken as the main dish alongside roasted vegetables and rice.

Day 2: Shred the remaining chicken to make chicken tacos. Sauté it with spices (like cumin and chili powder) and serve in tortillas with any fresh toppings you have.

Day 3: Use the chicken bones to cook a simple broth, then add leftover chicken meat and veggies to create a comforting chicken soup or stew."

In this example, ChatGPT turned one cooking effort (the roast chicken) into two additional distinct meals. Each meal feels different – the first is a classic roast, the second has a Mexican flair, the third is a cozy soup – keeping things from getting boring while using up all of the chicken. You could ask for variations on this plan too. If soup isn't your thing, you might prompt, *"What about something other than soup for Day 3?"* and it could suggest a chicken fried rice or a casserole using the last of the meat.

Batch cooking isn't limited to proteins. You can do the same with grains (like a big batch of rice or quinoa), beans, or roasted vegetables. ChatGPT knows plenty of ways to repurpose these. Let's say on Sunday you make a large pot of lentils or beans. You could ask, *"How can I use a big batch of cooked lentils for meals throughout the week?"* You might get suggestions such as: turn some lentils into a hearty lentil soup on Monday, toss them with veggies and vinaigrette for a salad on Tuesday, and spice them with curry powder to serve over rice on Wednesday. A simple pot of lentils suddenly becomes three different culinary experiences.

Another useful strategy is to get ideas for using specific leftovers. Perhaps you made a big lasagna and have half of it left, or you grilled a lot of vegetables and want to reinvent them. You can prompt ChatGPT with something like, *"I have a lot of grilled vegetables left over. What can I make with them tomorrow?"* The assistant might propose a grilled vegetable pasta, a frittata with those veggies, or even blending them into a rustic soup. If your leftover is a stew or chili, ChatGPT might suggest turning it into a filling for burritos or a topping for baked potatoes. The goal is to prevent "leftover fatigue" by transforming yesterday's dinner into something fresh and appealing.

ChatGPT can also help with planning out a cooking session that covers multiple meals. For instance, you could say, *"I want to meal prep for the week. I have ground beef, rice, and beans—how can I cook once and get a few different meals?"* The AI might advise cooking all the ground beef with a basic seasoning, then using part of it for tacos, part for a rice and beef bowl, and the rest for a quick chili with the beans. It could even suggest freezing one portion for later in the week. These suggestions act like a blueprint for efficient cooking: you do the main work (like browning the beef and cooking the rice) upfront, then assemble variations on subsequent days.

When it comes to reusing ingredients, don't forget you can ask ChatGPT for storage advice as well. If you're not sure how long something will keep, or the best way to store that soup you made, you can inquire: *"How should I store this soup and how long will it last?"* While not a food scientist, ChatGPT generally knows standard food safety guidelines and can tell you, for example, that soup will last a few days in the fridge or how to freeze it properly. This ensures your batch-cooked meals stay safe and tasty.

By leveraging ChatGPT for batch cooking and reuse ideas, you start to think of your kitchen as a continuous cycle rather than one-off projects. You'll buy and cook in larger quantities with confidence that nothing will be wasted, because the AI is ready with suggestions to reinvent leftovers. This not only saves time and money, but also adds a fun creative challenge to your cooking routine – it's satisfying to see a plan come together where Tuesday's dinner benefits from Sunday's preparation.

Having explored how to maximize ingredients across multiple meals, you're well on your way to a more efficient kitchen. But life isn't always so organized – what about those nights when you haven't planned at all and need something fast? Don't worry, ChatGPT has your back in those situations too, as we'll see in the next section on emergency meals and pantry rescues.

EMERGENCY MEALS AND PANTRY RESCUES

We all encounter those moments when it seems like there's nothing to eat and you need to whip up something *fast*. Maybe you skipped grocery shopping, or it's late at night and you're peering into a nearly empty fridge. The good news is that ChatGPT thrives in these "nothing to eat" scenarios. With a little creative prompting, you can find that there's almost always *something* you can make, even with a scant pantry.

When you're in a bind, start by listing whatever you *do* have – no matter how odd the combination may seem. ChatGPT doesn't judge; it will earnestly try to suggest a meal or snack from whatever inputs you give it. For example, you might type, "*I only have a box of spaghetti, an onion, and a bottle of ketchup. Help!*" While that sounds like a cooking nightmare, the AI can propose a survival meal: perhaps a simple spaghetti aglio e olio (spaghetti with sautéed onion in oil, if you have a bit of oil or butter) and a makeshift tomato sauce using diluted ketchup and spices to approximate a pasta sauce. It might not be gourmet, but in a pinch it will fill you up. The important thing is that ChatGPT will come up with ideas that you might not have considered in your hunger-induced panic.

Often, the AI will remind you of quick staples you might have overlooked. For instance:

- ***Eggs:*** Turn them into a quick omelet (you can throw in any leftover veggies or cheese you might find), or even crack one into a mug and microwave it for an almost instant scramble.
- ***Canned beans:*** Mash them with a bit of seasoning to make a speedy bean dip or spread; if you have any hot sauce or spices, stir them in. Or heat the beans with any condiments and water to create a simple soup or stew.
- ***A potato:*** Prick it with a fork and microwave it to create a "baked" potato in minutes. Top it with a little butter, salt, or even a leftover sauce packet for flavor. (If you have more time, you could dice it and pan-fry it for quick home fries.)
- ***Flour and water:*** Mix these into a simple dough or batter to cook a quick flatbread or pancake. It won't be fancy, but it can stave off hunger. Even just frying a bit of this dough in a pan can create a makeshift tortilla or crepe.

Speed is usually crucial in these situations, so you can explicitly tell ChatGPT you're in a hurry. Try a prompt like, *"I need something to eat in 10 minutes. I have rice, a jar of salsa, and a can of black beans."* The answer could be a very quick stovetop bean and rice bowl: heat the beans with the salsa to make a flavorful mixture and serve it over microwave-steamed rice. Or if the rice is already cooked, even better – it's basically an instant meal. The AI might even suggest wrapping that bean-and-rice combo in a tortilla if you have one, creating impromptu burritos.

Another "pantry rescue" trick ChatGPT uses is leveraging those long-forgotten items in the back of your cupboard. That dusty box of *instant ramen* can be transformed beyond just plain soup – the AI might suggest stirring in an egg to make it heartier, or draining the noodles and tossing them with a little oil and the seasoning packet to create a quick noodle stir-fry. If you mention any spices or sauces at all, no matter how seemingly incompatible, ChatGPT will try to incorporate them. Barbecue sauce and one can of chickpeas? Maybe you end up with BBQ chickpea sandwiches. A jar of pickles and some lentils? Perhaps a tangy lentil salad. The suggestions can sound a bit unconventional, but when you're truly scraping the bottom of the barrel, unconventional is fair game.

What's reassuring is the tone and encouragement ChatGPT often provides. In an emergency cooking situation, having a friendly assistant say "Here's something you can try!" is a relief. It takes away some of the stress and decision fatigue. You might even find it fun to see what crazy (yet edible) idea the AI comes up with for your odd assortment of ingredients. And because it's so quick to respond, you can go from despairing about an empty kitchen to actively cooking within minutes.

These last-minute meals might not be your most memorable gourmet experiences, but they can surprise you. You may discover a new favorite snack or a simple meal hack for the future. More importantly, you'll have satisfied your hunger without resorting to takeout or skipping dinner. And each time you use ChatGPT to solve a "nothing to eat" crisis, you become more confident that you can handle the next one.

By now, we've covered everything from using up pantry staples to dealing with emergency hunger. To wrap up this chapter, let's look at some *live examples* of pantry-based prompts and ChatGPT responses. In the next section, we'll walk through a series of real-world scenarios and see exactly how the AI tackles them, reinforcing all the techniques we've discussed.

LIVE EXAMPLES: PANTRY PROMPTS THAT WORK

Let's bring everything together with a few real-world examples. Below are sample prompts that a home cook might give to ChatGPT, along with brief excerpts of the AI's responses. These scenarios show how versatile ChatGPT can be – from ordinary pantry combinations to odd leftovers and last-minute scrambles.

Example 1: Turning Pantry Staples into Dinner

Prompt: "I have some chicken thighs, a can of diced tomatoes, and a can of beans. What can I make for dinner?"

ChatGPT: "You can make a hearty chicken and bean stew. Start by sautéing the chicken thighs in a pot until browned. Then add the diced tomatoes (with their juices) and the drained beans. Throw in some garlic or onion if you have it, and season with salt, pepper, and maybe a bit of cumin or chili powder for warmth. Let it simmer for 20 minutes. You'll end up with a cozy one-pot chicken chili that's perfect for dinner."

Example 2: Creative Meal from a Quirky Combo

Prompt: "All I have is a can of chickpeas and a jar of peanut butter. Is there anything I can make with that?"

ChatGPT: "It might sound unusual, but you can actually create a tasty West African-inspired peanut stew. Purée or finely chop some of the chickpeas to thicken the stew, and simmer them in water (or broth if available) with a couple spoonfuls of peanut butter. Add any spices you might have, like a pinch of cumin or curry powder, and salt and pepper. The peanut butter will melt into a creamy sauce. After about 15 minutes, you'll have a rich, nutty chickpea stew. It's surprisingly hearty and flavorful given the simple ingredients!"

Example 3: Specific Request (Tired of the Same Old Thing)

Prompt: "I have tofu and broccoli, but I'm tired of stir-fry. What else can I make with them?"

ChatGPT: "How about roasting them? Toss the broccoli florets and cubes of tofu with a little oil, salt, pepper, and any other seasoning you like (say, garlic powder and paprika). Spread them on a baking sheet and roast at 400°F (200°C) for about 20-25 minutes until the broccoli is tender and the tofu is golden and slightly crisp. Meanwhile, if you have soy sauce, ginger, or honey, you could mix up a quick sauce to drizzle on top afterward. This gives you a savory roasted tofu and broccoli dish that's a nice change from a stir-fry."

Example 4: Refining a Suggestion on the Fly

Prompt: "I have a bowl of cooked rice left over from yesterday. What can I do with it?"

ChatGPT: "Leftover rice is perfect for fried rice! Sauté the rice in a bit of oil. If you have an egg, scramble it in the pan and mix it in, and throw in any veggies or soy sauce you might have. In just a few minutes, you'll have a hot bowl of fried rice."

Follow-up: "I don't have any vegetables or soy sauce, unfortunately."

ChatGPT: "No worries. You can still make a satisfying dish. Try cracking an egg into the rice and frying it together to make a simple egg-and-rice scramble. Season it with just salt and pepper (and a dash of hot sauce or ketchup if you want to experiment). It's basic but comforting. Alternatively, form the rice into patties and fry them in a pan to make crispy rice cakes. Serve them with a little soy sauce or chili sauce on top if you have any. Even with just rice and an egg, you've got options for a quick meal."

Example 5: Batch Cooking Plan

Prompt: "I want to cook a big batch of ground beef now and use it for three different dinners. Any suggestions?"

ChatGPT: "Certainly! Here's one way you could use it:

- Taco Night: Season and cook the ground beef with taco spices. Serve some of it in tortillas as beef tacos (with any toppings you have like cheese, lettuce, salsa).
- Pasta Bolognese: Take another portion of the cooked beef and simmer it with a can of tomatoes or tomato sauce (plus garlic or herbs) to make a quick Bolognese sauce. Toss with pasta.

- Stuffed Peppers: Mix the last portion of the beef with cooked rice (if you have some) and a bit of seasoning. Stuff that into bell peppers and bake until tender. You've now made three distinct meals from one batch of cooking!"

In each of these examples, you can see how ChatGPT adapts to the situation: using what's available, following specific preferences, refining suggestions with user feedback, and planning ahead for multiple meals. Try imagining your own kitchen scenarios and test them out with ChatGPT. You'll gain confidence as you see these *AI-generated suggestions* come to life in your cooking.

In the next chapter, we'll continue expanding your AI-assisted kitchen skills, building on everything you've learned here.

3

MAKING IT WORK FOR YOU: DIETARY AND BUDGET FILTERS

Cooking at home becomes so much easier and more enjoyable when your meals fit *you*. Maybe you're trying to follow a new diet for health reasons, or you're keeping a close eye on your grocery spending. Perhaps you need recipes that meet specific nutritional targets or avoid certain allergens. Whatever your personal requirements – from dietary restrictions to budget limitations – this chapter will show you how to make ChatGPT cater to your needs. In other words, you'll learn to use dietary and budget filters so that every suggestion from your AI kitchen companion is practical and personalized for your life.

In this chapter, we dive into the art of custom cooking with constraints. Constraints might sound limiting at first, but think of them as guiding stars that help focus your cooking journey. Whether you need gluten-free weeknight dinners, high-protein vegan lunches, or family meals under $10, ChatGPT can be directed to filter its vast recipe knowledge and deliver ideas that check all your boxes. Instead of searching endlessly through cookbooks or websites for that perfect recipe that matches your diet and wallet, you can simply tell ChatGPT your criteria and let it do the heavy lifting.

You will discover how dietary filters (like keto, vegetarian, gluten-free, or low-sodium) can be combined with budget filters to yield meals that are both healthy and affordable. We'll discuss strategies for eating well on a tight budget – from bulk-friendly ingredients to low-waste cooking – and how to prompt ChatGPT for cost-effective meal plans. We'll also explore ways to maintain big flavor while sticking to diet plans, ensuring that "healthy" doesn't mean "boring." This chapter will give you plenty of real-world examples of how to phrase your requests so that ChatGPT understands your needs and provides spot-on recommendations.

Another focus of this chapter is learning to stack multiple requirements in a single prompt. Real life is complicated: you might be short on time *and* cooking for a picky eater, all while keeping things low-carb. We'll show you how to layer these needs in your questions to ChatGPT so it can handle complex requests like "quick, low-carb, kid-friendly dinners" without missing a beat. When you have lots of boxes to tick, a well-crafted AI prompt becomes your best friend in the kitchen.

By the end of this chapter, you'll also know how to turn ChatGPT's meal suggestions into actionable plans. This includes generating smart shopping lists with your budget in mind and getting advice on ingredient substitutions to save money or meet dietary rules. Finally, we'll walk through real-life scenarios where home cooks use ChatGPT to adapt their favorite recipes to new needs – like making a beloved comfort food gluten-free or trimming costs from a fancy dish. These examples will tie together everything you've learned, giving you the confidence to apply dietary and budget filters to any cooking situation.

In short, this chapter is all about making ChatGPT work *for you.* Cooking is not one-size-fits-all, and with a little guidance, your AI sous-chef can offer solutions tailor-made to your diet, your budget, and your household. Let's get started on cooking smarter within your limits – and turning limitations into delicious opportunities.

CUSTOM COOKING WITH CONSTRAINTS

Imagine walking into a huge library of recipes and meal ideas. It's exciting, but it can also be overwhelming if you have specific needs. This is where ChatGPT truly shines as a personal cooking assistant: you can tell it exactly what your constraints are, and it will narrow down that giant library to a curated selection that fits *you*. Dietary, nutritional, or financial goals — these are not obstacles, but parameters that guide ChatGPT's suggestions.

The first step is to be specific about your needs when prompting. ChatGPT will only know about your dietary or budget goals if you mention them. So, if you're trying to eat low-carb or you only have $20 to spend on dinners this week, make sure to include those details in your request. The more clearly you state your requirements, the better ChatGPT can filter its results. For example, consider the difference between these two prompts:

Prompt: "Tell me a healthy dinner recipe."

ChatGPT: *Provides a generic healthy recipe, perhaps a salad or grilled chicken dish, but it may not account for any specific diets or cost.*

Prompt: "Tell me a healthy dinner recipe under 600 calories that costs no more than $5 per serving."

ChatGPT: *Suggests a specific recipe (for instance, a hearty black bean and vegetable chili) noting that each serving is around 400–500 calories and uses budget-friendly ingredients like beans and seasonal veggies. The response might even mention the estimated cost per serving and a quick summary of how to prepare it.*

In the second prompt, we gave ChatGPT two clear filters: a calorie limit and a cost limit. As a result, the AI's answer becomes much more tailored and useful for someone counting calories and pennies. This is custom cooking with constraints in action. You guide the AI, and it delivers a recipe that works within your boundaries.

Dietary constraints are a common concern. If you have allergies or follow a specific eating plan (like vegetarian, keto, or gluten-free), always include that in your prompt. For instance, *"I need a gluten-free dessert idea"* or *"Suggest a keto-friendly breakfast high in protein"*.

ChatGPT has knowledge of many dietary substitutions and can often adapt traditional recipes to fit a diet. When you specify a diet, the AI will avoid ingredients you can't have (like flour for gluten-free or rice for keto) and suggest appropriate alternatives. It's like having a nutrition-savvy chef on call – one who remembers to skip the salt for low-sodium diets or to use dairy-free milk for a lactose intolerance.

Being **nutrition-specific** can help as well. If you have a particular nutritional goal, tell ChatGPT exactly what numbers you're aiming for. Are you watching your sugar intake or trying to boost protein? You could prompt: *"Give me a dinner under 500 calories with at least 20 grams of protein"* or *"I'm trying to eat 30 grams of fiber a day – what's a high-fiber lunch option?"*. The AI can calculate approximate nutritional content based on its knowledge of ingredients and common recipes. It might respond with something like, *"Try a quinoa and black bean salad with veggies – high in fiber and protein, around 400 calories per serving."* Including such details steers the answers toward recipes that truly align with your health objectives. And if you want the nutritional breakdown of a suggested recipe, you can ask for that too: *"Looks good – can you list the carbs, protein, and fat for each serving?"* ChatGPT can then break down the macros for you.

Financial constraints are another area where ChatGPT can make a huge difference in your meal planning. When money is tight, you'll want recipes that are inexpensive yet satisfying. Don't hesitate to mention your grocery budget or cost per meal limit. For example: *"I have $15 to spend on dinner for four people. What can I make?"* is a clear request. ChatGPT might answer with a cost-conscious meal like a vegetable frittata or a bean-and-rice burrito platter, along with notes on using affordable ingredients (eggs, beans, frozen veggies) and approximate costs: *"This whole meal comes in around $12, using ingredients like canned beans and seasonal vegetables."* By stating your budget up front, you filter out those recipes with fancy, expensive ingredients and get down to humble, hearty food that won't break the bank.

One handy tip is to also specify any **ingredient preferences or limitations** you already know. If you're cooking with what's on hand or you strongly dislike a certain food, that can be part of your prompt (even if it's not a dietary necessity, it's a personal constraint!). For example, *"Give me a dairy-free dinner under $10 that uses chicken and broccoli, and no mushrooms please."* Here you've combined a dietary filter (dairy-free), a budget filter (under $10), and even specific ingredients to include or exclude. ChatGPT can combine all of those elements to propose something like a stir-fry with chicken, broccoli, and a dairy-free sauce, ensuring it respects all parts of your request. The ability to mix and match these details is powerful – you are essentially programming the recipe parameters you care about.

As you begin using ChatGPT for personalized cooking advice, remember that you're in control of the criteria. Think of any factor that matters to you – health goals, ingredient availability, time constraints, or cost – and include those in what you ask. It might feel odd at first to spell everything out ("Can't the AI just know I'm on a budget?" we might wonder), but ChatGPT works best when we clearly communicate our needs. The good news is the more you practice writing these tailored prompts, the more naturally it comes.

Finally, don't be afraid to have a back-and-forth conversation with ChatGPT to refine the results. If the first answer it gives isn't quite right, you can clarify or add more constraints. For instance, *"Actually, I also need this recipe to be kid-friendly and not too spicy"* can be a follow-up if the budget-friendly curry it suggested sounds too bold for your children. ChatGPT will then adjust the recommendation (maybe a milder stew or a casserole) to better fit your family's needs. This interactive refinement is part of custom cooking with constraints – you start broad and then fine-tune the details. Now, with these prompting basics in mind, let's zoom in on one of the most common constraints for home cooks: cooking on a budget. It's entirely possible to eat well without overspending, and ChatGPT can be your guide to doing just that.

EATING WELL ON A BUDGET

Cooking on a budget doesn't mean settling for plain or unhealthy meals. With the right prompts, ChatGPT can help you maximize flavor and nutrition per dollar. The key is to ask for cost-effective ideas and include your budget constraints clearly. Whether you're a student trying to stretch a grocery allowance or a parent feeding a family of four on a single income, AI can assist in planning satisfying meals that won't break the bank.

Be clear and specific about your budget when you prompt. Instead of asking vaguely for "cheap recipes," put a number on it. For example: *"What's a dinner I can make for under $10 total?"* or *"Give me a week's meal plan for two people with a budget of $50."* By specifying an amount, you help ChatGPT understand exactly what "budget-friendly" means to you. It will then focus on economical ingredients and simple preparations. You might get suggestions like a hearty pasta dish or a bean chili – recipes known to be low-cost per serving. ChatGPT could even estimate the cost of each ingredient or the total meal, e.g., *"This soup uses lentils and vegetables and should come out to around $8 for four servings."* Keep in mind these are estimates, but they're useful for planning.

Focus on affordable ingredients in your requests. Staples like beans, rice, potatoes, pasta, canned tomatoes, and eggs are famously budget-friendly. If you prompt ChatGPT with specific cheap ingredients, it can build a meal around them. For instance: *"I have rice and beans – what can I make that's different and tasty?"* could yield a suggestion such as a spiced Mexican-style rice bowl or a Cajun red beans and rice recipe. Or if you say, *"Give me a dinner recipe using chicken thighs (an inexpensive cut) and seasonal vegetables"*, the AI might come back with a sheet-pan roasted chicken and veggies that makes use of whatever produce is cheap at the moment. You can also ask for *substitutions* to make a recipe cheaper. If ChatGPT offers a recipe with shrimp but shrimp is outside your budget, you could follow up: *"That sounds great. What's a cheaper protein I can use instead of shrimp?"* You'll likely get alternatives like chicken, tofu, or beans, along with advice on how to adjust seasoning or cook time for the swap.

Plan for leftovers and reduce waste – this is a budget-cooking golden rule where ChatGPT can help immensely. Wasted food is wasted money, so try prompts that encourage using up all your ingredients. For example: *"Plan a two-day menu that uses a whole roasted chicken – one day as a roast, the next day turning the leftovers into a new meal."* ChatGPT might suggest roasting the chicken for day one, then shredding the remaining meat for day two's tacos or soup. Another scenario: *"I have half a loaf of day-old bread and some wilting vegetables; what can I cook so I don't throw them out?"* The AI could respond with a strata or a panzanella (bread salad) that revives stale bread and veggies into a delicious dish. By prompting for low-waste ideas, you not only save money but also feel good about making the most of what you buy. If you ever find yourself with odd leftover ingredients, try a quick ChatGPT query: *"What can I do with leftover [ingredient]?"* – be it rice, cooked veggies, or even bones from a roast – and you'll get creative suggestions to turn scraps into a meal or ingredient for tomorrow.

Think bulk and multi-purpose when budgeting. Buying in bulk often lowers the unit price of ingredients, but you then need ways to use those larger quantities. You can ask ChatGPT for ideas that leverage a bulk buy across multiple meals. For example: *"I bought a big bag of quinoa because it was on sale. Can you give me three different dinner ideas to use it this week?"* Expect to see varied responses – maybe a quinoa salad, quinoa-stuffed peppers, and a warm breakfast porridge – which ensures you won't get tired of the same food. Similarly, you might prompt: *"Give me a big-batch recipe I can cook on Sunday and eat throughout the week."* The bot could suggest a large pot of vegetable soup or a tray of baked pasta, explaining how to store and reheat portions. This approach stretches your dollar and your time, since cooking one big batch is often more efficient than making separate meals every day.

Here are a few smart budgeting prompts and strategies to try with ChatGPT:

- ***Meal plans on a budget:*** *"Create a 5-day dinner plan for a family of 4 with a total budget of $75, using some ingredients in multiple meals."* – The AI may provide a structured plan (like Monday through Friday dinners), reuse a roast or a pot of beans in different ways, and list economical recipes (tacos, casseroles, stir-fries) that stay within the budget.

- ***Cheap ingredient focus:*** *"What are some meals I can make with just eggs, rice, and frozen vegetables?"* – Expect ideas like fried rice, omelets over rice, or a veggie rice casserole. ChatGPT will show how a few cheap staples can come together into satisfying dishes.
- ***Cost-saving swaps:*** *"Suggest a cheaper alternative to parmesan cheese in this pesto recipe."* – You might learn you can use sunflower seeds or walnuts instead of pricey pine nuts, and perhaps a less expensive hard cheese or even nutritional yeast in place of parmesan. The AI can explain how the flavor or texture might change with the substitution, ensuring you still get a good result.
- ***Local and seasonal picks:*** *"I'm on a budget and it's winter – what seasonal produce should I cook with?"* – The answer could highlight winter squash, cabbage, or root vegetables that tend to be affordable in season, along with recipe ideas (like a hearty cabbage soup or roasted root veggies) that make the most of them.

As you can see, eating well on a budget is about **strategy and creativity**, and ChatGPT is a great brainstorming partner for both. By clearly stating your spending limits and using smart prompts, you'll receive tailored suggestions – from thrifty recipes to grocery lists – that help you get the most meals for your money. This empowers you to enjoy home-cooked food even when money is tight. And remember, budget-friendly cooking often goes hand-in-hand with simpler, whole ingredients and less waste, which can benefit your health and the planet too. With your budget under control, you can focus on making those meals as enjoyable as possible. Now that your budget is under control, it's time to ensure that even healthy or diet-specific meals still burst with flavor and variety.

DIET-FRIENDLY, NOT FLAVORLESS

Special diets often get a bad rap for being boring or bland. Many home cooks have experienced the disappointment of a "healthy" recipe that just doesn't excite the taste buds. The good news is that with ChatGPT's help, diet-friendly doesn't have to mean flavorless. Whether you're following a keto plan, eating vegetarian, managing gluten-free meals, or cutting sodium, you can ask the AI for creative ideas that keep flavor front and center. The trick is to include keywords about taste and variety in your prompts – words like "flavorful," "spicy," "herb-seasoned," or "savory." This signals that you care about how the food *tastes*, not just the nutritional profile.

One way to ensure delicious results is to borrow flavors from global cuisines. Every culture has dishes that meet various dietary needs almost by accident of tradition, often bursting with taste. You can leverage this by specifying a cuisine or flavor profile along with your diet requirement. For example, instead of just saying, *"low-carb dinner,"* try *"a low-carb dinner with Mexican flavors"* or *"keto-friendly Italian-inspired recipe."* ChatGPT will then think in terms of spices, herbs, and traditional recipes from those cuisines that fit the diet. A Mexican-flavored low-carb dinner might yield lettuce-wrapped fajitas with cumin and chili seasoning, while an Italian keto idea could be grilled chicken topped with pesto and mozzarella (all low in carbs but high in flavor). By guiding the AI toward a flavor theme, you avoid the grilled-chicken-and-plain-salad rut and get something more exciting.

Let's talk **keto** first. Keto diets limit carbohydrates strictly, which means no regular pasta, bread, or sugary sauces. Yet, keto meals can be incredibly rich and tasty when done right (think garlic butter shrimp or creamy casseroles). When prompting ChatGPT for keto ideas, emphasize what you *do* want: indulgent, satisfying elements that are keto-friendly. For instance: *"Give me a flavorful keto dinner – something cheesy and hearty without carbs."* The AI might suggest a broccoli-cheese casserole with bacon, or a bun-less cheeseburger casserole loaded with spices. If you specifically miss a high-carb dish, ask for a keto version of it: *"I'm craving pizza but need it keto. Any ideas?"* ChatGPT could come back with options like mini pizza bites made with portobello mushroom caps or a cauliflower crust pizza. It will detail how to make the crust from cauliflower or almond flour and recommend flavorful toppings (garlic, basil, pepperoni, olives – all keto-friendly). The key is that you're not just saying "keto dinner" – you're expressing a desire for a certain taste (cheesy, pizza, etc.), and ChatGPT responds by balancing those cravings with the diet's rules.

Now consider a **vegetarian** diet. There's a world of vegetarian cooking beyond boiled veggies or plain salads. To keep things interesting, you can ask for recipes that highlight umami and hearty textures – elements that give vegetarian food that satisfying "meaty" character without meat. For example: *"Suggest a vegetarian dinner that even a meat-lover would enjoy, with bold flavors."* ChatGPT might propose a mushroom and lentil stew spiced with smoked paprika, or black bean tacos with roasted peppers and a tangy cilantro sauce. These dishes use ingredients like mushrooms, beans, soy sauce or miso (for umami), and spices to build deep flavor. If you're tired of the same old veggie dishes, prompt for variety: *"I eat vegetarian and love Indian and Thai flavors. Can you suggest something new for dinner?"* You might get back a suggestion like a Thai green curry with tofu and vegetables in a fragrant coconut broth, or an Indian chickpea-and-spinach curry (chana saag) with warming spices. Both are packed with flavor and align with a vegetarian diet. The lesson here is to ask for what you want – not just "a vegetarian dish," but perhaps "a spicy vegetarian dish" or "a comfort food made vegetarian." ChatGPT will pick up on those descriptors and deliver recipes that don't feel like a compromise.

For those who are **gluten-free**, the main challenge is replacing wheat-based foods with alternatives, while keeping texture and taste. If you have favorites that you miss, let ChatGPT know. Prompt something like: *"I need a gluten-free alternative to fried chicken that still has a crunchy coating."* The AI could suggest using crushed cornflakes or almond flour as a breading to mimic the crunch, and perhaps baking or air-frying to get it crispy. It might describe seasoning the coating with herbs and spices (paprika, garlic powder, pepper) so that the flavor is all there, just without the wheat. Another example: *"I'm gluten-free and craving pasta – what can I have instead that's just as satisfying?"* ChatGPT may come back with ideas such as rice noodle stir-fry (if you can have rice) or zucchini noodles (zoodles) tossed with a flavorful sauce. It might even mention alternative pastas like those made from chickpeas or lentils, explaining that they hold sauce well and taste close to the real thing. By specifying what kind of food or texture you want ("crunchy," "chewy like pasta," "fluffy like bread"), you help the AI pinpoint gluten-free solutions that hit the spot.

If you're watching your **sodium** (salt intake), you know that salt is a big flavor enhancer that's suddenly off the table. But this just opens up the opportunity to get creative with seasonings. When asking ChatGPT for low-sodium recipes, mention that you still want it well-seasoned or flavorful. For example: *"Find me a low-sodium chicken recipe that's packed with flavor – no bland diet food, please."* In response, you might receive a recipe for lemon-herb roasted chicken, emphasizing ingredients like fresh rosemary, thyme, garlic, and lemon juice to create brightness and depth without much salt. Or a suggestion for a curry or stew that uses salt-free spice blends and aromatic ingredients like onions, ginger, garlic, and peppers. You can also seek general advice: *"How can I make food taste good without adding salt?"* ChatGPT might list tips such as using acids (lemon, vinegar) to brighten flavors, toasting spices to intensify them, or adding a touch of natural sweetness or smoke (like a dash of smoked paprika) to give the illusion of savoriness without sodium. The guidance can be pretty comprehensive, giving you techniques to apply to any recipe.

Across all these diet scenarios, a few principles help keep food exciting: use herbs and spices generously, explore new ingredients (like nutritional yeast for cheesy flavor without dairy, or jackfruit as a pulled-pork substitute), and play with textures. You can prompt ChatGPT for any of these specifically. If a dish seems like it might be dull, you could ask: *"What can I add to this grilled vegetable dish to make it more interesting (but still vegan and low-salt)?"* The AI might recommend a drizzle of balsamic glaze, toasted nuts for crunch, or a fresh pesto-like sauce – all depending on your diet constraints.

Finally, don't forget to ask for variety. Sticking to a diet is easier when you're not eating the same two or three meals on repeat. Let's say you're on a heart-healthy diet which is low-fat and low-sodium – you could request: *"Give me a week's worth of dinner ideas that fit my low-fat, low-sodium diet, each with different cuisines or flavor profiles."* ChatGPT could then produce a mix: maybe a Mediterranean grilled fish one night, a Mexican-inspired quinoa bowl the next, an Asian stir-fry another, and so on, each adhering to your diet but keeping the palate entertained. When you see all the possibilities laid out, it's clear that dietary restrictions can actually spark creativity rather than stifle it.

By using ChatGPT to inject flavor and diversity into diet-friendly cooking, you turn what could be a chore (sticking to the rules) into an adventure in trying new seasonings and dishes. You'll quickly realize that phrases like "healthy" or "low-whatever" no longer mean "boring." We can take it a step further: what if you have *multiple* requirements at once? It's time to explore how to layer several filters together to get a recipe that checks all the boxes.

STACKING FILTERS LIKE A PRO

Life isn't one-dimensional, and your cooking requests to ChatGPT don't have to be either. Often you'll have several requirements for a single meal. Maybe you want something quick, healthy, and kid-friendly, or you need a dessert that is low-sugar *and* gluten-free. The great thing is, you can layer multiple filters in one prompt and ChatGPT will do its best to meet all of them. Think of it as giving the AI a checklist for your perfect recipe.

When stacking filters, it helps to state each requirement clearly. You can even list them. For example, you might write: *"I'm looking for a dinner idea that satisfies the following: 1) vegetarian, 2) under 30 minutes to cook, and 3) high in protein."* This explicit list makes it crystal clear to the AI what criteria must be met. ChatGPT will then cross-reference its mental cookbook for recipes that tick all those boxes. In this case, it might suggest something like a quick tofu stir-fry with vegetables and quinoa – vegetarian (no meat), high-protein (tofu and quinoa), and fast to prepare. If you phrase the prompt in a more natural sentence, it works too: *"Give me a high-protein vegetarian dinner that I can cook in under half an hour."* The AI will parse that just fine. The key is simply that all the important filters (vegetarian, high-protein, 30-minute cook time) are mentioned.

Here's an illustrative example of a multi-filter request:

Prompt: *"Please suggest a quick, kid-friendly dinner that's low-carb and costs under $15 total."*

ChatGPT: *"How about mini lettuce-wrapped turkey burgers with carrot sticks on the side? They're ready in about 20 minutes. Using ground turkey, lettuce leaves instead of buns, and simple seasonings, they keep the carbs low. Kids often enjoy mini burgers (especially if they can add their own toppings like cheese or ketchup), and the whole meal comes in around $10-$12. It's healthy, fun, and budget-conscious."*

In that response, notice how the AI addressed every requirement: it confirmed the meal is quick (20 minutes), kid-friendly (mini burgers that kids can customize), low-carb (no buns, using lettuce wraps), and under $15 (estimated $10-$12 cost). When you pack multiple criteria into one prompt, a good answer will touch on each aspect like this.

Sometimes you might get a response that misses one of your criteria – after all, ChatGPT might overlook something if the prompt is very complex. Don't be discouraged; instead, use a follow-up prompt to fix it. For example, if you said *"I need a vegan, low-sodium lunch idea that's high in fiber,"* and the answer looks great but includes a bit of added salt in the recipe, you can reply: *"Looks good, but please remove any added salt to keep it low-sodium."* ChatGPT will adjust the recipe (perhaps suggesting herbs or lemon juice in place of salt). Or if it gave you a dish that takes 45 minutes when you specified 30, you can remind it: *"Can you simplify this to be ready in 30 minutes?"* Iteration is part of the process. Usually, though, if your initial prompt is clear, ChatGPT will get it right on the first try.

A pro tip for stacking filters is to prioritize and mention the most crucial ones first in your prompt. While the order doesn't usually matter to the AI, putting the non-negotiables up front can help you mentally check that you've included them. For instance, "I need a nut-free dessert for 6 people that's also low-fat and takes under 1 hour to make" puts the allergy (nut-free) first, then servings (for 6), then other filters. This doesn't change how ChatGPT works internally, but it ensures you don't forget any important detail when typing out the request. Another tip is to ask for more than one option if you want to compare ideas. You could say, *"Give me two options for a gluten-free, dairy-free appetizer that's under 100 calories."* ChatGPT might respond with, say, cucumber hummus bites as one and roasted chickpea snacks as another. Having multiple options helps when balancing many requirements because you can choose the one that appeals most.

Don't shy away from mixing very different types of constraints. You can combine dietary needs, budget limits, time limits, cuisine preferences, and even equipment limitations in one prompt. For example: *"I have a slow cooker and need a dairy-free, low-sodium dinner recipe that will feed 5 people, with a prep time under 15 minutes."* This might lead to a suggestion like a slow-cooker lentil and vegetable stew, explaining how to toss everything in (within 15 minutes prep), using spices and herbs for flavor (no dairy or much salt), and yielding a big batch for 5. Or consider, *"I want an Italian-inspired dish that's vegan, under 500 calories, and I can make it with just a microwave."* That's a tall order, but ChatGPT could propose something unconventional yet clever, like a microwave polenta bowl with tomatoes and vegetables, using herbs for Italian flavor. The beauty of AI is that it can handle these cross-category combinations without getting flustered – it searches its knowledge for any intersection of those requirements.

Of course, common sense plays a role. If you pile on too many extreme filters, you might end up with a very narrow set of possible recipes or a slightly oddball suggestion. For instance, a prompt like "gluten-free, keto, vegan, low-sodium, French pastry under 30 minutes" is combining constraints that are nearly impossible together (a traditional French pastry that meets all those is basically nonexistent!). ChatGPT might do its best but the result could be something that barely resembles a pastry. In such cases, be ready to either relax a constraint or accept a creative compromise from the AI. On the flip side, you'll be surprised how often there *is* a sweet spot solution that you just hadn't thought of – and ChatGPT will find it. The trick is to be *flexible and collaborative*: treat the AI's first answer as a draft. If it's not perfect, refine your prompt or ask for tweaks until it meets your vision.

By mastering multi-filter prompts, you essentially become the director of your own custom recipe search. You're telling ChatGPT, "Here are all my criteria; now synthesize something that fits." It's incredibly empowering to see a complex request result in a real, cookable recipe that matches your needs. This skill is what truly makes you feel like you have an AI chef working under your guidance. Now, let's carry these tailored plans into the real world. We'll shift focus to organizing smart shopping lists and making savvy substitutions, so you can turn your chosen recipes into reality with ease.

SHOPPING SMARTER WITH AI

Once you have some meal ideas or a weekly menu from ChatGPT, the next step is turning those ideas into an actual grocery list. This is another task where your AI kitchen companion can save you time and help you stay on budget. Instead of manually writing out everything you need, you can simply ask ChatGPT to generate a shopping list based on the recipes or meal plan it gave you. Even better, you can request budget-conscious tips and substitutions along the way.

To get a useful grocery list, be specific in your prompt about what you want. For example: *"Provide a grocery shopping list for the above 5 recipes. List the items by category (produce, dairy, etc.), and keep the total cost around $50."* In response, ChatGPT might produce something like:

- **Produce:** 3 onions, 5 bell peppers, 1 head of garlic, 2 carrots, 1 bunch fresh basil (approx. $15)
- **Proteins:** 4 chicken breasts, 1 can black beans, 1 dozen eggs (approx. $12)
- **Dairy:** 1 gallon milk, 1 small block cheddar cheese (approx. $8)
- **Pantry:** 2 cans diced tomatoes, 1 box spaghetti, 1 lb rice, olive oil, salt, pepper (approx. $10)
- **Frozen:** 1 bag mixed vegetables (approx. $5)

Notice a few things in this example list: the items are grouped in a sensible way, and there are rough prices to help you budget. ChatGPT can often do that – it has a general idea of common prices – especially if you explicitly ask for cost estimates. The list also consolidates ingredients (like listing "3 onions" total if multiple recipes each need one onion). If you already have some staples or want to exclude certain items, mention that in your prompt: *"Make me a shopping list for these recipes, except I already have flour and sugar in my pantry."* The AI will then leave off flour and sugar from the list.

Another smart use of ChatGPT is getting substitution advice while making your shopping plan. Real-world shopping always has its curveballs: maybe the store is out of an item, or you find that one ingredient is too expensive. You can ask ChatGPT for alternatives that will still work in the recipe. Suppose a recipe calls for fresh cherry tomatoes but they're pricey or not available; you could ask: *"Cherry tomatoes are expensive now – what's a cheaper substitute in this recipe?"* The bot might suggest using canned diced tomatoes or less expensive Roma tomatoes, explaining that you can chop them up and still get a good result. Or say your recipe uses a specific herb like fresh basil, but you have dried basil at home – you might ask, *"Can I use dried basil instead of fresh? If so, how much?"* ChatGPT will tell you the conversion (usually about one-third the amount, since dried herbs are stronger) and any impact on flavor. In this way, you can adapt your shopping list on the fly based on what's available or affordable.

ChatGPT's advice can also align with local pricing or preferences if you provide that context. For example, you might include in your prompt, *"I shop at a discount grocery store that often has deals on chicken and rice. Can you base the meal plan around those and make a shopping list?"* The AI will likely lean into recipes using chicken and rice, taking advantage of those deals. Or if you mention, *"In my area, avocados are very expensive,"* and your recipe included avocados, ChatGPT could offer a substitution like cucumber or a different creamy element (perhaps yogurt in a sauce) to replace the texture or role of avocado. The more information you feed into the prompt about your local conditions or store habits, the more tailored the shopping advice. While ChatGPT doesn't have real-time pricing data, it knows general cost patterns (e.g., that beans and seasonal veggies are cheap, or that out-of-season produce and specialty items can be expensive).

Efficiency is another perk. You can have ChatGPT optimize the list to minimize waste and extra purchases. Maybe two recipes each require half an onion – the AI will list one onion for both. If one recipe suggests a rare spice you'll only use once, you can ask, *"Is there a common spice I can use instead of this one, so I don't have to buy it?"* For instance, it might recommend using regular paprika instead of smoked paprika if you don't want to buy a whole jar, noting you'll lose a bit of smoky flavor but the dish will still be good. These little adjustments make your shopping more streamlined and cost-effective. ChatGPT can even give storage tips if asked (like, *"Buy a larger pack of chicken and freeze the extra for next week"*), helping you think ahead.

It's also worth mentioning that you can do the reverse: give ChatGPT an inventory of what you already have at home, and have it generate recipes or a shopping list to complete those recipes. For example: *"I have rice, a can of tomatoes, some carrots, and eggs. What minimal additional ingredients do I need to buy to make a dinner?"* The AI might say you could make a simple fried rice (just pick up soy sauce and maybe green onions), or a tomato fried rice with egg (maybe grab some garlic and an onion). This way, you're shopping smarter by using what's on hand and only buying a few extras.

When you head to the store armed with a ChatGPT-generated list, you'll likely feel more organized. You have exactly what you need for your chosen recipes, along with backup plans for substitutions if you encounter high prices or empty shelves. It takes the mental load off – no more wandering aisles wondering what to buy, and less risk of forgetting an ingredient. As always, you'll want to double-check the list and adjust for package sizes and your preferences (ChatGPT might say "1 lb of rice" but maybe you'll buy a 5 lb bag because it's a better deal, and that's fine). The list is a starting point that you can tweak.

With groceries in hand (and money saved), you're ready to cook up those personalized meals. We've covered how to plan and shop for new recipes that meet your needs. But what about the recipes you already know and love? Next, let's see how ChatGPT can help transform your favorite dishes to fit your dietary and budget goals, allowing you to enjoy those old classics with a smart twist.

ADAPTING FAVORITE MEALS TO FIT YOUR NEEDS

We all have those tried-and-true recipes or favorite comfort foods we can't live without. But sometimes our circumstances change – maybe you've switched to a healthier diet, or someone in the family developed an allergy, or that special dish has gotten too pricey to make regularly. The great news is you don't have to say goodbye to your favorites. ChatGPT can help you adapt and reinvent beloved recipes so they align with your current dietary and budget needs.

To get started, tell ChatGPT about the dish you love and what needs to change. You can be general or very specific. For example: *"I love fettuccine Alfredo, but I'm watching my calories. How can I make a lighter, healthier Alfredo that still tastes good?"* The AI might respond with suggestions like using milk and a bit of flour to create a lighter creamy sauce instead of heavy cream and butter, adding some pureed cauliflower to the sauce for extra nutrition, and using whole-grain pasta or zucchini noodles to cut carbs. It could give a step-by-step modified recipe: perhaps sautéing garlic in a small amount of olive oil, adding skim milk with a little parmesan and Greek yogurt to mimic the creaminess, and tossing that with your pasta alternative. The result? You get the comforting essence of Alfredo with a fraction of the calories and fat.

If you have the original recipe on hand, you can even share key details from it in your prompt. Say you have a family chili recipe that calls for ground beef, canned beans, and a lot of salt, but now you need it to be lower in sodium and maybe vegetarian. You might prompt: *"Here are the ingredients in my usual chili: ground beef, kidney beans, canned tomatoes, chili powder, salt, etc. How can I make a vegetarian, low-sodium version of this that still has a hearty flavor?"* ChatGPT would likely propose swapping the ground beef for extra beans or perhaps lentils (to maintain a meaty texture and protein), using low-sodium canned tomatoes and beans (rinsing them to remove excess salt), and ramping up other seasonings like garlic, cumin, or smoked paprika to make up for using less salt. It might suggest adding vegetables like diced mushrooms or bell peppers to boost the savory satisfaction. The AI could then walk you through adjusting the cooking steps (for instance, sautéing those veggies and adding lentils which may need a bit more liquid to cook). By the end, you'd have a new chili recipe that aligns with your needs but still feels familiar and cozy.

Budget adaptations are another common request. Perhaps your favorite recipe is a steak stir-fry, but steak has become too expensive. You can ask: *"What's a cheaper alternative to steak in my favorite stir-fry, and will it taste as good?"* ChatGPT might suggest using chicken thighs or pork strips instead of beef, noting that you should stir-fry them similarly and maybe marinate to tenderize and boost flavor. Or maybe it will propose going vegetarian for that dish, using tofu or seitan with a flavorful sauce. It would reassure you that with the right seasoning (like soy sauce, ginger, garlic for an Asian stir-fry) you'll still get a delicious result. Another example: *"My grandma's cake recipe uses a lot of walnuts and almond flour, which are pricey – how can I reduce the cost?"* The AI could advise replacing part of the almond flour with regular flour if dietary needs allow, or using a less expensive nut (or a smaller quantity of nuts, toasting them to enhance their flavor so you can use less). It might even suggest making half the recipe if it's large, to save on ingredients.

Adapting for dietary restrictions often means finding substitutes that play a similar role in the recipe. For instance, if you adore tacos al pastor but no longer eat pork, you could ask for a substitute protein that works with the same seasonings. ChatGPT might propose using chicken thighs or even jackfruit (a popular plant-based substitute that mimics shredded meat) with the same marinade of chilies, pineapple juice, and spices. If your favorite brownies need to become gluten-free, the AI could recommend a one-to-one gluten-free flour blend, or even suggest a recipe that uses almond flour or sweet potato as the base for fudgy, flourless brownies. Importantly, it will explain how to adjust the recipe – maybe adding an extra binding agent like xanthan gum for structure in gluten-free baking, or baking a few minutes longer if the moisture content changes. These details give you confidence that the adapted version will succeed.

When you ask ChatGPT to transform a recipe, don't hesitate to specify what aspects are most important to you. For example: *"I have a great mac and cheese recipe from my mom. I need to make it lactose-free for my friend, but I want it just as creamy and delicious. What should I do?"* The assistant might suggest lactose-free milk and a dairy-free cheese substitute, or perhaps a creative solution like a sauce made from cashews or pureed butternut squash for creaminess. It could also mention using a small amount of real aged cheese if your friend can tolerate it (aged cheeses have less lactose) combined with other ingredients, to strike a balance. By stating that creaminess and flavor are your priorities, you guide the AI to focus on those elements in its answer.

This back-and-forth can be as detailed as you need. You can provide the whole original recipe for ChatGPT to modify, or just describe it loosely. For instance, *"I usually deep-fry my chicken wings, but I want a healthier method,"* is enough to prompt advice like oven-baking or air-frying the wings with a light coating of oil and still getting a crispy result. ChatGPT might even give you a full rewritten recipe for oven-baked buffalo wings with a tangy sauce, pointing out that you'll save on oil and calories while keeping the crowd-pleasing taste.

By adapting your beloved recipes with ChatGPT's help, you're effectively *future-proofing* them for your life changes. You get to enjoy the nostalgia and satisfaction of those dishes, minus any guilt or impracticality. Plus, you might discover tweaks that make the recipe even better – many people find that reducing salt or fat, or adding a new ingredient, actually improves a dish once they try it. Cooking is all about flexibility, and with an AI assistant, you have a world of substitution ideas and technique tips at your fingertips.

At this point, we've covered a lot of ground – from custom meal prompts to shopping lists and recipe makeovers. To bring it all together, let's walk through some real-life example prompts and ChatGPT responses. These examples will show exactly how a conversation with the AI can lead to practical, delicious solutions tailored to your needs.

PROMPT RECIPES: REAL-LIFE EXAMPLES WITH CONSTRAINTS

Nothing beats seeing the process in action. Below are a few sample exchanges between a home cook and ChatGPT, demonstrating how the AI generates useful, tailored cooking advice when given specific constraints. These examples tie together everything we've discussed, from budget and dietary needs to creative adaptations.

Example 1: Budget-Friendly Family Dinner

Prompt: *"I only have $10 left in my budget and I need to make dinner for a family of 4. We're hungry! What's a cheap and filling meal I can cook?"*

ChatGPT: *"How about a hearty bean and vegetable chili? It's budget-friendly and satisfying. You can use two cans of beans (like kidney or black beans), a can of tomatoes, an onion, some garlic, and chili powder to make a* *big pot of chili. If you have any ground meat you can add a small amount, but it's delicious and protein-packed even without meat. Serve it with rice or some homemade tortilla chips. You should be able to get all the ingredients within $10 (beans and rice are very inexpensive). This one-pot meal will be warm, filling, and have plenty of leftovers for second helpings."*

In this response, ChatGPT zeroed in on cheap staples – beans, rice, canned tomatoes – and outlined a simple, filling dish, even noting the cost and leftover potential.

Example 2: Big Flavor, Low Sodium

Prompt: *"I need to cut back on salt for health reasons, but I hate bland food. Can you suggest a low-sodium dinner that's still bursting with flavor?"*

ChatGPT: *"Certainly! Let's try a lemon-herb roasted chicken with vegetables. Use fresh herbs like rosemary and thyme, plus garlic and lemon juice to marinate chicken pieces (or tofu, if you prefer). Roast the chicken with a mix of potatoes, carrots, and broccoli. The herbs, garlic, and lemon will infuse everything with flavor so you won't miss the salt. You can also sprinkle a salt-free spice blend (like Mrs. Dash) for an extra kick. When it's done, you'll have tender, zesty chicken and roasted veggies that are deeply savory – all with very little sodium."*

Here, the AI focused on herbs, citrus, and roasting techniques to maximize flavor without relying on salt.

Example 3: Quick Vegan & Gluten-Free for Kids

Prompt: *"We need a quick dinner that's vegan and gluten-free. Oh, and it has to be kid-friendly – my kids are picky eaters!"*

ChatGPT: *"How about taco night with a twist? You can make* ***black bean and sweet potato tacos*** *using corn tortillas (they're naturally gluten-free). Roast or sauté small cubes of sweet potato and season them with mild spices like cumin and a touch of paprika. Warm up some black beans with a little garlic and onion. Then let the kids build their own tacos: fill corn tortillas with the sweet potatoes and beans, and top with fun stuff like diced avocado, chopped tomatoes, and a squeeze of lime. You can even add a dollop of dairy-free yogurt or guacamole on top. It's hands-on (which kids love), colorful, and everything in it is vegan and gluten-free. Plus, it'll be ready in about 30 minutes!"*

This answer manages to meet all three constraints: it's fast, adheres to vegan and GF requirements, and is playful enough for kids.

Example 4: Healthier Twist on a Fried Favorite

Prompt: *"I'm craving fried chicken, but I'm trying to eat healthier and avoid deep-frying. How can I make a lighter version of fried chicken that still tastes great?"*

ChatGPT: *"You can definitely satisfy that craving without deep-frying. One idea is* ***oven-"fried" chicken****. Take skinless chicken pieces (like drumsticks or thighs) and marinate them in a bit of buttermilk (or a non-dairy milk with a squeeze of lemon for a buttermilk substitute) and your favorite spices – say, garlic powder, paprika, and black pepper. For the coating, crush up some cornflakes or use whole-wheat breadcrumbs and season them as well. Dip the marinated chicken in beaten egg (or aquafaba for an egg-free option), then press it into the cornflake coating. Lay the pieces on a baking sheet lined with a rack and bake at a high heat (around 400°F/200°C) for about 30-35 minutes, flipping once, until they're golden and crispy. The result: chicken that's crispy on the outside, juicy inside, but with a fraction of the fat. All the flavor and crunch, much less oil!"*

As you can see from these scenarios, a well-crafted prompt can yield incredibly practical advice from ChatGPT. The AI takes into account all the details you provide – budget limits, dietary restrictions, time constraints, and personal preferences – and it responds with creative solutions that make cooking easier and more enjoyable. By experimenting with these kinds of prompts, you'll quickly get the hang of guiding ChatGPT to answer any kitchen query, no matter how specific your needs are.

By now, you've seen how ChatGPT can become an incredibly adaptable ally in your kitchen. You've learned how to clearly communicate your dietary needs and budget goals so that the AI can filter recipes and advice tailored just for you. Whether it's shaving dollars off your grocery bill or modifying a recipe to cut the sugar or salt, you have the tools to guide ChatGPT toward solutions that fit your life. You've also practiced layering multiple requirements, discovering that even complex requests (like "healthy, cheap, and kid-friendly") can yield spot-on suggestions. From generating meal plans and shopping lists to reimagining Grandma's famous casserole in a gluten-free avatar, you now know how to make ChatGPT work in harmony with your unique constraints.

The big takeaway is that cooking smarter with AI doesn't mean giving up what you love – in fact, it means finding new ways to enjoy everything under your own terms. Eating well on a budget, sticking to a diet, and accommodating personal preferences all become easier when you can ask an expert assistant for help anytime. As you continue to experiment with prompts, you'll get even better at this dialogue. Soon, you'll approach ChatGPT as confidently as you would a trusted friend who happens to know thousands of recipes and cooking tricks!

With your dietary and budget concerns well in hand, you're ready to broaden your culinary horizons further. In the coming chapter, we'll build on this foundation and explore the next frontier of the AI-assisted kitchen. There are always more tricks and techniques to discover, and ChatGPT will be right there with you as you continue your journey to cook smarter, not harder.

4

THE AI MEAL PLANNER

Meal planning doesn't have to be a dreaded chore at the end of a long day. Imagine if the answer to "What's for dinner this week?" could appear in seconds, tailored to your tastes and schedule. In this chapter, we'll show how ChatGPT can become your personal meal planner, taking the guesswork and stress out of planning meals. With a few well-crafted prompts, you can get a whole week's worth of dinner ideas – or even breakfasts, lunches, and snacks – laid out for you. The best part is that these meal plans can be customized to be as **balanced**, **varied**, and **practical** as you need, making healthy home cooking feel more achievable and even fun.

We'll explore how one prompt to ChatGPT can outline an entire week of meals that hit all the right notes: nutritional balance, diverse cuisines, and a sensible flow that makes cooking efficient. You'll learn how to design prompts that encourage reusing ingredients across multiple dishes, so that Wednesday's stir-fry might cleverly use Monday's leftover roast chicken. This not only saves you time in the kitchen, but also cuts down on food waste – some users report that with AI planning, they don't throw away any unused ingredients at all. It's a smart way to cook that ensures every carrot or chicken breast you buy earns its keep.

Another big advantage of ChatGPT as a meal planner is the time you save on both planning and shopping. People who normally spend hours flipping through cookbooks and compiling grocery lists find that ChatGPT can cut that planning time dramatically. In fact, one home cook observed that what used to take her an hour each week now takes less than 5 minutes – a **90% decrease** in time spent meal planning. That's time you can reinvest in relaxing, cooking, or doing anything else you love. And when it's time to shop, ChatGPT has your back there too: it can generate an organized grocery list from your meal plan, grouping items by category for a quick and painless shopping trip. No more wandering the aisles in circles; you'll have a clear list that gets you in and out of the store efficiently.

Crucially, an AI meal planner isn't one-size-fits-all – it's **your** meal planner. You can ask for meals that fit your dietary needs (maybe high-protein and low-carb, or vegan, or gluten-free), accommodate your budget, and cater to your family's preferences. Struggling to please a picky eater or balance different diet goals in one household can feel like playing a game of Tetris with meals. ChatGPT excels at solving these puzzles by considering all the pieces you give it: "We want vegetarian dinners twice this week, kid-friendly flavors every night, around 500 calories per meal, and nothing too spicy." Feed in the details, and it will juggle them to produce a plan that checks all the boxes. It's reassuring to see that what seemed like an impossible list of requirements – eating well, adding variety, reducing waste, saving money – can actually come together in a coherent plan **without** the usual headache.

Throughout this chapter, we'll cover step-by-step how to harness "The AI Meal Planner." We'll start with the magic of planning an entire week's menu in a single prompt, then look at using prep logic to batch-cook and reinvent leftovers. You'll learn how to turn a meal plan into a tidy grocery list at the press of a button, and how to tweak your plan with smart substitutions whether for seasonal produce, cost savings, or dietary swaps. We'll also address planning around your **real-life schedule** – because some nights you only have 20 minutes to cook, and other nights you might have time to simmer a stew – and show how ChatGPT can adapt plans to those time constraints. Then, we'll talk about tailoring meal plans for families, including strategies for picky eaters and making sure everyone from toddlers to grandparents looks forward to dinner. Finally, we'll bring it all together in a live demonstration: we'll walk through an example of going from zero to a complete meal plan and grocery list using ChatGPT, illustrating each step with example prompts and AI-generated ideas.

By the end of this chapter, you will have the confidence to let ChatGPT handle the heavy lifting of meal planning. You'll be equipped with prompt examples and practical tips to make sure the AI's suggestions truly fit your life. Cooking at home will feel more organized, more personalized, and more enjoyable. Let's dive in and learn how to plan a week of meals with your new AI kitchen companion.

PLANNING THE WEEK IN ONE PROMPT

What if you could plan an entire week of meals by asking one simple question? This section shows you how to do exactly that. With a single well-thought-out prompt, ChatGPT can generate a full week's meal plan that meets your needs for variety, balance, and even creativity. Instead of searching for recipes one by one or scribbling a list of dinner ideas on scratch paper, you can describe your goals and constraints in one go – and let the AI do the organizing for you. It's like telling a personal chef your weekly wish list and getting a tailored menu back instantly.

To start, think about the scope of your meal plan. Do you need just dinners for the next 7 days, or do you want breakfasts and lunches too? Let's say you want dinners for a week. A basic prompt could be: *"Hi ChatGPT, please provide a seven-day dinner plan for me."* ChatGPT will happily comply, but the real power comes when you add details. The more information you give, the more customized and useful the plan will be. For example, you might specify: how many people you're cooking for, any dietary preferences or restrictions, the type of cuisine variety you want, and so on. Here's an example of a detailed prompt:

User Prompt: "Generate a 7-day dinner plan for two adults. We prefer healthy, quick meals – ideally under 30 minutes to cook – and a mix of cuisines throughout the week. Include at least two vegetarian dinners, but the rest can include lean meats or fish. Make sure the meals are balanced with protein, vegetables, and some whole grains. List each day's meal with a brief description."

This one prompt gives ChatGPT a lot to work with: number of servings (two adults), an emphasis on quick & healthy, a requirement for diverse cuisines, some vegetarian meals, and balanced nutrition. In response, ChatGPT might produce something like:

ChatGPT Output: "Certainly! Here's a 7-day dinner plan for two people, focusing on quick, healthy, and balanced meals with some variety:

Day 1: Lemon Garlic Chicken with Roasted Vegetables – Chicken breasts marinated in lemon and garlic, roasted alongside a mix of broccoli, carrots, and bell peppers. A simple one-pan meal packed with protein and fiber.

Day 2: Veggie Tacos with Black Beans and Avocado – Soft tacos filled with spiced black beans, sautéed bell peppers and onions, topped with avocado and a dollop of Greek yogurt. A satisfying vegetarian dinner.

Day 3: Teriyaki Salmon with Brown Rice and Snap Peas – Pan-seared salmon glazed with a homemade teriyaki (soy sauce, ginger, garlic, honey) served over brown rice with a side of snap peas. Ready in about 20 minutes.

Day 4: Chickpea and Spinach Curry – A quick vegetarian curry using canned chickpeas, spinach, and tomatoes, seasoned with curry powder and served with basmati rice.

Day 5: Beef and Broccoli Stir-Fry – Thinly sliced lean beef stir-fried with broccoli, garlic, and ginger, tossed in a light soy-sesame sauce. Served over instant brown rice for a speedy cook time.

Day 6: Pasta Primavera – Whole grain pasta tossed with a variety of sautéed vegetables (like zucchini, cherry tomatoes, and bell peppers) in a light garlic and olive oil sauce. Sprinkle with parmesan cheese.

Day 7: Veggie-Packed Turkey Chili – A hearty yet healthy chili made with ground turkey, kidney beans, and plenty of vegetables (tomatoes, bell peppers, corn). Simmered with chili spices and served with a side of cornbread."

Notice how each day is clearly listed with a meal and a brief description. The plan above (a hypothetical ChatGPT response) demonstrates variety – we have chicken, vegetarian tacos, salmon, a chickpea curry, beef stir-fry, pasta, and turkey chili over the week. There's a good rotation of proteins (poultry, fish, legumes, beef, etc.) and cuisines (a bit of Mexican-inspired, Asian, Italian, and American comfort food). This keeps things interesting so you're "not eating the same five dishes on loop" as one meal-planning enthusiast put it. At the same time, the meals are balanced with vegetables and not overly time-consuming or complex.

When crafting your one-prompt meal plan, it helps to explicitly ask for **balance** and **variety**. Words and phrases you can include in your prompt: "balanced and nutritious meals," "variety of cuisines," "avoid repetition," "include plenty of vegetables," "mix of meat and vegetarian options," or whatever suits your dietary style. If you have specific nutritional goals (say, high-protein, or low-carb, or heart-healthy), mention those too. ChatGPT can adhere to guidelines like "keep each dinner under 600 calories" or "ensure each meal includes a source of protein, fiber, and healthy fats." It's equipped with general nutritional knowledge and can apply it to your plan.

Another tip is to mention any **themes or preferences for certain days** if you have them. For instance, maybe you like to do "Meatless Mondays" or "Taco Tuesdays." You could incorporate that: *"Make Monday's dinner vegetarian and keep Tuesday's meal a fun taco night."* The AI will then make sure Monday has a vegetarian dish and Tuesday might be some creative taco-based meal. By giving these hints, your resulting plan will feel more personal and aligned with your habits.

ChatGPT is also capable of planning beyond dinner. If you want an all-day meal plan, you can request: "a week's meal plan with breakfast, lunch, and dinner for each day." Be aware this will be a **lot** of information – potentially 21 meals listed out – so sometimes it's wise to focus on one meal category at a time (just dinners, or just weekdays, etc.) to avoid getting overwhelmed by the output. You could always ask day-by-day as well, but the beauty of the **one-prompt weekly plan** is how everything is laid out together, giving you a big-picture view.

Crucially, **don't be shy about including constraints or must-haves** in that single prompt. ChatGPT can handle quite a few instructions at once. For example: "We're on a budget, so keep the meals affordable" or "I have a well-stocked spice cabinet, so feel free to use herbs and spices" or "My partner dislikes mushrooms and eggplant, please avoid those." The AI is good at juggling multiple requirements. In fact, using ChatGPT for meal planning shines most when you have many specific needs – it can "take many specific and unique constraints and compile it into succinct directions and lists" as one expert noted. Instead of you having to manually cross-reference recipes with your requirements, the AI does that work for you.

To give a sense of how detailed you can get in one prompt, consider this example adapted from a power user's strategy:

Advanced Prompt Example: "I need a week of dinner recipes (5 recipes, Mon–Fri) for a family of 4. We have a total budget of $100 for the week. Each recipe should take under 30 minutes. Use a limited number of ingredients – ideally no more than 8 per recipe – and try to have recipes share some ingredients with each other to save money and reduce waste. We eat all cuisines, so vary the styles (e.g., one Italian, one Asian-inspired, one Mexican, etc.). At least one dinner should be vegetarian. Also, no shellfish or peanuts due to allergies. Please list each day's meal, and ensure they are balanced and kid-friendly."

That might look like a mouthful, but amazingly, ChatGPT can

process it and deliver a customized plan hitting each of those points. You might even get a response with notes like "Recipe X and Y both use spinach, so you can buy a big bag and split it" or "These two meals both use chicken breast, allowing you to cook extra on Tuesday for Thursday's recipe" – demonstrating that **smart prep flow** we want (we'll talk more about that in the next section). The prompt above asks to share ingredients across recipes, a clever tactic to minimize both cost and waste. One meal-planning prompt template suggests having recipes share at least 30% of ingredients with another recipe, which means, for example, Monday's and Wednesday's dinners have some overlap in ingredients. This way if you buy a certain item (say, a bunch of cilantro or a specific type of vegetable), you know it will get used in multiple meals instead of languishing in the fridge.

Don't worry if all these details feel overwhelming – you can start simpler and build up. Even a straightforward request like, "Give me 5 dinner ideas for this week that use chicken, fish, and vegetarian proteins, with lots of veggies, and different flavor profiles" will give you a decent plan. You can always refine in follow-up prompts. The key takeaway is that a single prompt can yield an entire week's roadmap for meals, especially if you clearly outline your needs and desires. It's a huge time-saver, and many folks find it oddly exciting to see what the AI comes up with – often it surfaces creative meal ideas you might not have thought of on your own, making your weekly menu more interesting.

By planning the week in one prompt, you shift the mental load off of yourself. ChatGPT can remember all the criteria you gave it and ensure each day's suggestion fits the puzzle. No more juggling nutritional goals, budget constraints, and recipe variety in your head – the AI handles that, presenting you with a plan that you can then adjust or approve. In the next section, we'll explore how to fine-tune these plans with **prep logic** – that is, using strategies like ingredient reuse, batch cooking, and leftovers to make your cooking process even more efficient. This will build on the idea of a weekly plan and making that plan work smarter for you.

THE POWER OF PREP LOGIC

Meal planning isn't just about **what** you'll eat, but also **how** you'll cook it in the most efficient way. This section is all about structuring your ChatGPT prompts (and your resulting meal plans) to take advantage of batch cooking, ingredient reuse, and planned leftovers – what we're calling "prep logic." By weaving these strategies into your meal plan, you'll reduce time spent in the kitchen and ensure that nothing you buy goes to waste. Essentially, you're teaching your AI meal planner to think like a savvy home cook who plans two steps ahead: if you grill extra chicken on Monday, you can have a ready-made ingredient for Wednesday's salad; if you make a big pot of chili, it can turn into Thursday's burrito filling, and so on.

ChatGPT is particularly good at optimizing with these kinds of instructions because it can consider the whole week at once. When we humans meal-plan, it's easy to treat each day's meal in isolation and end up with a disjointed list of recipes that use completely separate ingredients. Then we're stuck buying a ton of items and spending extra time cooking from scratch each night. But if you prompt ChatGPT with a request to **reuse ingredients or incorporate leftovers**, it will connect the dots between meals. It "doesn't give you a new set of stuff for every meal" – instead, it can smartly overlap ingredients, which saves you money and prep work. One person who tried an AI-generated meal plan loved that it "reduces waste by reusing ingredients smartly", meaning yesterday's ingredients find their way into tomorrow's recipe rather than ending up in the trash.

So how do you get ChatGPT to do this? It starts with the prompt. You can explicitly instruct it to plan for leftovers or batch cooking. For example:

Prompt: "Plan 5 dinners for the week that build on each other. Use one or two base ingredients multiple times. For instance, if one meal roasts a chicken or butternut squash, another meal should repurpose the leftovers. I'd like to batch-cook where possible to save time. Please note in the plan where I can cook once and eat twice."

With a prompt like that, ChatGPT might respond with a menu

where Monday you roast a whole chicken, Tuesday you shred leftover roast chicken into tacos, and maybe Wednesday you use the chicken bones to start a soup broth. It could also suggest, say, cooking a big pot of rice on one night and using the extra rice for fried rice a couple of nights later. In the plan it gives you, it may explicitly call out these opportunities: e.g., "Cook extra rice on Tuesday and reserve it for Thursday's fried rice to save time." These are the kind of **prep tips** an experienced meal planner would use, and ChatGPT can be prompted to include them.

In fact, you can ask ChatGPT not just for the meal plan but also for a short **prep guide** as part of the output. For instance: "Along with the meal plan, list any batch cooking or prep-ahead steps I can do to streamline cooking." This might produce a helpful list like "Sunday: chop all veggies and store, cook a double batch of quinoa for use on Mon and Wed" or "After Monday's dinner, store leftover grilled veggies for use in Wednesday's pasta." Some advanced prompt templates have a section for "Prep Tips" in the output, which includes notes on leftovers or ingredient reusability. Don't hesitate to ask for that – it's like getting a little meal prep coach built into your plan.

Let's consider a concrete example of reusing ingredients. Suppose you adore fresh basil and you bought a big bunch for Monday's pasta but won't use it all. You can plan another meal that uses basil on Tuesday or Wednesday so that it doesn't wilt away. When talking to ChatGPT, you could specify: "ensure that if I buy a fresh herb or specialty ingredient for one recipe, another recipe also uses it." If you forget to mention it up front, you might notice your grocery list has, say, a whole head of cabbage for one slaw recipe. Rather than waste the rest, you can go back to ChatGPT: *"Hey, can any other meal this week use some of that cabbage? If so, adjust the plan to include it."* The AI might then tweak a side dish on another day to be roasted cabbage or include it in a stir-fry. This adaptability is great for minimizing waste.

In the weekly prompt from the previous section, we hinted at sharing ingredients by asking for recipes to share a percentage of ingredients. Another way to phrase it: "Plan meals so that ingredients overlap. For example, use the same protein or vegetable in at least two different meals." If you explicitly mention a base ingredient, ChatGPT will find diverse ways to spin it. *"I have a large pack of chicken thighs – plan two different dinners that use them so I utilize it fully."* You'll likely get two distinct recipes (say, a chicken stir-fry and a baked chicken casserole) that collectively use up those thighs. This approach ensures you're buying in efficient quantities and using everything up.

Batch cooking is slightly different from simple leftovers. Batch cooking means cooking a larger quantity of something with the intention of using it for multiple meals. You can incorporate this by saying, for example, "Include one big batch-cook meal that I can eat across two nights," or even specify which day: "Make Friday's meal something I can easily double and reheat on Saturday." ChatGPT could then propose a large lasagna or a stew on Friday, noting "you'll have enough left for Saturday, just reheat." If you mention owning appliances like a slow cooker or Instant Pot, you can get suggestions for make-ahead friendly dishes on busy days. For instance: *"On Wednesday I only have 15 minutes to cook in the evening – suggest a slow-cooker meal I can start in the morning."* The plan might slot in a slow-cooker chili that cooks all day and is ready by dinner.

Let's illustrate a short scenario of how prep logic might look in a ChatGPT plan:

Prompt: "Create a 4-day dinner plan that uses batch cooking. I have time on Sunday to prep. Use one make-ahead recipe on Sunday that I can turn into a different dinner on Tuesday. Also, plan for a mid-week leftovers night. We want to minimize cooking effort on Wednesday because we get home late."

ChatGPT Output (excerpt): "...

Sunday: Big Batch Vegetable & Beef Stew – Make a large pot of hearty stew with beef, carrots, potatoes, and herbs. This will be dinner for Sunday, and you'll save the extra for Tuesday.

Monday: Baked Lemon Herb Chicken with Quinoa and Green Beans – A quick bake of chicken and vegetables. (Tip: While this bakes, you could also cook quinoa for Wednesday's dish.)

Tuesday: Shepherd's Pie using Sunday's Stew – Transform the leftover beef stew into a comforting shepherd's pie. Just add a simple mashed potato topping to the warmed stew and bake until golden. This way, you have a completely new dish with minimal effort by repurposing Sunday's meal.

Wednesday: Leftovers Buffet – Use any remaining portions from Monday or extra shepherd's pie from Tuesday. (This is an easy night —no new cooking needed. If you have leftover quinoa from Monday, you can toss it with some veggies for a quick side.)

Thursday: [Another meal...] ..."

In this hypothetical plan, the prompt's requirements are met: Sunday is a batch-cook that deliberately yields more than one meal. Tuesday explicitly reuses that into a new recipe (note how the AI explained the transformation). Wednesday is blocked off as a leftovers night to lighten the load. The plan even suggested an extra prep tip (cooking quinoa on Monday ahead of time) because we indicated we wanted to minimize effort on a late night.

Such synergy between meals is the real power of prep logic. You end up cooking smarter, not harder. You might find that your total active cooking time in a week drops because you're leveraging prior work. And beyond time savings, there's a satisfying reduction in **food waste**. When every ingredient serves a purpose in multiple meals, you're far less likely to discover sad, unused produce in the back of the fridge. In a trial of AI meal planning, one user happily reported that at week's end, they "didn't throw away any food – not even a single scrap", since they either ate everything the night it was cooked or as leftovers the next day. That's a huge win for both your grocery budget and the environment.

If you're someone who likes to meal prep (cooking parts of meals in advance), you can also get ChatGPT to incorporate that. Try a prompt like: "Give me a meal plan that uses a Sunday prep session: suggest two or three things I can cook or prep on Sunday that will make the week's dinners easier." The AI might respond with suggestions such as grilling a batch of chicken breast, chopping and portioning veggies, or cooking a grain base, and then it will list meals that make use of those pre-prepped components. For instance, "Grill chicken on Sunday, use it in Monday's salad and Wednesday's pasta," or "Cook a big batch of tomato sauce on Sunday, use it for Tuesday's spaghetti and Friday's pizza." These are strategies many seasoned home cooks use; the difference here is you have an AI helping you map it out systematically.

Remember that you are in control of how much or how little prep logic to apply. Some weeks you might not want any repeated ingredients because you crave something totally different each night – that's okay, you can skip reuse in your prompt. Other weeks, you might be extremely busy and welcome lots of shortcuts – that's when to lean in to batch cooking and leftovers. Let ChatGPT know your situation. As one meal planner advises, be clear on questions like "Are you OK with repeating meals or having leftovers?" when you set up your plan. If the answer is yes, you've unlocked a powerful tool: you can intentionally repeat or carry over parts of meals to save time.

By structuring your prompts with prep logic in mind, you turn ChatGPT into a true kitchen assistant that thinks ahead for you. The result is a weekly plan where the recipes aren't just a random collection, but a cohesive strategy. You'll spend less time cooking and more time enjoying meals. Plus, you'll likely notice your grocery list shrinking a bit (since ingredients do double duty) and your trash can staying emptier.

Now that you have a meal plan filled with great dinners and clever prep tricks, the next step is to get all the ingredients you need. But don't reach for pen and paper – ChatGPT can handle that, too. In the following section, we'll see how to go from **plan to pantry** by having the AI generate a complete, organized shopping list for your meal plan, making grocery shopping as straightforward as possible.

FROM PLAN TO PANTRY: GENERATING SHOPPING LISTS

Once you've got your week's meal plan, the logical next step is figuring out what groceries you need. This is another area where

ChatGPT shines as your kitchen companion. Instead of manually writing out each ingredient from each recipe (and inevitably forgetting something or mis-counting how many tomatoes you need), you can simply ask the AI to generate a shopping list. The result will be a clean, categorized list of everything required to cook the meals in your plan. This not only saves time, but also ensures you don't overlook any ingredient. Let's explore how to prompt ChatGPT for a grocery list and what kind of output to expect.

If you included "provide a grocery/shopping list" in your initial meal plan prompt, ChatGPT might have already given it to you. Some people prefer that one-and-done approach. For example, a very detailed prompt could end with: "... Also create a shopping list with all necessary ingredients, grouped by category (produce, dairy, pantry, etc.)." As we saw earlier, advanced users sometimes even ask for approximate costs, which ChatGPT can attempt to provide. If your meal plan prompt wasn't set up that way, no worries – you can do it in a follow-up query.

To get a shopping list from an existing meal plan, you can copy the plan (or refer to it) and instruct: *"Now list all the ingredients needed for these meals in a grocery list format, categorized by type of food."* ChatGPT will scan the meal descriptions or recipes it gave and compile a list of items. It usually groups them into categories such as Produce, Proteins/Meat, Dairy, Grains, Canned Goods, Spices, etc. This grouping is incredibly useful. One of the people who let ChatGPT plan their meals said their favorite part was "getting an accompanying grocery list" and that the app made the trip *"painless by grouping items by category for ultra convenience"*. You essentially get your shopping list sorted the way a pro organizer might do it – all the vegetables together, all the meats together, etc., which aligns with how you'd navigate a grocery store.

For example, after generating a weekly menu, you might ask:

User Prompt: "Create a grocery list for this meal plan. Organize it by categories like Produce, Proteins, Dairy, Canned Goods, Spices, etc., and list the items and quantities I need for the whole week."

ChatGPT Output: "Sure. Here's the grocery list for the week's meals:

Produce: 6 carrots, 2 onions, 1 head of garlic, 3 bell peppers, 2 zucchinis, 1 head of broccoli, 1 bunch fresh basil, 4 lemons, 2 avocados, 1 pint cherry tomatoes, 1 bag spinach (or about 5 oz).

Proteins: ~1.5 lbs chicken breasts, 2 salmon fillets (~1 lb), 1 lb ground turkey, 1 lb beef strips (or pre-cut stir-fry beef).

Canned/Dry Goods: 1 can black beans, 1 can kidney beans, 1 can diced tomatoes, 1 box whole wheat pasta, 2 cups rice (or 1 box instant brown rice), 1 package tortillas.

Dairy: 1 small container Greek yogurt (for taco topping), 1 block or bag shredded cheddar cheese, Parmesan cheese (if not on hand).

Spices/Sauces: Soy sauce, olive oil, chili powder, curry powder, ginger (fresh or ground), garlic powder, salt, pepper, honey (for teriyaki sauce)."

And so on, covering any other needed items like maybe a loaf of bread if there were sandwiches, etc.

This example list is illustrative – your actual list depends on your specific meal plan. But notice a few things: items are grouped logically, and whenever possible, quantities or estimates are given ("~1.5 lbs chicken breasts," "1 can black beans," etc.). ChatGPT can infer quantities especially if recipes were detailed, though sometimes it might leave it more generic (e.g., just "chicken breasts" without a number). If you want more precise amounts, ensure your request or the recipes have serving details, or you can follow up with: *"Please include quantities for each item assuming 4 servings per recipe."*

One prompt included a **budget** constraint when asking for the grocery list, and ChatGPT not only listed the items but also gave an approximate price for each. For instance, it might say "2 bell peppers ($5)" and so on, summing it up to an estimated total. The user found this helpful to get a ballpark sense of the cost and ensure they were sticking to their budget. If that interests you, you can prompt: "Include estimated prices for each item (assume typical prices) and keep the total under $X." Keep in mind these will be rough estimates – as that user noted, actual prices vary by location and brand– but it's a neat feature for budget-conscious planning.

Getting a computerized grocery list can feel like magic the first time. The list is usually comprehensive, but it's wise to double-check it against the meal plan or recipes to ensure nothing got missed or to adjust for your pantry. This leads to an important step: **cross-referencing with what you already have.** Before you rush off to the store with the AI-generated list, scan your kitchen. Do you already have some of these staples? Many AI meal plans will call for common pantry items (rice, spices, olive oil, etc.). As one home cook advises, "take a moment to double-check what we already have" to reduce food waste and unnecessary purchases. ChatGPT isn't connected to your pantry (not yet, anyway!), so it will list everything needed for the recipes, not knowing you might have, say, a bag of rice or a can of beans sitting on your shelf. You can strike those off the list yourself. If you want, you could even tell ChatGPT in advance what you have, and ask it to exclude them from the list: *"I already have rice and canned tomatoes, so don't include those in the shopping list."*

The format in which ChatGPT gives the list is usually text-based and easy to copy into a notes app on your phone or to print out. If you find the wording not to your liking, you can also customize it by asking: "List the grocery items in a bullet-point format by category" or "Sort the list alphabetically within each category" – whatever suits you. The AI is quite flexible in reformatting information.

One thing to be mindful of is how ChatGPT handles **quantities for combined recipes.** If two different dinners each need 1 onion, the list should ideally say "2 onions." Generally, ChatGPT does aggregate amounts when it's straightforward. But occasionally it might list the same item twice under different categories or contexts. For example, if one recipe calls for green onions and another for regular onion, it might list "green onions" and "1 onion" separately under produce. It's up to you to notice such things and adjust (in that case, those are indeed different types of onions). Or if it said "soy sauce" for one recipe and "teriyaki sauce (or soy sauce + honey)" for another, it might list both soy sauce and honey in pantry, which is correct. Just give the list a quick sanity check. When I use it, I like to skim and think, "Is anything missing or duplicated?" If you do spot something off, you can even ask ChatGPT again to clarify: *"Does this list account for all meals? I see chicken listed once, but we have two chicken recipes – do I need more?"* It can correct or explain the reasoning.

Another scenario: say one of your recipes has an optional ingredient or a garnish (e.g., "serve with cilantro on top"). ChatGPT might still include that item (cilantro) in the list. If you know you might skip the garnish, you could remove it. The AI tends to err on the side of completeness.

If you want to take it a step further, ChatGPT can also incorporate **store preferences** or **delivery formats.** For instance, "Provide the list formatted for online grocery shopping" might result in a list that's already separated in a way you could plug into a shopping app. Or "I only shop at X store, which has these brands... adjust if needed." These are more advanced uses and may vary in success, but it's interesting to experiment with if you have a particular shopping style.

So at this point, you have:

- A tailored meal plan.
- A neatly organized shopping list covering everything you need.

The feeling of walking into the grocery store with that list is empowering. You know exactly what's for dinner every night, and you have a checklist to make sure you get all the ingredients. It streamlines the trip; one person said with the AI-generated list on their phone, they were "in and out of the store within 30 minutes", which is impressively quick for a full week's shopping. The list grouped by category means you hit each section once – produce, then grains, then meats – no backtracking because you forgot something in Aisle 1.

Before we move on, one last pro-tip: after shopping, you can save that list or meal plan for future reference. If it turned out well, you might reuse a similar plan later, or even ask ChatGPT to generate a variation of it for another week. For example, "Use the same meal plan as last month but introduce two new recipes and a different cuisine for variety" – this can keep things fresh over time.

Now that your pantry (and fridge) is stocked with everything you need, you're almost ready to cook. But what if, while looking over your grocery list or recipes, you spot an ingredient you're not keen on or can't find? Maybe the store was out of eggplant, or you realize one meal might be too costly due to an expensive ingredient. That's where the art of substitutions comes in. In the next section, we'll discuss how to have ChatGPT suggest smart swaps for ingredients before you start cooking, whether to accommodate what's available, to save money, or to meet dietary needs. This will ensure your meal plan stays on track even when you need to make changes.

MAKING SUBSTITUTIONS BEFORE YOU SHOP

Meal plans are great, but real life can throw curveballs: perhaps an ingredient in your plan is out of season, too pricey, or simply something your family won't eat. The good news is you don't have to abandon the whole plan – ChatGPT can help you seamlessly adjust it. In this section, we'll cover how to prompt the AI for substitutions and modifications so that your meal plan stays flexible and practical. This could mean swapping out ingredients for dietary reasons, finding seasonal alternatives, or adjusting recipes based on availability and cost. Think of ChatGPT as your **culinary problem-solver** – if something doesn't fit, it can suggest a replacement.

Let's start with the scenario of **dietary needs or dislikes.** Say your meal plan comes back and one of the dinners is a mushroom risotto, but you absolutely hate mushrooms (or are allergic to them). If you didn't mention this in your original prompt, ChatGPT wouldn't have known. No problem: you can simply tell it now. For example: *"I noticed one recipe uses mushrooms, but my family doesn't eat mushrooms. What's a good substitute ingredient in that recipe?"* ChatGPT will analyze the role of mushrooms in the dish (texture, flavor) and come up with alternatives. It might say, "You can substitute zucchini or eggplant for the mushrooms, or even bell peppers, to provide a similar hearty texture." In fact, one user shared that they forgot to tell ChatGPT about a dislike – the husband hated mushrooms – so the AI's meal plan included mushrooms in multiple meals. They quickly asked for replacements and got a list of "equally nutritious yet more palatable" alternatives from ChatGPT. The fix was easy, and the plan was updated without mushrooms.

Substitutions can also be about **seasonality**. Maybe your plan suggests a fresh tomato salad in the dead of winter when good tomatoes are hard to find. You could ask: *"Tomatoes aren't great this time of year. Can you suggest a seasonal alternative for the salad on Day 3?"* ChatGPT might propose roasted root vegetables or a cabbage-based salad if it's winter, or swap in citrus segments for brightness. It has general knowledge of seasonal produce, so it can tailor suggestions to what's likely to be fresh. Similarly, if a recipe calls for an ingredient that's not available locally, you can request an alternative. For example, "The recipe uses bok choy but I can't find that – what could I use instead?" and you might be advised to use Napa cabbage or spinach, depending on the dish.

Cost is another reason to substitute. Perhaps the meal plan includes salmon, but salmon is very expensive in your area right now. You can ask ChatGPT to swap it for a more budget-friendly protein. *"Salmon is a bit out of my price range – could this recipe be done with a cheaper fish or chicken instead?"* The AI may suggest, "Yes, you can use chicken breast with a similar marinade, or try tilapia which is usually more affordable than salmon. Adjust cooking times accordingly (chicken will need longer to cook through than a salmon fillet)." In that suggestion, ChatGPT is not only giving a swap but also a tiny bit of cooking guidance for the new ingredient, which is helpful.

Sometimes the substitution is about **nutrition or diet**. If you decide you want the plan to be low-carb, for instance, and one dinner is pasta primavera, you could ask for a lower-carb version. *"What's a low-carb alternative to the pasta in the Day 5 recipe?"* and ChatGPT might suggest using zucchini noodles or spaghetti squash in place of pasta, or maybe swapping the dish entirely to something like a stir-fry without rice. If someone in your household needs a meal to be gluten-free or dairy-free, you can systematically request those adjustments: "Make sure all recipes are gluten-free – substitute any wheat products with gluten-free equivalents." The AI will then adjust ingredients (flour -> cornstarch for thickening, soy sauce -> tamari, etc.) as needed.

Keep in mind, you can either ask for substitutions for a specific recipe *or* ask ChatGPT to regenerate that part of the plan entirely with the new constraint in mind. For example, if one planned meal just doesn't appeal to you at all (maybe ChatGPT suggested shrimp tacos but you just had shrimp recently and want something else), you can say: *"Can you replace Tuesday's dinner with a different meal? Perhaps something with chicken instead of shrimp, and still fitting the overall healthy theme."* ChatGPT will swap out that meal for a new suggestion that meets your criteria, and update the ingredients accordingly. This way, you don't have to throw out the whole plan, you just tweak one day.

Another approach: if you anticipate substitutions in advance, you can **bake flexibility into your initial prompt**. For instance, you could prompt: "Provide a substitute for any ingredient that might be hard to find or very expensive, in parentheses next to it." The output might then list meals with notes like "(if salmon is too expensive, you can use chicken thighs instead)." This pre-empts the issue, giving you options upfront. Not everyone does this, but it's a clever use of AI to prepare backup plans.

Let's illustrate a substitution dialogue with ChatGPT based on a meal plan scenario:

User: "The meal plan looks good overall. However, one recipe is a spicy curry and my kids won't eat spicy food. How can we modify that meal to be kid-friendly?"

ChatGPT: "You can easily adjust the curry to make it milder. Use half or none of the chili powder called for. You can also add a bit of yogurt or coconut milk to mellow out any heat. Alternatively, if the recipe allows, you could replace it with a non-spicy dish altogether. For example, instead of a spicy chickpea curry, you could do an herbed chickpea and vegetable sauté with similar ingredients minus the hot spices."

User: "Great. Let's replace it with something non-spicy. Maybe a stir-fry?"

ChatGPT: "Sure. Replacing the spicy curry, how about a Ginger Garlic Vegetable Stir-Fry with Chickpeas? It uses the bell peppers, chickpeas, and spinach that were already on the list, but flavors them with ginger and garlic instead of chili. It's very mild and kid-friendly, but still nutritious. I'll update the plan and grocery list: remove 'curry powder' and add a bit of ginger if it's not already in your pantry."

In this exchange, ChatGPT not only provided a way to tone down the spice (for picky eaters, in this case children who don't do spicy) but also offered a completely different recipe idea that uses similar ingredients. The mention of removing curry powder and adding ginger in the list shows it is updating the shopping needs accordingly. The user could then ask, "Do I need to buy anything else for that replacement?" and the AI would clarify if any new item is needed.

We saw a real example earlier from a mom using ChatGPT: she said, "I have picky eaters that don't like spicy foods... I have chicken, rice, seasoning, oil. Create a recipe." The result was a kid-friendly golden chicken and rice dish that pleased her children. This highlights how clearly stating *what won't work* (e.g., no spicy) plus *what ingredients or goals you have* can yield a tailored solution that keeps everyone happy. After using the AI for a while, she noted her kids were pleased with the diverse meals and even looked forward to dinner, which is a huge victory for any parent.

Substitutions are not only for ingredients; you might also substitute methods or timing if needed. For example, if a recipe is grilled but you don't have a grill, you can ask how to cook it on the stove or in the oven instead. Or if something is meant to marinate for 8 hours and you don't have that time, you can ask the AI for a quicker marinade or alternative seasoning. Essentially, any aspect of a recipe that doesn't suit you – be it ingredient, tool, or time – can be brought up and ChatGPT will do its best to accommodate.

One more angle: **nutrition swaps**. If your plan included, say, a dessert or a sweet treat (some plans do include desserts or snacks), and you want a healthier alternative, you can request that. "Instead of the chocolate cake suggested, can ChatGPT recommend a healthier dessert with fruit?" could yield a baked apples recipe or a yogurt parfait suggestion. Or swapping refined carbs for whole grains in the plan, etc. The AI has knowledge of healthier alternatives (like using Greek yogurt instead of sour cream, or applesauce instead of sugar in baking) and can weave those in if asked.

When you make a substitution, remember to adjust your grocery list. If you use ChatGPT to make the change, it will often update the list if you prompt it to. In practice, you might just mentally note the changes. For instance, if we dropped "salmon" and went with "chicken" instead, obviously you'll buy chicken and not salmon. You could explicitly say, "Update my grocery list accordingly," and ChatGPT would regenerate the list with that change. It might be overkill for one or two swaps, but useful if you made several adjustments.

By using ChatGPT for these pre-cooking tweaks, you maintain the benefit of planning while introducing flexibility. Traditional meal plans (like those you might find in a magazine or a set weekly plan) can feel rigid – if Tuesday's recipe doesn't work for you, you're on your own to fix it. But with an AI meal planner, nothing is set in stone until you're happy. You have a virtual chef friend who can adapt any part of the plan on the fly. This adaptability means your meal plan can evolve with changing circumstances: seasonal produce, a great sale on a different protein, a last-minute guest with a peanut allergy, or just a craving for something else.

Now that you've fine-tuned your plan and list – you have your ingredients and any necessary substitutions in place – it's time to put the plan into action. The next consideration is making sure the plan fits into your life **time-wise.** Not every night is equal; some evenings you can luxuriate in cooking, and other nights you barely have 15 minutes to throw dinner together. How does ChatGPT handle that? In the upcoming section, we'll focus on time-sensitive planning: how to use prompts to ensure the meals align with the time you have available on each day, including strategies for "busy night" dinners and make-ahead options for those hectic days.

TIME-SENSITIVE PLANNING

One of the greatest feelings in cooking is knowing that the meal you planned matches the time and energy you actually have that day. There's no use planning a from-scratch lasagna for a night when you get home at 8 PM after the kids' soccer practice. In this section, we'll explore how to use ChatGPT to create meal plans that are **synchronized with your schedule** – including quick meals for busy nights, slower recipes or batch cooks for days when you have more time, and even make-ahead dishes that you can prepare in advance. By communicating your real-life time constraints and routines to ChatGPT, you can get a plan that not only sounds good on paper, but also works in practice on Monday through Sunday.

To start, it helps to map out your week in terms of cooking time. Ask yourself: which days are busy, which are moderate, and which (if any) are you free to spend a while in the kitchen? Maybe Monday and Wednesday you have late meetings or classes and need dinner on the table in 20 minutes. Perhaps Saturday you usually don't cook at all (maybe that's your takeout night or you eat out), and Sunday afternoon you could devote a couple of hours to cooking if needed. All these details can be incorporated into your prompt. Essentially, you're giving ChatGPT a bit of your schedule, so it can play the role of a personal planner that knows, for example, Tuesday has to be an easy night and Friday could be a fun, more involved cooking night.

When prompting, you might say something like: *"I only have about 30 minutes to cook on weeknights, except Thursday when I have even less time (maybe 15 minutes). On Saturday I usually eat out, and on Sunday I have plenty of time to cook or meal prep. Please design a meal plan around this schedule."* This way, ChatGPT will tailor the recipes accordingly. It might ensure that Monday-Wednesday have recipes labeled as "quick" or things like stir-fries, salads, or simple one-pan bakes. For the super busy Thursday, it could suggest a make-ahead meal or something almost no-cook (like using leftovers or a slow-cooker meal that's ready when you get home). Then perhaps Friday or Sunday it will place a recipe that takes longer or involves a special cooking method, since you indicated you have time then.

A real-world example: one blogger detailed how she considers her week's schedule before planning, noting things like an early soccer game one evening (needing a crockpot meal that's ready when they return), or a night when her spouse works late (so maybe a simpler meal for just her and the kids). You can do the same with ChatGPT: simply bullet out those time constraints. Here's an example prompt incorporating such details:

User Prompt: "This week, I have some specific schedule constraints:

Monday: Home by 6:30, can cook ~30 minutes.

Tuesday: Very busy, only ~15 minutes to make dinner (need something super quick or already prepared).

Wednesday: Moderate, about 30 minutes available.

Thursday: Husband is working late, so it's just me and the kids for dinner. Need something easy the kids will eat.

Friday: I have time (about 1 hour) and wouldn't mind a more involved recipe.

Saturday: We will likely order takeout, so no meal needed.

Sunday: I can meal prep for up to 2 hours in the afternoon. Now plan 6 dinners (Mon–Fri and Sunday, skipping Saturday) around this schedule, with appropriate recipes for each day's time constraints. Include notes if any prep can be done Sunday for the week."

This prompt is long, but it paints a clear picture of the week's rhythm. ChatGPT can use this information to, for example, assign a slow-cooker stew to Tuesday (so you can set it up in the morning and eat in the evening with 15 minutes or less of finishing touches), a simple kid-friendly meal on Thursday (maybe grilled cheese sandwiches with tomato soup, or a quick quesadilla, since only one adult is present and kids might be picky), and a more elaborate dish on Friday when you have time (perhaps homemade pizza or a roast). It might also suggest utilizing Sunday's prep time, something like: "On

Sunday, cook a double batch of rice and chop vegetables for Wednesday and Thursday." This merges our prep logic from earlier with time-awareness.

ChatGPT is quite good at understanding descriptors like "quick," "easy," or "make-ahead." If you specifically say "I need a 15-minute meal," it tends to propose very simple recipes or even partially pre-made solutions (for example, using rotisserie chicken to make a fast soup or salad). You can also mention appliances in relation to time: "I have an Instant Pot and a slow cooker," which signals to the AI that it can schedule an Instant Pot recipe (fast cooking, hands-off) or a slow-cooker recipe (long cooking time but very hands-off, good for busy days). One user wrote that ChatGPT can suggest meals that take 30 minutes or less to prepare, perfect for busy evenings, which is exactly what we want for those jam-packed weekdays.

Another strategy is to explicitly label certain days as "leftover night" or "no-cook night." For instance, if you know Wednesday you will be too tired to cook anything, you can plan Tuesday's meal to be a larger batch so that Wednesday you just reheat leftovers. We touched on this in prep logic, but here it's about scheduling. You could say in your prompt, "Plan for one day to be a leftover night (Wednesday) so I don't have to cook then." ChatGPT might then ensure Tuesday's recipe yields extra portions and list Wednesday as "Leftovers from Tuesday's lasagna" or something along those lines. This ties directly into time management – using leftovers is a classic time-saver.

Busy night hacks can also be requested. For example: "Include at least one meal that is basically assemble-and-eat, with minimal cooking, for the busiest day." This could lead to a suggestion like a loaded salad (where maybe you only have to quickly cook or open a can of beans), or breakfast-for-dinner (quick scrambled eggs and toast), or a sheet-pan meal that you can just shove in the oven and do other things for 20 minutes until it's done. The AI has learned from countless recipes and meal plans, so it knows typical quick meals versus more elaborate ones. It will likely tag words like "stir-fry," "tacos," or "sandwiches" for quick, and things like "braised" or "marinated" for longer recipes.

Now, on days you have *more* time and want to capitalize on it, you can ask for "make-ahead" or "time-intensive" recipes accordingly. Maybe Sunday is your day to try that recipe that takes longer or to meal prep for the week. You can prompt something like: "On Sunday I have a couple of hours; give me a recipe that takes advantage of that time (like a stew, a roast, or something I can also use for leftovers)." ChatGPT could respond with a Sunday roast chicken with roasted vegetables (and then note you can use leftover chicken for Monday's quick meal, for instance), or a large pot of chili that feeds into multiple days. Essentially, it will treat Sunday as the anchor of batch cooking if you suggest it.

Remember that your time constraints might also influence the **complexity** of recipes. ChatGPT usually assumes an average skill level and time commitment unless told otherwise. So if you say "quick" or "15 minutes," it will keep things simple. Conversely, if you have a free evening and want a challenge, you could actually say, "Friday I'd like a fun kitchen project meal since I have time (like homemade dumplings or pizza from scratch)" – and it might oblige with something more ambitious for that day. The beauty is that you can calibrate each day's difficulty.

One prompt style some people use is to integrate time into each meal description, like: "create a plan with labels for each meal such as (15-min meal), (30-min meal), (make ahead, 4 hours slow cook) etc." ChatGPT can format the output with those labels, making it super clear. For example:

Monday: (15-min meal) Veggie Quesadillas and Salad...

Tuesday: (Slow Cooker, 8 hours) Beef Stew, started in the morning...

Wednesday: (Leftovers) ...

Thursday: (30-min meal) Quick Shrimp Stir-fry...

Friday: (1 hour, indulgent) Homemade Pizza Night... And so on. You get an at-a-glance view of the time each one takes.

A key point to emphasize is that by conveying your schedule, you're ensuring the meal plan is **realistic**. This prevents a common pitfall where you might abandon a meal plan mid-week because Tuesday's recipe was just too much effort and you ordered pizza instead. By having, say, tacos or a stir-fry (something known to be quick) on Tuesday because you planned it that way, you set yourself up for success. One person who used ChatGPT noted that while the AI's meals were simple, they appreciated that you can ask for exactly the type of meals you need – like under 30 minutes, vegetarian, etc. – to get just what suits your lifestyle. You are effectively customizing not just the *food* but the *effort* level.

If your schedule includes mornings, you could also plan breakfasts by time. For instance, "weekday breakfasts need to be <5 minutes (cereal, toast, or make-ahead), but Sunday brunch can be a 1-hour affair." Then you'd see quick suggestions for those weekdays and maybe pancakes or a frittata for Sunday.

Let's paint a mini example to see it in action:

User Prompt: "Plan 3 dinners. On Day 1, I have a busy evening (only 20 minutes to cook). Day 2, I have plenty of time (around 1 hour) and would like to try something new. Day 3, I have moderate time (~30 minutes). Use this info to choose appropriate recipes and mention the expected cooking time for each."

ChatGPT Output: "Sure, here's a 3-day dinner plan with time considerations:

Day 1 (20-minute meal): *Turkey and Cheese Paninis with Side Salad* – Use deli turkey and cheese to make quick panini sandwiches (you can use a pan if no press). While they toast, throw together a mixed green salad. *This meal comes together in about 20 minutes.*

Day 2 (1-hour meal): *Homemade Baked Orange Chicken with Broccoli* – Marinate chicken in an orange-soy glaze and bake it, while stir-frying broccoli on the side. This recipe is a bit more involved but yields a takeout-style treat at home. *Expect about 1 hour total, including marinating and baking time.*

Day 3 (30-minute meal): *Shrimp Stir-Fry with Snow Peas and Rice* – A quick stir-fry using shrimp (which cook fast) and crunchy snow peas. Serve over pre-cooked or microwave rice to save time. *Ready in roughly 30 minutes.*"

In the above, ChatGPT clearly tailored each meal to the time available and even gave the duration. Day 1's paninis are very quick (leveraging partially prepared ingredients). Day 2 introduced a more complex dish since time allowed. Day 3 kept it moderate. This is the kind of alignment that makes following the plan much easier because it respects your time constraints.

By integrating time-sensitive planning with ChatGPT, you essentially eliminate the disconnect between your meal plan and your life schedule. Many of us have made meal plans that looked great on Sunday, only to find by Wednesday we're too busy to cook what we planned. With ChatGPT, you can plan with foresight: the AI can help you allocate simpler meals to busy days and more elaborate ones to free days. It's like having an assistant who not only suggests *what* to cook, but also *when* to cook it.

We've now covered customizing your plan for personal preferences, ingredient swaps, and scheduling. But what if you're cooking not just for yourself, but for a whole family with different ages and tastes? Keeping everyone satisfied – the toddler, the teen, and the adults – adds another layer of challenge. Fear not: our AI kitchen buddy can handle that too. In the next section, we'll discuss **family-friendly and picky-eater planning** – how to get ChatGPT to account for various preferences and quirks in your household so that dinnertime is happy for all.

FAMILY-FRIENDLY AND PICKY-EATER PLANNING

Cooking for a family can sometimes feel like running a short-order diner – different people have different tastes, and what one child loves, another might refuse to touch. The beauty of using ChatGPT as your meal planner is that it can take into account all these **household quirks and preferences** and help you craft a plan that is broadly family-friendly. In this section, we'll explore how to prompt the AI to consider age-appropriate meals, picky eaters, and even ways to customize dishes so that everyone can enjoy dinner (perhaps with slight modifications per person). The goal is to minimize dinnertime battles and make meals enjoyable for the whole family.

First, it's important to **outline your family's profiles** to ChatGPT. How many people are you cooking for, and who are they? For example: two adults, a teenager, and a preschooler. Are there general preferences or aversions? Maybe "the 4-year-old is very picky and only reliably eats pasta and chicken," or "the teen is adventurous and loves spicy food, but mom can't handle too much heat." List any dietary restrictions across the family: allergies (like nuts, shellfish?), intolerances (gluten, lactose?), or lifestyle choices (perhaps one person is vegetarian but others eat meat). Also mention any **compromises or strategies** you already use, like "We try to have at least one meal everyone will definitely eat, and others where we can deconstruct the components."

When prompting, you might write something like: *"Plan 5 family dinners for 2 adults and 2 kids (ages 6 and 10). The 6-year-old is a picky eater who prefers simple flavors and dislikes spicy food and most vegetables (but will eat carrots and corn). The 10-year-old is more open but doesn't like mushrooms. The adults enjoy a wide range of foods but we want to keep meals relatively healthy. Please choose dinners that can either be made palatable for the kids or easily have components separated (for example, build-your-own taco night or serve sauces on the side). Include at least one or two veggies in each meal (maybe hidden if needed for the kids)."*

This prompt sets the stage for ChatGPT to be clever. It might come up with ideas like tacos or burrito bowls where each person can pick what they want (the kids can skip the salsa if they find it spicy, etc.), or a mild chicken stir-fry where the adults can add hot sauce at the table. It could also suggest familiar favorites with healthy twists, like baked chicken tenders (picky-kid-friendly) with a variety of dipping sauces (to make it fun and also suit adult tastes). If you mention "hidden veggies," it might incorporate, say, finely grated carrots in a sauce or spinach in a pesto that kids won't notice but still get some nutrition.

One strategy for pleasing picky eaters is to ask ChatGPT for recipes that are **customizable or modular.** For instance, a base meal like *Make-Your-Own Pizza* or *Loaded Baked Potatoes* where each family member can choose their toppings. You can prompt: "Include a dinner that is interactive or customizable for the kids." The AI might give you a plan with one night being personal mini-pizzas (adults might put gourmet toppings, kids just sauce and cheese), or a taco bar, or even something like rice bowls where everyone adds their preferred protein and veg. These meals tend to go over well because each person has some control.

Another approach is to ask for **lighter seasoning** or sauces on the side for certain dishes. Kids often prefer plain elements (like plain pasta, plain chicken) while adults want more flavor. If you tell ChatGPT "the kids prefer plain foods," it might suggest serving things deconstructed: for example, if the meal is a chicken teriyaki with veggies, the kids' portion could be plain chicken with the sauce on the side for dipping, and raw veggies or fruits on the side instead of mixed in. The AI can present the recipe in a kid-friendly way if prompted, or at least you can infer how to adapt it.

Age-appropriateness can also mean considering texture and form. Younger kids might do better with finger foods or dishes that aren't too mixed up (many kids at a certain age don't like casseroles where everything is touching). ChatGPT, if told the ages and pickiness levels, might avoid certain formats like "spicy chili" or "sushi bowls" that could be a hard sell, and lean more towards items like pasta, tacos, sandwiches, etc., which are typically kid-approved. One parent humorously pointed out the challenge: wondering *"which of my kids is going to randomly reject a meal I've cooked this week?"*. While AI can't eliminate all whimsical kid refusals, it can at least stack the deck in your favor by choosing more universally appealing meals.

We can also leverage ChatGPT to introduce **variety in a gentle way.** Maybe your kids eat only a few staples and you want to expand their palate slowly. You can ask the AI to incorporate new foods alongside familiar ones. For example: "My child likes pasta and cheese. Can you include a pasta dish that sneaks in a vegetable and maybe a new flavor for them to try (but not too far from what they know)?" The AI might come up with a macaroni and cheese that includes pureed butternut squash in the cheese sauce (hidden veggie!) or a mild broccoli cheddar pasta bake. Or if a kid loves burgers, it might suggest homemade sliders where one could be a chicken or veggie patty as an introduction to something new, served with their favorite ketchup to keep it agreeable.

Another useful trick: involve the kids via ChatGPT. You could actually have your child help "ask" ChatGPT for a meal they want. For instance, say to your kid, "Let's have the computer help us. What would you like to eat? Pizza? Okay." Then to ChatGPT: "Include a kid-chosen meal: homemade pizza with pepperoni." If kids feel they got to choose one meal of the week, they might be more excited about the week overall. For the others, you can say, "Now the computer will choose some other dinners that I think you'll like." This inclusion can sometimes get buy-in from picky eaters because they find it neat that "the computer suggested this just for us."

From an adult perspective, family-friendly doesn't mean adult-boring. You can ask ChatGPT to find ways to add flavor for grown-ups without alienating the kids. For example: "Ensure the meals are flavorful for adults, but any strong sauces or spices can be added at the end or as a condiment." The AI might then explicitly say, "Serve adult portions with chili flakes or extra herbs." Or it might design a meal like a mild base curry and note "those who like heat can add hot sauce." One mom who used ChatGPT mentioned it gave her recipes that were easy, nutritious, and filling, and while some of the AI's portion suggestions were off (like the one protein bar example), overall the output was balanced and workable for her family. The key is that you as the cook can always adjust portion sizes (you know your family's appetite better), but the plan ensures a baseline that feeds everyone.

Also consider if any family member has specific needs – e.g., a toddler who needs softer foods, or an elderly family member who needs low-sodium. These details can be included. "Plan meals that are easy for a toddler to chew" might result in more casseroles or meatballs instead of steaks, for instance. Or "low salt for grandma, but others can salt at the table" – the AI could suggest seasoning with herbs and then adding salt individually.

Let's imagine a snippet of a family-oriented plan:

"**Tuesday:** Build-Your-Own Taco Night – Everyone can assemble tacos to their liking. We'll provide seasoned ground turkey, warm tortillas, lettuce, tomato, cheese, and mild salsa. (For adventurous eaters, we have hot salsa and jalapeños on the side, but kids can stick to just turkey and cheese if they want.) This way, the meal is fun and interactive, and each person gets what they like. Serve with a side of corn (which the kids love) and avocado slices.

Wednesday: Sneaky Veggie Pasta – A creamy pasta where the sauce is blended cauliflower and cheddar (it tastes like mac and cheese!). The kids just see a yummy creamy pasta, and adults get the satisfaction of a veggie-rich meal. We can top adult servings with a sprinkle of chili flakes and chopped parsley for extra flavor. The kids can have theirs plain. Add a side of roasted carrots (the 6-year-old's favorite vegetable) so there's something familiar on the plate.

Thursday: DIY Pizza Pita Bread – Give each family member a small pita. Provide pizza sauce, mozzarella, and various toppings (pepperoni, bell peppers, olives, etc.). Kids can make simple cheese pizzas or funny faces with the toppings. Adults can load theirs up with veggies and a bit of goat cheese from the fridge for extra flavor. Bake all the pitas together for 10 minutes. This is a hit because the kids are involved in making it, which often means they're excited to eat it."

This example shows a few approaches: customizable meals (tacos and DIY pizzas) and a stealth health meal (veggie pasta disguised as mac & cheese). It also considered specific kid-friendly sides and adult add-ons. The suggestions are written in a friendly tone, as if guiding a family plan.

ChatGPT can also provide tips like "If one child won't eat the casserole, set aside some of the chicken and serve it with ketchup for them" – sometimes it explicitly gives those kind of accommodations if it knows about a picky eater. This can validate your own strategies and maybe give new ones.

Another use-case is doubling up elements to suit different ages. For example, if you grill chicken, the adults get grilled chicken over salad, and the toddler gets small cut-up pieces of the same chicken with some buttered noodles. You could ask: "Suggest how to serve the meal so that a toddler will eat it as well." The AI might then describe plating options or slight modifications (like reserving some ingredients before adding spicy sauce).

What about **volume and leftovers** in families? With multiple people, leftovers might not be as abundant, but you can plan to cook a bit extra of kid-approved dishes so you have something easy to reheat for them on a night when the adult meal is too adventurous. If you foresee that, ask ChatGPT: "Maybe include one very kid-favorite meal that I can double and use as leftover lunch or backup for the kids on a night they refuse the main meal." It could pick something like chicken nuggets with homemade breading or a big spaghetti that yields extra portions.

One family-oriented user story from earlier: a mom using ChatGPT found that it "incorporates my children's dietary preferences and the ingredients I have available". For example, she typed in specifics about her picky eaters (no spicy food, had certain ingredients) and got a recipe that satisfied them. She no longer had to spend hours coming up with new meal ideas, and her kids started looking forward to dinner because it was diverse yet still within their comfort zone. That's a great summary of what AI can do in a family context: save the parent's mental energy and bring some harmony to the dinner table.

In summary, to use ChatGPT for family meal planning, be as clear as you can about:

- Who's eating (ages, how many).
- What each person likes or won't eat.
- How you prefer to handle meal differences (one meal for all, or slight modifications per person).

- Any shared family goals (like "we all eat the same meal together" or "we want to introduce more veggies to the kids").
- Preferences for meal formats that engage kids (like DIY style, finger foods, etc.).

The AI will then juggle these needs. It might not be 100% perfect on the first pass – you may need to clarify ("Actually, my kid won't eat anything mixed like a stew, can we swap that out?") – but it's easy to refine, as we discussed in substitutions. Over time, you'll notice patterns of what works for your family, and you can re-use those ideas or have ChatGPT generate fresh ones in the same vein.

Now that we've covered planning for variety, prep efficiency, shopping, substitutions, scheduling, and family needs, it's time to see it all come together. In the final section, we'll walk through a **live demo** scenario: from asking ChatGPT for a meal plan to refining it and getting the grocery list, step by step. This will serve as a concrete example of how you might interact with ChatGPT in a conversation to build your week of meals from scratch.

LIVE DEMO: MEAL PLAN + LIST FROM SCRATCH

In this section, we'll walk through a realistic example of using ChatGPT to plan a week of meals and generate the shopping list. Think of it as looking over the shoulder of a home cook (let's call her Alex) as she chats with ChatGPT to get her meal plan in place. This "live demo" will tie together all the concepts we've discussed: giving ChatGPT your requirements, refining the plan, leveraging prep logic, dealing with preferences, and finally producing the grocery list. By following this dialogue, you can get a feel for how you might conduct your own session with the AI to achieve a customized meal plan.

Step 1: Alex requests a meal plan.

Alex begins by telling ChatGPT about her household and what she wants:

User (Alex): "Hi ChatGPT! I'd like some help planning dinners for the next 7 days (Monday through Sunday). Here's what I need: It's for a family of 4 (2 adults, 2 kids ages 8 and 5). We try to eat fairly healthy: lean proteins, whole grains, and veggies if possible. The 5-year-old is a bit picky (likes plain foods, not too spicy). The 8-year-old is more adventurous but doesn't like mushrooms. I only have about 30 minutes to cook on weeknights. On Saturday, I have more time and wouldn't mind doing something a bit special or complex. Sunday we often do a make-ahead meal or something easy. Also, I have some ingredients already I'd love to use: there's some chicken breast in the freezer, a can of black beans in the pantry, and a lot of cheddar cheese in the fridge that should get used. We don't have any allergies, but I prefer the meals not to be super spicy. Could you please create a 7-day dinner plan for Monday-Sunday that takes all this into account? Please list each day with the meal name and a brief description or any notes (like if it's a quick meal or uses leftovers). Thanks!"

This prompt is detailed, which is great. Alex has covered number of people, dietary style, specific picky eater info, time constraints per day, existing ingredients to incorporate, and other preferences. ChatGPT now has a lot to work with.

ChatGPT: "Certainly! Let's create a 7-day dinner plan for your family, keeping it healthy, kid-friendly, and time-conscious. I'll note the cooking time or special prep where appropriate:

Monday: *Lemon Herb Chicken with Quinoa and Steamed Broccoli* – A simple, light meal. Season and bake the chicken breasts (you have these in your freezer) with lemon, garlic, and herbs. While they bake, cook quinoa (a whole grain) and steam broccoli. *(Approx. 30 min total. Kid-friendly: the chicken can be served plain or with a little ketchup on the side for the 5-year-old, and you can sprinkle cheese on the broccoli to make it more appealing.)*

Tuesday: *Build-Your-Own Burrito Bowls* – These are fun and customizable. Base of rice (or lettuce for a lighter option) topped with seasoned ground turkey (or beef), black beans (use the can you have), corn, tomatoes, and cheddar cheese (you have plenty). Serve with mild salsa and Greek yogurt as a stand-in for sour cream. *(Quick to* *prepare, ~25 min, especially if you cook extra rice on Monday or use microwave rice. Each family member can assemble their bowl – great for the picky eater who can choose what to include.)*

Wednesday: *Cheesy Veggie Pasta Bake* – A weeknight casserole using whole wheat pasta, lots of veggies (like spinach and diced carrots hidden in the sauce), and a cheese sauce made with that cheddar you have. Mix cooked pasta, sautéed veggies, and cheese sauce, then bake until bubbly. *(This takes a little longer, ~40 min, but you can prep it the night before or earlier and just bake at dinner time. Kids usually love anything cheesy; you can also let the top get crispy which is yummy.)*

Thursday: *Teriyaki Salmon with Green Beans and Brown Rice* – Oven-baked teriyaki salmon (in a foil packet for easy cleanup) served with green beans and brown rice. *(Prep is ~10 min, cook time ~20 min. If the kids are unsure about salmon, you can drizzle a little honey on theirs to make it sweeter, or give a small portion and more rice. You could also substitute chicken in teriyaki style for them if needed, but trying fish once a week is great.)*

Friday: *Turkey and Veggie Tacos* – Classic taco night. Use ground turkey sautéed with mild taco seasoning. Offer soft or hard taco shells. Fillings: lettuce, tomato, shredded cheese, mild salsa, avocado slices. Include a side of corn (the 5-year-old likes corn) and maybe some black beans left from Tuesday. *(Quick and interactive, ~30 min. Everyone can customize their tacos. You can even make "taco bowls" for the kids if they prefer to eat deconstructed.)*

Saturday: *Homemade Pizza Night* – Use store-bought whole grain pizza dough or crust. Everyone can help assemble. One pizza could be plain cheese (for the kids), and another loaded with veggies like bell peppers, onions, maybe some leftover chicken pieces for the adults. Use your cheddar in addition to mozzarella for a sharp flavor. *(Fun family activity; takes about 1 hour including baking. This is the 'special' meal for the week where you have more time and can involve the kids in cooking.)*

Sunday: *Slow Cooker Chili* – A mild ground beef and bean chili that simmers in the slow cooker while you relax. Include kidney beans, tomatoes, bell peppers (finely diced so they melt in), and you can sneak in grated carrots or zucchini. Season with chili powder but on the milder side. Serve with a sprinkle of cheddar on top and some bread or rice. *(Minimal morning prep, cooks 6-8 hours. Make a big batch – leftovers can be lunch or frozen. It's flavorful but not too spicy, pleasing for both kids and adults. The 5-year-old can pick out the beans if needed, but often the sweetness of slow-cooked carrots and the cheese on top win them over.)*

I hope this menu sounds good! It uses your chicken (Monday), black beans and cheddar (Tuesday, Friday, etc.), keeps things balanced and not too spicy, and includes some fun meals. Let me know if you'd like any changes or the recipes for any of these."

ChatGPT's plan is detailed and each day is tailored. Let's analyze it: It spread out the use of Alex's existing ingredients (chicken Monday, black beans Tuesday, cheddar in multiple places). It accounted for the kids – for example, suggesting cheese on broccoli, or honey on salmon, or making one pizza plain. It noted time: most are ~30 minutes, the slightly longer one (pasta bake) could be prepped ahead, and the special one (pizza) on the weekend when time allows. It even integrated leftover logic subtly (like using Tuesday's beans on Friday, and making extra chili for leftovers). This is a solid first draft.

Step 2: Alex reviews and adjusts the plan.

Alex likes most of it but has a couple of tweaks in mind. For one, she recalls that her kids really don't eat fish well, and she's not sure about doing salmon on Thursday. Also, Wednesday's pasta bake sounds good but maybe a bit heavy after having burrito bowls and before tacos; perhaps she'd prefer something lighter on Wednesday. Let's see how she refines it:

User (Alex): "This looks awesome! Thank you. A couple of adjustments:

- Instead of salmon on Thursday, can we substitute a chicken dish? Maybe teriyaki chicken thighs or something, because my kids might eat that better than salmon.

- Also, the pasta bake on Wednesday sounds tasty, but I wonder if it might be too heavy or time-consuming mid-week. Could you suggest a lighter quick meal for Wednesday, perhaps something like a soup and salad or a stir-fry?
- Everything else looks great. Please update the plan for Wednesday and Thursday with those changes."

Alex asks for changes, specifying alternatives (teriyaki chicken instead of salmon, and a lighter meal for Wednesday).

ChatGPT: "Sure, no problem! I'll adjust Wednesday and Thursday:

Wednesday (updated): *Vegetable Soup & Grilled Cheese Sandwiches* – A lighter, comforting meal. A quick veggie soup using carrots, celery, tomatoes, and any other veggies on hand (even throw in some of that broccoli stems chopped up, etc.), simmered in broth with herbs. Serve with whole-grain grilled cheese sandwiches (you can even use cheddar for these) for a bit of fun. *(About 30 minutes total. The kids can dip their grilled cheese in the soup if they like. It's lighter than a pasta bake but still satisfying, and a good way to get veggies in.)*

Thursday (updated): *Teriyaki Chicken & Green Beans* – Swap the salmon for chicken thighs (or breasts sliced) cooked in a teriyaki sauce. You can do it stir-fry style or bake in the oven. Serve with the same green beans and brown rice as planned. *(Around 30 minutes. The chicken in teriyaki sauce should be a hit with the kids – it's savory-sweet. You can even cook it in one pan on the stovetop for convenience.)*

All other days remain the same. Does this work better?"

This update reflects Alex's requests. Now Wednesday is an easy soup & grilled cheese (still uses some cheddar, nice!). Thursday is teriyaki chicken instead of salmon, keeping the spirit but aligning with family preference. Alex is satisfied.

Step 3: Alex asks for recipes (if needed).

Alex might already know how to cook most of these, but perhaps she's curious about a specific recipe or wants instructions for one of the meals she hasn't made before (say, the slow cooker chili or the teriyaki sauce). She can either ask for a recipe for each meal individually or as a batch. To keep things simple, maybe she wants just one recipe in detail: the slow cooker chili, since that's something she plans to do on Sunday and maybe freeze leftovers.

User (Alex): "Great, thanks! Can you provide me with the recipe for the Slow Cooker Chili on Sunday? I want to make sure I do it right."

ChatGPT: "Certainly! Here's a simple Slow Cooker Chili recipe tailored to Sunday's plan:

Slow Cooker Beef and Bean Chili (Makes about 6 servings)

Ingredients:

- 1 lb ground beef (you can use lean)
- 1 onion, diced
- 2 cloves garlic, minced
- 2 carrots, peeled and grated (sneaky veggie)
- 1 red bell pepper, finely diced (you can also use half green, half red for color)
- 1 zucchini, grated or finely diced (optional extra veg)
- 1 can (14-15 oz) kidney beans, drained and rinsed
- 1 can (14-15 oz) black beans, drained and rinsed (or pinto beans)
- 1 can (28 oz) diced tomatoes (with liquid)
- 2 tablespoons mild chili powder (use less if you want it very mild)
- 1 teaspoon ground cumin
- 1 teaspoon salt (adjust to taste)
- 1/2 teaspoon black pepper
- 1 cup of water or broth (if needed for more liquid)

To serve: Shredded cheddar cheese, plain yogurt or sour cream, and bread or rice.

Instructions:

- **Prep Beef and Aromatics:** In a skillet over medium heat, brown the ground beef for 5-6 minutes, breaking it into crumbles. If there's excess fat, drain it. Add the diced onion and minced garlic to the beef and cook for another 2-3 minutes until the onion begins to soften.
- **Transfer to Slow Cooker:** Put the beef-onion-garlic mixture into the slow cooker.
- **Add Veggies and Beans:** Add the grated carrots, diced bell pepper, and grated zucchini to the slow cooker. Then add the kidney beans, black beans, and the can of diced tomatoes (with their juices).
- **Season:** Stir in the chili powder and cumin, salt, and pepper. If you want it very mild, you can start with 1 tablespoon chili powder and add more later if needed.
- **Add Liquid:** If the mixture looks a bit thick (not much liquid), add about 1 cup of water or broth. The veggies and tomatoes will also release liquid as it cooks.
- **Slow Cook:** Cover and cook on **Low for 6-8 hours** or **High for about 3-4 hours.** Longer is fine on low if you need. The flavors will meld together and the veggies will become almost invisible (which is great for the kids).
- **Finish:** Taste and adjust seasoning at the end. You can add a bit more salt or pepper if needed. If you want more spice for the adults, you could add a pinch of cayenne or serve hot sauce on the side.
- **Serve:** Ladle the chili into bowls. Top with shredded cheddar cheese and a dollop of yogurt or sour cream. You can serve with crusty bread for dipping or over rice if you like.

This chili should be very family-friendly (nice and hearty but not too spicy). And you'll have leftovers which you can freeze or use for lunches. Enjoy!"

Now Alex has the recipe she wanted. ChatGPT gave a detailed, step-by-step recipe, including the "sneaky" veggies and notes about adjusting spice, which is very useful. It also reminded her of leftovers usage.

If Alex wanted recipes for each day, she could ask, but that would be a lot of information all at once. Often it's easier to request recipes one by one as needed.

Step 4: Alex generates the grocery list.

Finally, Alex will ask for a grocery list covering all the meals Monday-Sunday, excluding what she already has. She mentioned she had chicken, black beans, and cheddar initially. Also now from the recipe, she might recall she has some spices, etc. She can mention those items to be safe.

User (Alex): "Thanks for the recipe! Now, could you help me with a grocery list for the entire week's dinner plan (Monday to Sunday)? Please group items by category (Produce, Meat, Dairy, Canned Goods, etc.). I already have: chicken breasts (for Monday), a can of black beans, and plenty of cheddar cheese. Also, assume I have basic spices and cooking oil. List everything else I'll need to buy for these dinners."

Alex is making sure the list won't include what she has and is grouped nicely.

ChatGPT: "Sure! Here's the grocery list for the week's dinner plan, excluding the chicken breasts, black beans, and cheddar you already have, and assuming basic pantry items (salt, pepper, basic spices, oil) are on hand. I'll group the items by category:

Produce:

- Lemons – 2 (for Monday's lemon chicken marinade and any garnish)
- Garlic – 1 bulb (several cloves used across recipes)
- Yellow or White Onions – 3 large (1 for chili, 1 for soup, 1 for general use)
- Carrots – 6-7 medium (Broccoli night, soup, chili; includes extra for snacks or sides)
- Broccoli – 1 large head (Monday, and can use stems in soup)

- Celery – 2-3 stalks (for soup; you can buy a bunch and use some with peanut butter snacks)
- Bell Peppers – 3 (1 green, 1 red for chili; 1 extra red for topping or salad)
- Tomatoes – 4-5 (for burrito bowls, taco toppings, soup)
- Avocado – 2 (for burrito bowls, taco night toppings – optional but nice)
- Lettuce – 1 head or 1 bag of shredded lettuce (for burrito bowls and tacos)
- Green Beans – ~1 lb fresh (Thursday side)
- Cilantro – 1 small bunch (for burrito bowls and tacos garnish, optional)
- Zucchini – 1 medium (for chili, grated hidden veggie)
- Spinach – 1 bag (for salad with soup or to toss in soup, and can sneak some in burrito bowls)
- (Optional) Mushrooms – **omit** (we skip because family doesn't like)

Meat/Protein:

- Ground Turkey – 2 lbs (for burrito bowl and tacos; you could buy 2 separate 1lb packs)
- Ground Beef – 1 lb (for Sunday's chili)
- Chicken Thighs – ~1.5 to 2 lbs (for Thursday teriyaki chicken)
- (You already have chicken breasts for Monday)
- (Beans: you have black beans; also need kidney beans below)

Canned Goods & Pantry:

- Quinoa – 1 package (if you don't have ~1-2 cups for Monday)
- Whole wheat pasta – 1 box (for pasta bake originally; but since we changed Wednesday, you might not need this

now. You could get small pasta for soup like elbow or ditalini instead.)

- Taco shells or small tortillas – 1 package (for taco night)
- Whole wheat flour (or regular) tortillas – 1 package (for burrito bowls if making wraps or just have on hand)
- Brown Rice – enough for 2-3 cups cooked (if you don't have at home for Tuesday and Thursday; could be 1 box or bag)
- Kidney Beans – 1 can (for chili)
- Diced Tomatoes – 1 can (28 oz, for chili)
- Tomato sauce or crushed tomatoes – 1 small can (to enrich soup or chili if needed)
- Mild Salsa – 1 jar (for burrito bowls and taco night)
- Corn kernels – 1 bag frozen or 2 cans (for burrito bowls, taco side, etc.)
- Chicken or Vegetable Broth – 1 quart (for soup base)
- Bread – Whole grain bread for grilled cheese (Wednesday)
- Pizza crust or dough – enough for 2 pizzas (could be 2 pre-made crusts or dough balls)
- Pizza sauce – 1 jar (for Saturday pizza)
- Yeast (if making dough from scratch, but assuming store-bought dough)
- (Also ensure you have rice or bread to serve with chili, as preferred)

Dairy:

- Greek Yogurt or Sour Cream – 1 small container (used as topping for burrito bowl and chili, and sour cream can go in mashed potatoes if you like)
- Mozzarella Cheese – 2 cups shredded or 1 block (for pizza night, since you have cheddar already to mix)
- Milk – if needed for the soup or mac n cheese sauce (1 quart, if not already stocked)

- Butter – (for grilled cheese and general cooking, ensure you have some)

Other:

- Eggs – 1 dozen (for breakfast or if making dough, and can use in the breading or just general use)
- Honey – 1 small bottle (for teriyaki sauce if you don't have, and to sweeten kids' portions if needed)
- Soy Sauce – (for teriyaki; likely a pantry staple, but get a bottle if low)
- Whole grain crackers or bread for soup side – (optional)
- Your favorite hot sauce (adults can use on chili or tacos, optional)

This should cover everything you need for the dinners. You mentioned having spices, but double-check you have chili powder, cumin, and Italian herbs (for soup) on hand. Also, since we swapped the pasta bake for soup, you won't need as much pasta or cheese for that, but the list includes ingredients for all current meals.

Happy shopping and cooking!"

Now the list is compiled and categorized. Alex will review it and likely cross off the things she truly has. The assistant even made a note about the pasta bake being swapped (so pasta not needed unless for soup). It also omitted mushrooms as noted.

The list is comprehensive; Alex can trim or adjust based on pantry (maybe she already has rice, etc.). It grouped produce, meats, etc., which is convenient.

With this, Alex has successfully gone from planning to pantry: she got her meal plan, refined it, grabbed a recipe, and now has a shopping list.

Recap of the Live Demo:

We saw how Alex:

- Provided details to ChatGPT (family, preferences, time).

- Received a tailored week plan.
- Asked for modifications (substitutions and schedule tweaks).
- Got an updated plan.
- Requested a specific recipe.
- Got the recipe instructions.
- Asked for a shopping list, mentioning what she already has.
- Received a categorized shopping list to use.

Throughout the process, ChatGPT was warm, accommodating, and detail-oriented – just the kind of helper you'd want in planning meals. It's easy to see how this saves Alex mental effort and ensures she's prepared for the week. She can now head into Monday confident that dinner is all set, with a clear plan (and even contingency tips like simpler kid versions of each meal).

This concludes the live demo and, with it, Chapter 4. Over the course of this chapter, we've covered everything from one-prompt weekly planning to advanced techniques for making that plan efficient, cost-effective, and family-friendly. You've learned how to leverage ChatGPT to reduce your meal-planning time drastically while also improving the variety and nutritional balance of your meals. The AI can help you think ahead – reuse ingredients, plan leftovers, and organize your shopping – so that you're cooking smarter, not harder, all week long.

As you start applying "The AI Meal Planner" approach in your own kitchen, remember that it's a flexible tool. You can start small, maybe planning just a few days at a time, or dive into full weekly plans. You can chat back and forth with ChatGPT to tweak things until the plan feels just right for you. The more you use it, the more you'll develop a sense of what to ask for and how to phrase your prompts to get your ideal results. Soon, you'll have a rhythm: each week, a quick session with ChatGPT will produce a plan that once might have taken you hours of brainstorming and list-making.

The benefits go beyond saving time. Many people find that with

AI meal planning, they eat more diverse meals and waste less food. It's easier to stick to a budget because you have a clear list and plan. And perhaps most importantly, it takes away the daily stress of the "what's for dinner?" scramble. You've set yourself up for success, with an AI assistant ensuring you have a thoughtful answer to that question every day.

In the next chapter, we'll continue to build your AI-assisted kitchen skills. Now that meal planning and prep are under control, it's time to see how ChatGPT can be your sous-chef during cooking itself – helping with techniques, timing, and even on-the-fly adjustments as you cook. With planning out of the way, you can enjoy the cooking process more, and Chapter 5 will show you how AI can support you from the moment you tie on your apron to the moment you plate the food. Let's keep cooking smarter together!

5

RESCUE ME DINNER: WHEN YOU'RE TIRED, BROKE, OR OVERWHELMED

Imagine it's 7 PM on a weeknight. You're staring at an open fridge with glazed eyes, body weary from a long day, and brain running on empty. Maybe you're running low on groceries or cash until payday. Perhaps you've got a couple of fussy kids in the next room or just a grumbling stomach of your own. *Sound familiar?* We've all been there: those nights when figuring out what to make for dinner feels like solving a riddle while you're half-asleep. This chapter is all about those moments. It's about how to *rescue dinner* when you're tired, broke, or completely overwhelmed.

In these pages, you'll learn how to turn to ChatGPT as your personal kitchen lifeline on the toughest days. Think of it as your friendly AI sous-chef who never gets tired of helping out. When your energy is at zero, ChatGPT can suggest fast, low-effort meals to fill your plate with minimal fuss. When you barely have ten minutes to spare, it can brainstorm recipes that come together in a snap. When you can't handle a sink full of dishes, it will find one-pot or one-pan wonders that leave almost nothing to clean up. When money is tight, it will conjure up *cheap, filling, and surprisingly good* dinner ideas from basic ingredients. And if you don't even have a recipe in mind – just a random assortment of pantry items – ChatGPT can guide you through an improvised, on-the-fly meal like a seasoned chef helping you wing it.

Throughout this chapter, we'll explore seven life-saving strategies for dinnertime, each with plenty of real-world examples and ChatGPT prompts you can try. You'll see how to handle the nights when you're too exhausted to think, how to craft a meal in mere minutes, and how to simplify cooking so it doesn't add to your stress. We'll also dive into using ChatGPT when you're multitasking or literally have your hands full, and we'll walk through actual "panic cooking" scenarios to show how an AI helper can turn things around. The tone here is warm and supportive – because the last thing you need when you're overwhelmed is more pressure. Consider this a friendly conversation with a kitchen buddy who's got your back.

By the end of this chapter, you'll have a toolkit of ChatGPT prompts and techniques for surviving any dinner crisis. You'll feel more confident knowing that even on your worst days, you can lean on a virtual helper to get a decent meal on the table. No matter your cooking skill level, these tips are here to encourage and empower you. Dinner emergencies happen to everyone, but with an AI-first kitchen companion at your side, you'll be ready to tackle them head-on – and maybe even find some fun and creativity in the process.

Now, let's step into the first scenario: the *dinner triage*. What do you do when you have nothing left in the tank to cook? ChatGPT is standing by to assist… so let's put it to work.

DINNER TRIAGE: WHEN YOU HAVE NOTHING LEFT IN THE TANK

Picture this: you drag yourself into the kitchen after an exhausting day, and even the thought of cooking *feels like climbing a mountain*. This is the dinner emergency room – the *triage* situation – when you have nothing left in the tank but still need to feed yourself (and maybe a couple of others). In these moments, the goal isn't a gourmet feast; it's simply survival with something warm and nourishing on a plate. We're talking fast, low-effort meals that basically cook themselves. Fortunately, ChatGPT can step in as your on-call culinary medic, ready with ideas that require minimal energy and time.

Think of ChatGPT as a stress-free decision maker. When you're bone-tired, deciding *what* to cook is often the biggest hurdle. It's okay if all you can muster is typing a single sentence into your phone. Just tell ChatGPT how you feel and what you have on hand – or even what you *don't* have energy for – and let it do the thinking. You might say something like, *"I'm exhausted and can barely cook. I have a box of pasta, a jar of sauce, and some cheese. What's the easiest dinner I can make?"* In seconds, ChatGPT will likely suggest a minimalist meal like a simple baked pasta: cook the pasta, mix with sauce and cheese, and throw it under the broiler for a couple of minutes. Voilà – dinner with almost no effort.

When energy and patience are zero, *simplicity is key*. One of the best things to ask for are meals with *very few ingredients or steps*. For example, you could prompt: *"Give me an idea for the simplest one-pan dinner possible – I'm too tired to chop or do a lot of cleanup."* ChatGPT might respond with something like: *"Make a quick veggie omelet or frittata: beat eggs, pour into a pan with any veggies or cheese you have, let it set, and dinner is done."* Or perhaps it will suggest a sandwich night – something like grilled cheese and tomato soup (where you just heat up canned soup and make a quick sandwich). These aren't fancy meals, but when you're exhausted, they hit the spot and require almost no brainpower.

It also helps to use what's already cooked or requires no cooking. Tell ChatGPT what pre-made or leftover items you have, and watch it assemble a meal for you. Let's say you have leftover rice in the fridge and zero motivation. Try asking, *"I have some leftover rice and I'm too tired to really cook – what can I do with it for dinner?"* You might get a suggestion for a quick fried rice: throw the rice in a pan with a scrambled egg, frozen peas, and a splash of soy sauce. Suddenly you have a hot meal in about 10 minutes, using just one pan. Or if you have a rotisserie chicken from the store, ChatGPT might tell you how to turn it into *no-cook tacos*: shred the chicken, warm it in the microwave with some spices, then wrap it in tortillas with any sauce or cheese you have.

Don't hesitate to be *blunt about your limits* in your prompt. If you literally only have the strength to press a microwave button, say so. *"I can only use the microwave tonight. What's an actual dinner I can make with it?"* is a perfectly valid question. ChatGPT might remind you that baked potatoes can be made in the microwave: poke a potato and microwave it until soft, then top it with whatever (butter, cheese, canned chili, etc.). It could also suggest a microwave "omelet in a mug" or steaming some vegetables in a bowl covered with a plate. The key is that you're telling the AI exactly how little you can do, so it tailors the solution to your reality.

Here are a few example prompts for those *running-on-empty* nights:

- "I'm completely drained. What is the absolute easiest dinner I can make with a can of soup, some bread, and cheese?"
- "I have almost no energy. Give me a one-step recipe – like something I basically just assemble and eat."
- "Too tired to cook or clean – can ChatGPT suggest a meal that uses only one pot and maybe paper plates?"
- "I've got a hungry family and zero motivation. What's a quick dinner hack using stuff like eggs or pasta so I don't have to order takeout?"

Each of these prompts will get ChatGPT thinking about ultra-simple solutions. Maybe it will say to jazz up that can of soup by heating it and making cheese toast on the side (hardly any work at all). For the one-step recipe, it could propose a hearty salad if you have pre-washed greens (just dump ingredients in a bowl), or even something like nachos for dinner where you layer chips with beans and cheese and microwave them. Using one pot and paper plates might lead to a suggestion like a *one-pot mac and cheese*, eaten straight from the pot if you're that tired (we won't judge!). And the hungry family prompt could yield ideas like breakfast-for-dinner: quickly scrambling a dozen eggs with some veggies or cheese – high protein, filling, and done in 10 minutes.

The magic of using ChatGPT in these dire moments is that it removes the mental strain. Instead of mentally cycling through options while your stomach growls, you outsource that brainstorming to an always-cheerful assistant. Often, just seeing a suggestion pop up is enough to get you moving, because you realize "Hey, I can do that. Five minutes, a pot, and I'm done." ChatGPT can also throw in a bit of encouragement or a tip – like "you can even use paper towels instead of plates for easy cleanup" – which feels like a friend giving you permission to take shortcuts.

By the end of your *dinner triage* session with ChatGPT, you'll hopefully have something simple and satisfying ready to eat, and you'll have conserved precious energy. It's all about cutting corners and being kind to yourself. And once you've survived the crisis with a no-sweat meal, you can rest up. After all, tomorrow's a new day – hopefully with a bit more pep in your step. But sometimes, even after a good rest, you might still find yourself short on time. In that case, speed is the name of the game. It's time to unleash ChatGPT's *10-minute meal* ideas — perfect for those evenings when even fifteen minutes feels too long.

THE 10-MINUTE MEAL PROMPT

Some nights, the biggest challenge isn't lack of energy – it's lack of time. Maybe you got home late, or you have to head out soon, or everyone's already *hangry* and waiting. This is when you need dinner on the table *stat*, and a bowl of cereal just won't cut it. The good news: ChatGPT can help you rustle up a satisfying meal in around 10 minutes. The key is knowing how to prompt for ultra-quick recipes that use minimal prep, minimal cleanup, but still deliver maximum flavor.

When every minute counts, be direct about your time limit. For example, try something like: *"I only have 10 minutes to cook dinner. What's a quick meal I can make with [ingredient X], [ingredient Y], and maybe [ingredient Z]?"* By specifying that 10-minute window, you're telling ChatGPT to think in terms of very short cook times or even no-cook assembly. It might suggest ideas such as a speedy stir-fry (if you have something like pre-cut veggies and a protein), or perhaps a quick pasta dish using fresh pasta (which cooks faster than dry) and a simple sauce. If you include specific ingredients in your prompt, the AI can focus the suggestions on what you have, which saves even more time.

One useful trick is to mention *"minimal prep"* or *"no chopping"* if you truly can't spare a minute for knife work. Imagine you have some cherry tomatoes and spinach and want to use them fast. You could ask: *"Give me a healthy dinner I can make in 10 minutes with no chopping, using cherry tomatoes, spinach, and whatever common pantry items."* ChatGPT might respond with something like: *"Make a quick pasta toss: Boil pasta (spaghetti or any kind) – it will cook in about 8-10 minutes. While it boils, in a pan combine cherry tomatoes (no need to cut them) with olive oil and garlic powder (so you don't even have to chop garlic). Toss in the spinach to wilt at the end. Mix with the drained pasta and add salt, pepper, and a sprinkle of cheese. Dinner is ready in ten minutes."* Notice how the solution cleverly avoids chopping by using garlic powder instead of fresh garlic and lets the stove do two things at once (boiling and sautéing). ChatGPT is great at optimizing like this when you prompt it to eliminate prep steps.

For *minimal cleanup*, you can specify that too – though in a 10-minute scenario, often the simplest meals naturally don't use many pots. Still, you might say: *"I need a 10-minute dinner with basically zero cleanup – ideally something I can cook on one pan or not dirty any dishes."* This could lead to an idea like a quick quesadilla (cooked in one skillet, eaten off a cutting board) or even a microwaved meal in a single bowl. ChatGPT might suggest, for instance, *"Black bean and cheese quesadillas: spread canned beans and cheese in a tortilla, fold and toast it in a pan until crispy. Serve with salsa (you can even eat it straight out of the jar). Only one pan to wash!"* This kind of meal is done in under 10 minutes and hardly makes a mess.

Another powerful use of ChatGPT in time-crunch mode is *parallelizing tasks*. You can ask for instructions that take advantage of every minute. Maybe you have a scenario: *"I have 10 minutes and a pound of ground beef – what can I make quick?"* The AI might come back with a plan to make crumbled beef tacos: *"Put the ground beef in a skillet to brown (no need for oil if it's not too lean). While it's cooking, warm some tortillas in the microwave and gather any toppings (shredded cheese, salsa, lettuce). Season the beef in the pan with whatever spices you have (chili powder, salt, garlic). By the time the beef is cooked (8-10 minutes), you can assemble tacos."* This way, there's zero idle time. The prompt didn't explicitly mention multitasking, but ChatGPT often includes it instinctively, and you can encourage it by asking for a step-by-step timeline for a 10-minute recipe.

If you're completely unsure what you want, you can even ask for a list of options and then choose. Try a prompt like: *"What are some dinner ideas I can make in 10 minutes or less? I have eggs, bread, a can of tuna, and some frozen vegetables."* ChatGPT might give you a handful of suggestions: maybe a quick tuna melt (toast bread, mix tuna with mayo, spread and broil with cheese), or an egg fried rice using the frozen veggies and eggs, or even a hearty salad topped with tuna and a quick vinaigrette. By listing a few ideas, it lets you pick what sounds best, which is great when you're in a hurry but still a little indecisive.

Remember, a "10-minute meal" sometimes assumes you have water boiling already or an oven pre-heated – things that in reality might add a couple of minutes. If ChatGPT suggests something that seems like it would actually take longer than 10 minutes, you can reply and say, *"I really only have 10 minutes of actual cooking – can we make it even faster?"* The AI can then adjust, maybe suggesting you use the microwave or choose ingredients that cook faster (like couscous instead of rice, or shrimp instead of chicken since shrimp cook in a flash). This back-and-forth can hone the plan to truly fit your time crunch.

In essence, the 10-minute meal prompt is about *stripping down a recipe to its essential quick-cooking elements.* You'll find that many cuisines have their speedy dishes – think of a simple stir-fry, an omelet, a sandwich, or pasta aglio e olio (garlic and oil pasta) which takes no more time than boiling the pasta. ChatGPT has a vast library of such ideas to pull from. And unlike searching the web, it won't make you scroll through a long story or ads – it jumps straight to the instructions.

Armed with these ultra-fast dinner techniques, you can beat the clock on even the busiest evenings. Ten minutes might sound impossibly short, but with a smart prompt and an AI helper, you'll be amazed what's doable. Of course, cooking fast is only half the battle – cleaning up is the other half. Wouldn't it be nice if dinner left behind just one dish to wash? In that spirit, let's explore the realm of one-pot and one-pan wonders that make cleanup a breeze.

ONE-POT WONDERS AND SHEET PAN SAVIORS

After a meal, nothing kills the post-dinner vibe like a sink full of dirty dishes. That's why one-pot and sheet-pan dinners are a busy cook's best friends. Here we'll look at how to use ChatGPT to simplify dinner into a single dish – and as a bonus, only one pot or pan to clean. It's the ultimate win-win: you get a hearty meal, and cleanup is a breeze.

One-pot meals are exactly what they sound like: everything cooks in one pot (or one pan on the stove) together. This could be a soup, a stew, a pasta dish, a casserole – you name it. *Sheet pan meals* are similar in spirit: you toss all your ingredients on one baking sheet and roast or bake them together in the oven. Both methods keep things simple. When prompting ChatGPT for these, you can explicitly say "one-pot" or "sheet-pan" to get recipes that meet those criteria.

For instance, try asking: *"What's a good one-pot dinner I can make with chicken, rice, and carrots?"* ChatGPT might give you a cozy answer like: "*How about a one-pot chicken and rice stew? Start by sautéing pieces of chicken in a large pot, then add chopped carrots, rice, and broth. Simmer everything together until the rice is tender and the chicken is cooked through. You'll have a complete chicken, rice, and veggie dinner in one pot.*" This way, you've got protein, starch, and veggies all in a single vessel, and it likely even tastes better because the flavors meld as they cook together.

Sheet pan prompts work similarly. You could say: "*I want a simple sheet-pan supper with fish and vegetables. What do you suggest?*" The AI may respond with something like: "*Try a sheet-pan roasted salmon with broccoli and cherry tomatoes. Preheat your oven, place salmon fillets on a greased pan, scatter broccoli florets and cherry tomatoes around them. Drizzle everything with olive oil, salt, and pepper (and maybe a squeeze of lemon on the fish). Roast for about 12-15 minutes until the salmon is flaky and the veggies are tender. Dinner is served straight from the pan!*" With that, you've cooked an entire meal on one tray, and cleanup is basically washing that tray.

Don't hesitate to include cleanup preferences in your prompt. You could tell ChatGPT, "*I hate doing dishes. Give me a dinner recipe that only uses one pot (and maybe a cutting board).*" It might suggest something like a one-pot pasta where even the pasta cooks in the same sauce, so you don't need a separate boiling pot. In fact, one-pot pasta has become a popular trick: ChatGPT could walk you through dumping dry pasta, water or broth, sauce ingredients, and veggies all together in a pot and cooking it until the pasta is done – magically, it often works and makes a creamy pasta without draining water. Another example: "*I have ground beef and want as few dishes as possible.*" The AI might come up with a one-skillet ground beef stroganoff or a chili – basically browning the beef with onions and spices, then adding everything else (like noodles for stroganoff, or beans and tomatoes for chili) into the same pot to simmer.

With one-pan or one-pot cooking, timing and arrangement can be important, and ChatGPT can help with that too. If you mention multiple ingredients, it will often guide you to add them in the right order so nothing overcooks or undercooks. For a sheet pan meal, you could ask, *"I have potatoes and bell peppers that take longer to cook than my shrimp. How can I make them all on one sheet pan without overcooking the shrimp?"* The assistant might advise cutting the potatoes smaller or giving them a head start in the oven, then adding the shrimp later, all on the same pan. It can provide those kind of tips automatically, but you can always ask directly for help coordinating cook times on one pan.

Here are a few one-pot or one-pan dinner ideas that ChatGPT might suggest, to spark your imagination:

- *Hearty Lentil Stew*: Using dried lentils, an onion, and a couple of carrots or celery stalks, you can make a big pot of savory stew for just a few dollars. ChatGPT can give you spices suggestions (like cumin or bay leaf) to make it extra tasty.
- *Peanut Butter Pasta*: It sounds odd, but a quick peanut sauce (peanut butter, soy sauce, a bit of sugar or vinegar) tossed with noodles creates a sort of budget satay noodle dish. If you ask for cheap and flavorful, you might get this unconventional idea.
- *Rice and Eggs, Any Style*: Eggs are cheap protein. You could fry up cooked rice with a couple of eggs (like egg fried rice) or serve a veggie stir-fry over rice with a fried egg on top. ChatGPT might recommend shakshuka too – eggs poached in tomato sauce – which is inexpensive and satisfying, especially with bread.
- *DIY Personal Pizzas*: Got flour and yeast or even just some store-bought flatbread? You can make cheap pizzas. ChatGPT might walk you through a quick dough or suggest using tortillas as crusts, then top with whatever you have (even just tomato sauce or canned tomatoes and a bit of cheese or veggies). It's fun, cheap, and comforting.

These are the kinds of suggestions you can either ask for explicitly or discover through ChatGPT's answers. You might even take a conventional recipe and ask, *"Can I do this in one pot instead?"* For example, if you find a recipe for baked mac and cheese that uses multiple steps and pots, you could paste the gist into ChatGPT and say, "Simplify this to a one-pot version for me." Often, it will find a way (like cooking the pasta in milk and cheese directly).

By embracing one-pot and sheet-pan cooking with ChatGPT's guidance, you not only save on dishwashing duty, but you often end up with deeply flavorful meals. Everything sharing the same cooking space means sauces get richer and veggies soak up juices from the proteins. It's efficiency meets deliciousness. And when your dinner cooks in one vessel, you're free to relax for a bit instead of juggling multiple pans.

Now that we've conquered the *Mount Everest of dirty dishes*, let's tackle another common dinner challenge: money. Cooking on a shoestring budget can be tough, but ChatGPT has you covered with meals that are cheap, filling, and still surprisingly good.

CHEAP, FILLING, AND SURPRISINGLY GOOD

Let's face it: food can get expensive, and there are times when your wallet is as light as your appetite is heavy. Whether you're between paychecks, a student on a shoestring budget, or just trying to save some cash, you still deserve dinners that are comforting and satisfying. The great thing is, cooking cheaply doesn't mean sacrificing taste or fullness. With ChatGPT's help, you can find meals that are incredibly budget-friendly yet still hit the spot. This section is all about using prompts to get cheap, filling dinner ideas that will make both you and your bank account happy.

When you need to pinch pennies, start by telling ChatGPT exactly that. For example: *"I only have a few dollars' worth of ingredients at home – things like rice, beans, and some spices. What can I make for dinner that's cheap but filling?"* A prompt like this signals the AI to think of hearty, low-cost staples. You'll likely get suggestions such as: *"How about a simple beans and rice burrito bowl? Cook the rice, season and warm the beans (canned is fine), and serve them together with any spices or a little sauce. You can top it with a fried egg or some cheese if you have it for extra richness."* This kind of meal costs next to nothing and is quite filling. ChatGPT might also mention variations, like adding canned tomatoes or frozen corn if available, showing how to adapt a basic formula with whatever cheap ingredients you've got.

Another approach: ask for *"budget recipes"* or mention a specific dollar amount if you want to challenge the AI. For instance, *"Can you give me a dinner idea that costs under $5 total?"* You might get a recipe for something like a hearty lentil soup (dried lentils are very cheap) with carrots and potatoes, or perhaps a classic like *spaghetti aglio e olio* (pasta with garlic and oil) which has basically three ingredients but is delicious. If you say, *"I'm cooking for three people on a very low budget,"* ChatGPT could suggest a big pot of chili or vegetable stew that uses inexpensive beans and veggies and makes plenty of servings.

In many cases, the cheapest meals are also comfort foods. ChatGPT might revive some thrifty classics: think grilled cheese sandwiches with a side of tomato soup, or tuna casserole, or pancakes for dinner (breakfast items like pancakes or French toast are super cheap to make). Don't be shy about specifying what you have a lot of, because bulk ingredients are your goldmine when money is tight. A prompt like *"I have a big bag of potatoes and not much else. What dinner can I make for almost free?"* could yield ideas like homemade potato soup (just add water or milk, salt, and maybe a bit of onion or bouillon if you have it), or oven-baked potatoes topped with whatever bits you can find (butter, a sprinkle of herbs, maybe leftover cheese or beans).

Notice that many budget meals rely on pantry staples – things like beans, rice, pasta, potatoes, canned tomatoes, or frozen vegetables. If you tell ChatGPT what staples you have, it will combine them in interesting ways. And it can suggest flavor boosters that don't cost much, like spices or a little bit of butter or cheese for richness. Sometimes, it's as simple as knowing a new way to season or combine basics: ChatGPT might introduce you to curry powder in your lentils, or how a splash of soy sauce can transform simple fried rice.

One more tip: use ChatGPT to prevent waste, which is just as good as saving money. If you say, *"I have some leftover roast chicken and a bunch of vegetables that are about to go bad. How can I stretch them into a meal?"* you might get a fried rice or a casserole suggestion that uses up every bit of those leftovers. By using what you already bought (and might otherwise toss), you're effectively making a free meal. Cheap and eco-friendly!

The beauty of asking an AI for cheap meal ideas is that it has a huge mental library of world cuisines and creative tricks. Maybe you haven't heard of a certain bean stew from another country that is super cheap to make, but ChatGPT has. It can bring global inspiration to your budget cooking. So even if you're broke, you can eat well and maybe even learn a new favorite dish.

Now that we've proven you can dine on a dime with satisfaction, let's remove another safety net: what if you have *no recipe at all*? In fact, what if you hardly even know what you want to cook, or you have a weird assortment of ingredients? That's the perfect time to test ChatGPT's improvisational skills.

NO RECIPE, NO PROBLEM

Up to now, we've talked about dealing with low energy, little time, one-pan strategies, and tight budgets – usually with a specific *type* of meal in mind. But what if you don't even have a recipe idea to start with? Perhaps you just have a mishmash of ingredients and no clue what to do with them. This is where ChatGPT truly shines as a creative kitchen companion. You can literally say, *"I have this and that... what can I make?"* and it will guide you through an improvisational dinner like a friendly chef by your side.

Start by surveying what you do have. You don't need exact measurements or fancy ingredient names – just give ChatGPT a candid rundown of the pantry and fridge odds and ends. For example: *"I've got half an onion, a can of chickpeas, some spinach, and a little bit of cooked rice. Can I turn that into dinner somehow?"* Even though that might sound like a Chopped mystery basket, ChatGPT can instantly recognize a pattern: those ingredients could become a tasty chickpea sauté or stir-fry, or perhaps a curried rice dish. It might respond with something like: *"Sure! How about a quick chickpea pilaf? Sauté the chopped onion in oil, add the chickpeas (drained) and some spices like cumin or garlic. Toss in the spinach until it wilts. You can stir in the cooked rice to make it more filling and season with salt, pepper, and maybe a squeeze of lemon if you have it. It's like an improvised chickpea bowl."* Suddenly, you have a recipe where there was none – and you've learned a way to combine those ingredients.

The beauty of this "no recipe" approach is that you can keep the conversation going with ChatGPT. Maybe its first suggestion doesn't quite fit what you're craving. You can reply with something like, *"Hmm, I was thinking of something more like a soup."* ChatGPT can then pivot: *"No problem. You could do a quick chickpea and spinach soup. Put that onion in a pot with oil, add a bit of tomato paste or diced tomato if you have it, then the chickpeas, spices, and water to make a broth. Simmer and wilt the spinach in it. If you have any of that rice, you can throw it in at the end to make the soup heartier."* In effect, you're co-creating a recipe on the fly. This back-and-forth is something you just can't do with a static cookbook.

You can also be *really vague* and let ChatGPT ask you questions to clarify. For example, you might say, *"I have a bunch of random stuff in my fridge, I don't even know what goes together. What should I make?"* ChatGPT might then prompt you for details: *"List out the main items you have and I'll come up with options."* This interactive process is great when you're overwhelmed by a disorganized fridge. It's like having a patient cooking coach who asks, "Tell me what we're working with, and we'll figure something out." Once you list things (even if it's as odd as "a jar of olives, some feta cheese, a bag of peas, and ramen noodles"), the AI can string them into a concept (maybe a sort of fusion pasta or noodle dish, in this case).

In these improvised scenarios, ChatGPT can also help you substitute and adapt. Suppose a suggestion it gives includes an ingredient you're missing; you can ask, *"I don't have cumin, what else can I use?"* and it will come up with alternatives (maybe coriander, or just black pepper and a little chili powder). Or if it suggests an oven method and you only have a stove, you can say, "How about a stovetop version?" and it'll rewrite the plan. Essentially, you're getting a live recipe developer tailoring instructions to your exact situation.

One fun way to use this ability is to pretend you're on a cooking show challenge. You can prompt: *"I feel like playing Iron Chef with my pantry. I have canned tuna, a sweet potato, peanut butter, and some spices. Can you help me make something edible out of that?"* Don't be surprised if ChatGPT comes back with a surprisingly plausible idea – maybe a Thai-inspired peanut sauce tuna stir-fry over roasted sweet potato, who knows! The point is, it will earnestly try to combine whatever you throw at it into something coherent. And often it works, or at least gives you a starting point that you can tweak.

This approach not only saves dinner on those disorganized nights, it teaches you to be a more flexible cook. As ChatGPT suggests combining odd ingredients, you might discover flavor pairings you hadn't thought of. Over time, you'll get more confident peeking into your fridge and conjuring up a meal without a recipe, because you've sort of absorbed the "improv cooking" mindset from these interactions.

Even with all these tricks, life can still throw curveballs. What if you're juggling so much that you literally have only one hand free to cook? Let's see how ChatGPT can help in that situation.

COOKING WITH ONE HAND (FIGURATIVELY OR LITERALLY)

Sometimes life demands your attention while dinner still needs to get made. Maybe you're rocking a baby to sleep in one arm, or answering work emails on your phone, or you've injured an arm and truly only have one hand available. Cooking with only one hand (or half your attention) is a real challenge, but ChatGPT can help streamline things so you can still put together a meal with minimal active effort. The trick is to ask for the *simplest possible method* and be upfront about your limitations.

When you prompt ChatGPT in this scenario, mention exactly

what's restricting you. For example: *"I only have one hand free and I can't do much chopping or stirring. What's an easy dinner I can make?"* A well-phrased query like this will nudge the AI to think of very hands-off recipes. One likely suggestion: a slow cooker or crockpot meal. ChatGPT might say, *"Try a slow-cooker chili: in the morning, dump canned beans, canned tomatoes, some ground meat (you can just break it up with a spoon), and spices into a slow cooker. By dinner time, it'll be ready and you only dirtied one pot."* Slow cookers are a one-hand cook's best friend, because you can often just throw everything in and press a button. If you have an Instant Pot (pressure cooker), that's another gadget ChatGPT might recommend using similarly for dump-and-go meals.

But let's say you don't have those appliances. You can still get advice for simplifying normal recipes. Perhaps you write: *"I have to cook while tending to a toddler. Can you give me a recipe that requires almost no monitoring?"* The AI could suggest an oven-baked dish that you prep in 5 minutes and then ignore. For instance, *"Make baked BBQ chicken and veggies: put chicken thighs in a baking dish, pour store-bought BBQ sauce over them, toss chopped potatoes and carrots (you can use baby carrots to avoid chopping) around the chicken with a bit of oil, then bake for about 45 minutes. You can play with your toddler while it cooks."* This kind of meal requires a tiny bit of prep (which you might manage during nap time or in a quick break), and then your hands are free until the oven timer rings.

If even that prep sounds daunting, tell ChatGPT you need something with *no prep at all*. It might get creative and propose something like: *"Loaded baked potatoes in the microwave: poke a potato and microwave it until soft. Then just slice it open and throw on shredded cheese, maybe canned chili or beans if you have them. Minimal work, one hand can handle it."* Or even, *"a platter of snacky foods"* — for example, putting together a plate of cheese, crackers, pre-cut fruits, and deli meat, which is more assembly than cooking but still a decent meal when you truly can't cook actively. The key is that you can be honest about needing essentially *zero* intense cooking, and ChatGPT will accommodate without judgment.

Here are a couple of prompt examples for one-handed or distracted cooking:

- *"I only have one hand free and 15 minutes. What's a meal I can basically just stir once or twice and be done?"*
- *"I'm caring for a sick family member, so I can't stand at the stove. How can I make dinner that more or less cooks itself?"*
- *"Any tips for cooking dinner with literally one hand? I have an injury and can't chop things."*

ChatGPT's responses to these might include things like skillet meals where you can dump ingredients and let them simmer, or using frozen pre-chopped veggies to eliminate knife work, or casseroles that only require mixing and baking. For the 15-minute one-hand prompt, an answer might be, *"Make a quick stir-fry with frozen veggies and pre-cut meat: you can pour them straight from the bag to the pan and use one hand to stir occasionally. Season with soy sauce or any sauce you like, and it'll be done in 10 minutes."* For the caring-for-family scenario, it could suggest a simple soup that simmers on its own, or even sandwiches for dinner (nothing wrong with a sandwich night when you're stretched thin). And for the injury scenario, ChatGPT might advise using kitchen shears (which are easier one-handed) to cut up anything, or opting for meals that require no cutting – like heating up soup and making a grilled cheese by assembling bread and cheese and flipping it carefully with one hand.

This kind of tailored advice can be a lifesaver. It reminds you of shortcuts: pre-washed salad greens, microwaveable pouches of rice, frozen chopped onions, rotisserie chicken (already cooked and tender, easy to shred one-handed). ChatGPT can suggest all these hacks if you mention your constraints, because it has learned from countless recipes and tips. The tone of its advice will likely be encouraging, reassuring you that it's okay to take every shortcut in the book when you need to.

In the end, cooking with one hand or a scattered mind is about minimizing steps and leveraging any tool or convenience at your disposal. ChatGPT can act like that helpful friend who says, "Just do tacos tonight – use pre-made tortillas, and you barely have to cook," when you're overwhelmed. And you know what? That's still a home-cooked meal to be proud of given the circumstances.

So far, we've tackled almost every tough cooking scenario: exhaustion, hurry, cleanup, budget, no plan, and even physical limitations. For a final challenge, let's step into some real-life "panic cooking" situations people have faced and see how ChatGPT came to the rescue with clever solutions.

THE AI HELPLINE: REAL-LIFE RESCUE PROMPTS

Let's bring everything together with a few *panic cooking* stories. These are the kinds of real-world dilemmas where home cooks turned to ChatGPT as an emergency helpline. We'll see exactly what they asked and how ChatGPT responded to save the day.

Scenario 1: The Missing Ingredient Meltdown

Sarah was boiling pasta for a spaghetti dinner when she realized she had no jarred sauce left. It was late, stores were closed, and plain pasta sounded sad. In a moment of desperation, she typed into ChatGPT:

User: "I'm halfway through making spaghetti for dinner and just realized I have no tomato sauce or canned tomatoes. What can I do to save this pasta? Please help!"

Within seconds, ChatGPT offered a solution:

ChatGPT: "Don't worry! You can make a quick garlic and olive oil sauce (aglio e olio). Drain the pasta, but save a bit of the cooking water. In the same pot, add a good amount of olive oil (a few tablespoons) and toss in minced garlic (or garlic powder if that's what you have). Gently sauté the garlic until fragrant (be careful not to burn it). If you have any red pepper flakes, add a pinch for heat. Return the cooked pasta to the pot and toss it in the garlic oil. If it seems dry, add a splash of the pasta water you saved to loosen it up. Season generously with salt and pepper. If you have some herbs like dried oregano or basil, throw a little in. And if you have parmesan or any cheese, grate it on top. It's not tomato sauce, but it's a delicious Italian classic that lets the pasta shine!"

Relieved, Sarah followed these steps and in no time had a flavorful garlic pasta ready. What started as a meltdown turned into a cooking victory, all thanks to a quick prompt and ChatGPT's clever workaround.

Scenario 2: Burnt Dinner, Plan B

Mike had planned to serve roast chicken, but an unfortunate distraction meant the chicken got overcooked – dry as a bone. With hungry family waiting, he needed a fast Plan B using whatever was on hand. He asked ChatGPT:

User: "Uh oh, I ruined the roast chicken I was making – it's totally dried out. I have about 30 minutes to come up with something else for dinner. I do have some eggs, bread, and cheese, and a few veggies. Any chance I can turn those into a quick meal to save the night?"

ChatGPT quickly responded with an alternative:

ChatGPT: "Absolutely. How about whipping up some savory omelets or scrambles? You can make 'breakfast for dinner' in under 30 minutes. Here's an idea: chop up those veggies (for example, if you have a bell pepper, tomato, or even some of the overcooked chicken meat you can salvage, dice it up). Sauté the veggies in a pan with a little butter or oil. Beat the eggs and pour them over the veggies to make a big omelet (or just scramble them together). Sprinkle cheese on top to melt. Serve with the bread toasted on the side – maybe buttered or rubbed with a bit of garlic if you have it. It's comforting, quick, and uses what you have. Alternatively, you could make grilled cheese sandwiches and serve some sliced veggies or a quick salad on the side. But an egg scramble with veggies and cheese will be fastest."

Mike went with the veggie and cheese scramble, and within 15 minutes dinner was back on track. The family even thought it was intentional and loved the "brinner" (breakfast for dinner). Crisis averted!

Scenario 3: Surprise Guest Stretch

Alicia cooked a pot of chili that normally fed two, but just as they were about to eat, two friends dropped by unexpectedly. She had more mouths to feed than anticipated. She turned to ChatGPT on her phone for help:

User: "I made about 2 servings worth of chili, but now 4 people are here for dinner. How can I stretch this meal or add sides to feed everyone without running to the store?"

ChatGPT had a resourceful answer:

ChatGPT: "One easy way to stretch that chili is to serve it over rice or pasta. Do you have any instant rice or even bread? If you have rice, quickly cook a cup or two – it will bulk up the servings (chili over rice is delicious and filling). You can also add a can of beans or corn into the chili to increase volume if you have them. As for sides, you could whip up some quick quesadillas or grilled cheese with the bread and cheese – cut them into smaller pieces for everyone to share. Even plain tortilla chips or crackers on the side can make the meal feel more complete. And if you happen to have lettuce and a few veggies, a simple side salad will help fill everyone up. In summary: add starch (rice, pasta, or bread), add any extra beans/veggies to the chili, and serve a little something crunchy or fresh alongside. No one will go hungry!"

Alicia had rice and a can of black beans. She stirred the beans into the chili and served it over rice. She also toasted and buttered some leftover hamburger buns as impromptu garlic bread. The four friends ended up happily full, and they marveled at how she pulled together a feast out of thin air.

In each of these scenarios, a kitchen disaster or challenge was averted by treating ChatGPT like an emergency hotline. The prompts were specific about the problem and what was available, and that allowed the AI to respond with tailor-made solutions. Notice how ChatGPT's answers often not only give a recipe but also encourage and reassure (reminding you that *breakfast for dinner is okay*, or suggesting creative tweaks confidently). It's like having a calm voice in the kitchen saying "We've got this."

By now, you've learned how to formulate prompts to tackle just about any dinner crisis. From zero-energy meals to split-second recipes, one-pot cleanups, budget feasts, improvisational cooking, and juggling life's chaos, you've seen ChatGPT rise to each occasion.

In the next chapter, we'll build on this foundation and explore even more ways your AI kitchen companion can make cooking easier, more fun, and endlessly creative. With the "AI helpline" in your back pocket, no cooking challenge is too great to conquer.

6

CUSTOMIZING LEFTOVERS: A SECOND LIFE FOR YESTERDAY'S DINNER

Open your refrigerator door and there it is: last night's dinner, sitting in a Tupperware container, looking a bit less enticing than it did fresh off the stove. We've all been there—faced with leftovers that we know we *should* use, but the excitement of that meal has faded. It's easy to feel uninspired by yesterday's food. You might sigh and think, "Not chicken curry *again*..." or worse, feel tempted to toss it out. But before you resign yourself to a repeat dinner (or a guilty bit of food waste), take heart: this is where your AI kitchen companion can come to the rescue.

In this chapter, we'll explore how to give a second life to yesterday's dinner using ChatGPT as your creative partner. Think of it as having a friendly chef at your side, one who never runs out of ideas. Leftovers don't have to be a dreaded rerun of a meal – with the right prompts, ChatGPT can help you transform that chicken curry into spiced empanadas, that plain rice into a fragrant stir-fry, or that half-eaten pasta into a hearty soup. The possibilities are surprisingly endless when you start asking the right questions.

"Customizing Leftovers" is all about turning meh into marvelous. You'll learn how to describe your leftovers and prompt ChatGPT to completely reimagine them into a new dish – often something that doesn't resemble the original at all. We'll dive into ways to boost flavors so yesterday's meal tastes fresh and exciting, how to change the texture and form of a dish to keep your palate guessing, and how to mix multiple leftover items into one cohesive new creation. And since not every suggestion needs to be a taco or casserole (we all love them, but variety is the spice of life), we'll talk about pushing beyond the obvious answers to get truly creative solutions.

This chapter will also show you how to think ahead. With ChatGPT's guidance, you can plan initial meals that turn into "planned-overs" – dishes that actually get better the next day or are designed to be reinvented. Imagine cooking once and eating twice (or more), without feeling like you're stuck on repeat. By storing and portioning smartly and knowing how to ask for remix ideas later, you'll soon approach cooking with leftovers in mind from the start.

Finally, we've compiled a leftovers prompt bank – a set of example questions and ChatGPT responses for common leftover ingredients like roast chicken, pasta, rice, grilled vegetables, and beans. These examples will serve as a handy reference whenever you're staring down a container of last night's dinner unsure of what to do. Use them as inspiration to craft your own prompts tailored to whatever you find in your fridge.

Throughout this chapter, the tone is warm, practical, and confidence-building – just like a good friend helping you make the most of what you have. By the end, you'll feel empowered to tackle any leftover challenge with ChatGPT's friendly assistance. So, let's open that fridge, embrace those leftovers, and discover how a little AI creativity can turn yesterday's meal into today's triumph.

LEFTOVERS, REIMAGINED

When we talk about reimagining leftovers, we mean truly giving yesterday's meal a makeover. The goal here is to prompt ChatGPT in a way that it doesn't just tell you to reheat your food, but rather to *transform* it into a completely different dish. Think of it like culinary recycling: you're not just warming up that lasagna, you're turning it into a savory lasagna soup or even crispy fried lasagna bites. To do this, you'll want to guide ChatGPT with the right details and an open mind for creativity.

The key to this transformation is in how you phrase your request. A simple question like "*What can I do with leftover lasagna?*" might yield a few ideas, but you can push ChatGPT further by being specific about the change you want. For instance, you might say: "*I have a few slices of cooked lasagna from last night. I don't want to just eat it as-is—how can I turn it into a different meal?*" By explicitly stating that you want a *different* meal, you signal to ChatGPT that it should step away from the original form and flavor profile.

ChatGPT thrives on details, so don't be shy about providing context. Tell it what the original cuisine or flavor was, and if you have any thoughts on what direction you'd like to go next. Maybe last night's dinner was Italian and tomato-based, and today you're craving something with a different vibe—say, a Mexican dish or an American comfort-food classic. You could prompt: "*I have a bowl of leftover beef chili. Can you help me transform it into a new dish? Perhaps something like a pie or a casserole, not just chili again.*" This gives ChatGPT both the raw material (chili) and a hint of the form you're imagining (pie or casserole). In response, ChatGPT might get inventive:

User: I have a bowl of leftover chili from yesterday. How can I turn it into a completely new meal? Maybe something like a pie or even a filling for another dish?

ChatGPT: One idea is to create a *chili pot pie*. You could use the chili as a filling by thickening it a bit with some flour or corn starch, then spoon it into a baking dish, cover with a layer of pie crust (or even just a circle of puff pastry on top) and bake until golden. This way it feels like a totally new comfort-food dish. Another option: use the chili as a filling for *stuffed bell peppers*. Mix the chili with some cooked rice, fill the peppers, sprinkle cheese on top, and bake – you'll have a Southwest-style stuffed pepper that's a far cry from just reheating a bowl of chili.

In that example, notice how the prompt led to two distinct ideas (a pot pie and stuffed peppers). ChatGPT often responds with several suggestions if you leave the request open-ended. That's great when you're fishing for inspiration. You can then choose the idea that appeals to you most and ask for more details. If the chili pot pie idea sounded exciting, your follow-up might be: *"That chili pot pie sounds great! What steps should I follow to make it?"* ChatGPT can then break down a simple set of instructions for you, turning your leftover chili into a brand new dish step-by-step.

Here are a few tips for prompting ChatGPT to reimagine leftovers into a new creation:

- **Clearly identify the leftover:** Mention what the dish is and what's in it. For example, "leftover grilled salmon with lemon and herbs" or "half a pot of mushroom soup" gives the AI a good starting point for flavor and ingredient ideas.
- **Specify the transformation goal:** If you want a different cuisine or format, say so. "Turn this into an Italian-style appetizer" or "make a vegetarian dish out of my beef stew leftovers" guides the kind of answer you'll get.
- **List any additional ingredients:** If you have other ingredients on hand that could be used, include them. "I have leftover plain rice and also some eggs and green onions" might prompt ideas like fried rice or rice fritters because ChatGPT knows you have eggs.
- **Ask for multiple options:** A prompt like "Give me three new meal ideas using my leftover roasted vegetables" can yield a range of options (perhaps a soup, a wrap, and a hearty salad), letting you pick your favorite.
- **Encourage creativity:** Use phrasing like "completely different meal," "unexpected twist," or "something creative" if you want to push the AI toward more imaginative suggestions.

The fun part of using ChatGPT is that it can act like a brainstorming partner. No idea is too crazy to throw at it. If you have leftover spaghetti with marinara sauce, you might even ask it to reimagine that in an Asian stir-fry context—it sounds wild, but ChatGPT could suggest chopping the spaghetti as noodle bits in a stir-fry with soy-ginger sauce, creating a quirky East-meets-West dish. Or if you have a bunch of plain cooked chicken breasts, you might prompt, *"This chicken was originally lemon-herb flavored. I've had it as-is already—what completely new dish can I make that uses it? Perhaps a curry or something creamy?"* ChatGPT could respond with: *"How about making a quick coconut chicken curry? Sauté some onions and curry powder, add coconut milk, and toss in the chopped chicken to simmer so it absorbs those new flavors."* Suddenly your mild lemon-herb chicken is reborn as a spiced, aromatic curry.

Another example: imagine you made a big tray of roasted vegetables as a side yesterday (zucchini, bell peppers, eggplant, and the like). Today, you don't want just warmed-up veggies again. You can say to ChatGPT, *"I have a container of mixed roasted vegetables from last night. Can I create a whole new dish with these?"* You might get an answer like, *"Certainly! You can chop those roasted veggies and use them as the base for a* ***vegetable frittata****. Just beat some eggs, mix in the veggies and a handful of cheese, and cook it until set. It'll feel like a brand new meal."* Alternatively, ChatGPT might propose blending the veggies with broth to make a creamy **roasted vegetable soup**, or rolling them into a wrap with fresh greens and a tasty spread for a **Mediterranean veggie wrap.** The idea is that by asking for a transformation, you're giving the AI license to be inventive.

Remember, you're not limited to one round of suggestions. Reimagining leftovers can be a back-and-forth conversation. If ChatGPT's first suggestions still feel too close to the original, you can clarify further: *"Those sound good, but I had that flavor profile yesterday. What about using these veggies in an Asian or Middle Eastern inspired dish instead?"* This nudge can lead to ideas like folding the veggies into a curry, stuffing them in a pita with hummus and tahini (for a Mediterranean spin), or stir-frying them with soy sauce and ginger (for an Asian twist). Each follow-up tweak to your prompt refines the direction, and ChatGPT will adjust its ideas accordingly.

By the end of this reimagining process, you should have at least one exciting plan for that leftover. It's a great feeling when you realize that the dinner on your plate tonight shares almost nothing with last night's meal, even though you cleverly repurposed the same ingredients. With practice, you'll get better at envisioning possibilities on your own, but even if you're stumped, ChatGPT is there to provide a creative spark.

Next, let's tackle one of the most common complaints about leftovers – the fact that they can taste a bit bland or "samey" the next day. In the following section, we'll use ChatGPT to help breathe new life into leftover flavors with bold spices, sauces, and seasonings.

FROM BLAND TO BOLD

One of the biggest letdowns with leftovers is that they often taste a bit bland or "flat" compared to the first time around. Maybe the seasoning that was perfect yesterday has muted in the fridge overnight, or the dish just lacks the excitement it had when it was freshly cooked. The good news is that you can bring those flavors back to life (or add entirely new ones) with a few smart tweaks. In this section, we'll use ChatGPT as a flavor consultant, asking it for spice upgrades, sauce pairings, and little flavor-bombs that can make yesterday's dinner taste fresh and exciting today.

A great way to start is by telling ChatGPT exactly what you didn't love about the leftover's current flavor. For example, *"My leftover stir-fry tastes kind of bland now"* or *"This curry isn't as spicy as I'd like on day two."* By pinpointing the issue—be it lack of spice, saltiness, freshness, or complexity—you give the AI a clear target for improvement. Let's say you have leftover roasted potatoes that turned out underseasoned. You could ask: *"These roasted potatoes are a bit bland. What can I add to them or serve with them to pack more flavor?"* ChatGPT might suggest something like tossing the potatoes with a generous sprinkle of paprika and garlic powder and reheating them until crispy, or perhaps drizzling them with a quick herb dressing (olive oil, lemon, and chopped rosemary) to give a zingy finish.

Often, what a leftover needs is a *flavor boost* in the form of spices or herbs. Don't hesitate to ask ChatGPT direct questions like, *"What spices would go well in my leftover chicken soup to make it more flavorful?"* If your soup was fine yesterday but tastes a bit dull today, ChatGPT might recommend adding a pinch of cumin and chili powder to give it a southwestern flair, or stirring in some fresh grated ginger and a dash of soy sauce for an Asian twist. It could even suggest dropping in a Parmesan rind or a splash of vinegar (depending on the soup) to enrich or brighten the flavor. The beauty is that ChatGPT can tailor the suggestion to the cuisine of the original dish or take it in a new direction—just let it know what you're aiming for.

Besides spices, *sauces and condiments* are your best friend for reviving leftovers. Imagine you have grilled chicken breasts from yesterday; they were delicious then, but today they're a bit dry and lackluster. Try prompting: *"I have some cooked chicken breast that's a little dry. What sauce or flavoring can I add to make it more interesting?"* You might get several ideas: a quick creamy garlic sauce (using yogurt or sour cream as a base), a spicy buffalo-style sauce to coat and reheat the chicken, or slicing the chicken and simmering it in barbecue sauce for a fast faux "BBQ pulled chicken." ChatGPT might even give you a simple recipe:

User: My leftover roast chicken is pretty bland on its own. Could I toss it with a sauce or spices to liven it up?

ChatGPT: Absolutely! Here are a couple of options. One: you can make a *tangy teriyaki glaze* by mixing soy sauce, a bit of honey or brown sugar, minced garlic, and ginger, then simmering it for a few minutes. Toss the shredded chicken in this glaze and warm it up – you'll have sweet and savory teriyaki chicken. Two: if you prefer something spicy, coat the chicken pieces in a *quick buffalo sauce* (melted butter mixed with hot sauce) and heat them under the broiler for a minute. This will give you spicy buffalo chicken bites. Serve with a side of ranch or blue cheese dressing to complete the flavor upgrade.

In this answer, notice how ChatGPT not only suggested what kind of sauce to use, but even how to make it from scratch using common ingredients. This is where the AI really shines as a kitchen companion: it can walk you through a flavor-boosting technique step by step. If one of those options sounded appealing, you could follow up by saying, *"That teriyaki glaze sounds perfect. How do I make it in detail?"* and ChatGPT would list out the measurements and steps in order, like a mini recipe.

Here are some flavor-boosting ideas you can prompt ChatGPT for when reviving leftovers:

Fresh Herbs and Aromatics: Ask "What fresh herbs would brighten up this dish?" A sprinkle of cilantro or parsley, or a bit of freshly chopped garlic or ginger added during reheating, can wake up flavors.

Spice and Heat: If the food is too mild, you can ask for ways to add heat or depth. A dash of cayenne, smoked paprika, curry powder, or even a squirt of sriracha can transform the flavor profile.

Acid and Zing: Leftovers often benefit from a hit of acidity. You could prompt, "It tastes a bit heavy – what can I add?" and get suggestions like a squeeze of lemon or lime, a splash of vinegar, or a spoonful of pickled jalapeños or capers to brighten the dish.

Creamy or Cheesy Elements: For something that's dry or too spicy, adding richness can help. ChatGPT might suggest stirring in a dollop of sour cream or coconut milk, or grating some cheese on top and melting it. A bland casserole portion, for example, can get new life with a fresh cheesy crust: *"How can I make this leftover casserole less dry?"* might yield "top it with shredded cheese and bake until bubbly."

Condiments and Global Sauces: You can literally pick a cuisine and ask for a corresponding sauce. "What Indian spices or sauces could I add to this plain leftover rice?" might lead to an idea like frying the rice with cumin seeds, turmeric, and a bit of tomato to create a quick biryani-like flavor. Or "What Mexican flavors can I add to these leftover beans?" could prompt ChatGPT to suggest stirring in cumin, chili powder, and tomato, or making refried beans with onion and garlic, then adding a splash of lime.

When prompting for flavor upgrades, it's helpful to mention the original flavors *and* the direction you'd like to go. If your leftover pasta was originally tossed in olive oil and garlic, but you're craving something spicy, let ChatGPT know: *"My leftover spaghetti aglio e olio is bland now. Can I turn it into a spicy dish?"* This context allows the AI to suggest, say, heating the pasta with chili flakes, sun-dried tomatoes, and a bit of sausage or smoked paprika to create a new spicy pasta variation.

Another tip is to consider *pairings*: sometimes the leftover itself might be fine, but it needs an accompaniment to shine. You can ask ChatGPT for a sauce or side that would complement it. For instance, leftover sliced pork could be served in lettuce wraps with a ginger-soy dipping sauce – the pork hasn't changed, but the way you eat it has, and now it's an exciting dish. Or that leftover lentil stew might be a little boring on its own, but if ChatGPT suggests serving it over rice with a fresh squeeze of lemon and some chopped herbs plus a spoonful of yogurt, suddenly it's vibrant again.

By regularly asking for these flavor enhancements, you'll start to build an intuition for what spices or condiments wake up different dishes. ChatGPT can be your training wheels for this learning process. Over time, you might remember "Oh, roasted potatoes go well with rosemary and garlic" or "Stir-fry can be revived with a dash of soy sauce and chili." But even then, when in doubt, you know you can always brainstorm with your AI kitchen buddy.

So now that we know how to fix flavor boredom, let's move on to another aspect of leftovers that can be less than ideal: texture. In the next section, we'll explore how ChatGPT can help you change up the texture of a leftover dish—turning soggy or mushy foods into crispy delights, or repurposing soft foods into new forms altogether.

SWITCHING UP THE TEXTURE

Sometimes it's not the flavor of a leftover that's the issue, but the texture. Foods can turn soggy, dry, or just texturally monotonous after sitting overnight. The good news is that by changing the form of the dish, you can often make it much more appealing. ChatGPT can help brainstorm ways to *reshape* your meal—literally changing its texture.

Whether it's transforming a stew into a hand-held wrap, turning soft vegetables into crispy fritters, or using leftover rice to create a silky soup, a few strategic prompts can lead to delightful textural makeovers.

Let's talk about soggy foods first. Maybe you have leftover stew or curry that, while delicious, is just a mushy mix of ingredients on day two. To introduce some texture, you could ask ChatGPT: *"I have leftover beef stew. The flavors are great, but it's kind of one-note in texture. How can I turn it into a dish with some crunch or different mouthfeel?"* ChatGPT might suggest straining out the chunky pieces (meat and veggies) and using them as a filling for *beef stew wraps* or burritos. For instance, it could say: shred the beef, mash the soft carrots/potatoes a bit and spread them on a tortilla, add some crunchy coleslaw or fresh bell pepper strips for contrast, then wrap it up. Now you've got a tender, flavorful filling *and* a crisp fresh crunch from the veggies—plus the handheld format is fun and different. The remaining gravy from the stew could even be repurposed as a dipping sauce for the wrap, so nothing goes to waste.

Another common scenario: leftover roasted or steamed vegetables that have lost their crisp edges and are just limp. Instead of eating them as sad soggy veggies, think *crispy fritters* or patties. You could prompt: *"I have a bunch of cooked vegetables (like broccoli, carrots, and cauliflower) that are soft now. How can I make them crispy or give them a new texture?"* ChatGPT might walk you through making vegetable fritters. It could respond: *"Chop up those veggies and mix them with a beaten egg, a couple of spoonfuls of flour (or breadcrumbs), and some seasonings like salt, pepper, and maybe a spice you like (curry powder or chili flakes for example). Form that mixture into small patties and pan-fry them in a bit of oil until they're golden brown on each side. You'll end up with veggie fritters that are crispy on the outside and soft inside."* What was once a bowl of lifeless vegetables can become savory little cakes with a satisfying crunch. If ChatGPT doesn't automatically give you the full recipe in its first answer, you can always ask, *"That sounds good—what quantities and steps should I use for the fritters?"* and it will spell it out.

On the flip side, sometimes a leftover is too dry or tough, and you want to *soften it up*. Leftover cooked rice is a prime example—it often dries out in the fridge and the grains harden. Rather than just microwaving it with a damp paper towel (the usual fix to rehydrate rice), you can ask ChatGPT for a completely different approach: *"My leftover rice has dried out. Can I turn it into a soup or another dish so it gets soft again?"* One idea ChatGPT might give is to use the rice in a comforting *rice soup*. It could suggest sautéing some onions and garlic, adding broth, and then stirring in the cooked rice to simmer for a while. The rice will absorb the broth and soften, essentially turning into a quick congee or a thickened soup. Throw in any other bits (like that handful of spinach or diced tomato you have lying around) and season it, and you've got a brand new dish—warm, soothing, and with a completely different texture profile than plain rice. Another example: leftover grilled chicken that feels a bit rubbery cold could be shredded and cooked down in a sauce or broth to make it tender again (like adding it to soup or a saucy curry, where the moisture can penetrate and soften the meat).

Here are some textural transformations ChatGPT can help you achieve with leftovers:

- **Make It Crispy:** For anything that's gone soggy (fries, breaded foods, roasted potatoes), ask "How can I crisp this up again?" Often the answer will involve high heat: spreading items on a baking sheet and broiling or re-baking them, or pan-frying in a little oil to bring back crunch. For example, *"These leftover french fries are limp—how can I make them crispy?"* might yield a tip to toss them in a hot oven or air fryer for a few minutes.
- **Make It Crunchy Outside, Soft Inside:** This is the fritter/croquette approach. You can take soft leftovers (mashed potatoes, beans, vegetables) and ask how to form them into patties or balls and fry or bake them. Leftover mashed potatoes can become potato pancakes, leftover

risotto can become crispy arancini (risotto balls), and so on.

- **Make It Soft or Soupy:** For dry or dense leftovers, incorporating them into a soup or stew can give them new life. "How can I use this leftover roast pork in a soup?" might lead to shredding the pork into a broth with noodles and veggies. Dry turkey meat can be chopped and turned into a creamy pot pie filling, which both softens the meat and provides a new velvety texture in the form of a sauce.
- **Blend or Puree It:** Some textures can be improved by pureeing. If you have, say, leftover cooked carrots or squash that no one wants to eat as is, ask ChatGPT if you can puree them into something. It might suggest blending into a creamy soup (add stock, maybe a splash of cream), or even making a spread or dip (puree with some tahini or olive oil for example, like a twist on hummus).
- **Add Crunchy Toppings:** Sometimes the simplest fix is to add a new texture on top. If you have leftover casserole or mac and cheese that's just uniformly soft, you could ask, "What can I sprinkle on this for texture?" ChatGPT might propose adding buttered breadcrumbs and reheating until they crisp up, or simply garnishing with toasted nuts or seeds. Even a handful of crispy fried onions (the kind that often top green bean casserole) can do wonders on a plain soup or stew.

Another neat trick is using *wrappers and breads* to change texture. We saw the stew-in-a-wrap idea; similarly, almost any leftover stew, chili, or chunky sauce can be spooned into a tortilla, pastry dough, or lettuce leaf to add a new textural element. You could transform leftover lentil curry into samosa-like turnovers by spooning it into squares of store-bought puff pastry and baking them. Or take that soft shredded pork and pan-sear it between tortillas with cheese to make crispy quesadillas. Whenever you encase a soft leftover in something starchy and cook it, you'll get a contrast between the crisp shell and the tender filling. Ask ChatGPT things like, *"Can I use this in a sandwich or wrap somehow?"* or *"Could I bake this filling into a pastry?"* and see what creative vehicle it suggests.

By now, you can see that texture is just as important as taste in making leftovers exciting. With ChatGPT's help, you can brainstorm whether to crisp it, soften it, wrap it, or blend it—depending on what you have and what you're craving. After tackling flavor and texture, there's another potential pitfall to avoid: falling into a rut of the *same old* leftover solutions. Next, we'll look at how to break out of the usual patterns and avoid the obvious ideas when reinventing your leftovers.

AVOIDING THE OBVIOUS

By now, you have a solid handle on transforming leftovers in terms of flavor and texture. But one more hurdle remains: avoiding the *leftover rut*. We humans are creatures of habit, and when it comes to leftovers, we often cycle through a handful of go-to solutions. Tacos, casseroles, stir-fries... sound familiar? There's nothing wrong with any of these dishes—they're classics for a reason. Yet if you find yourself turning every leftover into a taco or a generic stir-fry, things can get boring fast. The beauty of ChatGPT is that it's not limited by your personal routine or even by cultural norms; you can prompt it to think outside the box and suggest remix ideas that go well beyond the usual suspects.

The first step to breaking out of the obvious is to literally tell ChatGPT what *not* to give you. It might feel strange at first, but it's a powerful technique. For example, you could say: *"I have leftover roast beef, but I don't want the usual ideas like tacos or beef stew or stir-fry. Can you suggest something different I could do with it?"* By excluding the common answers in your question, you push the AI to dig deeper into its recipe toolbox. Perhaps it will come back with, "How about making beef empanadas? You can chop the roast beef, mix it with sautéed onions, spices, maybe a bit of cheese, and use it as a filling for pastry turnovers." Or it might suggest a beef and barley hand pie, or even something like Vietnamese summer rolls with shredded beef and herbs for a fresh twist. These are ideas that may not immediately spring to your own mind if tacos and stew are front-and-center, but by banning them, you've uncovered new territory.

Let's illustrate this with a mini dialog. Suppose you normally turn leftover grilled chicken into a quick quesadilla every time, but today you're craving something new:

User: I have two pieces of grilled chicken left over. I usually do tacos or quesadillas, but I want to avoid those this time. What else can I make with the chicken?

ChatGPT: You could try a *Mediterranean chicken pita*. Slice the grilled chicken and toss it with a little olive oil, lemon juice, and oregano. Stuff it in a pita bread with hummus, chopped tomatoes, cucumbers, and feta cheese. It'll be a completely different flavor direction from tacos. Another idea: make a *chicken Thai curry*. Cut up the chicken and simmer it briefly in a sauce of coconut milk, curry paste, and vegetables. The chicken will soak up the new flavors, and it won't remind you of quesadillas at all.

Now, imagine ChatGPT's first answer wasn't quite what you wanted. Maybe it still suggested something like "chicken tacos" even though you hoped it wouldn't (perhaps you didn't explicitly forbid it). You can follow up to steer it away: *"That sounds a bit too similar to what I usually do. Any more unique ideas? Maybe something like a soup or a baked dish I haven't tried?"* ChatGPT will take the feedback and generate new options, perhaps coming up with a hearty chicken pot pie or a spicy chicken tortilla soup (which, okay, is still sort of like tacos in soup form—but you get the idea). The key is that you can iterate until the suggestion strikes you as sufficiently fresh.

Another approach is to ask for ideas in a specific *cuisine or meal type* you wouldn't normally associate with that leftover. For example, *"Can I use this leftover pasta to make a breakfast dish?"* might yield a surprising idea like pasta frittata (pasta baked with eggs and cheese into a sliceable breakfast pie) or even pasta pancakes. Or *"What's a Japanese-inspired way to use leftover cooked pork chops?"* could lead to a suggestion such as slicing the pork thin and using it as a topping for ramen or folding it into okonomiyaki (a savory Japanese pancake). By giving ChatGPT an unusual angle, you invite creative answers that transcend the default leftover playbook.

Here are some uncommon leftover remix ideas that go beyond tacos, casseroles, and stir-fries, which you can try prompting ChatGPT about:

- **Leftovers to Breakfast:** Ask how to turn last night's dinner into a breakfast. For instance, leftover vegetables or meat can go into an omelet or a quiche. Leftover rice can become a sweet rice pudding or a savory breakfast porridge. This isn't the usual dinner-to-dinner transformation, so it can produce fun results.
- **Savory Bakes and Pastries:** Instead of a standard casserole, think hand pies, turnovers, or savory muffins. You might prompt, "Other than a casserole, how can I bake my leftover curry into something?" ChatGPT might suggest spooning it into puff pastry for curry puffs, or layering it with mashed potatoes in a muffin tin to bake mini shepherd's pies.
- **International Twists:** If you always do Italian with your leftovers, ask for an Indian or Thai or Moroccan twist, for example. Leftover roast lamb could become Moroccan tagine-inspired filling for wraps if you add the right spices. Leftover roast veggies could be rolled in rice paper for Vietnamese spring rolls with a peanut dipping sauce. By specifying a cuisine—e.g., "Give me a Mexican-inspired idea for these leftover grilled veggies (but not fajitas)"—you steer clear of default ideas and into more niche territory.
- **Unconventional Formats:** Perhaps turn something into a soup, a dip, or a sushi roll. Leftover turkey meat could be blended with cream cheese and herbs to make a spread for crackers – far from the typical turkey sandwich. Leftover chili could top a pizza (not a usual combo, but

chili pizza with cheddar and onions could be amazing). Or leftover mac and cheese could be rolled into balls, breaded, and fried to make mac-and-cheese bites. These ideas are a bit offbeat, and that's the point.

- **Dessert from Dinner?** This one's really outside the box: occasionally you can transform a savory item into a sweet-ish dish, or at least a completely different course. For example, leftover plain rice might be repurposed into rice pudding with milk, sugar, and cinnamon – turning a side dish into dessert. Or leftover bread from dinner becomes a bread pudding. While you won't turn steak into dessert, you get the idea – thinking in terms of a different course can spur unconventional suggestions.

The goal of avoiding the obvious is to keep your kitchen adventures interesting. With ChatGPT, you have a tireless idea generator that doesn't get stuck in a rut unless you let it. So feel free to push it: use phrases like "something I haven't seen before with X" or "an unconventional way to use Y." You might be delighted by the suggestions that pop up.

Now that you're breaking free of the standard leftover formulas, you can really start to play mad scientist in the kitchen. In fact, you don't have to limit yourself to reworking one leftover at a time. The next step is to **combine** leftovers—taking a little of this and a little of that to create something cohesive and delicious. In the following section, we'll explore how to ask ChatGPT to mix and match multiple leftovers into one harmonious dish.

MIX AND MATCH: MULTI-LEFTOVER COMBOS

Not every night leaves you with a generous portion of a single dish. Sometimes, it's a little bit of this and a little bit of that: half a chicken breast, a scoop of rice, and a few roasted veggies, for example. These odds and ends might not look like much separately, but combined, they can become the base of an inspired, "kitchen-sink" creation. In this section, we'll see how ChatGPT can help you play matchmaker with your leftovers, turning random components into one cohesive dish.

The strategy here is to present ChatGPT with a list of what you have on hand and explicitly ask for one dish that uses as many of those components as possible. For instance, you might say: *"I have a cup of cooked rice, a small piece of grilled salmon, and some roasted broccoli from last night. What can I make that combines all of those?"* By listing each item, you ensure the AI knows the playing pieces. And by asking to combine them, you steer it toward integrated solutions (as opposed to suggesting separate uses for each item).

Let's walk through an example scenario. Your fridge contains a hodgepodge: say, *leftover roast chicken*, *steamed rice*, and *sautéed vegetables* (like bell peppers and onions). You could prompt ChatGPT with: *"I have leftover roast chicken, some cooked rice, and sautéed peppers and onions. Can I make a single dish out of all this?"* A good ChatGPT response might be: *"Absolutely! You can make a quick chicken fried rice. Shred or chop the roast chicken, and in a hot pan, sauté some garlic (and ginger if you have it). Toss in the peppers and onions to reheat, add the rice and a splash of soy sauce (and an egg if available). Stir-fry it all together, and you'll have a flavorful chicken fried rice, using everything you mentioned."* That's one cohesive dish that uses all three leftovers. If you wanted something less obvious, maybe ChatGPT could propose a *burrito or wrap* where you layer the rice, veggies, and chicken with a sauce in a tortilla, or a *chicken rice casserole* binding them with a bit of cheese and broth then baking.

The fried rice suggestion in this case might have been low-hanging fruit, because those ingredients naturally lend themselves to it. If you want to avoid the most obvious combo (as we discussed in the previous section), you can specify a particular cuisine or format. For example: *"I have that same leftover chicken, rice, and veggies, but I just had Asian food yesterday – can you suggest a non-Asian dish using them together?"* ChatGPT might then pivot and suggest something like a *chicken and rice soup* (with herbs and maybe a touch of cream) or *stuffed bell peppers* (mix the rice, chopped chicken, and veggies with some seasoning, stuff into hollowed bell peppers, top with cheese and bake). It's all about how you frame the question.

When combining multiple leftovers, consider if you have or need a "binder" or a unifying element. ChatGPT often accounts for this. For example, if you list ingredients that seem disparately seasoned, the AI might suggest adding a sauce or broth that ties everything together flavor-wise. Say you have a bit of teriyaki chicken and some plain pasta. A direct combination might seem odd (teriyaki pasta?), but you could ask for a way to use them together. ChatGPT could suggest chopping the chicken and adding some extra stir-fry veggies to make a lo mein-like noodle dish (essentially treating the pasta like chow mein noodles). In doing so, it uses soy/ginger flavors to bridge the gap between the teriyaki and the pasta. Alternatively, it might propose slicing the teriyaki chicken and tossing it in a pasta salad with an Asian-inspired dressing (using soy sauce, sesame oil, etc.) to make the combination coherent.

It's a lot like solving a puzzle: you have these pieces (leftovers), and ChatGPT helps figure out how they might fit together. Another scenario: imagine you have **two slices of meatloaf, a cup of mac and cheese**, and **some roasted Brussels sprouts** sitting in the fridge. Instead of eating them separately (a somewhat mismatched plate), you could ask: *"Here's an odd mix: a bit of meatloaf, some mac and cheese, and roasted Brussels sprouts. Is there a creative way to combine them into one dish?"* An inventive answer could be: crumble the meatloaf and mix it with the mac and cheese and chopped sprouts, maybe add a little extra binder like a beaten egg, then spoon into muffin tins and bake until it sets and crisps on top. You'd get *savory mac and cheese muffins* or cups that have bits of meatloaf and veggie in each bite – essentially a quirky take on a casserole, but in a fun portable form. If that sounds strange, perhaps the AI might offer a simpler route: chop the meatloaf and sprouts, stir them into the mac and cheese, put the mixture in a baking dish, top with breadcrumbs, and bake as a *mac and cheese bake* until golden. The result is a single casserole that incorporates everything (and hey, cheese can unify almost anything!).

If ChatGPT ever suggests using only some of the leftovers and leaving one out, and you really want to use *all* of them, you can clarify: *"I'd like to include the Brussels sprouts too—any idea how to work those in?"* It will then adjust the plan to accommodate. Conversely, if you suspect one item might not fit well with the others, you can ask for confirmation. For example, *"I also have half an avocado. Could that be used here or would it be weird?"* ChatGPT might say, "You could slice it on top fresh after heating the dish, for a cool creamy contrast," or it might agree that avocado doesn't play well with those flavors once cooked. This way, you get guidance on what combinations make sense.

To get the most out of a multi-leftover prompt, try to include:

Quantity or role hints: If one ingredient is much larger in amount, mention it (e.g., "a lot of rice and a small piece of chicken") so the suggestion scales accordingly (maybe a rice-based dish with chicken as garnish).

Flavor details: Briefly note how each was seasoned originally, if it matters. "Leftover roasted potatoes (with rosemary), and leftover grilled steak (garlic marinade)" could yield different ideas (maybe a steak and potato hash with eggs) than if the steak was teriyaki and potatoes had cumin (which might steer toward a fusion taco filling with a new sauce).

Desired cuisine or dish type: If you have a hankering for a certain style, say it. "I'm in the mood for a warm salad or grain bowl" or "Maybe a baked dish?" This helps narrow down the infinite possibilities to something you're excited about.

Mix-and-match leftover cooking is incredibly satisfying because you're not only reducing waste but also creating something new out of what looked like random scraps. And truth be told, some of these impromptu combinations end up being surprise hits you'll want to make again (planned next time!). With ChatGPT's suggestions, you'll become more confident in combining ingredients in unconventional ways.

At this point, we've covered transforming a single leftover and even blending several leftovers into one meal. The last major piece of the puzzle is learning to think ahead – to plan your cooking and storage so that leftover transformations become even easier. In the next section, we'll look at storage-savvy cooking: how to set yourself up with meals that taste great the next day or are primed for remixing, and how to use ChatGPT to guide that forward-thinking approach.

STORAGE-SAVVY COOKING

We've all heard the saying "Cook once, eat twice." This section is about embracing that philosophy with the help of ChatGPT, by planning meals that not only yield delicious leftovers but might even taste better the next day or easily morph into a new dish. It's about being strategic: choosing recipes that age well or making a bit extra of a component that you can remix. With a little foresight (and some AI guidance), you can save time and reduce waste, all while enjoying flavorful meals throughout the week.

Planning for flavorful leftovers: Some dishes are famous for being *better the next day*. Stews, chilis, and curries often fall into this category—after a night in the fridge, the flavors have mingled and deepened. Braised meats and soups can also develop richer taste. You can ask ChatGPT directly, *"What meals actually taste better as leftovers?"* and expect a helpful list. For example, it might mention beef stew, lasagna, chili con carne, chicken curry, or bean soup, explaining that these are dishes that benefit from a rest period. Armed with that knowledge, you could decide to cook a big pot of chili knowing that Day 2 chili will be even more satisfying.

ChatGPT can also help you plan the remix while you're still cooking the original meal. Imagine you're making a hearty tomato-based pasta sauce on Saturday and you'd love to use the leftovers for a quick meal on Monday. You might prompt: *"I'm cooking marinara sauce tonight. What can I do with the extra sauce later this week that isn't just more spaghetti?"* The AI could suggest using the extra sauce as a base for shakshuka (a dish where you poach eggs in simmering tomato sauce) or turning it into a soup (adding broth and veggies to make a minestrone). It might even say: freeze a portion for next week's pizza night. The idea is that while you have something simmering, ChatGPT can already be plotting its second act.

Designing "planned-overs": One pro move is to intentionally cook more than you need of a versatile ingredient, specifically with future meals in mind. For example, roast two chickens instead of one, cook extra rice or quinoa, or double the amount of grilled vegetables. Then use ChatGPT to brainstorm how those planned leftovers can serve you. You could ask: *"What different meals can I make later this week if I roast a whole extra chicken today?"* A sample answer might be:

- Shred some of the chicken for tacos or enchiladas tomorrow (with spices and sauce so it feels new).
- Use the carcass to make a stock or soup base, and toss in remaining bits for a chicken soup in a couple of days.
- Slice some breast meat for a chicken stir-fry or a chicken fried rice midweek, adding fresh veggies and a new sauce.
- Chop up whatever is left to mix with mayo, grapes, and celery for a chicken salad sandwich for lunch.

That's four different uses from one extra chicken! By getting these ideas in advance, you can store your chicken accordingly (maybe keep some pieces whole, shred some while it's easier to do warm, freeze the stock).

When planning meals with remixing in mind, it's also important to think about **storing components separately** if needed. ChatGPT can remind you of this. For instance, if you make a big batch of pasta with sauce but know you want to reuse it, you might ask, *"If I want to reuse this pasta dish later, should I store the noodles separate from the sauce?"* and likely it will advise yes – to keep the noodles from getting too soggy, store them apart and combine when reheating. Similarly, if you grill a bunch of veggies, it might suggest storing them in portions and not all tossed with dressing if you plan to repurpose them in multiple ways (one day in a salad with vinaigrette, another day in a curry).

Storage and food safety: While creativity is great, we mustn't forget practical aspects like how to store leftovers safely. You can absolutely consult ChatGPT on these points too: *"How should I store my leftover soup and how long will it keep?"* or *"Can I freeze this cooked lentil curry, and if so, what's the best way to reheat it later?"* ChatGPT can give general guidelines like cooling food properly, using airtight containers, keeping most leftovers 3-4 days in the fridge, and how to thaw and reheat for best results. For example, it might remind you that curry often tastes even better after freezing and reheating, because the spices continue to infuse; just add a little fresh cilantro or a squeeze of lemon when serving to brighten it up.

Another neat use-case: ask ChatGPT what you can cook today that will make your life easier tomorrow. For example, *"I have a busy day tomorrow. What can I cook tonight that will be even better tomorrow for dinner?"* might yield suggestions like a casserole (which you can bake halfway and finish tomorrow, and that also tastes great reheated), or a marinated dish (like a bean salad or coleslaw that develops flavor overnight). It could also suggest doing prep tonight, such as chopping ingredients or making a sauce, so that tomorrow's meal assembly is a breeze. In this way, ChatGPT functions as a meal-planning assistant, not just for recipes but for timing and prep strategy.

Some dishes almost seem designed for remixing. Think of a basic pulled pork or slow-cooked jackfruit: the first night you enjoy it as BBQ sandwiches, but you can easily turn the leftovers into tacos with a different set of spices, or a topping for baked potatoes. ChatGPT can enumerate these variations if you ask ahead of time, *"What can I do with the leftovers from this pulled pork to make it a new meal?"* So while you're cooking it initially, you're already looking forward to that transformed leftover dinner.

Cultivating an AI-assisted habit: The more you use ChatGPT to plan and reinvent, the more you'll start naturally cooking with leftovers in mind. It's almost like having a meal planner friend who nudges you, "Hey, if you cook a few extra servings, I have ideas for how you can use them!" This approach reduces waste, saves money, and frankly, saves mental energy on subsequent nights. You're not scrambling to think of what to cook – Past You (with a little help from ChatGPT) has set up Future You with a head start.

By planning storage-savvy meals, you'll find that leftovers are no longer an afterthought or a burden – they're an integral, delicious part of your meal routine. And you're doing it with confidence, knowing that ChatGPT's got your back on safety and creativity. To wrap up this chapter, let's compile some of the great ideas we've explored into a handy prompt bank. In the next section, we'll provide example prompts and ChatGPT responses for some of the most common leftover ingredients, so you have a quick-reference guide for your own kitchen adventures.

PROMPT BANK: LEFTOVERS EDITION

We've covered a lot of ground. To help cement these ideas, let's look at some concrete examples of how you might prompt ChatGPT for specific leftover situations. Below are sample prompts and abbreviated ChatGPT-style answers for five common leftovers: roast chicken, pasta, rice, grilled vegetables, and beans. These examples are meant as a starting point – you can modify and expand on these prompts based on what's in your fridge and your personal cravings.

Leftover Roast Chicken

User: I have a bunch of leftover roast chicken. I already used some for sandwiches, but I still have about two cups of chicken pieces left. What interesting dinner can I make with it? (Something other than chicken salad or soup, please.)

ChatGPT: One tasty idea is to make *chicken enchiladas*. Shred the roast chicken and mix it with a little salsa or canned enchilada sauce (to keep it moist and add flavor). Take tortillas and roll up the chicken mixture in each, then place them in a baking dish. Pour more enchilada sauce on top, sprinkle with cheese, and bake until bubbly. You'll have a delicious Mexican-inspired dinner that's totally different from the original roast chicken. If enchiladas aren't your style, another idea is a *creamy chicken pasta bake*: combine the chicken with cooked pasta, a simple white sauce (or even a jar of Alfredo), and some vegetables. Put it in a casserole dish, top with breadcrumbs and bake. That turns your roast chicken into a comforting, cheesy bake.

Leftover Pasta (Cooked)

User: I made more spaghetti (with marinara sauce) than we could eat. Now I have a bowl of fully cooked spaghetti in tomato sauce. I don't just want plain reheated pasta – what can I do with it?

ChatGPT: A fun option is to turn that leftover spaghetti into a *spaghetti frittata* (also known as pasta pie). Beat some eggs in a bowl, add a bit of salt, pepper, and maybe some grated Parmesan or mozzarella. Stir in the spaghetti with its sauce, coating the pasta with the egg mixture. Heat a nonstick pan with a little oil, pour in the pasta-egg mixture, and cook on medium until it's mostly set. Then finish it under the broiler (or flip it, if you're adventurous) to cook the top. You'll end up with a firm, sliceable pie of spaghetti that you can cut into wedges. It's great because it transforms the texture – crispy edges, soft inside – and feels like a brand new dish. Serve it with a fresh salad on the side. Another idea: use the spaghetti to make a hearty *minestrone soup*. Cut up the pasta a bit, then simmer it in broth with some extra vegetables and herbs; the spaghetti acts like the noodles in the soup and soaks up new flavor.

Leftover Rice

User: I have about 3 cups of cooked white rice left from takeout. I do fried rice a lot, so I'd like a different idea. What else can I make with day-old rice?

ChatGPT: Since you want to skip the usual fried rice, how about making *stuffed bell peppers*? Mix that rice with anything tasty you have – for example, some browned ground beef or turkey (or chopped mushrooms for a vegetarian route), plus spices, a bit of tomato sauce, and maybe cheese. Stuff that mixture into halved bell peppers and bake until the peppers are tender and the filling is heated through. It's a whole new meal, and the rice gets seasoned and moistened in the process. Alternatively, you could go in the opposite direction and use the rice for a **dessert**: turn it into a quick rice pudding. In a saucepan, combine the cooked rice with milk, a little sugar, and a pinch of cinnamon and simmer until it thickens into a creamy pudding. Stir in raisins or vanilla if you have them. It's a sweet way to give leftover rice a second life, completely different from its original role as a side for your takeout.

Leftover Grilled Vegetables

User: I have a container of assorted grilled vegetables (zucchini, eggplant, bell peppers, and onions). They were simply seasoned with olive oil, salt, and pepper. How can I use them to make a vegetarian lunch that's not just re-heating them as is?

ChatGPT: Those grilled veggies are flavor gold and can become the star of many dishes. One delicious idea is to make a *grilled vegetable panini*. Take some good bread (like ciabatta or sourdough), spread pesto or goat cheese on it if you have some, pile on the chopped grilled vegetables, maybe add a slice of cheese, and then press it in a panini press or toast it in a skillet with a weight on top. You'll get a crunchy sandwich with melty, marinated veggies inside. For something lighter, transform the veggies into a *Mediterranean salad bowl*: chop them up and toss with fresh cherry tomatoes, cucumber, maybe some chickpeas or feta cheese. Drizzle a vinaigrette over it and serve on a bed of greens or grains – a hearty salad that makes the most of those smoky vegetables. In both cases, the goal is to use the vegetables as ready-made ingredients that just need reassembling into a new form.

Leftover Beans (Cooked or Canned)

User: I have a lot of cooked beans (about 2 cups of black beans) from earlier this week. I've already had them with rice. What creative dish can I make with these beans so they don't go to waste?

ChatGPT: Black beans are super versatile! One idea is to turn them into *black bean burgers*. Mash the beans in a bowl, and mix them with some binders and flavor: a beaten egg, breadcrumbs or cooked rice, chopped onion or scallion, and spices (like cumin, chili powder, garlic). Form into patties and pan-fry until they have a crust. Serve on buns with your favorite toppings (avocado, salsa, etc.). It's a satisfying way to reuse beans and you can even freeze extra patties for later. Another idea: make a flavorful *bean dip*. Sauté some garlic in olive oil, add the beans with a bit of cumin and paprika, and mash it all together (or blend for a smoother texture). Stir in a squeeze of lime and some chopped cilantro. In minutes, you have a tasty refried-bean–like dip or spread. You can enjoy it with tortilla chips, or spread it on a tortilla with cheese and make a quick quesadilla. Either way, those beans get a yummy makeover.

You've now learned how to see leftovers not as a burden, but as an opportunity. In this chapter, we took yesterday's dinner and gave it a second life in countless ways. We explored how a well-crafted prompt to ChatGPT can help you completely *reimagine a leftover*, turning it into a brand-new meal. We saw how to inject bold flavors and spices to banish blandness, and how to switch up textures so each bite feels fresh and exciting. You've practiced going beyond the obvious solutions, daring to try creative ideas that even seasoned cooks might not think of at first. And you discovered the art of combining multiple leftovers into one harmonious dish, essentially creating something from nothing.

Beyond the immediate cooking tricks, you also picked up a forward-thinking habit: planning and cooking with tomorrow in mind. By using ChatGPT to guide storage-savvy cooking, you can choose meals that age like fine wine (or at least like a good chili) and set yourself up for easy remix opportunities. Instead of dreading a fridge full of odds and ends, you can approach it with curiosity and confidence, knowing you have an AI partner ready to brainstorm alongside you.

With these leftover strategies in your toolkit, you're well on your way to running an efficient, waste-conscious, and wonderfully inventive kitchen. Embracing an AI-first approach doesn't end here – it just keeps opening up new possibilities. In the next chapter, we'll continue our journey into the many ways ChatGPT can empower and inspire your home cooking. Until then, enjoy giving your leftovers a delicious second life, and happy cooking!

7

COOKING FOR ONE, A COUPLE, OR A CROWD

Cooking isn't a one-size-fits-all activity. Some days you're just feeding yourself and looking to avoid an entire week of left-overs. Other times you're cooking a cozy dinner for two, or maybe you've got a full house of family and friends to feed. **How do you adjust your recipes and plans to fit the occasion without stress or waste?** This chapter tackles that very question, showing how ChatGPT can be your adaptable sous-chef whether you're cooking for one, a couple, or a crowd.

In the pages ahead, you'll learn how to **scale any recipe up or down** to get the perfect number of portions. We'll discuss prompts that help you halve a big recipe or stretch a small one without losing flavor or balance. You'll find out how to avoid common pitfalls when resizing recipes – like over seasoning or underestimating cooking times – with a little help from AI guidance.

We'll also dive into the art of **cooking for one** without getting bored or wasting food. Solo meals don't have to mean eating the same dish five days straight. With ChatGPT's help, you can keep your single-serving dinners varied, fun, and efficient. You'll see how to prompt for creative ideas that use up leftovers and minimize fuss, so cooking for yourself feels just as rewarding as cooking for a group.

Next, we'll explore strategies for **dinner for two**, from casual weeknight meals to special date nights. Cooking for a couple comes with its own joys and challenges – you want just enough food and maybe something a little special, but not so much that you're stuck with unnecessary leftovers. You'll learn how ChatGPT can help you plan **cozy, well-portioned meals for two** that hit the sweet spot between simple and satisfying.

Of course, we can't forget those times you need to **feed a whole family or a flock of guests.** Big gatherings can be intimidating for any home cook. How much do you need to make? What recipes scale up gracefully? We'll cover how to use ChatGPT to calculate quantities and choose dishes that serve 6, 10, or even 20 people with ease. From potlucks to holiday feasts, your AI kitchen companion can help ensure everyone leaves the table happy (and you aren't pulling your hair out).

Finally, we'll get into **batch cooking and make-ahead meals.** Preparing food for future you – whether later in the week or months from now – is a smart way to save time and reduce waste. You'll learn how to prompt ChatGPT for batch-cooking plans that turn one day of cooking into many days of delicious meals. We'll also look at prompts for freezer-friendly recipes, so you can make it now and enjoy it much later.

By the end of this chapter, you'll have the confidence to handle any serving size or meal plan. Whether it's dinner for one or thanksgiving for twenty, ChatGPT will be by your side helping you cook smarter, not harder. Let's jump in and see how to make every meal, large or small, a success!

RIGHT-SIZED RECIPES FOR ANY TABLE

Cooking for the right number of people often means adjusting recipes up or down. Maybe you found a fantastic chili recipe that serves 8, but tonight it's just you and your partner. Or perhaps your favorite pasta dish is written for two servings, and you need to feed a family of six. **Scaling recipes** can be tricky – nobody wants to do fraction math in their head while cooking – but that's where ChatGPT shines. With the right prompt, you can instantly get a recipe tailored to the exact number of portions you need.

To prompt ChatGPT for scaling, be specific about the original recipe and your target servings. For example, you might say: *"I have a recipe for 4 servings of vegetable curry. Can you adjust it to make only 2 servings?"* ChatGPT can then recalculate each ingredient quantity, effectively halving the recipe for you. It will list the new ingredient amounts (like "1 cup of broth instead of 2 cups") and can even tweak the cooking instructions if needed. The AI handles the arithmetic so you can focus on cooking confidently.

The same goes for **scaling up a recipe**. You can ask, *"This casserole serves 3, but I need enough for 6 people. How should I multiply the ingredients?"* ChatGPT will double everything for you, and it might offer tips if anything doesn't scale neatly. For instance, if the original recipe called for 1.5 eggs (which is awkward to measure), ChatGPT could suggest using 2 small eggs or adjusting another ingredient to balance it out. In our experience, it's great at doing the heavy lifting on calculations, sparing you from manual conversions or mistakes.

Keep in mind that when you scale recipes, **certain elements may not scale linearly**. ChatGPT often knows this from its training: it can warn you to be cautious with strong spices or salt. For example, doubling a spicy stew doesn't always mean exactly double the chili powder – you might start with 1.5 times the amount and add more to taste. You can include a request in your prompt like, "Adjust the ingredients for 10 servings and let me know if any seasoning should be modified." The AI might reply with a scaled ingredient list and notes such as "start with 2 teaspoons of salt, then adjust to taste," helping you avoid over seasoning in the larger batch.

Scaling down recipes is another common use-case. Maybe you love lasagna but don't want to be eating it all week. ChatGPT can assist by, say, quartering a lasagna recipe meant for a crowd so you can bake a personal-sized portion. You might prompt: *"Give me a lasagna recipe for one or two people, scaled down from the classic 9x13 pan version."* The AI will shrink the ingredient list (perhaps using 1/4 of the noodles, sauce, and cheese) and suggest using a smaller baking dish. *Personal loaf pan lasagnas* (like the one pictured above) are a perfect example – all the flavor, but right-sized for a couple of servings. ChatGPT can even adjust the cooking time (likely a bit shorter for a mini-lasagna) so it comes out perfectly cooked in its smaller form.

Another handy trick is asking ChatGPT to convert measurements while scaling. If a recipe is originally in metric for 2 servings and you want imperial units for 5 servings, just include that in your prompt. For instance: *"Scale this 2-person recipe for beef stir-fry to 5 people and give ingredient amounts in cups and ounces."* In one go, you'll get the quantities multiplied and converted – maybe it'll tell you to use "1 1/4 pounds of beef" or "about 3 cups of sliced veggies" to feed five. No more juggling unit conversions; ChatGPT will format the recipe in whatever measurement system you prefer.

You can also use ChatGPT to **double-check your own math or adjustments.** Suppose you roughly estimated how to triple a cookie recipe. You can run your new ingredient list by ChatGPT: *"I want to make 3 times this cookie recipe. Will these ingredient amounts work?"* It will compare against the original and confirm or correct your numbers. This is a comforting backstop that can catch a mistake before you end up with, say, overly salty dough or cookies that spread too thin.

By leveraging ChatGPT for scaling, you'll save time and avoid waste. No more guessing or ending up with either skimpy portions or far too many leftovers. And if you do end up with extra, it might be on purpose – after all, making a bit more than needed can set you up for tomorrow's lunch. But that's a strategy we'll explore soon. For now, with the fundamentals of resizing recipes under your belt, you're ready to tackle one of the most common scenarios: **cooking for just one person.**

COOKING FOR ONE WITHOUT GETTING BORED

Cooking for yourself is a wonderful act of self-care, but it can sometimes feel like more trouble than it's worth. A common complaint from solo cooks is boredom – eating the same big batch of stew four nights in a row, or letting half of your groceries go bad because recipes aren't scaled down. The good news is that with ChatGPT's help, **cooking for one can be exciting, efficient, and far from repetitive.** The key is to use prompts that focus on variety and smart use of ingredients.

One strategy is to ask ChatGPT for recipes that are **single-serving by design.** Instead of trying to divide a large recipe (though you can do that too), you could prompt: *"What's a simple dinner I can make just for myself tonight?"* The AI might respond with a quick dish like a one-pan chicken and veggies, a personal-sized frittata, or a hearty grain bowl – all tailored to one portion. These suggestions often use minimal ingredients and steps, perfect for a low-fuss evening. If you specify your preferences (say, "I'm in the mood for Italian" or "I need it to be vegetarian"), ChatGPT will incorporate that and still keep the portion small.

Another approach is to **plan for variety using one main ingredient.** Maybe you bought a pack of tofu or a bunch of cilantro and don't want the remainder to languish in the fridge. You can tell ChatGPT what you have and ask for multiple ideas: *"I'm cooking for one and have half a block of tofu left. Can you give me two different dinner ideas to use it up this week?"* Don't be surprised when ChatGPT comes back with, say, a tofu-veggie stir-fry for one night and a spicy tofu taco for another. By splitting one ingredient into two distinct recipes, you avoid feeling like you're eating the same thing on repeat. Plus, you use up that ingredient completely – no waste, no boredom.

Using leftovers creatively is a solo cook's secret weapon. ChatGPT can turn last night's dinner into a new culinary experience. Let's say you roasted some chicken thighs for yourself and have one left over. Instead of microwaving the same meal again, you might prompt: *"I have a cooked chicken thigh from yesterday. What can I make for dinner for one using it, that's different from roast chicken?"* The AI could suggest shredding the chicken into a single-serving barbecue chicken sandwich, or chopping it into a quick curry for one. It might add ideas to freshen things up, like tossing in some frozen veggies or a dash of a spice you haven't tried before. Leftovers don't have to be dull – with a little imagination (and AI help), they can be reinvented into something just as delicious as the original meal.

Of course, cooking for one also means being mindful of **simplicity and cleanup.** You can ask ChatGPT for recipes that use only a few dishes or ingredients. For example: *"Give me a dinner recipe for one person that only uses 5 ingredients and one pan."* A prompt like this might yield a suggestion for a simple stir-fry or an oven-baked foil packet meal. The idea is to keep your solo cooking from feeling like a huge production. The chatbot might even include tips like how to scale down the cooking vessel (using a smaller skillet, for instance) so you're not washing a giant pot for a little meal.

It's also helpful to involve ChatGPT in **meal planning for the week.** If you're cooking for yourself regularly, try something like: *"Plan a week of dinners for one person. I want different cuisines each night, and I'd like to reuse ingredients smartly so nothing goes to waste."* This kind of prompt will get ChatGPT to think holistically. It might come back with a Monday-through-Friday plan: perhaps a pasta for one that uses half a tomato can, a taco for one on Tuesday that uses the other half, a stir-fry on Wednesday with leftover veggies from Monday, and so on. Each meal will be unique, but you'll see ingredients carrying over efficiently. Not only do you save money and avoid waste, but you also get the fun of a varied menu.

Here are a few prompt ideas that can level-up your solo cooking game:

- **"I only have a microwave in my dorm. What single-serving dinner can I make?"** – ChatGPT might suggest a clever microwave mug recipe or a steamed fish and rice bowl for one.

- **"I love chili, but I don't want to eat a whole pot of it alone. Can I make a small batch of chili for one or two servings?"** – Expect the AI to provide a scaled-down chili recipe, maybe using one can of beans and a single portion of ground meat (or a meatless version), plus advice on seasoning gradually for the smaller volume.
- **"Cooking just for me tonight – I have eggs, a bell pepper, and some cheese to use up. Any ideas?"** – The bot could propose a quick veggie omelette or a shakshuka for one, ensuring you enjoy a fresh-cooked meal that uses what you have.

By experimenting with prompts like these, you'll discover that cooking for one is anything but lonely or monotonous. In fact, it can be an adventure in personalizing your food. ChatGPT becomes your kitchen companion, brainstorming alongside you so you're never short on ideas. You'll eat well, waste less, and gain confidence that you can whip up something delicious *just for you* any day of the week.

After mastering the solo meal, the next step up is cooking for two. Whether it's a romantic dinner or just Tuesday night with your roommate, feeding a pair has its own tricks – and yes, ChatGPT can help with those too.

DATE NIGHT, DINNER FOR TWO, AND BEYOND

Cooking for two opens up a world of possibilities – it's intimate and efficient. Whether you're planning a romantic date night or just a cozy Tuesday dinner with your roommate, you want meals that are **just the right size and effort** for a pair. With ChatGPT, you can strike that balance easily. Think of it as having a virtual sous-chef who helps you tailor recipes and menus so you end up with satisfied diners and minimal waste.

For a special occasion like date night, ChatGPT can help you craft a memorable meal without overdoing it. You might prompt: *"Give me a simple three-course Italian dinner for two, something romantic but not too time-consuming."* In response, you could get a lovely menu: perhaps a caprese salad to start (with just two portions prepared), a scaled-down pasta primavera for the main course, and two individual tiramisù cups for dessert. The instructions would be geared toward feeding exactly two people – no huge salad bowl or giant pot of pasta, just enough for you and your loved one. By specifying that you don't want it too time-consuming, you'll likely get dishes that can be made in about an hour or less, so you spend more time at the table and less in the kitchen.

Even for everyday dinners, **efficiency and balance** are key when cooking for two. Let's say you have a recipe that technically serves four, like a stir-fry. You can ask ChatGPT if it's okay to make the full recipe and save half for tomorrow, or how to cut it down. Often, it might suggest going ahead and cooking the four servings, since stir-fry makes great leftovers, and then provide tips on storing the extra for the next day. On the other hand, if you really only want two portions total, ChatGPT will help halve all the ingredients and might note, for example, to use a slightly smaller pan so the ingredients don't spread too thin and burn.

One handy use of ChatGPT is to **get ideas for two-person meals that use up ingredients smartly**. For instance, if a pack of tortillas comes with 8 and you only need 4 for tonight's dinner, you can ask: *"I'm making fish tacos for two, which will use 4 tortillas. What can I do with the remaining tortillas later this week?"* The AI might suggest a quick quesadilla lunch for two or homemade tortilla chips for a snack. This way, even though you're cooking a small meal, you're planning ahead to use everything up. Cooking for two doesn't have to mean lots of half-used ingredients lounging in the fridge – ChatGPT can always come up with a follow-up recipe so nothing gets wasted.

Another scenario: you and your cooking partner want to **cook together**. This can be a fun part of date night or a family activity. You could prompt, *"We want to cook dinner together as two people. Can you suggest a recipe where we can both have tasks to do?"* The AI might propose something like homemade pizza: one of you kneads and stretches the dough while the other preps toppings, then you assemble together. Or it might suggest making sushi rolls as a duo, or assembling tacos with each person in charge of different fillings. The point is to turn cooking for two into a shared experience. ChatGPT can outline roles or steps so that both cooks stay engaged and the meal comes together smoothly.

When it comes to portions, **meals for two** have the benefit of flexibility. You can cook exactly enough for one meal, or intentionally make a little extra for tomorrow. ChatGPT can help either way. If you say, "I want a dinner for two with no leftovers," it will aim for precision – maybe two steaks, two baked potatoes, and just enough salad for two plates. If you say, "We wouldn't mind some leftovers for lunch," it might give you a pasta recipe that yields 3-4 servings so you have extra. Being clear in your prompt will guide the AI to tailor the recipe size.

Importantly, cooking for two should feel **rewarding, not wasteful**. There's something satisfying about finishing a meal and not scraping plates of untouched food into the trash. With recipe-scaling and clever planning from ChatGPT, you'll hit that sweet spot. You'll also find you can afford to be a bit more experimental or indulgent when cooking for two – after all, buying a small specialty cheese or herb to use in a dinner for two isn't as daunting cost-wise as needing it for a huge batch. So you can ask ChatGPT to jazz things up: *"We're two adventurous eaters; give us a creative dinner for two that uses an unusual ingredient."* Such a prompt might lead to a unique suggestion like a two-serving paella with cuttlefish ink or a spiced-up shakshuka for two with exotic spices – just enough to try something new without a lot of leftovers.

By using ChatGPT for inspiration and adjustments, **dinners for two** can be perfectly scaled and delightful. You'll spend less time second-guessing portions and more time enjoying the meal with your companion. Now that we've covered solo and duo cooking, let's turn to the challenge of feeding bigger groups. How do you satisfy six, ten, or twenty people without breaking a sweat?

FEEDING A FAMILY OR A FLOCK

Cooking for a larger group can feel like a high-wire act: you want to have plenty of food, but not so much that you're overwhelmed (or throwing away tubs of leftovers). Whether it's a family of six or a party of twenty, **planning is everything.** ChatGPT can be an incredible aid here, acting like a seasoned chef who's done the "cooking for a crowd" math and logistics before. With the right prompts, you can figure out how much to cook, what to cook, and how to get it all done without last-minute panic.

One of the biggest questions when feeding a crowd is **how much food is enough.** You can directly ask ChatGPT for portion guidelines. For example: *"I'm making beef tacos for 12 people. How many pounds of ground beef should I use, and how many tortillas do I need?"* Based on standard catering rules, the AI might tell you something like: *"For 12 people, use about 4 to 5 pounds of ground beef (around 6 ounces per person) and roughly 24–30 small tortillas (2–3 per person)".* It understands general portion sizes – often around 6 ounces of protein and 5 ounces of starch per adult – and can adjust for the specifics of your meal (for instance, people might eat a bit less meat if you have substantial sides). If you mention kids are involved, ChatGPT will likely account for smaller appetites (maybe one taco per young child instead of two). By getting these numbers upfront, you'll shop and cook with confidence that everyone will get fed.

ChatGPT is also great for **suggesting crowd-friendly recipes.** Some recipes scale up more easily than others. If you prompt, *"What's a good dinner to serve 15 people that isn't too labor-intensive?"*, you might get recommendations like a big batch of chili, a couple of large casseroles, or a build-your-own taco bar. These are dishes that naturally accommodate large quantities and can often be prepared in advance. The bot could say: *"How about two large trays of baked ziti? Prepare the sauce and pasta ahead, then bake just before serving. Add a big green salad and garlic bread for a complete meal."* It not only gives you the main dish idea but also suggests complementary sides, so you have a full menu that works for a crowd.

When recipes need to be **scaled up**, ChatGPT will once again handle the math. If you have a favorite recipe for 4 and you want to serve 8, it can double the ingredients for you (just like we discussed earlier) and more importantly, point out any technique adjustments. For example, doubling a soup recipe might mean you need to simmer it a bit longer or use two pots if one pot isn't big enough. The AI might gently remind you of such details. It can also warn if a certain dish doesn't multiply well – perhaps a delicate soufflé is riskier to make in a huge batch – and suggest alternatives that achieve a similar vibe with less hassle.

Another crucial aspect is **timing and equipment.** If you only have one oven and you're trying to feed 10 people a roast chicken dinner, you could ask: *"How can I time a meal for 10 people with one oven?"* ChatGPT might help you strategize: maybe it suggests roasting two chickens sequentially earlier in the day (then keeping them warm), and focusing on stove-top sides closer to serving time. Or it could propose using a slow-cooker for one dish and the oven for another to spread out the cooking load. Essentially, you can describe your kitchen constraints and guest count, and get a plan that fits. This can significantly cut down on stress, because you'll have a clear game plan rather than juggling everything last minute.

Here's an example of a prompt and answer for a large gathering: *"I have 20 people coming for a backyard barbecue. I want to serve burgers and salad. How much ground beef should I buy, and can you suggest a big salad that goes well with burgers?"* ChatGPT might respond: *"For 20 people, get about 10 pounds of ground beef (assuming ~1/2 pound per person for burgers, which accounts for some having double patties or extra). For the salad, consider a large pasta salad with veggies and a vinaigrette – it's hearty, can be made in advance, and will hold up outdoors. You'll need roughly 3 pounds of dry pasta to make enough for 20 people, plus assorted mix-ins...."* This kind of answer gives you both the quantities and a practical menu idea. Notice it also errs on the side of having a little extra (nobody complains about leftover pasta salad the next day).

With crowd cooking, it's often better to have a bit too much than not enough. ChatGPT understands that and usually builds in a slight buffer. If you do end up with leftovers, you can always ask it for ideas to repurpose them – but by planning well, you'll cut down on excessive surplus.

Finally, don't forget that **you don't have to do it all alone.** ChatGPT can help you delegate or simplify. It might suggest, "Have someone bring dessert, while you focus on the main and sides," or propose store-bought shortcuts (like using pre-chopped veggies or bakery bread) to lighten your load. The goal is a successful, low-stress feast. With an AI assistant mapping out recipes, portions, and timing, feeding a family or flock becomes much more manageable.

Next, we'll shift gears from one-time meals to a different tactic: cooking in bulk for yourself. It's time to talk about batch cooking – making big batches now to save time later.

BATCH COOKING LIKE A PRO

In the busy modern world, many home cooks swear by **batch cooking** – preparing a large quantity of food that can be enjoyed over multiple days. The idea is simple: cook once, eat several times. But batch cooking isn't just about making a giant vat of soup and eating it all week (unless you love soup that much!). It's also about cooking smartly so you can create different meals from a common set of components. ChatGPT can act like your personal meal prep planner, helping you maximize variety and minimize daily effort.

To get started, you might ask ChatGPT for a **meal prep plan.** For example: *"I have a free Sunday afternoon. Help me batch cook dinners for the next 5 days for a family of four."* The AI could respond with a step-by-step plan: maybe roast two chickens (to eat as roast chicken one night and use in tacos another night), cook a big pot of rice or quinoa (to serve as a side for a couple of meals and later turn into a fried rice), and chop a load of vegetables (some to roast, some to throw into a soup). It would outline recipes for each day, like: Monday – roast chicken with veggies; Tuesday – chicken tacos using leftover chicken; Wednesday – vegetable soup using the roasted veggie leftovers; Thursday – fried rice with the remaining chicken, veggies, and rice;

Friday – maybe a simple pasta using any remaining ingredients. It might even generate a grocery list for you if you ask, ensuring you have all the ingredients for the week. With one prompt, you've essentially obtained a full meal prep game plan.

The beauty of ChatGPT's approach is that it can emphasize **variety.** One common issue with batch cooking is you get tired of eating the same thing. But if you prompt the AI to "use shared ingredients in different ways," it will intentionally switch up the flavor profiles. For instance, those roast vegetables from Monday can taste entirely new when they're simmered into a curry on Wednesday with some spices and coconut milk added. ChatGPT might say something like, *"Save two cups of the roasted carrots and broccoli. On Wednesday, use them in a quick Thai curry for a totally different taste,"* giving you explicit instructions to transform leftovers. This way, you still reap the efficiency of batch cooking (cooking and chopping done ahead) without the monotony.

Storage and safety are important in batch cooking, and ChatGPT can advise on that too. It can remind you to let food cool properly and get it refrigerated in a timely manner, and to store portions in airtight containers. If you ask, *"How long will these meals stay good in the fridge?"* it might respond with general guidelines: cooked meats and most prepared dishes are best within 3-4 days in the fridge. Perhaps it'll suggest freezing Friday's portion on Sunday if you won't get to it until the end of the week, just to be safe. The AI can also tell you the best way to reheat each dish (for example, reheat soup on the stove, reheat roasted meats in the oven covered so they don't dry out, etc.), so that Wednesday's dinner is just as enjoyable as the day you cooked it.

Another great use of ChatGPT is coming up with **big-batch recipes that serve as building blocks.** Think of staples like a large batch of tomato sauce, a pot of beans, or a base grain like barley. You can prompt: *"I want to batch cook one base item and use it in 3 different dinners. What do you suggest?"* The assistant might propose cooking a large batch of black beans, then using them throughout the week: one night in burrito bowls, another night mixed into a hearty chili, and a third time turned into bean burgers. It will give you three distinct recipes, all leveraging that initial batch of beans. Not only is this economical, but it also saves time (you only had to cook the beans once) and ensures nothing goes to waste.

By now you can see how ChatGPT can make you feel like a pro meal prepper. It organizes the process, so you know what to cook and in what order. It can suggest doubling recipes when it makes sense, and repurposing leftovers cleverly. The result is that you spend a few focused hours cooking, and then you get to relax on the weeknights while still enjoying homemade dinners.

Batch cooking is all about foresight, and with an AI assistant, you gain an extra pair of eyes on your plan. It's like having a coach reminding you, "Hey, while you have the oven on, roast some extra potatoes for later," or "Cook a double batch of rice, you'll need it Thursday." The more you include those hints in your prompts, the more ChatGPT will integrate them. Soon you'll have a streamlined routine: **cook once, clean once, and eat well all week.**

Up next, we'll extend this idea even further – beyond just a week. What if you could cook now and have meals ready months from now? That's where your freezer (and ChatGPT's planning) becomes your best friend.

MAKE IT NOW, FREEZE IT FOR LATER

Batch cooking often goes hand in hand with **freezer-friendly meals.** Freezing is like hitting the pause button on your food – make a dish now, enjoy it weeks or months from today. For busy folks (which, let's face it, is most of us), having a stash of homemade frozen meals is a lifesaver. ChatGPT can help you plan and execute this strategy, from identifying the right recipes to providing instructions on how to store and reheat them.

If you're new to making freezer meals, a great prompt is something like: *"What are some dinners that freeze and reheat well? I'd like to cook now for meals next month."* The AI might suggest classics like lasagna, chili, curries, stews, and casseroles – dishes known to survive the deep freeze and come out tasty. It could also surprise you with ideas like marinating meat and then freezing it (so you can thaw and cook with the flavor already infused), or assembling a pie or enchiladas and freezing before baking. Each suggestion will typically come with tips, e.g., *"Let the chili cool completely before portioning into freezer containers,"* or *"Wrap the unbaked lasagna tightly in foil to prevent freezer burn."* These details are crucial for quality, and ChatGPT has learned many best practices to pass on.

You can get very specific with your freezing questions. For instance: *"I want to freeze a homemade casserole. Should I bake it first or freeze it raw?"* Expect a nuanced answer. ChatGPT might say, *"You can do either. If you freeze it unbaked, add a few extra minutes to the baking time when you cook it later. If you bake it first, let it cool, then freeze, and when reheating, cover it so it doesn't dry out."* This kind of guidance can remove the guesswork from the freezing process. Similarly, you can ask, *"Can I freeze creamy soups?"* The AI might caution that soups with heavy cream can sometimes separate upon thawing, but then suggest a fix like stirring in a bit of fresh cream when reheating to bring it back together. It's like having a kitchen consultant who knows the quirks of frozen food.

Another helpful use of ChatGPT is figuring out **how long frozen meals will last** and how to label them. You could ask: *"How far in advance can I make and freeze meals? What's the shelf life in the freezer?"* Generally, the bot will remind you that most cooked dishes maintain good quality for 2-3 months in the freezer, and are safe to eat beyond that but might start to lose flavor or texture. It will likely advise using airtight containers or freezer bags (pressing out excess air), labeling each with the name and date (so you don't play mystery freezer Tetris later), and possibly arranging your freezer so newer meals go to the back and older ones up front. These are the kind of kitchen habits that seasoned meal-preppers use, and your AI assistant will happily teach them to you.

And what about reheating those frozen treasures? ChatGPT can walk you through that too. For example: *"I froze a batch of beef stew. What's the best way to reheat it?"* The answer might be, *"Thaw the stew overnight in the fridge if possible. Reheat it in a pot on the stove over medium heat, stirring occasionally, until it's hot all the way through. You can also microwave individual portions, stirring in between, but be sure to cover it so it doesn't splatter."* This saves you from trial and error, and ensures your make-ahead meal tastes just as good when you finally dig in.

Perhaps one of the most satisfying prompts is when you plan to double a recipe – eat half now and freeze half for later. For example: *"I'm making beef enchiladas for 4, but I want to make double and freeze an extra pan. Any tips?"* ChatGPT might provide the adjusted ingredient list for 8 servings, and then suggest how to package the second pan (tightly wrap in foil, maybe even do two layers if it's going to be in the freezer for a while). It will note to label and date it, and include reheating instructions like *"Bake from frozen at 350°F for about 45 minutes, covered, then uncover for 15 minutes to brown the cheese."* In essence, you get a full plan to not only cook more now, but also enjoy a home-cooked meal later with zero prep.

By leveraging your freezer and ChatGPT's knowledge, you can future-proof your dinners. On days when you're too busy or tired to cook, you'll have a ready meal waiting – one that you made yourself, with all the love and quality of home cooking. It's an empowering feeling to look at a well-stocked freezer and know that you've got a safety net for dinner. And with ChatGPT's help, building that safety net is easier than ever.

We've now looked at cooking for all sorts of scenarios: from one solo dinner to big gatherings, from eating now to eating much later. To wrap up, let's see some concrete example prompts that demonstrate adjusting recipes for any crowd and occasion, reinforcing everything we've learned.

PROMPT RECIPES FOR EVERY CROWD SIZE

Let's bring together everything we've learned by looking at a variety of example prompts. These show how you can adjust recipes for any number of people, whether you're cooking solo or for a whole party.

In each case, notice how the prompt clearly states the desired serving count, and how ChatGPT's response provides the right ingredient amounts (and sometimes extra tips).

Cooking for One: Imagine you have a recipe for 4 servings of pancakes but you only want to make enough for yourself. You could prompt ChatGPT with: *"This pancake recipe serves 4 and uses 2 cups of flour, 2 eggs, and 1 cup of milk. How do I scale it down to 1 serving?"* ChatGPT might reply with a scaled-down ingredient list, for example:

"For 1 serving of pancakes, use about 1/2 cup of flour, 1/2 teaspoon of baking powder, a pinch of salt, 1/2 cup of milk, and 1 egg. This will yield roughly 2-3 pancakes." It rounded the eggs to 1 whole egg (since you can't easily use half an egg) and adjusted the other ingredients accordingly. It might also mention that the batter consistency should be checked (since very small batches sometimes need a touch more liquid) – helping ensure your single serving comes out just right.

Dinner for Two: Now let's say you found a stew recipe for 8 people, but you're only feeding two. Your prompt might be: *"I have a beef stew recipe for 8 (calls for 2 lbs beef, 8 carrots, 4 potatoes, etc.). Can you adjust the ingredient amounts for just 2 servings?"* ChatGPT's answer would scale everything down to a quarter:

"For 2 servings, use about 1/2 pound of beef, 2 carrots, 1 potato, half an onion (instead of 2 onions), and halve all the spice amounts. Keep the broth to around 2 cups. Simmer time might be a bit shorter, so start checking sooner." In addition to the new measurements, see how it noted using half an onion – acknowledging you might not need a whole one – and reminded you to watch the cooking time. This way, your cozy dinner for two won't be swimming in leftovers, and the stew will still turn out flavorful.

Family Dinner (6 people): Perhaps you have a casserole recipe that serves 4, but you need to feed a family of 6. You ask: *"The original baked pasta recipe is for 4 servings. What quantities do I need for 6 servings?"* ChatGPT will calculate a 1.5x increase:

"To serve 6, increase the pasta from 8 ounces to 12 ounces, use about 1.5 lbs of ground turkey (up from 1 lb), 3 cups of tomato sauce (up from 2 cups),

and 3 cups of shredded cheese (instead of 2 cups). Use 1 and 1/2 of each spice measurement (e.g., if it was 2 teaspoons oregano, use 3 teaspoons). Bake time should remain roughly the same, but check for a bubbly center." Here it precisely adjusted each ingredient by 1.5, giving you the numbers in common kitchen units. It also addressed the baking time (which in this case doesn't change much). Feeding the whole family is as straightforward as basic math – which you didn't have to do by yourself.

Big Crowd (Party of 20): Now picture planning a big chili cookout. The recipe you love serves 5, and you expect 20 people. That's 4 times the amount. You prompt: *"I have a chili recipe for 5 people. How much of each ingredient do I need to serve 20?"* ChatGPT will multiply everything by 4:

"For 20 servings, use 4 times the ingredients: e.g., 4 pounds of ground beef (if originally 1 lb), 4 onions (if originally 1 onion), 4 cans of beans (15 oz each), 4 cans of tomatoes, etc. Add 4 times the spices, but you might start with 3 times the salt and chili powder and add more to taste, since seasoning can be adjusted. You'll likely need a very large pot or split the chili into two pots for cooking." This response not only gives the raw numbers, but also wisely advises caution with spices (to avoid overspicing) and a practical tip about using multiple pots. It's exactly the kind of insight you need when scaling up a recipe dramatically.

Custom Large Recipe: Finally, you can use ChatGPT to directly generate recipes tailored to a specific number of people. For example: *"Give me a lasagna recipe that serves 10 people."* Rather than starting from an existing recipe, the AI will create one with the desired yield:

"Lasagna for 10: Use 2 pounds of ground beef, 2 jars of tomato sauce, 18 lasagna noodles, 4 cups of ricotta, 4 cups of mozzarella, and 2 eggs for the ricotta mixture... Bake in two 9x13 pans..." It will list all ingredients in appropriate amounts and provide the cooking steps. By specifying the serving count upfront, you get a recipe that is already sized for your crowd, no math needed. This is incredibly handy for party planning – you can ask for any dish "for 12 people" or "for 3 people" and get a ready-to-cook recipe.

As you can see, whatever the crowd size – 1, 2, 6, 20, or anything in between – ChatGPT can adjust and produce recipes to fit. The prompts combine the techniques we've covered: mentioning the original serving (if scaling a known recipe), specifying the new serving target, and asking for any additional advice. And the results are recipes that take the guesswork out of scaling.

With these examples in mind, you should feel empowered to tackle any serving-size challenge in the kitchen. ChatGPT is like a flexible recipe book that rewrites itself to suit your needs, ensuring you always have the right amount of delicious food on the table.

Cooking for one, a couple, or a crowd – you've now got strategies for all these situations, with ChatGPT as your trusty kitchen sidekick. In this chapter, we explored how to scale recipes up or down without losing flavor, how to keep solo meals interesting, and how to plan perfect portions for two. We tackled the challenges of feeding whole families and larger gatherings, leaning on AI for math, menu ideas, and timing tips. We also reviewed batch cooking and freezing meals, unlocking the ability to enjoy home-cooked food on your busiest days. By walking through real-world prompt examples, you saw how a few well-chosen words can get ChatGPT to handle everything from halving a recipe to multiplying it for a feast.

The big takeaway is confidence: no matter the headcount at your table, you have an approach to cook smarter and reduce stress. Instead of juggling mental math or worrying if you'll have enough, you can ask ChatGPT and get instant, reliable guidance. You've learned to phrase your requests to get precise ingredient adjustments and clever advice, whether it's cautioning you to season gradually when scaling up or suggesting a creative way to use leftovers when scaling down. Cooking should be enjoyable, and with AI help, it stays that way even as the scope changes.

Equipped with these skills, you can stride into any cooking scenario knowing that portion size is under control. In the next chapter, we'll build on this momentum and tackle another key aspect of smart cooking. Get ready to explore new ways ChatGPT can elevate your kitchen game – turning the challenges of mealtime into opportunities for creativity and ease.

8

GLOBAL FLAVORS, LOCAL INGREDIENTS

Ever wanted to take a trip around the world using nothing but your taste buds and your home kitchen? This chapter is all about exploring global flavors while using the ingredients you already have at hand. With ChatGPT as your kitchen companion, you'll learn how to bring international flair to your meals without needing a plane ticket or a pantry full of rare spices. It's like having a friendly chef from every country available to coach you through dinner.

In the pages ahead, you'll discover practical ways to prompt ChatGPT for globally inspired recipes that make the most of local ingredients. We'll demystify the essential flavors that define different cuisines, from the fragrant basil and oregano of Italian cooking to the warm spices of Indian curries. Don't worry if some cuisines feel unfamiliar or if you're not sure how to pronounce the dish names—ChatGPT can guide you step by step, making the journey fun and unintimidating.

Cooking internationally at home often raises questions: *What if I can't find that special spice?*, *How do I make it taste authentic?*, or *Why is this dish prepared this way in its culture?* This chapter will show you how to use ChatGPT to answer all those questions and more. You'll see how to substitute ingredients creatively without compromising on flavor, and how to ask for the cultural context that turns a recipe into a story. We'll even venture into the realm of fusion cooking—blending cuisines to create something new (and delicious) with what you have on hand.

By the end of this chapter, you'll be equipped with an arsenal of ChatGPT prompts for culinary inspiration across the globe. Whether you crave a Thai-inspired stir-fry using local vegetables, a Mexican dish with ingredients from your neighborhood market, or a twist of Moroccan spice in your weeknight stew, you'll know how to get ChatGPT to help you make it happen. The tone is warm and practical, because cooking should be joyful and approachable, even when the flavors are from faraway places. Consider this your passport to new cuisines, stamped by creativity and curiosity.

Home cooks of all skill levels will find something useful here. If you're a beginner, you'll gain confidence to try recipes from different cultures, knowing ChatGPT has your back with tips and encouragement. If you're an experienced cook, you'll find new ideas and maybe fill gaps in your knowledge about certain cuisines. Cooking with an AI assistant is a collaborative adventure—one that can make your kitchen feel connected to the wider world.

So, tie on your apron and get ready to explore. In this chapter, we'll journey through seven key areas—from sparking global recipe ideas with local foods, to learning foundational flavors, to understanding cultural stories behind dishes, and beyond. Each step of the way, you'll see example prompts and suggestions that you can try out yourself. Let's embark on this flavorful trip around the world without ever leaving your kitchen.

AROUND THE WORLD WITHOUT LEAVING YOUR KITCHEN

Cooking dinner can feel like a mini vacation when you use your kitchen to explore another country's cuisine. With ChatGPT, you have a tour guide to global flavors right at your fingertips. You can ask for dishes from India, Italy, Mexico, or anywhere else, and tailor those suggestions to what you have on hand. The magic lies in the prompts: how you ask ChatGPT to bridge the gap between faraway flavors and local ingredients sitting in your pantry.

Think about a time you craved something exotic but only had everyday groceries. Perhaps you wanted Thai curry, but all you had were chicken and some vegetables. Instead of giving up, you could prompt ChatGPT with something like: *"I have chicken, carrots, and broccoli. How can I make a Thai-inspired dinner with these common ingredients?"* In response, ChatGPT might suggest a simplified Thai stir-fry. It could tell you to sauté the chicken and veggies with garlic and ginger, add a dash of soy sauce and peanut butter to mimic Thai peanut sauce, and squeeze in some lime if you have it. Suddenly, your plain chicken and broccoli turn into a dish that *tastes* a bit like Thailand, all without a special trip to the store.

The key is to be clear about the flavors or cuisine you want, and what ingredients you have (or even what you don't have). For example, imagine you usually make spaghetti with tomato sauce but tonight you're in the mood for something Mexican. You might ask: *"What Mexican-inspired dish can I cook using ground beef, tomatoes, and beans?"* ChatGPT could come back with an idea for a quick chili or a homemade taco filling. It might suggest seasoning the beef with cumin, chili powder, and garlic, stirring in the tomatoes and beans, and serving it with rice or tortillas. In effect, you've just guided the AI to combine your ingredients with Mexican flavors, giving you a satisfying meal that feels like a trip to Mexico via your dinner plate.

You can also start with a cuisine in mind and let ChatGPT fill in the blanks based on common ingredients. Let's say you want an Italian flair in your meal but only have basic staples. You could prompt: *"I'm craving Italian food. I have pasta, olive oil, garlic, and a can of tomatoes. What can I make?"* In this case, ChatGPT might walk you through a simple pasta dish reminiscent of Italy. For instance, it could suggest a garlicky tomato pasta: heat the olive oil, sauté chopped garlic until golden, toss in the canned tomatoes to simmer into a sauce, maybe add dried basil or oregano if you have some, and then mix with cooked pasta. It's a basic idea, but it transforms pantry staples into a dish with an Italian soul.

Notice how these prompts work: you're pairing *cuisine keywords* (like "Thai-inspired" or "Mexican-inspired") with the ingredients you have. You can also mention any limitations or preferences, such as quick meals or dietary needs. For example: *"Give me a quick Indian-inspired vegetarian dish using potatoes and peas."* ChatGPT might suggest an easy curry like aloo matar (a North Indian potato and pea curry), guiding you to fry some cumin seeds and onions, then add potatoes, peas, tomato and spices to create a fragrant, spicy-sweet stew—all with a few simple ingredients. If you specify *"quick,"* the assistant will likely keep the steps straightforward and time-saving.

The beauty of using ChatGPT is that it's interactive. If the first suggestion it gives doesn't sound appealing, you can ask for another idea. Maybe ChatGPT's first idea for your potatoes and peas was samosas, but you don't want to fry anything. You could follow up: *"That sounds good, but I'd prefer not to deep fry. Any other Indian dish with potatoes and peas?"* It might then pivot to the curry idea or perhaps a spiced potato-pea stir fry. This back-and-forth is like brainstorming with a creative chef friend who has encyclopedic knowledge. You're not just getting one recipe—you're having a conversation that leads to the perfect dinner for your mood and ingredients.

By experimenting with prompts, you'll get a feel for how to 'travel' anywhere through cooking. One night, you can be in Morocco by asking for a tagine-style dish with the carrots and chickpeas you have; another night, you're in Japan, asking how to make a teriyaki-like glaze for the salmon from your local market. It's all possible just by describing what's in your kitchen and choosing a destination for your taste buds.

Before long, you'll realize that no ingredient is "too boring" if you have a world of cuisines to apply it to. A simple carrot can become part of a spiced Moroccan stew or a Thai salad depending on how you prompt ChatGPT to use it. This opens up infinite variety in your daily meals—picky eaters in the family might even get excited, because Tuesday's chicken dinner is never the same if one week it's teriyaki chicken bowls and the next it's chicken tacos.

In summary, this first step in cooking globally at home is all about using ChatGPT to imagine *possibilities*. Be specific about the flavors you want and honest about what you have, and you'll receive a tailored suggestion that turns your kitchen into a new country for the evening. It's a wonderful way to keep cooking interesting and to learn a bit about other cuisines in a practical, hands-on way. Now that we've seen how to spark these global ideas with local ingredients, let's dive deeper: how do you make those dishes taste truly authentic? The answer lies in understanding each cuisine's foundational flavors and techniques.

BUILDING FLAVOR WITH REGIONAL FOUNDATIONS

Every cuisine has its own "language" of flavors—the essential ingredients and techniques that make Italian food taste Italian or Thai food taste unmistakably Thai. Learning these building blocks is like picking up key phrases in a new language, and ChatGPT can be your teacher. By asking the right questions, you can uncover the base spices, herbs, and methods that define different regional cuisines. Once you know these, you'll not only cook better recipes but also understand *why* certain ingredients show up again and again in dishes from the same culture.

Try prompting ChatGPT to explain the fundamentals. For example: *"What ingredients form the flavor base of Mexican cooking?"* or *"How do French chefs build flavor in their dishes?"* You might discover that Mexican cuisine often starts with a *sofrito* of onions, garlic, and chili peppers, cooked in oil to create a savory base. French cuisine might be defined by the *mirepoix* (onions, carrots, celery) sautéed in butter, and the use of techniques like making a roux (butter and flour cooked together) to thicken sauces. If you asked about Indian cooking, ChatGPT could tell you about the practice of frying whole spices in oil at the start of a dish (a technique called tadka or tempering) to release their flavors, along with the holy trinity of garlic, ginger, and onion as a common base for curries.

The answers you get will highlight what's non-negotiable for authentic flavor. Here are a few examples of regional flavor foundations you might learn about through ChatGPT:

Italian: Olive oil, garlic, and often a mix of onions, carrots, and celery (called *soffritto*) form the base of many sauces and soups. Herbs like basil and oregano, tomatoes, and a bit of wine or broth build up the flavor.

Chinese: A common base is ginger, garlic, and scallions, quickly stir-fried in hot oil. Add to that soy sauce, rice wine, and a touch of sesame oil, and you have the makings of countless stir-fries and braises.

Thai: Many dishes start with a curry paste of chili peppers, garlic, lemongrass, and sometimes ginger or galangal, pounded together. Thai cooking balances four key tastes—sweet (palm sugar), salty (fish sauce or soy sauce), sour (lime or tamarind), and spicy (chili)—so expect advice to include achieving that balance.

Indian: Slow-cooked onions, ginger, and garlic create a flavorful base for curries. Warm spices like cumin, coriander, turmeric, and chili powder are added early to bloom in the oil. Later, a finishing spice mix like garam masala or fresh cilantro might be suggested for that final aromatic touch.

Mexican: Onions and garlic are often paired with tomatoes or tomatillos and chili peppers to make salsas and stews. You'll hear about spices such as cumin and oregano, and herbs like cilantro. Techniques like charring ingredients (for example, roasting tomatoes, garlic, and chilies to make a salsa) add depth.

Middle Eastern (e.g., Moroccan): A foundation of sautéed onion and garlic is common, with spices like cumin, paprika, cinnamon, and coriander layering in warmth. You may be advised to simmer ingredients slowly (as in a tagine) with components like preserved lemon or dried fruits to add complexity.

These are just highlights—whatever cuisine you ask about, ChatGPT will outline its key flavors and methods. Armed with this knowledge, you can approach new recipes with more confidence. Say you've learned from ChatGPT that Greek cuisine relies a lot on olive oil, lemon, garlic, and oregano. The next time you want a Greek flair, you could ask for a recipe or even create your own knowing those elements should be involved. Or, if you remember that Japanese cooking often uses soy sauce, dashi (a kind of broth), and mirin (a sweet rice wine), you might ask ChatGPT how to use some soy sauce and sugar to mimic a teriyaki sauce when you don't have mirin on hand.

Another neat trick is to compare cuisines or ask for substitutions within a flavor profile. For instance: *"If I like the flavors of Thai cooking but don't have lemongrass or kaffir lime leaves, what common ingredients can I use instead?"* The AI might remind you that a squeeze of lime and some lemon zest can mimic the citrusy aroma of those Thai ingredients. Or you could ask: *"What's the difference between Italian and Spanish sofrito?"* and learn that Italian *soffritto* usually includes carrots for sweetness, while a Spanish sofrito might lean more on tomatoes and garlic. Each insight helps you see the patterns and differences among cuisines.

By engaging in this kind of dialogue, you're essentially taking a mini cooking class in regional cuisine basics. You can follow up with more questions too. If ChatGPT tells you, *"Chinese stir-fries often use ginger, garlic, and scallions,"* you might ask, *"How should I cut those for a stir-fry, and in what order do I add them?"* Then you'll learn that adding garlic too early can burn, so maybe start with ginger and scallions, then add garlic shortly after. Or if you're told that French cooking uses a roux, you can ask, *"How do I make a roux and when do I add it to my dish?"* to get a simple explanation (for example, whisk flour into melted butter and cook it before adding liquid to make a sauce).

This foundational knowledge makes your future prompts more effective. The next time you're cooking, you won't just say *"I have chicken, what can I do?"* You might add, *"...and I'd like it to have French flavors,"* because you now know roughly what that entails (perhaps butter, thyme, and a wine sauce). And sure enough, ChatGPT's answer will likely incorporate those elements. It's a feedback loop:

the more you learn from ChatGPT, the better your prompts become, and the more personalized and authentic the recipe suggestions get.

Understanding regional foundations also makes the cooking experience more rewarding. Instead of blindly following instructions, you'll start noticing, *"Ah, we're starting with cumin seeds because that's what gives many Indian dishes their depth,"* or *"This recipe has cilantro at the end, just like ChatGPT mentioned most Mexican dishes do for freshness."* It feels like uncovering the secrets behind your favorite takeout foods or grandma's recipes from the old country.

Now that you have a grasp on the "what" and "how" of global flavors, you might find yourself curious about the "why." Why do Italians use those herbs? Why is a tagine cooked slowly in Morocco? Cooking is not just technique; it's also about tradition and culture. Understanding that context can add even more meaning to your cooking—and ChatGPT can help you uncover it.

CULTURAL CONTEXT IN THE KITCHEN

Food is more than a list of ingredients and steps—it's a reflection of culture, history, and tradition. When you cook a dish from another part of the world, knowing the *why* behind it can make the experience richer. ChatGPT isn't just a recipe generator; it can also be a storyteller. By prompting it for background information, you can learn the stories and traditions that give global dishes their soul.

Imagine you're making a traditional Japanese miso soup. Beyond just asking for the recipe, you might wonder why miso soup is so ubiquitous in Japan. You could ask ChatGPT: *"Why is miso soup important in Japanese cuisine?"* In response, you might learn that miso soup is a staple of Japanese meals, often served at breakfast, and that it has been enjoyed for centuries as a comforting, nourishing start to the day. ChatGPT might explain that the fermented miso paste is valued not only for its flavor but also for health benefits, and that serving soup with meals reflects a balance that's central to Japanese dining. Suddenly, as you stir your pot, you're connected to a Japanese morning routine, appreciating your soup in a new light.

Or say you're preparing a batch of Mexican tamales. You can ask: *"When do people in Mexico typically make and eat tamales?"* ChatGPT could share that tamales are often made for special occasions and holidays—like Christmas or Día de los Muertos (Day of the Dead)—where families gather to cook together. It might paint a picture of a grandmother teaching her grandchildren how to spread masa on corn husks, filling them with meat or cheese, and steaming dozens of tamales for a festive gathering. Knowing this, the tamales you cook on an ordinary weekend suddenly carry a bit of that celebratory spirit, and maybe you'll even invite family or friends to help, turning it into an event.

These cultural nuggets can be both fun and useful. For one, they make great dinner conversation. If you serve an Indian biryani and have learned from ChatGPT that biryani was historically a royal dish or is a beloved Sunday family meal in parts of India, you can share that story at the table. It turns a simple meal into a cultural experience for everyone eating. You might ask while cooking: *"What is the story behind Indian biryani?"* and discover tales of how this spiced rice and meat dish was born in the kitchens of Mughal emperors, or how different regions of India have their own spin on it (Hyderabadi biryani vs. Lucknowi biryani, for example). Those insights don't just educate you; they also honor the culture that created the recipe.

Another example: you try your hand at a Moroccan vegetable couscous. Alongside the cooking instructions, you prompt: *"Tell me about couscous traditions in Morocco."* ChatGPT might describe how couscous is often prepared on Fridays in many Moroccan households or for family gatherings, served in a large communal dish. It might explain that it's traditionally steamed multiple times to make it fluffy and light, and that the meal symbolizes hospitality and community. Picture yourself fluffing up your couscous, knowing that in homes across Morocco this dish brings families together at the end of the week—that understanding can give your cooking an extra layer of meaning.

There's also practical value in cultural context. Some techniques or ingredients make more sense when you know their origin. For instance, if you learn that a certain Ethiopian stew is spicy because historically it helped people sweat and stay cooler in a hot climate, you might understand why so much chili is used—and decide if you want to tone it down or embrace the heat. Or you might ask, *"Why do Italians traditionally eat lentils on New Year's Eve?"* and find out it's because lentils resemble coins and symbolize prosperity for the coming year. Don't be surprised if you start adopting some of these fun traditions yourself, like making that lentil dish every New Year for good luck!

To get these insights, try prompts that go beyond "how" and ask "why" or "when." Here are some ideas:

- *"What is the history of [dish name]?"* – for example, *"What's the history of pad Thai?"*
- *"Is there a special occasion for making [dish]?"* – like *"Do people in Greece eat roast lamb for a holiday?"*
- *"What does [dish name] mean in its original language?"* – you might ask, *"What does 'Coq au Vin' translate to and why is it called that?"*
- *"Why is [ingredient] used so much in [cuisine]?"* – for example, *"Why is yogurt common in Middle Eastern cooking?"*

The answers can surprise you and deepen your appreciation. You may learn that pad Thai became popular due to a national unity campaign in Thailand, or that Greek Easter is a time when a whole community might roast lamb together. You might discover that *Coq au Vin* simply means "rooster in wine," a rustic French dish born of necessity to tenderize tough meat. Or that yogurt's cooling effect and availability made it a staple for balancing spicy and rich foods in Middle Eastern cuisines.

By weaving this kind of curiosity into your use of ChatGPT, you turn cooking into a form of cultural exploration. It's like traveling via stovetop: even if you can't visit Morocco or Mexico in person, you get a taste of the culture along with the meal. Plus, having this background knowledge shows respect. It acknowledges that each recipe comes from real people and a real place. When you cook a dish with its story in mind, you're more likely to handle it with care and authenticity—perhaps you'll crush spices with a bit more reverence if you know they were once considered as valuable as gold in trade, or you'll take the time to brew that Japanese tea to go with your meal when you remember the tradition of tea ceremonies.

One more benefit: this context can guide your improvisations. Suppose a recipe calls for an ingredient you don't have, but you remember from ChatGPT's cultural notes why that ingredient is used. Maybe you don't have an authentic fish sauce for a Vietnamese dish, but you learned it's used for saltiness and umami because refrigeration was scarce in tropical climates. That knowledge will help you find a clever substitute (like a mix of soy sauce and a bit of anchovy paste, or a splash of Worcestershire sauce) to mimic the intended flavor role. Which brings us to a practical hurdle every global cook faces: what to do when you're missing a traditional ingredient. You now have the know-how and the "why" behind a dish. Now, how can you adapt when your pantry isn't a perfect match for the recipe?

SUBSTITUTING WITHOUT COMPROMISING

No galangal for your Thai curry? Can't find paneer cheese for that Indian dish? Don't worry—ChatGPT is an expert in culinary improvisation. One of the greatest challenges in global cooking is running into an ingredient that your local store doesn't carry. The beauty of asking ChatGPT is that it can suggest smart swaps so you don't have to abandon the recipe. The goal is to substitute without compromising the essence of the dish, and a well-crafted prompt can get you there.

When you realize you're missing something, try prompts like: *"I want to make [dish], but I don't have [ingredient]. What can I use instead?"* or *"I can't eat [ingredient] – how can I adjust this recipe?"* By specifying the dish, you help ChatGPT give a more context-aware answer. For instance, if you ask, *"I'm making Thai green curry but can't find lemon-*

grass. What's a good substitute?" the assistant might recommend using lemon zest and a bit of ginger. It could explain that while nothing perfectly replaces lemongrass's unique citrusy flavor, lemon zest gives a bright citrus note and ginger adds some zing, combining to mimic the intended effect.

Let's look at a few common substitution scenarios:

Hard-to-find spices or herbs: Say a Moroccan tagine recipe calls for *preserved lemons*, but you don't have any. ChatGPT might suggest using fresh lemon zest and a pinch of salt to approximate the salty-citrusy punch of preserved lemons. Or if a recipe needs *kaffir lime leaves* (common in Thai cooking), a smart swap could be a combination of lime zest and a bay leaf. The lime zest provides the fragrance, and the bay leaf adds a subtle herbal note.

Specialty condiments: Perhaps you're cooking a Vietnamese dish that uses *fish sauce*, but you either don't have it or prefer not to use it. A prompt like *"What can I use instead of fish sauce?"* could yield options: soy sauce for saltiness, plus a squeeze of lime or a bit of mushroom powder to add depth (since fish sauce has a deep umami flavor). If you mentioned you're vegetarian, ChatGPT might specifically recommend soy sauce with a dash of seaweed or miso to replace the ocean-like savoriness of fish sauce.

Dairy and other basics: World recipes often call for things like buttermilk, yogurt, or ghee. If you lack *buttermilk* for an American Southern fried chicken or an Irish soda bread, ChatGPT would likely remind you that you can sour regular milk with a tablespoon of vinegar or lemon juice as a perfect substitute. If a curry needs *ghee* (clarified butter) and you don't have it, the assistant might simply tell you to use regular butter or oil, maybe with a note that the flavor will be slightly less nutty but still good.

Proteins and produce swaps: Maybe you found a Spanish paella recipe but live nowhere near fresh seafood, or you're vegetarian. You could ask, *"Can I make paella without seafood? What can I use instead?"* ChatGPT might suggest a vegetable paella variant, using mushrooms and artichoke hearts to give meaty texture and flavor, and perhaps extra smoked paprika to evoke some of the depth seafood would provide. Or if a Japanese recipe uses pork but you only have chicken, it can walk you through adapting the cook time and seasoning for the different meat.

Heat and spice adjustments: If you're aiming for a Szechuan Chinese dish that calls for Szechuan peppercorns (which create a unique tingly heat) and you don't have them, ChatGPT might advise a mix of black pepper (for peppery flavor) and a pinch of chili flakes, acknowledging it won't be the same tingle but will keep some heat in the dish. It often will tell you frankly when a substitute can't fully replicate the original (like "nothing truly replaces the aroma of saffron, but a pinch of turmeric can give the color and a subtle earthy note"). That honesty helps you set expectations and perhaps use a lighter hand or add extra of something else to compensate.

A great feature of ChatGPT is that it can provide *recipes for substitutes* as well. For example, if you're out of *garam masala* (an Indian spice blend), you can prompt: *"I don't have garam masala. How can I mix common spices to replace it?"* The assistant might give you a quick DIY spice blend to toast and grind using cumin, coriander, cinnamon, pepper, and maybe cardamom. Similarly, no *harissa* paste for a North African recipe? ChatGPT might guide you to blend paprika, cumin, chili powder, garlic, and olive oil to make a make-shift spicy paste.

It's not only about missing ingredients; it's also about dietary needs. If you love a Thai peanut sauce recipe but someone has a peanut allergy, you can ask for alternatives: *"Allergic to peanuts – what can I use instead in this satay sauce?"* Chances are, you'll get suggestions like almond butter or sunflower seed butter, or even a completely different sauce that still matches the dish's flavor profile (perhaps a soy-ginger glaze instead of peanut sauce for the satay). If you don't eat dairy and a Turkish dessert calls for milk, ChatGPT could suggest coconut milk or almond milk as replacements, noting any flavor differences.

When ChatGPT suggests a swap, it often preserves the role of the ingredient. Think of it like this: every ingredient has a job, whether it's adding sweetness, sourness, thickness, or aroma. By asking the AI for a substitute, you're basically saying, "I need something else that can do a similar job in this dish." And because ChatGPT knows the cuisine context, it might also mention if the dish will still be considered authentic or if you're creating a variant. Sometimes it will reassure you: *"Using yogurt instead of sour cream in this taco recipe is fine—many people do that,"* or *"Without the traditional chilies, it won't be exactly the same, but it will still taste good."* Such guidance gives you confidence to proceed with your version of the recipe.

To make the most of it, don't hesitate to follow up. If the suggestion is "use yogurt instead of sour cream," and you're unsure how much, you can ask: *"Should I use the same amount of yogurt as the recipe called for sour cream?"* ChatGPT will clarify, perhaps saying the quantity is one-for-one or if any adjustments are needed due to differences in consistency. It's like having a cooking hotline where no question is too small.

By mastering substitutions with ChatGPT's help, you truly free yourself from strict recipes. You learn that missing an ingredient is not a deal-breaker for enjoying global cuisine. This flexibility means you can venture into cooking dishes from, say, Korea or Nigeria, even if you can't get the exact chili paste or spice blend—they're no longer off-limits. You also start building your own intuition for swaps: after a few suggestions, you might predict what the AI will say ("hmm, I bet it will tell me to use cinnamon and nutmeg for allspice—and there it goes!"). That's a sign you're internalizing the knowledge.

With the obstacle of missing ingredients overcome, the entire world of cuisine is truly open to you. Now it's time to use that freedom for a bit of *culinary tourism*—journeying to new cuisines from the comfort of your kitchen.

CULINARY TOURISM, PANTRY EDITION

Now that missing ingredients aren't a roadblock, you can truly globetrot in your kitchen. Think of ChatGPT as your travel agent for a culinary tour. The idea of "pantry edition" tourism is that you explore far-off cuisines using the staples you already have. It's a fantastic way to broaden your cooking repertoire and taste new flavors without needing a suitcase—or a long shopping list of exotic items.

Perhaps you realize you've never cooked anything from Korean cuisine before, and you're curious. You might prompt ChatGPT: *"I've never made Korean food. What is an easy Korean dish I can cook with chicken and rice?"* The assistant could introduce you to *dak bulgogi*, a Korean BBQ chicken, explaining how to make a simple marinade with soy sauce, sugar, garlic, and sesame oil—all ingredients you might already stock. It might suggest pan-frying or grilling the marinated chicken and serving it over rice with some sautéed veggies. Just like that, you're trying Korean flavors for the first time, guided step-by-step, using familiar items in a new way. Along with the instructions, ChatGPT might tell you, "This dish is a common home-style recipe in Korea, kind of like making teriyaki chicken but with a different flavor profile," which helps you connect it to something you know.

The key to exploring a new country's cuisine is to communicate both your curiosity and your constraints. You can say you're a beginner and mention what ingredients you do or don't have. For example: *"I'd like to cook a simple dish from Ethiopian cuisine, but I only have basic vegetables (potatoes, carrots, cabbage) and common spices. Any suggestions?"* ChatGPT could suggest *Atakilt Wat*, a spiced Ethiopian vegetable stew. It would describe how to use turmeric, cumin, and maybe a bit of curry powder as a stand-in for the traditional *berbere* spice blend, instructing you to stew the cabbage, potatoes, and carrots with those spices and some tomatoes. It might also share a bit about Ethiopian food culture, like how such stews are often eaten with injera flatbread (and even give you an easy flatbread alternative if you're interested). Suddenly, you've cooked an Ethiopian meal with everyday ingredients—an experience you might never have attempted without an AI gently encouraging you.

You can also take a broader approach: ask for a tour of flavors. Try something like, *"Give me a list of 5 countries and a simple dish from each that I can make with chicken or vegetables."* This kind of prompt invites ChatGPT to become a global menu planner. It might come back with:

- **Italy:** A basic pasta primavera (pasta with sautéed vegetables, garlic, olive oil, and parmesan).
- **India:** A mild vegetable curry using potatoes and peas (along with curry powder or common spices).
- **Thailand:** A quick stir-fry with peanut sauce (using peanut butter, soy sauce, and chili to mimic Thai peanut flavors).
- **Mexico:** Vegetable fajitas (bell peppers, onions, and spices, served with tortillas).
- **Greece:** Lemon herb grilled chicken or tofu with a side of tomato-cucumber salad (using oregano, lemon, and olive oil for that Greek taste).

For each, ChatGPT would outline how to make it and why it represents that country's flavors. You could then decide which of these "destinations" to cook tonight. It's like having a curated list of must-try dishes on your world tour.

Another fun idea is to use ChatGPT to plan a thematically global week. Maybe you tell it, *"I have chicken, ground beef, rice, and assorted veggies. Could you plan a week of dinners, each from a different cuisine, that aren't too hard to make?"* Don't be surprised if the assistant delivers an exciting plan, like: Monday – Japanese teriyaki chicken bowls; Tuesday – Italian spaghetti with homemade sauce; Wednesday – Indian spiced lentils (using that ground beef in a keema curry or swapping for a vegetarian version); Thursday – Mexican burrito bowls; Friday – Middle Eastern-style kebabs with garlic yogurt. With the plan in hand, you can then ask for individual recipes. This turns meal planning into an adventure rather than a chore—one night you're "in" Tokyo, the next in Rome.

As you explore, you'll likely encounter new ingredients or terms. Don't hesitate to ask follow-ups. If ChatGPT suggests a Japanese dish and mentions *mirin* (a sweet rice wine) which you don't have, you can reply: *"I don't have mirin, what can I use instead or can I skip it?"* You'll get guidance, like using a bit of honey or sugar plus extra soy sauce to compensate. This way, even a suggestion that initially includes something unfamiliar can be adapted to your pantry. Every time you ask and learn, you become more fluent in the world's cuisines.

Culinary tourism from home can be eye-opening. You may discover you love the bright, tangy flavor of a Peruvian ceviche (which you tried with locally available fish and a lime you had), or that Hungarian goulash (made with your trusty paprika and beef) becomes a new family favorite. You might even keep a journal or list of the countries and dishes you've tried, essentially mapping out your journey. ChatGPT can help here too—ask it for a brief description of each dish to note down, so you remember that, say, "Gado Gado" is an Indonesian salad with peanut sauce you made on a whim and really enjoyed.

By now, you've traveled quite far using taste and creativity, and your confidence is growing. You've learned that no cuisine is off-limits, even if you start with zero knowledge about it. Each new dish is like a postcard from a friend abroad, and ChatGPT is helping deliver those postcards to your kitchen. After sampling so many distinct flavors, you might start wondering: what if you bring some of these flavors together? Can you mix and match what you've learned from different cuisines to invent something new? This is where fusion comes in, and yes, ChatGPT can guide you there too.

FUSION WITHOUT CONFUSION

Once you've dabbled in cuisines across the globe, you might find yourself thinking, "What if I mix some of these together?" Fusion cooking is where creativity really kicks in—combining elements from different culinary traditions to create something new and exciting. With ChatGPT as your brainstorming partner, you can attempt bold flavor mash-ups while still making sure the result is harmonious. The goal is to be inventive *and* respectful: blending cuisines in a way that celebrates them rather than muddling them.

To get started, be clear about what you want to combine. For instance: *"Help me create a fusion of Italian and Japanese cuisine. I have pasta, tomatoes, soy sauce, and chicken."* This prompt gives the AI a clear picture of the two cuisines and key ingredients. ChatGPT might come back with a creative idea like a *teriyaki chicken pasta*: marinate and sauté the chicken with a soy-ginger sauce (Japanese teriyaki style), then toss it with spaghetti, garlic, and a touch of tomato for an Italian-meets-Japanese noodle dish. It could suggest garnishing with fresh basil and a sprinkle of sesame seeds—blending an Italian herb with an Asian condiment. The result? A fusion dinner that surprisingly works, and you might never have invented it without a little AI inspiration.

Fusion can be as simple as taking a familiar dish and giving it a twist from another culture. Imagine you love tacos and you also love Indian spices. You could ask: *"Any ideas for an Indian twist on tacos using chicken?"* ChatGPT might propose *tandoori chicken tacos*. It would describe marinating chicken in yogurt and Indian spices (like a classic tandoori), roasting or grilling it, then stuffing it in taco shells or flatbreads instead of the traditional naan. Top it with a chutney-inspired salsa (maybe tomatoes, cilantro, and a dash of cumin) and you have a cross-cultural hit. It's respecting the essence of both cuisines: the taco format from Mexico and the flavor profile from India, in a way that complements each other.

The magic of asking ChatGPT for fusion ideas is that it has knowledge of flavor profiles from around the world, so it can highlight what might go well together. You can even ask it outright: *"Do Thai flavors and Italian flavors have any common ground I can play with?"* It may find a connection, like how both Thai and Italian cooking value fresh basil (Thai basil vs. Mediterranean basil) albeit with different varieties. Perhaps it suggests a *Thai-inspired pesto* for pasta: blending Thai basil, peanuts (instead of pine nuts), garlic, chili, and lime in place of the usual lemon, creating a spicy green sauce that you toss with noodles. That's fusion – and also a use of local ingredients if Thai basil grows in your area or you substitute regular basil but add Thai seasonings.

Respect is an important word in fusion. It's easy to throw random ingredients together, but a thoughtful approach makes a better dish. ChatGPT can help by explaining the role of each ingredient, so you don't, say, overpower a delicate Japanese broth with too much Italian cheese, or vice versa. If you propose something unusual, like *"I want to put kimchi in a grilled cheese. Would that taste good?"* the assistant might respond enthusiastically that kimchi's tangy, spicy crunch is actually terrific with melty cheese (a known Korean-American fusion combo), and even give you tips like using cheddar or mozzarella and adding a little butter on the bread to balance the kimchi's acidity. On the other hand, if you suggested something that might clash, ChatGPT could warn you gently. For example, *"I'm thinking of adding curry powder to my spaghetti carbonara"* might prompt a response that it would certainly be an experiment—perhaps it will suggest a better way to integrate those flavors, like making a cream sauce with curry spices instead of altering the classic carbonara technique directly.

You can also approach fusion from the angle of necessity. Maybe you started making a Chinese stir-fry and realize you only have Italian seasoning herbs available—why not create a one-of-a-kind *Italian–Chinese stir-fry*? You could prompt: *"I'm stir-frying chicken and broccoli, but instead of soy sauce I only have olive oil, garlic, and Italian herbs. Any fusion idea for this?"* ChatGPT might suggest a garlic and herb stir-fry, essentially an Italian-flavored sauté but done in a stir-fry style: high heat, quick cooking, maybe adding a splash of vinegar for tang (as a nod to Chinese stir-fry sauces). It might not be a traditional dish anywhere, but it could turn out delicious. And importantly, it uses what you have and validates that it's okay to break rules as long as the result tastes good.

For a high-level fusion challenge, you can even ask for a blend of three cuisines, though it helps to have a unifying idea. For instance: *"Create a fusion appetizer mixing Japanese, Mexican, and Mediterranean flavors."* That's a wild mix, but ChatGPT might find a creative solution, like *seaweed hummus tacos* or *sushi falafel bites* (imagine falafel with edamame and wasabi in it, served in a mini tortilla with tahini sauce and pico de gallo—crazy, but could be tasty!). The point is, the AI can generate ideas you might not think of, grounded in its knowledge of what flavors typically go together.

As always, feel free to iterate. If the first fusion suggestion sounds too complicated or not to your taste, tell ChatGPT. *"Hmm, I don't have Thai basil for that pesto idea. Any other Italian-Thai fusion suggestion using shrimp?"* might lead it to propose a lemongrass risotto with shrimp, using a bit of coconut milk in place of cheese for a Thai twist. Each tweak gets you closer to a dish that's practical for you and intriguing to eat.

By experimenting with fusion, you really become the chef of your own global bistro. It's a playful process, and ChatGPT is there to offer ideas, adjust them, and even suggest how to present or name your creation if you ask. You could end up serving "Mexi-Indian Curry Tacos" or "Asian Alfredo Noodles" at dinner, turning a weeknight meal into a conversation piece. And because you've been learning about ingredients and cultural significance along the way, you handle this fusion with an understanding of both sides—that's the respectful part. You're not claiming to reinvent another culture's cuisine; you're simply creating something new that nods to them.

We've covered a lot of ground: from finding global recipes with local ingredients, to understanding traditional flavors, to substituting ingredients and even merging cuisines. Sometimes it helps to see everything come together in examples. Let's take a quick trip around the world through a series of sample ChatGPT cooking prompts and imagine the responses. This will showcase just how much you can do with a little curiosity and the right question.

PROMPTS FROM ACROSS THE GLOBE

India – Weeknight Chickpea Curry:

Prompt: "I have canned chickpeas and tomatoes. What Indian-inspired dinner can I make easily?"

ChatGPT suggests: A quick *chana masala*-style curry. It instructs you to sauté a chopped onion, minced garlic, and grated ginger in oil until golden. Then, add common spices like ground cumin, coriander, and turmeric (and a pinch of chili powder if you like heat). Next, you stir in the canned tomatoes and chickpeas and let them simmer together. The assistant notes you can finish with a sprinkle of garam masala or fresh cilantro for extra flavor. In about 20 minutes, you'll have a fragrant chickpea curry to ladle over rice, satisfying that Indian food craving with pantry staples.

Thailand – Easy Pad Thai-ish Noodles:

Prompt: "I have rice noodles, some shrimp, and peanut butter, but no tamarind paste. Can I make a Thai-inspired noodle dish?"

ChatGPT suggests: A simplified version of *Pad Thai*. It tells you to soak or boil the rice noodles until tender, then stir-fry them with a beaten egg, the shrimp, and any veggies you have (like bean sprouts or carrot slices). For the sauce, since you lack tamarind, the assistant proposes a mix of soy sauce (for salt), a spoonful of peanut butter (for nuttiness and a hint of sweetness), a bit of brown sugar, and a squeeze of lime or splash of vinegar (to mimic tamarind's tang). Toss the noodles in this sauce. ChatGPT might add: "garnish with crushed peanuts and a squeeze of lime if you have them." The result is a peanutty, tangy noodle dish reminiscent of pad Thai, made entirely with ingredients in your kitchen.

Mexico – Cheesy Black Bean Tacos:

Prompt: "I want a Mexican-inspired vegetarian dinner. I have black beans, corn, and cheese. Any ideas?"

ChatGPT suggests: Tasty black bean and corn tacos. It guides you to warm up some canned or cooked black beans in a pan with a little oil, adding cumin, chili powder, and garlic (powder or fresh) to give them a kick. Then stir in the corn kernels (even frozen corn works) until everything is seasoned and heated through. It tells you to spoon this filling into warmed tortillas. Top with shredded cheese and let it melt. The assistant also throws in serving ideas: if you have an avocado, slice it on top, or add a quick salsa by chopping tomatoes and cilantro. In no time, you have hearty veggie tacos that bring Mexican flavors to your table, no meat needed.

Morocco – Spiced Chicken Stew:

Prompt: "I have chicken, carrots, and chickpeas, and I want something Moroccan-flavored for dinner."

ChatGPT suggests: An easy take on a Moroccan *tagine* (slow-simmered stew). It advises cutting the chicken into pieces and browning them in a pot with oil. Then you add chopped carrots, a can of chickpeas, and spices to evoke Moroccan cuisine: ground cumin, paprika, ginger, and a pinch of cinnamon. The assistant might say, "toss in a handful of dried apricots or raisins if you have them, for a touch of sweetness." Pour in some broth or even water, cover, and let it simmer until the chicken is tender and the aromas of warm spices fill your kitchen. ChatGPT explains that this mimics a chicken tagine, using a regular pot. Serve it over couscous (or rice, if that's what you have). You end up with a gently spiced, hearty stew that conjures the markets of Marrakech using everyday ingredients.

Italy – One-Pot Puttanesca Pasta:

Prompt: "I have spaghetti, canned tomatoes, garlic, and some olives. What Italian dish can I make?"

ChatGPT suggests: Pasta *alla puttanesca*, a classic Italian pantry pasta. It tells you to heat olive oil in a pan, sauté the minced garlic (and a pinch of red pepper flakes if you like a little spice). Add the canned tomatoes to create a sauce, and toss in those olives (chopped up). If you have capers or dried oregano, it says to add a bit for authenticity, but it notes that just olives and garlic will still give a nice briny, savory kick. Meanwhile, boil your spaghetti until al dente and then combine it with the sauce. The assistant might add a tip like, "save a little pasta water to stir into the sauce if it's too thick." In the end, you've got a tangy, garlicky puttanesca using just a few simple ingredients.

China – Simple Fried Rice:

Prompt: "How can I make a Chinese-style fried rice with leftover rice, an egg, and some frozen vegetables?"

ChatGPT suggests: A basic but satisfying fried rice. It explains how to scramble the egg first in a bit of oil and set it aside. Next, heat more oil and add your cold leftover rice (cold rice fries up better). Toss in the frozen vegetables (like peas and carrots mix), and stir-fry everything on high heat. The assistant says to season with soy sauce as your primary flavoring—drizzle it around the pan and stir so the rice turns light brown and picks up the savory taste. It might suggest adding a dash of garlic or onion if you have it, and a few drops of sesame oil at the end for aroma. Finally, mix the scrambled egg back in. In just a few minutes, you've transformed scraps into a comforting Chinese-style fried rice, all with a simple technique and basic ingredients.

Greece – Lemon Oregano Potatoes:

Prompt: "I need a Greek-inspired side dish. I have potatoes, lemon, garlic, and oregano. What can I make?"

ChatGPT suggests: Greek lemon-roasted potatoes. It instructs you to cut the potatoes into wedges and toss them with olive oil, lots of lemon juice, minced garlic, and dried oregano (plus salt and pepper). Then spread them on a baking sheet or in a roasting pan. The assistant recommends roasting them in a hot oven until they're golden brown outside and tender inside, flipping them once. Partway through cooking, it even suggests pouring a little water or broth into the pan and covering it for a bit, which is a trick to get the potatoes extra creamy and infused with lemony flavor. Remove the cover to let them crisp up at the end. What comes out: slightly tangy, herb-infused roast potatoes that would be right at home next to a Greek grilled chicken or salad. With just a few ingredients, you've nailed the taste of Greece.

You've traveled the world in this chapter, all from the comfort of your kitchen with ChatGPT as your guide. We started with the simple idea that you can enjoy *around-the-world* meals using everyday ingredients, and you've seen that in action—from Indian curries whipped up with pantry staples to Thai noodles improvised with peanut butter. You learned how each cuisine has its own backbone of flavors and techniques, and how asking ChatGPT the right questions can teach you those cooking "languages." We explored how to bring a dish to life with cultural context, turning recipes into stories that you can share. When ingredients were missing, you discovered that there's almost always a creative substitute to keep your dish on track. You even ventured into uncharted territories, cooking cuisines you've never tried before, proving no country's food is off-limits. And finally, you played the role of flavor DJ, mixing cuisines to invent fusion creations—all with a little help from AI.

By now, you've likely gained not only new recipes but a new mindset. With ChatGPT, the fear of cooking something "wrong" or unfamiliar fades away. You can approach any global recipe with confidence, knowing you have a smart assistant to coach you through unfamiliar steps, explain the *why* behind them, and help you adjust as needed. Your kitchen has become a place of exploration and experimentation. Feel free to keep this adventurous spirit alive: the next time you crave something different, you know exactly how to ask for it. Each prompt is an invitation to learn and to taste something new.

As you continue to the next chapter of *Cook Smarter with ChatGPT*, you'll build on this foundation. The world of cooking is endless, and so are the ways an AI assistant can support you. With global flavors now part of your skill set, you're well-equipped for whatever culinary challenge or curiosity comes next. Keep that sense of curiosity and confidence, and get ready to discover even more ways to make your kitchen truly AI-first and fun.

9

HOLIDAY FEASTS AND SPECIAL EVENTS

Holiday gatherings are when home cooks truly shine – and also when the pressure is on. Whether it's a cozy family Christmas dinner, a bustling New Year's party, or a culturally significant celebration, cooking for special occasions is as rewarding as it is challenging. The kitchen comes alive with the aromas of seasonal spices and family recipes, but behind the scenes it can feel like a high-wire juggling act. In these moments, having a helping hand to plan, organize, and inspire can make all the difference. This chapter explores how ChatGPT can be that extra pair of hands (and brains) in your kitchen, guiding you through planning and executing memorable feasts with confidence and creativity.

In Holiday Feasts and Special Events, you'll learn to harness AI as your secret weapon for stress-free celebration cooking. Imagine having a virtual sous-chef who never sleeps – ready to brainstorm menu ideas at 2 AM, suggest ingredient substitutions, or generate a timeline for the big day. We'll walk through how to prompt ChatGPT for full-course menus tailored to holidays, seasons, or any festive occasion you have in mind. The goal is to help you craft meals that wow your guests and still let you enjoy the party.

You'll also discover the art of themed dinners made easy with

ChatGPT's creative input. From a sun-soaked "Italian Summer Night" to a cozy "Rustic Winter Brunch," we'll see how an AI assistant can help design a menu around a fun concept or theme. Thematic menus turn meals into experiences, and you don't need to be an event planner to pull it off – just the right prompts.

Special events often mean diverse guests, so we haven't forgotten about dietary restrictions and preferences. This chapter shows you how to prompt for crowd-pleasing dishes that include everyone at the table, whether you have vegan cousins, gluten-free friends, or picky kids. Inclusivity in menu planning doesn't mean sacrificing flavor or creativity, and with ChatGPT's vast culinary knowledge, you can accommodate all your guests with ease.

Another skill you'll gain is balancing a multi-dish menu. A great feast isn't just a random collection of recipes – it's a harmonious ensemble. We'll use ChatGPT to coordinate flavors, cooking methods, and prep times across an entire menu, so your appetizer complements your main course and you're not stuck searing vegetables while the roast burns in the oven. It's like having a kitchen coordinator who helps you think of everything.

Of course, presentation matters when it comes to feasts. Ever wish you knew how to make your dishes look as good as they taste? In this chapter, we'll practice asking ChatGPT for presentation and plating tips that make meals look festive, elegant, or Instagram-ready – without piling on extra stress. Little touches like a drizzle of sauce or a sprinkle of fresh herbs can elevate the celebration, and your AI kitchen companion can suggest plenty of those.

We'll also explain the magic of make-ahead strategies. Big holiday meals don't have to mean big last-minute rushes. You'll see how to prompt ChatGPT for prep timelines and advice on which dishes or components can be made in advance. By spreading out the work, you free yourself up to actually enjoy the event – maybe even join your guests in a toast rather than stirring gravy all evening.

Finally, to bring everything together, we'll go through sample prompts for real celebrations. From Thanksgiving to birthdays to cultural festivals, we'll explore examples of how to use ChatGPT in planning and executing a feast. These scenarios will tie together all the techniques from this chapter and show you how an AI assistant can shine in different holiday situations. By the end of this chapter, you'll have a toolkit of AI-driven strategies for hosting spectacular feasts. Whether it's an intimate dinner or a big bash, you'll feel prepared, supported, and inspired – ready to cook smarter, not harder, with ChatGPT as your kitchen companion.

PLANNING A MEMORABLE MEAL WITH AI

Planning a big holiday meal or special event menu can feel overwhelming, but ChatGPT is here to lighten the load. Instead of juggling cookbooks and scribbled notes, you can simply ask your AI assistant to help design a **full-course menu** tailored to your occasion. The key is providing a clear prompt with the details of your event. Are you hosting an Easter brunch for 10 people? A summer backyard BBQ for a family reunion? Maybe a romantic anniversary dinner for two? Whatever the scenario, start by telling ChatGPT what kind of event you're planning, how many guests are attending, and any particular cuisines or dishes you have in mind.

For example, imagine you're hosting Thanksgiving for the first time and want a traditional but manageable menu. You might prompt ChatGPT with something like:

"I'm hosting Thanksgiving for 8 people. I want a classic American Thanksgiving menu with a twist, including appetizer, main course with at least two sides, and dessert. I have a vegetarian guest, so include a vegetarian option for the main. Please suggest a full menu with dish names and brief descriptions."

With a prompt like that, ChatGPT will get to work as your personal menu planner. It could respond with a line-up of courses such as a spiced pumpkin soup starter, a roast turkey as the main course (plus a stuffed squash as a vegetarian main alternative), sides like maple-glazed carrots and garlic mashed potatoes, and a dessert of apple cranberry pie with vanilla ice cream. Each item might come with a tempting description, giving you a clear vision of the feast. It's as if you've consulted a dozen holiday cookbooks in seconds – except all the ideas are neatly packaged and tailored to your needs.

The beauty of using AI for menu planning is that you can iterate on the ideas instantly. Maybe ChatGPT's first suggestion was a pumpkin soup but you'd prefer a salad to start. No problem – you can follow up with a tweak: *"That menu sounds great! Instead of pumpkin soup, what festive salad could I serve?"* In a flash, the assistant might swap in a harvest apple-walnut salad with cranberries, keeping the autumn theme intact. This back-and-forth is natural and encourages you to fine-tune the menu until it feels just right. It's like brainstorming with a friendly chef who never runs out of suggestions or patience.

ChatGPT is also fantastic at incorporating seasonal ingredients or themes into your menu. Let's say you want your special event to celebrate spring flavors. You could ask: *"Plan a three-course spring dinner menu for 6, highlighting seasonal produce like asparagus, strawberries, and peas."* The AI might come back with an appetizer of asparagus tartlets, a main of lemon-herb chicken with spring pea risotto, and a dessert of fresh strawberry shortcake. By specifying the season and key ingredients, you get a menu that matches the time of year, which often means fresher ingredients and more vibrant flavors. This is especially useful for farm-to-table enthusiasts or anyone who likes to shop at the farmer's market – you can plug in whatever produce is plentiful and have ChatGPT build a menu around it.

When planning a memorable meal with AI, don't forget to mention any themes or special touches you envision. If it's a birthday celebration, you might want the menu to include the guest of honor's favorite foods, or a nostalgic dish from childhood. If it's a cultural celebration, you might want to feature traditional recipes. For instance, *"Help me plan a full-course menu for a Lunar New Year dinner with traditional Chinese dishes, including a fish course for prosperity and a sweet rice dessert."* A prompt like this tells ChatGPT not just the event and courses, but also the cultural significance behind some choices. The AI can then weave in symbols and traditions – perhaps suggesting a whole steamed fish, longevity noodles, and sticky rice cake – giving you ideas that honor the celebration.

Another helpful tip is to specify the format of the meal in your prompt. Are you envisioning a buffet spread where people graze, or a formal sit-down dinner with plated courses? ChatGPT can tailor its suggestions accordingly. If you say "buffet," it might lean toward dishes that hold up well over time and can be made in large batches, like a big pot of chili or a build-your-own taco bar for a casual gathering. For a "formal sit-down" dinner, it might stick to a more structured progression of courses and elegant dishes. Always feel free to include practical details: *"I only have two hours to cook on the day of the event"* or *"My guests love Italian food"* – the more context you give, the better the AI can customize the plan.

Crucially, ChatGPT can help ensure your menu is cohesive. Home cooks sometimes throw together a mishmash of favorite recipes, only to realize too late that they don't complement each other (imagine serving three different heavy starches and no vegetables – it happens!). By asking for a full-course menu in one go, you get a set of dishes that are meant to go together. The AI often inherently balances flavors and textures – pairing a rich main with a lighter side, or acidic elements to balance sweet ones. If something seems off to you, you can always ask *"Does this combination work well together?"* and ChatGPT will explain or adjust as needed. We'll dive deeper into balancing menus in a later section, but even at the planning stage, the AI is considering these factors.

One more advantage: efficiency. In the flurry of planning a special event, time is precious. ChatGPT can not only dream up the menu, but also help you execute it. Once you have the menu, you can ask for the recipes for each dish, a consolidated grocery list, or timing tips (e.g., *"Which of these dishes can I make ahead?"* – which we'll cover soon). Having all this information generated for you means you spend less time researching and more time actually cooking – or enjoying the process. It's like having a project manager for your feast.

In short, using AI to plan a memorable meal transforms what could be a stressful planning session into a fun, creative collaboration. You bring your ideas and constraints to the table, and ChatGPT brings a world of culinary knowledge and inspiration. The result is a clear plan for a fantastic meal, custom-built for your holiday or event. With your menu mapped out, you're ready to dive into the next step: adding a unique twist with themed dinners that will make the occasion even more special.

THEMED DINNERS MADE EASY

One way to make a special meal even more memorable is to give it a theme. Themed dinners turn an ordinary gathering into an experience – think of a backyard luau with tropical dishes, or a medieval banquet with hearty old-world recipes. With ChatGPT's help, dreaming up a themed menu becomes a playful and easy task. Instead of spending hours researching recipes that fit your idea, you can simply describe the vibe or concept to the AI and let it suggest a cohesive set of dishes. It's like having a creative director for your dinner party living inside your computer.

To get started, decide on a theme that excites you or matches the occasion. It could be based on a cuisine ("Italian Summer Night"), a season or setting ("Rustic Winter Brunch"), a cultural idea ("Street Food Fiesta"), or even a story or movie ("Wizarding World Feast" for a Harry Potter fan gathering). Once you have a theme in mind, include it prominently in your prompt to ChatGPT along with any specifics you want. The more vividly you paint the picture for the AI, the better the suggestions will align with your vision.

For example, suppose you want to host an **"Italian Summer Night"** dinner on your patio. You imagine twinkling lights, red-checkered tablecloths, and the warm breeze of an August evening accompanied by Italian music. You could prompt:

"Help me design an 'Italian Summer Night' three-course dinner menu for 6 people. I'd like a light starter, a pasta dish for the main course (with a vegetarian option), and a cold Italian dessert. Include a suggestion for a suitable wine or drink for each course."

Within seconds, ChatGPT might whisk you away to the Italian

coast: suggesting a starter of bruschetta with ripe tomatoes and basil or perhaps a Caprese salad drizzled with balsamic glaze. For the main course, it could propose two options – say, spaghetti alle vongole (clam pasta) for seafood lovers and a rich eggplant parmesan as a vegetarian alternative – both fitting the summery Italian theme. It might pair these mains with a crisp Pinot Grigio for the pasta and a robust red for the eggplant dish. Finally, dessert could be a classic tiramisu chilled to perfection or scoops of lemon gelato with fresh berries, along with a suggestion of limoncello as an after-dinner liqueur. Not only do you have a menu that transports your guests to Italy for the evening, but you also got a curated drink pairing, making the experience feel that much more authentic.

Now let's try a different angle: a **"Rustic Winter Brunch"**. Perhaps the idea came to you after seeing a cozy cabin photo on social media – you envision serving comfort food on a chilly Sunday with friends gathered around the fireplace. Here's how you might prompt ChatGPT:

"I want to host a 'Rustic Winter Brunch' for 8 people. The theme is cozy and hearty. Please suggest a menu with a warm beverage, a main dish, a side, and a dessert, all with a rustic homemade feel."

ChatGPT could respond with something like: start off with steaming mugs of spiced apple cider or mulled cranberry punch to set the mood. For the main dish, it might suggest a country-style skillet hash with potatoes, sausage, and herbs, or a savory mushroom and cheddar quiche – both earthy and satisfying. A fitting side could be freshly baked sourdough bread with spiced butter, or perhaps a roasted root vegetable medley highlighting winter produce. And for the sweet finish, imagine a bread pudding with cinnamon and raisins or rustic apple crumble served warm with whipped cream. Each suggestion ties back into the theme of "rustic" and "winter," featuring hearty flavors and homestyle touches that feel like a hug on a plate. It's the kind of menu that makes your guests want to linger by the fire all afternoon.

Themed prompts can be as imaginative as you desire. Hosting a birthday party for a child who loves superheroes? Ask ChatGPT for a

"superhero-themed menu" – it might come up with power-packed "Mighty Veggie Burgers," "Cape Crusader Fries" with colorful dipping sauces, and a "Superhero Sundae Bar" for dessert. Throwing a New Year's Eve bash with an air of Gatsby-era glam? An **"Art Deco 1920s cocktail party menu"** prompt could yield elegant canapés, a champagne cocktail suggestion, and a decadent chocolate mousse to echo the Roaring Twenties. The AI draws on a vast library of culinary styles and eras, so it can blend historical menus or pop-culture references into your dinner planning. Don't be surprised if it even throws in a clever name or two for the dishes when it recognizes a theme – it adds to the fun!

When using ChatGPT for themed dinners, remember that you can ask for more than just dish names. You can inquire about serving ideas or small touches to reinforce the theme. For instance, for that Italian night, you might follow up with, *"Any ideas for making the table setting or presentation feel Italian?"* and get advice like using empty Chianti wine bottles as candle holders or playing opera music in the background. For the winter brunch, you might ask, *"How can I decorate or garnish the dishes to enhance the rustic feel?"* prompting tips like serving the cider in mason jars or garnishing the plates with fresh rosemary sprigs. While we'll talk more about presentation later in this chapter, it's worth noting that ChatGPT can integrate theme suggestions beyond just the food itself.

Themed menus can also accommodate practical needs. If you're on a budget but want a theme, include that in your prompt: *"Plan a Greek Isles-themed dinner for 4 that's budget-friendly, around $20 total, but still delicious."* The AI might pick simpler Mediterranean dishes like a classic Greek salad, lemon-oregano grilled chicken (an inexpensive cut), and yogurt with honey and walnuts for dessert – all evoking Greece but using few, affordable ingredients. Or perhaps you want a theme but have limited cooking facilities: *"Create a 'Tropical Beach' themed menu I can cook entirely on an outdoor grill, since my kitchen is under renovation."* ChatGPT would then ensure every suggested dish – maybe grilled fish wrapped in banana leaves, coconut lime rice (done in a foil packet on the grill), and caramelized pineapple slices – can be made with just the grill and no stove or oven.

The versatility of ChatGPT means no theme is too wild to try. You provide the imagination, and it provides the structure and details. For home cooks, this is incredibly freeing. You might not know a lot about, say, authentic Japanese tea ceremony snacks or medieval European cuisine, but if that's the theme you choose, ChatGPT can give you a starting point (with the caveat that for very specialized themes, you may want to double-check authenticity with additional sources). You're not left flipping through niche cookbooks or blogs – the AI does that research legwork and delivers concise ideas to you.

By leveraging themed dinner prompts, you transform cooking from a task into a creative project. It's gratifying to watch guests light up when they realize the meal has a concept behind it – "Oh, everything is from Grandma's recipe box!" or "Wow, we're eating like we're at a Spanish tapas bar!" And knowing that ChatGPT helped you orchestrate that experience can boost your confidence to try even more ambitious themes in the future.

Now that we've seen how to craft a menu around a unifying concept, it's time to ensure that menu works for everyone at the table. After all, a theme can fall flat if some guests can't partake in key dishes. Let's explore how to use AI to navigate dietary restrictions and preferences so that all your guests feel included and satisfied.

NAVIGATING DIETARY RESTRICTIONS AT THE TABLE

In any group of ten people, it's almost guaranteed that at least one will have a dietary restriction or strong food preference. When you're planning a holiday feast or special event, you want everyone to feel welcome and well-fed – no one should be relegated to nibbling on side salad because they can't eat the main dishes. Navigating dietary restrictions can seem daunting, but ChatGPT makes it much easier to create a menu where every guest finds something delicious. Whether it's allergies (nuts, shellfish), intolerances (gluten, lactose), or choices (vegetarian, vegan, keto, halal, kosher), your AI kitchen assistant can help you adapt and conquer.

The first strategy is to **build inclusivity into your menu from the start.** When you know in advance that, say, two guests are vegetarian and one is allergic to dairy, you can include those facts in your initial prompt to ChatGPT. For example:

"We're planning a holiday dinner for 12. Two guests are vegetarian and one has a dairy allergy. Please suggest a menu – appetizer, main (with a vegetarian alternative), two sides, and dessert – that will accommodate everyone. Ideally, the vegetarian dishes should be satisfying enough that even meat-eaters enjoy them."

A prompt like this tells the AI exactly what boundaries it's working within. The response might be a well-rounded menu such as: a roasted butternut squash soup (made with coconut milk to avoid dairy) for everyone to start, a main course of herb-crusted beef tenderloin for the meat-eaters with a show-stopping stuffed portobello mushroom as a vegetarian main, sides of garlic roasted potatoes (vegan and dairy-free) and a colorful quinoa-stuffed acorn squash, and for dessert, perhaps an olive oil orange cake that just so happens to be dairy-free. Notice how none of these dishes sound like "special diet food" – they're just appealing dishes in their own right. That's the sweet spot you're aiming for: dishes that meet dietary needs *and* delight all guests.

ChatGPT is great at coming up with creative substitutes and alternatives. Let's say you really want to make a classic dish, like creamy scalloped potatoes, but you have a guest who can't have dairy. You can ask: *"How can I make dairy-free scalloped potatoes that still taste rich and creamy?"* ChatGPT might suggest using coconut cream or a plant-based milk with a bit of cornstarch for thickening, and perhaps nutritional yeast or a dairy-free cheese for that savory flavor. It could outline a quick recipe: layering potatoes with a garlic-infused oat milk béchamel sauce, for instance. Suddenly, a dish that might have been off-limits is back on the table in an inclusive form. The same goes for baking – if you need an egg-free version of your famous holiday cookies for a vegan friend, you could prompt, *"Give me a vegan adaptation of a chocolate chip cookie recipe that tastes as good as the original."* The AI might point you to flax or chia "eggs" and vegan butter substitutes, resulting in a dessert no one will realize is vegan.

Allergies require careful thought, and ChatGPT can help there too. If you mention an allergy in your prompt, the AI will avoid suggesting any dangerous ingredients and might even remind you of cross-contamination precautions. For example, *"I have a guest who is severely allergic to peanuts and tree nuts. Suggest three dessert options for a holiday party that contain no nuts or nut oils, but still feel indulgent."* The recommendations could include things like chocolate mousse cups, a berry cobbler with oatmeal crumble, or sugar-dusted shortbread cookies – all nut-free. If you're unsure about hidden sources of allergens (like peanut butter in a sauce or almond flour in a cake), ChatGPT can double-check ingredients for you. You could list a recipe you're considering and ask, *"Does this recipe contain any hidden nuts or common allergens?"* and it will highlight what to watch out for, such as Worcestershire sauce containing fish or soy sauce containing wheat (gluten).

Another common scenario is the *picky eater* or someone with specific preferences. Maybe your nephew will only eat plain foods, or your friend just doesn't like spicy dishes. You can absolutely account for personal preferences in your prompts: *"One of our guests doesn't eat spicy food or any seafood. Can you adjust the appetizer and main course suggestions to be mild and no fish?"* ChatGPT will adjust its suggestions, perhaps swapping a chili-spiked dish for an herb-seasoned one, and it might remember to keep heat out of condiments or sides as well. This ensures you don't accidentally make your guest sweat over a too-hot curry or stare sadly at a shrimp cocktail they won't touch. What's nice is that the AI can do this without making the menu feel "less than" – a mild coconut curry soup can be just as delightful as a spicy one, and a grilled vegetable flatbread can replace a seafood appetizer so successfully that nobody misses the shrimp.

It's also wise to have *some dishes that are universally safe* – things like a big salad, a fruit platter, or a simply prepared vegetable side that almost any guest can eat. If you forgot to plan one, you can ask

ChatGPT at the end: *"What's a simple side dish I can add that has no common allergens (no nuts, dairy, gluten, or shellfish)?"* It might suggest something like honey-glazed carrots or roasted brussels sprouts with lemon, which you can add to the menu as a worry-free option. These kinds of additions ensure that even if someone is being cautious, they have at least one or two options to fill their plate.

One advanced use of ChatGPT is to handle *multiple overlapping restrictions*. Imagine you have one guest who is vegan, another who eats no added sugar, and another who is on a low-carb diet. That's a puzzle even seasoned cooks might groan at. But you could pose it to ChatGPT: *"I need a dessert that contains no animal products (vegan), has no added sugars (sweetened naturally), and is relatively low in carbs, yet will still satisfy a crowd of sweet-tooths at a holiday dinner."* It's a tall order, but the AI might propose something clever like a baked cinnamon apple crisp sweetened with dates and a crumble made from almond flour and coconut oil – vegan, no refined sugar, and lower carb than a typical pie. While not every restriction can always be met in one dish, the AI at least offers a starting point and often an innovative idea that you might not have thought of on your own.

Above all, when adapting your menu for dietary needs, communicate with your guests if possible. Here's where ChatGPT can help you phrase things diplomatically or come up with ideas if you get input like "I'm gluten-free." A quick use might be: *"What are popular crowd-pleasing gluten-free side dishes for a holiday meal?"* to broaden your ideas. Incorporating a person's dietary need into a dish that everyone can enjoy (like using gluten-free corn tortillas for tacos, or making an all-vegan pasta salad using egg-free pasta) avoids singling them out. ChatGPT can assist in finding those common-denominator solutions.

Thanks to AI assistance, accommodating dietary restrictions becomes an opportunity for culinary creativity rather than a headache. You'll end up with a menu where every guest feels taken care of. Often, guests with restrictions are used to making do with sparse options at parties; imagine their delight when they realize they can eat almost everything on your menu without worry. And the best part is, the inclusive dishes can be so tasty that guests without restrictions devour them too – it's truly a win-win.

With your menu now thoughtfully tailored to all your guests' needs, you've cleared one big hurdle of event cooking. The next step is to make sure those diverse dishes come together harmoniously and feasibly. After all, offering variety is wonderful, but you also have to cook it all! Let's turn our attention to balancing the multi-dish menu – coordinating flavors, cooking times, and kitchen workload so that your inclusive feast is not only delicious, but also manageable for you as the chef.

BALANCING A MULTI-DISH MENU

Once you've decided on all the dishes for your event, the challenge becomes making sure they all work together – both in terms of taste and in the practical reality of cooking them. It's one thing to have a great appetizer and a great main course; it's another for them to complement each other rather than fight for attention. Plus, when you're cooking multiple recipes, you have to juggle time and equipment. ChatGPT can act like a culinary project manager, helping you balance flavors, textures, and logistics across your menu so that everything harmonizes.

Let's start with **flavor and texture balance.** Imagine you've planned a winter dinner with a creamy potato soup as a starter, a rich beef stew as the main, and mashed potatoes as a side. Each of those might be tasty alone, but together they're one-note: heavy, soft in texture, and lacking contrast. An AI assistant can catch that kind of issue. You could explicitly ask: *"Do the dishes in this menu provide enough variety? Here's what I'm planning: [list of dishes]."* ChatGPT might analyze the list and point out, for example, that you have multiple starchy items and not much crunch or freshness. It might suggest swapping the mashed potatoes for a crisp green salad or roasted Brussels sprouts to bring in a different texture and a bit of bitterness to cut the richness. Or, if you have two very spicy dishes back-to-back, it could recommend making one of them milder to give your guests' palates a break.

Example Prompt – Checking Menu Balance: Let's say your menu is: spicy buffalo wings, followed by a spicy chili con carne, with a side of jalapeño cornbread, and a rich chocolate cake for dessert. You ask ChatGPT, *"Here's my menu for game night: Buffalo chicken wings, beef chili, jalapeño cornbread, and chocolate cake. Does this menu seem balanced, and how could I improve it?"* ChatGPT might respond that while each dish sounds great, the appetizer and main are both very spicy and meaty. It could propose a tweak such as starting with a lighter appetizer – maybe a tangy coleslaw or a refreshing avocado salad – to balance the heavy chili. Or it might suggest adding a cooling element like a sour cream and chive topping for the chili, to offer relief from the heat. For dessert, since everything before is bold and spicy, the AI might even suggest a lighter dessert like a citrus sorbet instead of a heavy cake, to cleanse the palate. These are the kinds of adjustments a seasoned chef would make, and ChatGPT can offer them to you just by analyzing the menu you provide.

Another critical aspect is **balancing cooking methods and timing.** If every dish you plan needs to be baked in the oven at the same time, you'll run into a bottleneck. ChatGPT can help foresee these issues. When you list your menu, include how each dish is cooked if you know it, then ask: *"Given this menu, are there any cooking or timing conflicts I should be aware of?"* For example, say your holiday menu includes a roast turkey, a tray of roasted vegetables, and a baked casserole – all of which typically need the oven, possibly at different temperatures. The AI might flag that you have three oven-dependent items. It could suggest alternatives like making the vegetables on the stovetop (perhaps sautéed green beans with garlic instead of roasted broccoli) or choosing a make-ahead casserole that you can reheat quickly under the broiler while the turkey rests. It might also advise a sequence: roast the vegetables first and keep them warm, then increase the oven temperature for the turkey, etc. Essentially, it helps you create a rough game plan so you're not panicking about oven space an hour before dinner.

You can also ask ChatGPT about **prep effort distribution.** A common pitfall is inadvertently picking multiple labor-intensive dishes that all need lots of last-minute attention. For instance, if you choose a made-to-order appetizer (like pan-seared scallops that must be done right before serving), a main course that requires constant stovetop stirring (like a risotto), and a delicate souffle for dessert (which waits for no one), you might be tied to the kitchen all night, unable to enjoy your guests. If you suspect you've got a high-maintenance menu, run it by the AI: *"These are the dishes I'm thinking of. Will it be too much for one cook to handle? If so, which dish could be simplified or changed?"* ChatGPT might spot that trio of high-effort dishes and recommend, say, swapping the scallop appetizer for something you can prep ahead and serve cold (like a ceviche or a fancy cheese board). Or instead of risotto that needs 20 minutes of stirring, maybe a pilaf that can sit happily on the stove. The souffle might be replaced with a cake you bake earlier in the day. The AI can give you these suggestions, prioritizing a smoother cooking experience without sacrificing the quality of the meal.

Sometimes **balancing a menu** means editing down. As home cooks, we often overestimate how much food we need or how many courses to serve, especially for a celebration. If you're unsure about quantities or number of dishes, ask ChatGPT for guidance. For example: *"I have a main course and three sides for 5 people – is that too much? Should I drop one side dish?"* It will give a reasonable take, perhaps noting that three sides might be more than necessary for a small group, and maybe suggest focusing on two really good sides to simplify things. Or conversely, *"I'm serving 15 people; is one salad enough or should I do two different vegetable sides?"* Getting a second opinion from AI can confirm your plan or gently nudge you to adjust the scale.

Another facet to consider is a **thematic or nutritional balance** – are you unintentionally serving three dishes in a row that are all similar in style or ingredients? If your first course is a tomato bruschetta and your main is tomato-based pasta, your menu might feel repetitive. ChatGPT can catch that if you list those dishes, likely pointing out the duplication of tomato and advising an alternative for one course. Nutritionally, while a special feast isn't usually about health food, you might still want some balance – e.g., one green vegetable among the sides, or not everything drowned in cheese. If you care about that, you can specify: *"Ensure at least one side dish is a green vegetable"* in your initial prompt, or ask after the fact *"How can I add something lighter or healthier to this menu?"* The suggestions could be as simple as adding a crisp cucumber salad to a BBQ spread or including a fruit platter along with rich desserts.

What's remarkable is how quickly ChatGPT can evaluate the big picture. Seasoned cooks learn these balancing acts through experience (often by making the mistakes first). But with an AI assistant, you can benefit from a vast collective experience. It will remind you, for example, "Your menu has no starch – maybe add rice or bread rolls" or "You've got three dishes that all have a lot of cheese; perhaps substitute one for a dairy-free option for variety." These nudges can save you from minor hiccups like too many similar flavors, or major ones like realizing you physically can't cook everything at once.

At the end of this balancing act, you'll have a menu that not only sounds delicious on paper but is also set up for success in your kitchen. Each dish has its place, in flavor, in timing, in effort – and they all play nicely together. With a cohesive, well-planned menu in hand, you can move on to the fun part: making your food look as incredible as it tastes. After all, we eat with our eyes too, and a bit of presentation flair can elevate your feast to the next level.

PRESENTATION AND PLATING TIPS

You've cooked a fantastic meal – now how do you make it look as spectacular as it tastes? Presentation is the final layer of love you can add to each dish, especially for holidays and special events when a little extra festivity on the plate goes a long way. Many home cooks shy away from "plating" like a restaurant, but with a few simple tips (and some guidance from ChatGPT), you can elevate the visual appeal of your food without a ton of effort. Think of it as setting the stage so when your guests feast their eyes, they're already delighted before the first bite.

ChatGPT can serve as your personal plating coach. If you're unsure how to present a particular dish, try asking something like: *"How can I plate [dish] to look elegant?"* For example, *"How can I plate a simple carrot soup in a festive way?"* The AI might suggest serving the soup in white bowls to make the orange color pop, then garnishing with a swirl of coconut cream or yogurt, a sprinkle of chopped parsley or toasted pumpkin seeds, and perhaps a small drizzle of chili oil for a splash of red. It could even recommend adding a decorative element like a Parmesan crisp on top or a sprig of rosemary. Suddenly, your humble soup has restaurant flair – and all it took was a question and a few garnish ingredients.

For **main courses and platters**, plating often involves arrangement and garnish. Let's say you've roasted a turkey or a whole cauliflower roast for the centerpiece. You could ask ChatGPT: *"What's an attractive way to present a roast turkey on the table?"* You might get tips such as: position the turkey on a large warm platter, surround it with roasted vegetables or fresh herb sprigs and citrus slices for color, and maybe brush the skin with a bit of oil or glaze right before serving so it glistens. If it's a carved meat, the AI might suggest arranging the slices fanned out, with a garnish of something green (like parsley or kale leaves) and bright (like pomegranate seeds or cherry tomatoes) to make the platter visually appealing. These suggestions turn a plain serving into a statement piece, and none are hard to do – it's just about that extra minute of assembly.

Color and contrast are big elements of plating that ChatGPT can remind you about. A quick prompt like *"Give me tips to make my plates look more colorful and photogenic"* can yield general advice: include a variety of colors on each plate (think green herbs, red pomegranate arils, yellow lemon zest) because a monochrome plate is less exciting. It might also mention using contrasting textures – like a crunchy topping on a creamy dish or a dollop of sauce on a solid piece of meat – to add visual interest. The AI can suggest little flourishes, such as a sprinkle of paprika on deviled eggs for a pop of red, or a few edible flowers on a salad to add beauty (edible flowers like pansies or nasturtiums are conversation starters!). For desserts, it could be as simple as a dusting of powdered sugar or cocoa to give a professional touch, or plating a slice of cake with a drizzle of sauce and a berry on the side to make it look straight out of a patisserie.

Themed presentation is another area where AI assistance shines. If you followed our earlier example of an Italian-themed night, you can ask for plating ideas that match that vibe: maybe rustic wooden boards for antipasto, or serving pasta in charming ceramic bowls like a trattoria. Or for a winter holiday theme, ChatGPT might suggest touches of green and red (like parsley and dried cranberries) as garnish to give a Christmas color palette. For a kid's birthday, it might recommend playful arrangements – like a smiley face made of fruit on a plate, or colorful cupcake toppings. All these ideas can be generated with simple questions, such as *"How can I decorate the plates or table to enhance the [theme] theme?"* The AI might go beyond food too – advising on table decor like scattering pinecones and holly for Christmas, or using themed napkins and plating on banana leaves for a tropical theme. While décor isn't our main focus, it's nice that the assistant can bridge the gap between food and ambiance if you ask.

One big thing to remember: **presentation shouldn't stress you out**. The goal is to add enjoyment, not pressure. So, use ChatGPT to find **simple** enhancements. If you're not skilled with piping bags, for instance, it might suggest an easier garnish rather than an intricate sauce swirl. For example, instead of painstakingly stacking ingredients MasterChef-style, you could simply slice the meat neatly, use a clean spoon to place your sides on the plate with intention rather than slopping them on, and wipe any spills off the plate edge (a classic restaurant trick). ChatGPT might remind you to use the rule of odds (odd numbers of items tend to look more artful than even), or to try layering textures (placing a crisp element on top of a soft one). These are straightforward once you know them, and the AI can explain them in a friendly way if you prompt, *"What are some basic plating principles I can use at home?"*

Another example: Let's say you've made a chocolate cake for a special occasion. Serving it straight from the pan might taste fine, but plating it could be so much more delightful. If you ask *"How can I present my chocolate cake for a wow factor?"* ChatGPT might suggest cutting it into neat slices, placing each slice on a dessert plate, adding a dollop of whipped cream or a scoop of vanilla ice cream, drizzling chocolate or caramel sauce in a zigzag on the empty side of the plate, and topping with a fresh berry or mint leaf. Alternatively, it might encourage you to add a decorative topper on the whole cake – maybe fresh flowers or chocolate shavings – and to present it on a cake stand for height. These tips turn a straightforward dessert into a centerpiece. And none of it requires professional training – just a bit of foresight, which the AI helps provide.

The AI can also advise on **photography-friendly plating** if you're keen to snap some Instagram shots before everyone digs in. It might mention using natural light, choosing plates that contrast the food color, and arranging the scene with props (like a fork or a linen napkin) to make the shot appealing. While this might be extra, it's something many home cooks enjoy doing nowadays. If that's you, a quick, *"Any suggestions to plate this dish so it looks great in photos?"* will get you tailored advice.

By incorporating ChatGPT's plating tips, you'll find that making food look good can be both fun and rewarding. Guests respond not just to taste but to visual cues – the sparkle in their eye when you bring out a beautifully arranged platter is priceless. Plus, you might discover a creative side of yourself in the kitchen you didn't know you had, experimenting with garnishes and layouts like an artist. And if something doesn't turn out exactly as envisioned, remember: the food is still delicious, and you can always adjust the presentation next time. The point is that you're learning and adding new skills to your cooking repertoire.

To really enjoy the presentation phase, it helps to have breathing room in your schedule. It's hard to artistically drizzle sauce when you're racing against the clock. This is where smart planning comes full circle. If you prepare well in advance, you can spare those few minutes to plate nicely. The key is to plan what to make ahead of time so you're not scrambling at the last minute – and ChatGPT can help with that too.

MAKE-AHEAD MAGIC FOR LESS STRESS

One of the best gifts you can give yourself as a host is time. When the day of your event arrives, you don't want to be chopping vegetables frantically or realizing you have three things to bake at once. This is where **make-ahead magic** comes in. By preparing some dishes (or parts of dishes) in advance, you distribute the workload and ensure that when your guests are about to arrive, you're calm, collected, and maybe even sipping a drink instead of breaking a sweat. ChatGPT can be an excellent planner for this make-ahead strategy, helping you figure out what can be done ahead of time and crafting a timeline for you to follow.

A good way to start is to have ChatGPT **outline a prep schedule** once your menu is set. You can prompt something like: *"Here's my menu for Saturday's party (list dishes). I want to do as much prep as possible on Friday. What tasks should I do on Friday, and what should I save for Saturday, so that everything is fresh and delicious?"* The AI will likely break it down for you. For example, if your menu includes a stew, a salad, and a cake, ChatGPT might suggest cooking the stew on Friday because stews often taste even better the next day as the flavors meld. It could advise to chop and refrigerate all your salad vegetables (except maybe delicate ones like avocado) and mix the dressing on Friday, but only toss them together on Saturday just before serving to keep things crisp. For the cake, it might tell you to bake it on Friday, wrap it well once cooled, and then do the frosting or final touches on Saturday so it looks fresh. You'd get a neat checklist like:

Day Before: Stew – cook completely, cool and refrigerate. Salad – wash and cut veggies (store in containers), mix dressing and keep separate. Cake – bake, cool, wrap in plastic.

Day Of: Gently reheat stew. Assemble salad with dressing right before serving. Frost the cake and set it out 1 hour before dessert time.

This kind of timeline, generated in seconds, can save you from a lot of last-minute chaos. It's like having a sous-chef who also acts as a project planner.

ChatGPT can also recommend **make-ahead friendly dishes** if you want to deliberately choose recipes that won't chain you to the stove on event day. If you ask *"Which parts of a Thanksgiving dinner can I prepare a day or two ahead?"* you might get tips such as: make cranberry sauce and pies a couple of days prior, prep the turkey stuffing ingredients (chop herbs, dice onions and celery ahead), even assemble the stuffing and refrigerate it uncooked, tear bread for stuffing so it gets stale (better texture), and perhaps brine the turkey a day ahead if you plan to. It could suggest peeling and parboiling potatoes the night before for mashed potatoes (then you just finish them on the day), or making turkey stock in advance for gravy. The guidance could be very granular: *"Toast the almonds and breadcrumbs on Wednesday, then on Thursday you can just sprinkle them on the green bean casserole before baking."* These specific suggestions help you break down seemingly huge tasks into manageable chunks over days.

If you're unsure about whether a particular dish can be made ahead without losing quality, just ask. For instance: *"Can I make the hollandaise sauce a few hours before brunch, or will it separate?"* ChatGPT would warn you that hollandaise doesn't hold well and is best made last minute, but it might propose an alternative sauce that's similar but more stable, or a method to keep it warm. Or you could ask, *"How far in advance can I assemble a lasagna before baking?"* and you'd learn that assembling it the night before is fine (even beneficial for flavor), just keep it refrigerated and add a few extra minutes to the bake time if it goes into the oven cold. Essentially, you can run any **"Can I make this ahead?"** question by the AI, and get either a yes, a no, or a "yes, but here's how" answer.

Besides dishes, think about **prep work.** Sometimes it's not the cooking but the chopping, mixing, and measuring that eats up time on the big day. Why not do it early? ChatGPT can guide you on mise en place: *"Which ingredients from these recipes can I prep the night before?"* It might respond: chop all the onions, garlic, and other veggies and store them in zip-top bags or containers (labelled by dish if you're really organized). Measure out all the dry spices and seasonings and set them aside. If a marinade is involved, make it and marinate the protein overnight. If dough is needed (for bread or rolls), perhaps you can make it ahead and let it do a slow rise in the fridge. The AI could give safe storage tips too: e.g., *"You can peel and cut potatoes the day before, just keep them submerged in cold water in the fridge so they don't brown."* Advice like this helps you avoid common pitfalls of advance prep.

Another area ChatGPT can assist with is **reminders for the day-of** so that make-ahead items turn out perfect. If you refrigerated that stew, you might need to take it out a bit early to let it come closer to room temp before reheating. If you froze a casserole last week (yes, you can plan even weeks ahead for some dishes!), the AI would remind you to start thawing it a day or two in advance. You could essentially have ChatGPT generate a full timeline: *"Create a detailed schedule for me for the day of the event, including preheating ovens, when to reheat each dish, and any finishing touches."* The output could be something like:

10:00 AM: Take stew out of fridge to start warming up.

11:00 AM: Preheat oven to 350°F for casserole.

11:15 AM: Put casserole in oven.

11:30 AM: Whip cream for dessert and keep in fridge.

12:00 PM: Remove salad ingredients from fridge.

12:15 PM: Reheat stew on stove on low heat, stirring occasionally.

12:30 PM: Remove casserole from oven, cover with foil to keep warm.

12:45 PM: Toss salad with dressing.

1:00 PM: Guests arrive, everything is ready to serve!

Having this kind of play-by-play can be a huge stress reliever because you're not keeping all the timings in your head – it's laid out for you. Of course, you can adjust on the fly, but even a basic roadmap is a confidence booster.

It's worth noting that not **everything** should be made ahead. Some things truly are best last minute – like that fresh green salad or anything fried (nobody wants day-old soggy fried food). If you include those in your menu, ChatGPT will likely flag them as day-of tasks. And that's fine; you'll at least know that those are the only things to focus on when the time comes.

By mastering the art of the make-ahead with AI's help, you transform the cooking experience. Instead of a frenzy, it becomes a steady, enjoyable process. You get to actually savor the holiday or event you're hosting, which is the whole point! With much of the work done before the big day, you'll find yourself more present with your guests, and maybe even able to sit down and enjoy the meal while it's hot. And when it's time for those last finishing touches – reheating, plating, garnishing – you can approach them with a clear head and even a touch of creative flair, since you're not utterly exhausted.

We've now covered planning, theming, accommodating, balancing, beautifying, and easing the execution of your special event meals with ChatGPT. The final piece of this chapter is to see it all in action with real-world scenarios. Let's walk through some example prompts for major celebrations – from Thanksgiving to New Year's and more – showing exactly how you can use everything you've learned to cook smarter (not harder) when it matters most.

SAMPLE PROMPTS FOR CELEBRATIONS

Now let's put it all together with a few real-world holiday scenarios. These examples show how you might interact with ChatGPT for different celebrations, applying everything we've discussed – from menu planning to make-ahead strategies. Each scenario includes sample prompts and a sense of how ChatGPT could respond, giving you a blueprint for using your AI kitchen companion when the occasion arrives.

Thanksgiving (USA): Thanksgiving is the ultimate multi-dish feast, which can intimidate even experienced cooks. Picture yourself a couple of weeks before Thanksgiving, getting organized. You might start with a prompt for an overall game plan: *"I'm hosting Thanksgiving for 10 people. I need a traditional menu (turkey, sides, dessert) with one vegetarian main option, and a prep schedule for the two days before. Help me plan the menu and timeline."* ChatGPT would likely come back with a classic menu: roast turkey as the star, a vegetarian-friendly main like a hearty wild mushroom stuffing or a vegetable pot pie, sides such as mashed potatoes, green bean casserole, cranberry sauce, and maybe a fresh twist like maple-roasted sweet potatoes with pecans. For dessert, it might list pumpkin pie and an apple crumble. What's more, it would break down a timeline: "Two days before: do grocery shopping, make cranberry sauce (it keeps well), bake the pie. One day before: prep vegetables (peel potatoes, trim beans), assemble the casserole and stuffing ready to bake, brine the turkey. Thanksgiving morning: roast the turkey, boil and mash potatoes an hour before dinner, reheat casserole and stuffing, toss salad last minute, etc." Imagine receiving this organized roadmap – suddenly the feast feels feasible. You could even follow up with more prompts, like *"Give me a recipe for the vegetarian pot pie"* or *"How do I make the turkey carving look nice for presentation?"* and ChatGPT would continue to guide you step by step. By using AI to orchestrate the big picture and the details, hosting Thanksgiving can transform from panic-inducing to a manageable (even enjoyable) project.

New Year's Eve Party: New Year's often means gatherings where people graze on finger foods and toast with drinks. Let's say you plan to host a cocktail party for New Year's Eve with about 20 friends. You might ask: *"Suggest a New Year's Eve party menu with 5 easy appetizers (some that I can make ahead) and a signature festive cocktail. I'd like a mix of vegetarian and meat options."* ChatGPT could propose a spread of crowd-pleasers: perhaps Caprese skewers (cherry tomato, mozzarella, basil) for a fresh vegetarian bite, mini spanakopita (spinach-feta pastries) that you can bake straight from frozen (a make-ahead win), bite-sized meatballs in a tangy glaze kept warm in a slow cooker, smoked salmon cucumber rounds for an elegant touch, and a plate of assorted cheeses, fruits, and crackers for simplicity. For the signature cocktail, it might suggest a sparkling pomegranate punch (with a non-alcoholic variation noted so everyone's included). Each appetizer might come with a brief note: "assemble the Caprese skewers in the morning, they'll hold up fine; spanakopita can be made ahead and frozen – just bake when guests arrive; meatballs can be pre-cooked and reheated in sauce," and so on. You could then drill down: *"Give me the recipe for the pomegranate punch"* – and you'd get a step-by-step, including how to make an ice ring with berries to float in the bowl (a classic party trick). If you worry about timing, you might say, *"In what order should I prepare these appetizers?"* and the assistant would likely advise doing any baking (spanakopita, meatballs) just before guests come, having cold items ready to go on a platter, etc. By asking ChatGPT, you essentially have an event planner helping you ensure your New Year's Eve starts and ends with sparkles, not stress.

Birthday Celebration: Birthdays come in all styles, but the common thread is making the honoree feel special. Suppose you're organizing a 40th birthday dinner for your best friend who adores Mexican food and chocolate cake. Your prompt could be: *"It's my friend's 40th birthday. She loves Mexican cuisine and I want a semi-formal sit-down dinner for 8 people. Can you help me design a menu with a fun theme (maybe an 'elevated taco night') and a show-stopping chocolate dessert? Also include one vegetarian option."* ChatGPT might run with that, suggesting an appetizer of individual mini guacamole cups or a warm street corn dip, a main course of a DIY gourmet taco bar – with options like achiote-marinated grilled chicken, beer-braised brisket, and a mushroom and roasted pepper filling for the vegetarian twist, accompanied by elegant sides like cilantro-lime rice and a jicama-orange salad for brightness. It could propose fun touches like a mango salsa and a chipotle crema to drizzle on the tacos, bringing that restaurant flair. For dessert, knowing the chocolate request, perhaps it proposes a Mexican chocolate cake (with cinnamon and a hint of chili) or molten chocolate lava cakes, served with a scoop of dulce de leche ice cream. The theme "elevated taco night" is achieved by combining the interactive fun of tacos with high-quality ingredients and beautiful presentation (maybe suggest plating tacos on wooden boards with small bowls of toppings, etc.). Once you have the menu, you might ask ChatGPT for help with timing (grill the meats just before serving, but have them marinated from earlier in the day; bake the cake in the morning and dust with cocoa before serving) or even wording a birthday toast. The AI can assist in those personal touches too, like *"What's a creative way to present the birthday cake?"* (perhaps with sparklers or a drizzle of caramel sauce on the plate). In the end, you've used ChatGPT to tailor an event that speaks to your friend's tastes and makes her feel celebrated, without you having to comb through hundreds of recipe sites for ideas.

Cultural Celebration (Lunar New Year): For a cultural or religious celebration, ChatGPT can help you honor traditions while planning practically. Imagine you're hosting a **Lunar New Year** dinner for your family and want to include symbolic foods for good luck. You could prompt: *"Help me plan a Chinese New Year dinner for 6 people with traditional dishes that symbolize prosperity and good fortune. I'd like to include dumplings, a whole fish, and a dessert. Provide brief cooking or serving tips for each."* Your AI assistant, drawing on cultural knowledge, might assemble a meaningful menu: start with pork and cabbage dumplings (symbolizing wealth because they resemble little purses of money, and it might note to fold them in a gold ingot shape if you can), a whole steamed fish with ginger and scallions as the centerpiece (fish represents abundance; it might remind you to leave the head and tail on to symbolize a good start and finish to the year), alongside a longevity noodle dish (perhaps a stir-fried noodle with vegetables, advising not to cut the noodles to preserve the symbolism of long life), and a side of garlicky gai lan (Chinese broccoli) for greens. For dessert, it could suggest sweet rice balls in syrup (tangyuan) symbolizing family togetherness, or sticky rice cake (nian gao) for rising fortune. In its response, ChatGPT might also weave in tips like, "Make the dumpling filling and wrap dumplings ahead of time and freeze, so on New Year's Day you just boil or pan-fry them," or "When steaming the fish, pour hot oil and soy sauce over it at the table for a dramatic final touch." These insights help you not only know *what* to cook, but *how* to pull it off authentically and efficiently. If you're unfamiliar with the recipes, you can naturally ask for them one by one (e.g., *"Give me a recipe for the tangyuan"*), and ChatGPT will oblige, complete with ingredients and steps. By embracing AI guidance, you ensure your cultural celebration is respectful of tradition, delicious, and well-organized – even if you didn't previously know all the customs by heart.

These scenarios are just a taste of what's possible. No matter the celebration – be it a casual Fourth of July barbecue, a Passover Seder, a graduation party, or a baby shower brunch – you can adapt these prompting techniques to fit. The key is to communicate your vision and needs to ChatGPT: the occasion, the vibe, any must-have dishes or dietary needs, and where you need help (ideas, logistics, recipes, etc.). The AI will respond as your knowledgeable, tireless helper, sparking ideas and solving problems. The more you practice with smaller events, the more confident you'll become in letting ChatGPT handle the heavy lifting of planning, so you can focus on adding your personal touch.

By seeing these examples, you've got a clear picture of how an AI assistant can lighten the load for special occasion cooking. From grand holiday feasts to intimate celebrations, ChatGPT is like a versatile toolkit at your disposal – ready to generate menus, refine them to your theme and guests, schedule your cooking, and even suggest garnishes for that wow factor. The days of tackling big cooking events alone, with stacks of recipe books and scribbled lists, are over. Now you can cook smarter, with a friendly AI by your side.

After exploring *Holiday Feasts and Special Events*, you've gained a comprehensive playbook for tackling even the most elaborate meals with ChatGPT by your side. We covered how to dream up full-course menus tailored to any occasion, from concept to dessert, and how to use the AI to inject creativity with themed dinners. You learned strategies to make every guest feel welcome by accommodating dietary needs, ensuring no one leaves your table hungry or unhappy. We also balanced the fine details of multi-dish cooking – aligning flavors and managing kitchen logistics – and added the finishing touches with plating and presentation tips to make your food shine. Crucially, you discovered how planning ahead (with a little AI magic) can turn a hectic cooking marathon into a smooth, enjoyable experience. By walking through real celebration scenarios, you saw these ideas in action, proving that with the right prompts, ChatGPT truly can be your co-host in the kitchen.

Armed with these skills, you can approach any holiday or special event with confidence and calm. Instead of dreading the complexities of big meals, you might even find yourself looking forward to them – an opportunity to flex your newfound "AI + cooking" muscles and impress your guests (and yourself!). You're not just cooking harder, you're cooking smarter, turning what used to be stress into a fun collaborative project between you and your AI assistant. Every successful feast will reinforce how far you've come as an AI-empowered home cook.

This journey doesn't end here. As you continue, you'll discover even more ways to weave ChatGPT into your culinary adventures. With each step, you're becoming more adept at leveraging AI to enrich your cooking – whether it's everyday dinners or once-in-a-lifetime events. So take a moment to celebrate your progress (perhaps with a leftover slice of that celebration cake!), and get ready for the next helping of insight as we move forward to another exciting facet of the AI-assisted kitchen.

10

SWEET AI DESSERTS FROM WHAT YOU HAVE

Imagine finishing dinner and suddenly craving something sweet. You peek into your pantry and fridge, only to find a few odds and ends: perhaps a lone banana starting to spot, half a bar of chocolate, and a cup of yogurt. In the past, you might have shrugged and assumed you didn't have the right ingredients to make a dessert. But now you have ChatGPT as your creative sous-chef. **Sweet AI Desserts from What You Have** is all about transforming those humble scraps and spontaneous cravings into delightful desserts with the help of artificial intelligence.

In this chapter, you'll learn how to use ChatGPT to whip up treats on demand using whatever ingredients you have on hand. We'll explore prompting techniques that turn a handful of pantry staples into a sweet creation, even when you haven't planned ahead. Whether you're missing key ingredients like eggs or flour, or adapting a recipe to fit dietary needs, you'll see how an AI assistant can suggest smart substitutions and clever workarounds without missing a beat.

You'll also discover how ChatGPT can satisfy a sweet tooth in record time. Late-night chocolate craving? Need a dessert in 10 minutes flat? We've got you covered with prompts for quick microwave mug cakes, no-bake snacks, and other speedy indulgences. And if you're watching your sugar intake, don't worry—AI can guide you to desserts that are low in sugar but high in satisfaction, so you can treat yourself a little more healthfully.

Beyond quick fixes and substitutions, ChatGPT can spark your creativity with flavor and texture. Ever wondered what unexpected ingredients might pair well together in a dessert, or how to give your treats that perfect balance of crispy and gooey? We'll show how you can ask ChatGPT for imaginative flavor pairings and textural contrasts that take your dessert game to the next level. You might discover a new favorite combo of sweet and salty, or a genius way to add crunch to a creamy pudding.

And if you're not a confident baker, ChatGPT has your back. You'll see how it can walk you through each step of a recipe, help convert measurements or temperatures, and explain baking techniques in simple terms. It's like having a patient, knowledgeable friend in the kitchen, ready to answer any question—no judgment, just support and encouragement.

Finally, we'll wrap up with a handy dessert prompt bank. We've compiled sample prompts for common ingredients like oats, bananas, chocolate, peanut butter, and yogurt—the kinds of everyday items that often sit around waiting to become something delicious. These examples will give you a head start the next time you find yourself wondering, *"What can I make with this?"*

By the end of this chapter, you'll feel empowered to create desserts anytime, anywhere, with whatever you have available. With ChatGPT as your guide, no ingredient is too humble and no craving is too last-minute to satisfy. So, let's dive into the sweet side of AI-assisted cooking and unleash your dessert creativity!

DESSERT ON DEMAND

Sometimes the best desserts are born out of necessity. Perhaps you weren't planning to make dessert at all, but now you have a sweet craving and only a handful of ingredients in your kitchen. The good news is that ChatGPT can be your personal dessert generator, brainstorming recipes based on whatever you've got. The key is knowing how to prompt it effectively. In this section, we'll explore how to ask ChatGPT for dessert ideas when you have "almost nothing" in the house, and we'll see examples of turning pantry staples into satisfying treats.

Start with What You Have: The first step is to take stock of your ingredients. Do you have a couple of fruits, some basic baking supplies, or even a leftover item from earlier in the week? List them out. When prompting ChatGPT, it helps to be specific about what's on hand. For example, you might type: *"I have two apples, a little bit of butter, some sugar, and a package of tortillas. What dessert can I make with these?"* This prompt clearly lays out your ingredients and asks for a dessert idea. ChatGPT can recognize these items and might respond with a creative suggestion – perhaps caramelized apple quesadillas or a quick apple tart using the tortillas as a crust.

Notice that in the prompt, you're not just saying "I don't have anything to make dessert," which might be too vague. Instead, you're giving the AI something to work with. ChatGPT has been trained on countless recipes and cooking tips, so even a short list of ingredients can trigger its recipe knowledge. It's like telling a friend, "Here's what I've got – any ideas?" Often, you'll be pleasantly surprised by the suggestions.

Be Open to New Ideas: When you're improvising a dessert from what you have, be prepared for unconventional ideas. Let's say you have a leftover cooked rice and some milk. You might not immediately think "dessert," but if you prompt ChatGPT with those ingredients – *"I have a cup of cooked rice, milk, and honey. Is there a dessert I can make from this?"* – you could get a suggestion like a quick rice pudding. In fact, rice pudding is a classic dessert that many home cooks forget about. ChatGPT might walk you through warming the milk with honey, stirring in the rice and a pinch of cinnamon, and before you know it, you've repurposed leftovers into a comforting sweet dish.

Here's another example: suppose all you find in your pantry are oats, peanut butter, and a bit of cocoa powder. It might not look promising at first glance. But try asking ChatGPT: "*What dessert can I make with oats, peanut butter, and cocoa powder? I don't have flour or eggs.*" This prompt tells the AI not only what ingredients are available, but also mentions a couple of common things you're missing (flour, eggs). ChatGPT could come back with an idea for no-bake chocolate peanut butter oat cookies – the kind you can stir together on the stovetop or even in the microwave. It might suggest mixing the oats with melted peanut butter, cocoa, and a little sugar or honey to bind it together, then chilling dollops of that mixture until they firm up into chewy, fudgy cookies. Suddenly, your bare-bones pantry is yielding a treat with zero baking required.

Specify Your Constraints: If you have any equipment or time limitations, include those in your prompt. The more details you provide, the more tailored ChatGPT's answer can be. For instance, you might say: "*I have half a loaf of bread, some sugar, and a can of coconut milk. I also have a sweet tooth right now but only a microwave to cook with. Any dessert ideas?*" Here, you've not only listed ingredients (bread, sugar, coconut milk) but also given context – you want something quick and you only have a microwave available. ChatGPT might suggest a microwave bread pudding: tearing up the bread, soaking it in a mixture of coconut milk and sugar (and maybe a pinch of cinnamon if you have it), then microwaving it briefly to set. It could turn out to be a surprisingly delicious coconut bread pudding that satisfies your craving in minutes.

Another scenario: "*I have a bar of dark chocolate and a handful of pretzels. No oven. What can I make that's sweet and salty?*" From this prompt, ChatGPT sees two specific ingredients and a flavor direction (sweet and salty). A likely suggestion could be chocolate-dipped pretzel clusters. ChatGPT might instruct you to melt the chocolate (even in the microwave, given no oven), toss in the pretzels to coat them, and let them set on parchment paper. In a short time, you'd have crunchy, sweet-salty bites – a dessert born entirely from an unplanned combination.

Iterate and Refine: One of the great things about using ChatGPT in the kitchen is that you can have a back-and-forth conversation.

The first idea it gives might not be exactly what you want, but you can refine your prompt or ask follow-up questions. Suppose ChatGPT's first suggestion sounds too complicated or you're missing one minor ingredient it assumed you have. You can reply with something like, *"That sounds good, but I actually don't have any cinnamon. Can I still make this, or is there a different idea using what I have?"* ChatGPT will typically adjust the recipe or offer an alternative. Maybe it will say you can omit the cinnamon, or it might propose a different dessert altogether.

For example, you might start with: *"I have frozen berries and yogurt. What dessert can I make?"* If ChatGPT suggests a berry yogurt parfait but you were in the mood for something frozen, you could clarify: *"Can I turn these into a frozen dessert instead?"* The AI might then pivot and guide you to blend the berries and yogurt into a simple frozen yogurt or smoothie bowl, perhaps telling you how to sweeten it a bit and freeze it for a quick sorbet-like treat.

Embrace Creativity: Some of the best ChatGPT dessert prompts are those where you just throw out a weird combination to see what happens. Don't be afraid to mention ingredients that you normally wouldn't combine. Maybe you have a jar of Nutella and a couple of wonton wrappers in your fridge – ChatGPT might suggest filling the wontons with Nutella and frying or baking them for impromptu chocolate pastries. Or you have a can of black beans and cocoa (yes, black bean brownies are a thing!), so it might generate a flourless brownie recipe. The AI can draw from diverse cuisines and recipe archives, so it sometimes offers ideas that mix and match culinary traditions. As a home cook, this can be a fun way to discover new desserts you wouldn't have tried otherwise.

For instance, one home cook asked ChatGPT to invent a dessert with just canned pumpkin, ginger, and milk. The AI came up with a spiced pumpkin pudding, combining those ingredients with a bit of creativity (suggesting a dash of cornstarch from the pantry to thicken, and a sprinkle of any spices on hand). The result was a silky pumpkin-ginger pudding that satisfied a sweet tooth and used up an otherwise puzzling set of ingredients. This kind of kitchen improvisation becomes much easier when you can bounce ideas off ChatGPT.

By using detailed prompts and an open mind, you'll find that "nothing to eat" often transforms into "maybe we can make dessert out of this!" Dessert on demand is about seizing the moment and trusting your AI helper to find the sweet possibility in your pantry. And once you've mastered prompting ChatGPT with what you have, even a sparse kitchen can turn into a source of delightful treats.

As you get comfortable creating desserts from thin air (or rather, from the back of your cupboard), you might run into situations where you *almost* have everything you need, but not quite. Maybe the recipe idea you got from ChatGPT calls for an egg and you're out, or you're baking for someone who can't have flour. Don't worry—that's where substitutions come in. With ChatGPT's help, missing ingredients or dietary restrictions don't have to derail your dessert plans. It can suggest alternatives so that "no eggs or no flour" is truly no problem at all.

NO EGGS, NO FLOUR, NO PROBLEM

Every home baker has faced this scenario: you're halfway through mixing a batter or you've got a craving to bake, and then you realize something essential is missing. No eggs in the carton, or the flour jar is nearly empty. Or maybe you're baking for a friend who's vegan or gluten-free and you need to adjust a recipe. In these moments, ChatGPT becomes an invaluable resource for finding substitutions. This section will show you how to prompt the AI for replacement ingredients and recipe tweaks so that "no eggs" or "no flour" doesn't stop you from making dessert.

Finding the Right Substitute: Let's start with a common emergency – you need eggs for a recipe and you have none. Instead of dashing to the store, you can ask ChatGPT for alternatives. For example: *"I'm making brownies but I just realized I have no eggs. What can I use instead of eggs in the recipe?"* This straightforward question lets the AI know the specific context (brownies, which need eggs for binding and moisture) and asks for a substitution. ChatGPT might respond with a list of egg replacers commonly used in baking: a flaxseed "egg" (ground flaxseed mixed with water), applesauce, mashed banana, yogurt, or even a commercial egg-replacer product if you have one. It could say something like, "For brownies, you can replace each egg with 1/4 cup of applesauce or 1/4 cup of mashed banana. If you have ground flaxseeds, mix 1 tablespoon of ground flax with 3 tablespoons of water for each egg and let it sit to gel – that works well as a binder."

This is incredibly helpful because not only do you get the substitute suggestion, but often ChatGPT will include the ratio or method to use it. You don't have to remember the exact measurements – the AI will remind you. If the recipe were something like cookies, ChatGPT might tailor its answer slightly (for a crispy cookie, it might suggest a different approach than for a fudgy brownie). The key is that by specifying what you're trying to make, the AI can give the best substitute for that situation.

Adapting to Dietary Needs: Now consider flour – perhaps you're out of all-purpose flour, or you want to bake a cake for someone who can't eat gluten. Try a prompt like: *"How can I bake chocolate chip cookies without any flour? I have oats and almond flour though."* In response, ChatGPT might offer a couple of solutions. It could propose using ground oats (oat flour) in place of regular flour, and might mention that adding a bit of almond flour could improve the texture. Or it might recall a classic flourless peanut butter cookie recipe (which typically uses just peanut butter, sugar, and an egg, for example) if it thinks you have those ingredients. If you specifically mention almond flour, the AI can give tips such as "almond flour can often substitute for regular flour at a 1:1 ratio by volume in cookies, but the texture will be softer and more crumbly; you might need an extra binding agent."

For a gluten-free adaptation, you could also prompt: *"I have a great muffin recipe but I need it to be gluten-free. What should I use instead of flour?"* ChatGPT might suggest a gluten-free all-purpose blend if available, or a mix of almond flour and a bit of tapioca starch to mimic the regular flour's properties. It could even recall specific proportions from known gluten-free recipes. The AI might warn you that gluten-free batters sometimes need an extra egg or a spoon of xanthan gum for binding – useful tips that save a lot of trial and error.

Substitutions for Dairy and Other Ingredients: Eggs and flour are big ones, but what about other common ingredients? ChatGPT can help there too. Imagine you're making a pudding and it calls for milk, but you only have almond milk on hand. You could ask: *"Can I use almond milk instead of regular milk in a pudding recipe?"* The AI is likely to respond with encouragement and perhaps a slight caution: yes, almond milk can work, though the pudding might be a bit thinner unless you use a thickener, since almond milk has less fat. It might suggest adding a teaspoon of cornstarch extra or using full-fat canned coconut milk if you have it for a creamier result. Essentially, ChatGPT will give you the confidence to use what you have – be it almond milk, soy milk, or even water with a bit of butter – and explain any trade-offs.

Another common scenario: no butter. Maybe you're in the middle of baking cookies and discover you're out of butter, or you're baking for someone who is dairy-free. A quick prompt such as *"What can I use instead of butter in cookies?"* will get ChatGPT listing options like vegetable oil or coconut oil (with a typical guideline like use 3/4 cup oil for 1 cup of butter since oil is 100% fat and butter is about 80% fat plus water). It might mention margarine or shortening as a direct 1:1 substitute, or even cream cheese or mashed avocado in some cases, depending on the recipe. You'll likely see notes about how each substitute affects the outcome – e.g., "cookies made with oil may spread more and be a bit greasier, but they'll still taste good," or "using applesauce instead of butter will make the cookies cakier and lower in fat." This kind of guidance helps you choose the best option from what's available and manage expectations on how the dessert might turn out.

Sugar is another ingredient you might need to substitute, either because you're out of one kind or for health reasons. Suppose you're out of white granulated sugar. You could ask: *"I have no white sugar –*

can I use brown sugar in a cake recipe instead?" ChatGPT would likely reassure you that brown sugar can work pretty well as a replacement in most cases, and it might add that the cake could come out a bit moister and darker in color due to the molasses in brown sugar. If you only have liquid sweeteners like honey or maple syrup, you might prompt: *"Can I substitute honey for sugar in this recipe, and how much should I use?"* Expect ChatGPT to tell you that you can, usually using a smaller amount of honey (since it's sweeter than sugar) and reducing other liquids slightly – for example, use about 3/4 cup of honey for 1 cup of sugar and cut a couple of tablespoons of other liquid in the recipe. The AI might also note that honey will make things brown faster, so you might need to bake at a slightly lower temperature or watch carefully. These are the kind of nuanced tips that you'd otherwise have to look up in various cookbooks or websites, but ChatGPT can consolidate them in one helpful answer, tailored to your situation.

Here's a quick list of some handy baking substitutions that ChatGPT can help you with at a moment's notice:

- **Eggs:** 1 egg ≈ 1/4 cup applesauce, or 1/2 a mashed banana, or 1 tablespoon ground flaxseed + 3 tablespoons water (mix to gel), or 1/4 cup yogurt. Ask ChatGPT which is best for your recipe type (cakes vs. cookies vs. brownies).
- **All-Purpose Flour:** Substitute by weight with oat flour (blend oats to a powder) or try almond flour (though recipes may need extra binding). ChatGPT can guide how to adjust recipes that are naturally flourless (like meringues or flourless chocolate cake) if you have the other necessary ingredients.
- **Milk:** Use equal amounts of non-dairy milk (almond, soy, oat milk) – the result may be slightly less rich, but usually it works fine. If you have dry milk powder, ChatGPT can tell you how to reconstitute it. No milk at all? It might suggest water with a bit of butter or cream to mimic milk's fat content.

- **Butter:** Use about 3/4 of the amount in oil (e.g., ~3/4 cup oil for 1 cup butter) for baking, or swap with margarine 1:1. In some recipes, coconut oil works well (solid at room temp like butter), and ChatGPT will remind you coconut oil might add a slight coconut flavor. For certain baked goods you can replace some of the butter with applesauce or nut butter to experiment with flavors.
- **Buttermilk:** Make your own by adding 1 tablespoon of vinegar or lemon juice to 1 cup of regular milk and letting it sit a few minutes. This is a classic tip ChatGPT often gives if you ask, "I don't have buttermilk – what do I do?"
- **Baking Powder/Soda:** If out of baking powder, use 1/4 teaspoon baking soda plus 1/2 teaspoon vinegar or lemon juice for each teaspoon needed. If you're out of baking soda but have baking powder, you can use about 2-3 times the amount of baking powder (though large amounts might affect taste slightly).

One neat aspect of using ChatGPT for substitutions is that it can adapt to multiple constraints at once. If you say, *"I want to bake brownies that are vegan and gluten-free – what substitutions do I need?"* you'll get a coordinated answer. It might suggest a known vegan, GF brownie recipe (using flax eggs and almond flour, for instance) or walk through replacing eggs, butter, and flour all in one go. It's like consulting a very knowledgeable cookbook that instantly cross-references all your needs.

Follow-Up Questions Welcome: Just as with creating a dessert from odd ingredients, don't hesitate to ask follow-ups when working with substitutions. If ChatGPT says, "use applesauce instead of eggs," and you're not sure how that integrates (do you mix it in at the same stage as eggs? do you need to adjust baking time?), you can ask: *"How do I add the applesauce – at the same time I would have added the eggs?"* The AI can clarify each step. It can also help troubleshoot if you're unsure about quantity: *"The recipe calls for 2 eggs, so do I use 1/2 cup of* *applesauce?"* and ChatGPT will confirm or adjust the advice accordingly.

By leveraging AI to solve these little kitchen dilemmas, you'll become a more flexible and confident baker. You'll start remembering some of your favorite substitutes, but you'll always have ChatGPT as backup in case you encounter a new situation (like "can I use jelly instead of sugar?" – an actual question someone might have when really improvising!). With no ingredient truly indispensable, you can forge ahead with dessert-making even when your pantry is seemingly lacking.

After tackling ingredient swaps and substitutions, you might be curious about saving another precious resource: time. After all, what about those moments when you want something sweet *right now*? ChatGPT can help you whip up treats in record time – perfect for late-night cravings or surprise guests – proving that even on short notice, a sweet fix is within reach.

QUICK FIXES FOR A SWEET TOOTH

Some cravings just can't wait. It's late in the evening, or you're just not in the mood for an hour of baking – you want something sweet *now*. The good news is that ChatGPT can come to the rescue with super-fast dessert ideas. In this section, we'll focus on prompts that yield treats you can whip up in around 10 minutes or less, including no-bake delights perfect for those late-night indulgences. These are the kind of desserts that satisfy your sweet tooth without a long wait or a lot of fuss.

When Time Is of the Essence: Let's set the scene: it's 10:30 PM, the kitchen is mostly clean from dinner, and suddenly you're prowling the pantry for a quick sweet fix. Instead of resorting to plain chocolate chips straight from the bag (we've all been there), you can ask ChatGPT for a speedy dessert solution. Try prompting with something like: *"I'm craving dessert but I only have about 10 minutes and I don't want to use the oven. What quick sweet treat can I make?"* This prompt clearly states your time limit and the no-bake requirement.

ChatGPT might respond with a few ideas. A very common suggestion is a **microwave mug cake** – essentially a single serving of cake batter mixed in a coffee mug and "baked" in the microwave in about a minute or two. The AI could give you a simple recipe: for example, mix 4 tablespoons of flour, 2 tablespoons of sugar, 2 tablespoons of cocoa powder, a pinch of baking powder, 3 tablespoons of milk (or water), 2 tablespoons of oil, and maybe a drop of vanilla right in a mug; then microwave for around 90 seconds. Voila – a warm, chocolatey cake for one, ready in no time.

ChatGPT might also mention variations: if you don't have cocoa powder, make a vanilla mug cake by leaving it out and adding a bit of extra vanilla and a spoon of milk powder or just accept a lighter-colored cake. If you have some peanut butter, it might suggest swirling a spoonful into the batter for a peanut butter chocolate mug cake. The beauty of asking the AI is that it can adjust the base idea to whatever you have. The first time you try a mug cake, it feels a bit like kitchen magic – and with ChatGPT's guidance, you'll get the proportions right without having to look up a recipe in a book.

No-Bake and Minimal Effort Treats: Another category of quick desserts involves no baking at all – often just mixing or assembling a few ingredients. For example, you could prompt: *"Give me an idea for a no-bake dessert I can make in 5 or 10 minutes. I have peanut butter, oats, and honey on hand."* ChatGPT will likely suggest something like **no-bake peanut butter oat cookies** or energy balls. It might instruct: mix peanut butter, oats, and honey (and a little cocoa powder if you crave chocolate) into a dough, roll it into balls and chill them briefly (or if you can't wait, just eat them as chewy bites). You'll have a sweet, satisfying treat with the flavors of a peanut butter cookie, made in minutes and with zero baking. If you mention you have chocolate, the AI might instead guide you to melt the chocolate and stir in the oats and peanut butter to make quick **chocolate peanut butter clusters** spooned out onto wax paper to set.

Consider another scenario: you have some yogurt and fruit, and you want a dessert that feels a bit more special than just eating them separately. You can ask: *"What dessert can I make with yogurt and berries in just a few minutes?"* ChatGPT could suggest a layered **fruit and yogurt parfait.** It might tell you to alternate layers of yogurt, berries, and something crunchy like granola or crumbled cookies in a glass. In 5 minutes, you have a dessert that looks pretty and feels like a treat – no cooking required at all. If you have a bit of whipped cream or mint sprig to top it off, the AI might even throw that idea in to make it feel fancy.

Late-Night Cravings and Single Servings: When it's late at night, you probably don't want a huge batch of dessert (and you definitely don't want a sink full of dishes). ChatGPT can help you make *just enough* to satisfy the craving. Try a prompt like: *"I want a single-serving dessert because it's late and I don't want leftovers. What can I make quickly for one person?"* Besides the mug cake mentioned above, ChatGPT may propose a quick **microwave brownie in a mug** (similar concept, slightly different ratios for a denser, fudgier result). Or it might suggest something like a **one-minute cookie:** mixing a few spoonfuls of flour, sugar, a dab of butter (or oil) and a bit of water in a small bowl, pressing it into a cookie shape and microwaving for 40-50 seconds. It won't be golden brown like an oven-baked cookie, but it can be surprisingly cookie-like and definitely cures the cookie craving fast.

Another late-night idea ChatGPT might give is **banana "nice cream"**, especially if you mention you have a ripe or frozen banana. For instance: *"It's late and I want ice cream but have none. I have a banana though. Any ideas?"* The AI could walk you through making a quick banana ice cream by mashing a ripe banana and mixing it with a spoon of peanut butter and a dash of milk, then freezing it for just a little bit (or if it's already a frozen banana, blending it until smooth). In a few minutes, you get a creamy, soft-serve-like dessert that feels indulgent but is basically just fruit – a neat trick for a sweet tooth. If you have cocoa powder, ChatGPT might suggest adding that for a chocolate banana ice cream. Because it's smart about ingredients, it might also say: if you have a blender or food processor, use that for a better ice-cream consistency; if not, just do a hand-mashed version which will be more like a pudding but still yummy.

Leveraging Store-Bought Stuff Creatively: Quick desserts often mean remixing things you might already have that are ready-to-eat. Don't be shy to tell ChatGPT about any store-bought items in your kitchen that could be part of a dessert. For example: *"I have vanilla ice cream in the freezer and some instant coffee. Can I make a quick dessert with these?"* You might get the suggestion of an **affogato**, which is an Italian dessert where you pour a shot of espresso (or in our case, strong instant coffee) over a scoop of ice cream. It's dead simple but feels elegant. Or say you have graham crackers, chocolate, and marshmallows – the AI may very well guide you to make **microwave s'mores** (stacking them and zapping for a few seconds to melt the chocolate and marshmallow). If you mention just marshmallows and no chocolate, it could suggest making marshmallow cereal treats by melting them with a bit of butter and tossing in any kind of cereal to set into bars (a riff on the classic Rice Krispies treats, adaptable to what you have).

By including brand names or packaged foods in your prompt, you'll see that ChatGPT can incorporate them. *"I have half a pack of Oreos – what can I do for a quick dessert?"* might lead to a suggestion like crushing them and mixing with a little melted butter to press into a mini pie crust, then filling with that yogurt or ice cream we talked about for an instant pie. Or it could be as simple as sandwiching some peanut butter between Oreo cookies and chilling them as a makeshift cookie sandwich.

Prompt for Multiple Ideas: If you're not sure what you're craving exactly, you can ask ChatGPT for a list. Try something like: *"Give me three ideas for a dessert I can make in under 10 minutes with no baking."* The AI might list, for example: 1) a fruit and yogurt parfait, 2) chocolate-dipped fruit (like strawberries or pretzels if you have them – just melt chocolate, dip, and let set for a minute), and 3) a quick mug brownie. This way you get a menu of options to choose from. You can then pick one and say, "Great, how do I make that chocolate-dipped fruit?" and ChatGPT will then give you the steps. This iterative approach – first brainstorming, then drilling down – works especially well when you know your constraint (quick/no-bake) but you're open-minded about the actual treat.

These quick-fix desserts show that with ChatGPT's help, you never have to go to bed without dessert if you want one. From a warm mug cake to a cool yogurt parfait, there's an instant gratification sweet for any mood. And importantly, you'll learn techniques that you can reuse: once you've made a 5-minute mug cake with AI's guidance, you'll remember the gist for next time (though ChatGPT will be there if you forget the exact amounts).

Many home cooks want to indulge their sweet tooth without loading up on sugar. The good news is, ChatGPT can help satisfy your sweet cravings while cutting down on the sugar – showing that you can have low-sugar treats that still delight your taste buds just as much.

LOW-SUGAR, HIGH-SATISFACTION

Dessert doesn't have to mean *sugar overload.* Many of us love a sweet treat but are trying to cut back on sugar for health or personal preference. The challenge is making desserts that still taste rich and satisfying, even when the sugar is reduced. ChatGPT can be your ally here, suggesting clever ways to sweeten naturally, use alternative ingredients, and adjust recipes to maintain delicious flavor and texture with less sugar. In this section, we'll explore how to prompt ChatGPT for lower-sugar desserts that don't skimp on enjoyment.

Healthier Sweet Tooth Cravings: Suppose you're in the mood for something sweet but want to keep it light on sugar. You might prompt ChatGPT with: *"I'm looking for a dessert idea that uses very little sugar or only natural sweeteners. What can I make?"* With a query like this, the AI might propose options such as baked apples with cinnamon (where the sweetness comes mostly from the fruit itself), a yogurt-based dessert with berries and a drizzle of honey (just a small amount of added sugar), or perhaps oatmeal cookies sweetened with mashed bananas instead of cups of sugar. For example, ChatGPT might describe a simple recipe for **banana oat cookies:** mash a ripe banana, mix it with a cup of oats, a dash of cinnamon and a handful of raisins or nuts, then bake spoonfuls of that mixture. The banana and raisins provide natural sweetness, and you end up with cookie-like bites that have no processed sugar at all. If you prompt for it, the AI can give you exact oven temperature and timing (say, bake at 350°F for about 12-15 minutes) – all the details needed to actually make the recipe.

Another idea ChatGPT often suggests for a low-sugar sweet fix is a **fruit parfait or smoothie** that relies on the fruit's sweetness. If you ask for a dessert with no added sugar, you might get something like a blended frozen mango smoothie (mango is quite sweet on its own) topped with a dollop of unsweetened whipped cream, or a bowl of mixed berries with a splash of vanilla and a spoonful of whipped ricotta cheese, which tastes creamy and indulgent without needing sugar. The key is that the AI can highlight ingredients that naturally satisfy our sweet tooth – fruits, dairy, spices – so that you can enjoy dessert without dumping in sugar.

Using Sugar Substitutes and Alternatives: Perhaps you want to remake a favorite dessert in a healthier way. ChatGPT can help you figure out how to replace refined sugar with alternatives like honey, maple syrup, or even zero-calorie sweeteners. Imagine you have a great muffin recipe that calls for a cup of sugar, and you want to cut that down. You could prompt: *"How can I reduce the sugar in this muffin recipe? It calls for 1 cup of sugar – what if I only use 1/2 cup? Do I need to add anything to replace the missing sweetness or moisture?"* The AI could respond with a nuanced answer: maybe suggesting that with half the sugar, the muffins will be less tender (since sugar helps retain moisture), so you might add an extra spoonful of milk or some applesauce to keep them moist. It might also mention that you can boost flavor with spices like cinnamon or vanilla to make the muffins taste sweeter without actually adding sugar. In testing that prompt, you might see ChatGPT walk through the considerations: "Using 1/2 cup sugar instead of 1 cup will definitely reduce the sweetness. You could compensate by adding 1/4 cup of applesauce for moisture and natural sweetness. Also, add a bit more cinnamon and a teaspoon of vanilla extract – those will enhance the perception of sweetness. Your muffins will be a little lighter in color and might not caramelize as much on top, but they should still be tasty and moist."

If you're considering sugar substitutes like stevia or erythritol, ChatGPT can guide you on using them (for example, noting that a specific stevia blend might replace sugar 1:1, or that pure stevia requires only a tiny amount and some recipe adjustments for texture). For instance, you might ask: *"Can I use stevia or erythritol to bake a cake instead of sugar?"* ChatGPT will likely explain that yes, you can, but results may vary. It might caution that some sweeteners like pure stevia are much sweeter than sugar, so you'd use far less and might need to add extra bulk (like more flour or applesauce) since sugar provides structure and moisture. Or it might recommend using a baking blend (some products mix stevia with bulking agents to measure similarly to sugar) for simplicity. It could also mention the aftertaste some substitutes have, so you're prepared.

Maintaining Flavor and Texture: One worry when reducing sugar is that the dessert won't taste as good or have the same mouthfeel. Sugar does more than sweeten – it helps with browning, moisture, and even the thickness of things like custards. ChatGPT can help you navigate these issues. For instance, you could ask: *"I want to make chocolate chip cookies with less sugar. How will it affect them, and can I do anything so they still come out chewy?"* The AI might explain that less sugar will make the cookies spread less and they may be more cake-like. It could then suggest using a touch more butter or a tablespoon of honey to encourage browning and chewiness even with reduced granulated sugar. Or perhaps it will recommend forming the cookies smaller and flattening them a bit before baking to help them spread since the sugar isn't there to do it. These are the kind of practical tips that ensure your lower-sugar experiment still yields a treat that's enjoyable.

Often, ChatGPT will remind you about the power of **spices and flavorings** when you cut sugar. It might say, "Add a bit of almond extract to those cookies – it gives an impression of sweetness and richness, so you won't miss the sugar as much," or "Consider adding orange zest to your low-sugar cake; the fruity aroma can make the cake seem sweeter." By incorporating such advice into your recipe, you learn ways to maximize flavor. In our prompt about low-sugar chocolate chip cookies, for example, ChatGPT might mention using a darker chocolate (which actually has less sugar than milk chocolate) so each bite has intense chocolate flavor, making the overall cookie taste more satisfying even if the dough is less sweet. Or it may propose adding nuts or a pinch of salt on top to create a sweet-salty contrast, enhancing the perception of sweetness.

Examples of Low-Sugar Desserts: If you ask ChatGPT directly for recipe suggestions, you can specify your sugar goal. Try something like: *"Suggest a dessert recipe with no refined sugar. I don't mind natural sweetness from fruit."* The AI may give you an idea like **date-sweetened brownies** (using pureed dates in place of sugar, which gives a rich sweetness along with fiber and nutrients). It could also suggest a classic **chia seed pudding** where you soak chia seeds in milk (or almond milk) with vanilla and just a touch of sweetener or mashed fruit – by morning, it's thick like a pudding and you can top it with berries. That dessert can easily be low-sugar by relying on the fruit topping and maybe a few drops of stevia or a spoon of honey for the whole batch. Another option might be **baked pears or peaches:** roasting fruit concentrates its natural sugars, and ChatGPT might instruct you to sprinkle a little cinnamon and just a teaspoon of honey or a pat of butter on a halved peach and bake it until soft and caramelized. The result tastes like pie filling but without the crust and heavy sugar.

For a no-added-sugar treat, the AI might go as simple as suggesting frozen grapes or a fruit salad with a squeeze of lime and mint – incredibly straightforward, but sometimes we forget how satisfying fresh fruit can be as a dessert until an "assistant" reminds us. On the slightly more elaborate side, it might propose something like blending Greek yogurt with a bit of honey and freezing it to make a quick frozen yogurt, or making a crustless pumpkin pie custard sweetened with maple syrup. The level of complexity is up to you – you can always specify, "give me something very easy and low-sugar," versus, "I don't mind a longer recipe as long as it's healthy," and ChatGPT will tailor its suggestion.

Learning to Adjust Sweetness with AI's Help: Over time, using ChatGPT for these tips can train your own instincts too. You'll start to remember tricks like adding fruit puree or yogurt to keep things moist when sugar is reduced, or boosting spices when sweetness is low. But whenever you're unsure, you can run your idea by the AI. Say you're inventing a recipe yourself – "I want to create a banana bread with half the sugar; here's what I'm thinking of doing [and you list your planned ingredients]. Do you think it will work?" – and ChatGPT can evaluate and give feedback, almost like a baking coach. It might say, "That looks good overall. With only half the sugar, I'd increase the banana by one for more sweetness and maybe add an extra egg to keep it tender. Also, don't expect it to brown as much, but that's okay."

Using ChatGPT in this way not only gives you recipes to follow, but also teaches you the science behind sweets. You become more confident creating or tweaking desserts on your own, knowing you have a safety net of advice. And most importantly, you'll have a roster of go-to treats that satisfy your cravings without derailing your goals. Just because something is low-sugar doesn't mean it has to be boring! This is a great opportunity to tap into ChatGPT's creativity in combining flavors and textures, helping you dream up desserts that are not only healthier or faster, but also more inventive in taste and mouthfeel.

FLAVOR PAIRING AND TEXTURAL PLAY

Cooking is as much an art as a science, and desserts are a perfect playground for creativity. One way to take your desserts from good to unforgettable is by combining flavors and textures in interesting ways. Sweet with salty, creamy with crunchy, fruity with a hint of savory – these contrasts make each bite exciting. In this section, we'll see how ChatGPT can act like your personal flavor consultant. By asking the right prompts, you can get ideas for inventive dessert combos that balance different tastes and textures, bringing a professional chef's flair into your home kitchen.

Exploring New Flavor Matches: If you've ever wondered "What flavors go well together?" you can literally ask ChatGPT that. For example: *"I'm thinking of making a dessert with chocolate, but I want to add a surprising flavor twist. Any suggestions?"* The AI might deep dive into its culinary knowledge and suggest pairings like chocolate with a pinch of chili pepper (for a Mexican chocolate vibe), chocolate with sea salt and olive oil (if you're feeling adventurous and gourmet), or chocolate with citrus zest for brightness. It could even propose more unusual ideas like infusing the chocolate dessert with Earl Grey tea or lavender. The beauty here is that ChatGPT can surface combinations that are tried-and-true (like chocolate and peanut butter – not surprising but always good) and also some that are lesser-known but delightful. If something like "olive oil in chocolate dessert" catches you off guard, you can always follow up: "How would I use olive oil with chocolate in a dessert?" and ChatGPT might describe drizzling a good olive oil and flaky salt over chocolate mousse or brownies to bring out the flavor.

You can prompt ChatGPT for specific pairings too. Say you have a flavor in mind and want to find it a partner: *"What fruit would pair well with ginger in a dessert?"* You're likely to get answers like pear (a classic combo with ginger), pineapple (for a tropical zing), or even things like peaches or oranges. The AI might explain, "Ginger adds warmth and a bit of spice, so it goes nicely with fruits that are sweet and slightly tangy. Pears or apples baked with ginger are lovely in a crumble, or you could do pineapple with ginger syrup for a tropical dessert." This gives you not just a pairing, but also an idea of the form the dessert could take. Another example: *"I want to use rosemary in a dessert – what would taste good with it?"* ChatGPT could suggest lemon (rosemary lemon shortbread cookies are amazing), or perhaps strawberries (a rosemary-infused syrup over strawberries and cream), or even chocolate (less common, but rosemary can work with dark chocolate in small amounts for a sophisticated twist).

Balancing Sweet and Salty: Many modern desserts play with sweet-salty balance – think salted caramel everything. You can use ChatGPT to brainstorm how to add a salty element to a sweet dessert. For instance: *"Give me an idea for a dessert that combines something sweet and something salty."* The AI might come back with suggestions like salted caramel brownies (sweet chocolate and caramel with flaky salt on top), pretzel-crust cheesecake (a buttery, salty pretzel base under a sweet cheesecake), or even bacon maple cupcakes (if you're open to meat in dessert, the salty smoky bacon contrasts with sweet maple syrup – an indulgence some people love). If one of these catches your interest, you can then ask for the recipe or more details: "That pretzel-crust cheesecake sounds great – how do I make the crust?" and ChatGPT will happily provide the steps (crushing pretzels with butter and a bit of sugar, for example).

Even without diving into a full recipe, ChatGPT can suggest quick sweet-salty touches. You could ask: *"What salty topping can I add to my vanilla ice cream to make it more interesting?"* You might get answers like crumbled potato chips (yes, really – it's an addictive sweet-salty crunch!), salted nuts, or a sprinkle of coarse sea salt with a drizzle of olive oil (again, trust the foodies on this one, it's a thing!). By experimenting with these ideas, you turn a plain dessert into something with a gourmet feel, and it's as simple as sprinkling a bit of salt or crunch on top.

Texture: Crunchy, Gooey, Creamy, Chewy: Flavor is one dimension of dessert; texture is another that can bring big enjoyment. ChatGPT can help you introduce a missing texture to a dessert. For example, you could say: *"I have a creamy pudding for dessert, but I feel it needs some crunch. What can I add?"* The AI might suggest easy fixes like crushed cookies or granola on top, candied nuts, or even a bruléed sugar topping (if you have a kitchen torch or can put it under a broiler briefly, like the top of a crème brûlée). It could also get creative and suggest something like a sprinkle of popped quinoa or toasted coconut flakes – things you might not think of offhand.

If you start with a texture idea, ChatGPT can build a dessert around it. *"I want a dessert that has both a crispy element and a gooey element. Any suggestions?"* A prompt like this could yield ideas such as s'mores bars (crisp graham cracker layers with gooey marshmallow and chocolate in between), churros with chocolate sauce (crunchy fried dough to dip in a gooey sauce), or a classic baked Alaska (toasted crisp meringue outside with cold ice cream and soft cake inside – giving hot, cold, soft, and crisp all at once). Another idea the AI might give is a skillet cookie (cookie dough baked in a cast iron skillet so it's crispy at the edges and gooey in the middle, often served with ice cream on top – which adds cold and creamy to the mix too).

The key is that you can describe what experience you want – *"I want something chewy and fruity"* or *"I want a dessert that's light and fluffy but also has a little crunch"* – and ChatGPT will try to figure out a dessert that matches that description. For "chewy and fruity," maybe it suggests raspberry mochi bites or apricot oat bars. For "light and fluffy with crunch," perhaps a meringue with nuts or a soufflé with a crispy topping. It's like having a pastry chef to bounce ideas off of; you supply the adjectives, and the AI supplies the concept.

Mixing in Savory or Unusual Ingredients: Some of the most memorable desserts incorporate a touch of the unexpected – an herb, a spice, even a vegetable (carrot cake and zucchini bread have long proven that veggies can shine in sweets). If you're curious about using an unconventional ingredient, go ahead and ask ChatGPT. *"Can I use basil in a dessert? What would that look like?"* might lead to the suggestion of strawberry basil sorbet or basil-infused panna cotta with a strawberry sauce. *"What's a dessert that uses cheese in a sweet way?"* could bring up ideas like a ricotta-based cheesecake (ricotta is cheese after all) or a simple pairing of fresh figs with honey and a slice of parmesan (an Italian-style minimalist dessert), or even cheddar baked into an apple pie crust (a tradition in some regions). By asking the AI these offbeat questions, you tap into a wealth of culinary tradition and innovation. You might not have thought to put black pepper in cookies, but if you ask about unusual spices in dessert, ChatGPT could recall that a pinch of black pepper or cayenne can actually accentuate chocolate or fruit flavors.

One user asked ChatGPT for a dessert that was "sweet, spicy, and fruity all at once," and got the suggestion of mango slices sprinkled with a tiny bit of chili powder and a squeeze of lime – a simple treat inspired by Mexican street snacks. Another time, someone wanted to use miso (a savory fermented soybean paste) in a dessert, and ChatGPT suggested making a miso caramel sauce to drizzle over vanilla ice cream (miso caramel is a trendy twist that gives a salty, deep complexity to the sweetness). These are the kinds of ideas that can really impress if you serve them, and they're accessible thanks to a little prompting and an open mind.

From Idea to Implementation: When ChatGPT gives you a cool flavor or texture idea, it doesn't leave you hanging. You can always follow up for the how-to. If it says "try a rosemary lemon cake with a crunchy almond topping," and that intrigues you, your next prompt could be, "Great, can you give me a recipe or steps for a rosemary lemon cake with almond topping?" And you'll get a step-by-step game plan. In this way, flavor brainstorming seamlessly transitions to actual cooking. You don't have to know how to execute an unusual idea – you just have to ask, and the AI will guide you.

This approach of starting with a sensory idea (like a flavor combo or texture contrast) can really expand your baking repertoire. It encourages you to think beyond the standard recipes and have fun, while still having the safety net of ChatGPT's knowledge to make sure it works.

With a notebook (or app) full of exciting dessert ideas, the next step is actually bringing them to life. But what if you're not very experienced in the kitchen? No worries – ChatGPT can boost your confidence in baking even if you're a complete beginner. From explaining techniques to adjusting oven temperatures, your AI kitchen companion will guide you so you can turn those creative ideas into delicious reality.

BAKING WITH CONFIDENCE (EVEN IF YOU DON'T BAKE)

Not everyone grew up baking cookies or feels at home with an oven – and that's okay. ChatGPT can be like a patient tutor by your side, guiding you through recipes and techniques one step at a time. Whether you're unsure how to measure ingredients, need to convert temperatures, or want a clear explanation of a confusing instruction, this AI assistant can boost your confidence. In this section, we'll see how to use ChatGPT to demystify baking, so you can tackle dessert recipes even if you've never considered yourself a "baker."

Step-by-Step Guidance: One of the most helpful ways to use ChatGPT is to literally have it walk you through a recipe. For instance, you might say: *"I've never baked brownies before. Can you guide me step by step through a simple brownie recipe?"* ChatGPT will not only provide a recipe, but it can break it down into very clear stages. The response might start by listing the ingredients you'll need, then move on to step 1: preheat the oven to a certain temperature, step 2: melt butter and chocolate together (with tips like using a microwave or double boiler), step 3: stir in sugar, then eggs one at a time, and so on. Each step can be as detailed as you need – you can even prompt, *"Explain it to me like I'm a complete beginner who doesn't know baking terms."* In that case, if the recipe says "fold in the flour," ChatGPT would clarify: "This means gently stirring the flour into the batter using a spatula, turning the mixture over itself rather than beating or whisking. It helps keep the batter airy."

Having such granular guidance is like having a cookbook that anticipates your questions. You don't have to feel embarrassed for not knowing something; you just ask. Suppose you're in the middle of a recipe and something isn't clear. You encounter: "cream the butter and sugar until light and fluffy" – a very common phrase in baking. If you're not sure how to do that, you can pause and ask ChatGPT: *"What does it mean to cream butter and sugar, and how do I know I've done it right?"* The AI would explain that creaming means beating the butter and sugar together (with an electric mixer or by hand with a wooden spoon) until the mixture turns pale, fluffy, and increases in volume a bit. It might give you an estimate of time ("about 2-3 minutes with a mixer, longer by hand") and a visual cue ("it should look almost like frosting and you shouldn't see individual grains of sugar as much"). With that kind of answer, you can return to your bowl and carry on with more confidence.

Conversions and Measurements Made Easy: Baking often involves numbers and units that can trip people up, especially if you're dealing with recipes from different countries or an unfamiliar scale. ChatGPT is excellent for on-the-fly conversions. For example, you have a British recipe that calls for a "gas mark 4" oven or 180°C, but your oven is in Fahrenheit. Just ask: *"What is 180 degrees Celsius in Fahrenheit for baking?"* You'll get the answer (which is about 356°F, usually rounded to 350°F for practical purposes). Or you might find a recipe that gives flour in grams but you only have measuring cups. You could prompt: *"How many cups is 300 grams of flour?"* and ChatGPT will provide an approximation (around 2.5 cups, though it might note that exact conversion can vary based on flour type and how you scoop). This saves you from either doing math by hand or searching the internet – it's all right there in the chat.

Another common need is scaling recipes. Maybe you have a recipe for 24 cupcakes but you only want to make 12. Try asking: *"Can you help me halve this cupcake recipe that uses 3 cups of flour, 2 cups of sugar, etc...?"* ChatGPT can list the halved ingredient amounts (like 1.5 cups flour, 1 cup sugar, and so on). It can also warn you about any tricky parts of scaling down – for instance, if the original calls for 1 egg, halving is awkward, but the AI might suggest using just 1 egg (since 0.5 egg is impractical) and perhaps a touch less flour to balance, or using an egg substitute for the half. It's like having a knowledgeable friend double-check your math and logic.

Even equipment size conversions are within reach. If a recipe is for a 9-inch round cake pan and you only have an 8-inch, you could ask: *"I have an 8-inch round pan but the recipe calls for a 9-inch pan. How should I adjust?"* ChatGPT might tell you that an 8-inch pan will make the batter deeper, so you should either not fill it all the way (and maybe make a cupcake or two with extra batter) or bake a little longer at a slightly lower temperature to ensure the center cooks through without burning the top. These are the little pieces of practical wisdom that can prevent mishaps.

Technique Basics and Troubleshooting: For a beginner, recipes sometimes assume you know techniques. ChatGPT can fill in those blanks anytime. If you're unsure how to separate egg yolks from whites, you can ask and get a quick tutorial (perhaps recommending the shell-to-shell method or using clean hands to let the white slip through your fingers, along with a note to be careful not to get yolk in the whites if you plan to whip them). If you don't know how to tell when a cheesecake is done (a bit jiggly in the center is okay, it will set as it cools – something not all recipes clearly say), you can inquire, and the AI will explain it.

Troubleshooting is another area where ChatGPT shines, even after the fact. Let's say you attempted a cake and it came out dense or it sank in the middle. You could describe what happened: *"My cake sank in the middle after I took it out of the oven. What might have caused that?"* ChatGPT can list common reasons: perhaps the cake was underbaked (needed a few more minutes), or the batter was over-mixed (developing too much gluten, leading to collapse), or maybe too much leavening was used causing it to rise fast and fall. It might then give you tips to avoid it next time, like checking doneness with a toothpick or opening the oven door more gently. While this is advice for the future, it's comforting and educational to diagnose kitchen hiccups so you can improve.

Even during a recipe, if something looks off – "My cookie dough seems much wetter than usual, is that okay?" – you can ask ChatGPT. It might ask back what ratio you used, or it might guess that maybe butter was too warm and suggest chilling the dough before baking to prevent cookies from spreading too much. These mid-course corrections can save a recipe from failure. It's similar to having a baking forum at your fingertips, but faster and personalized.

Encouragement and Confidence-Building: Beyond just facts and steps, ChatGPT can provide moral support. Baking can be stressful when you're unsure. If you express worry, like *"I'm nervous about rolling out pie dough, it always breaks. Any advice?"* – you might get both practical tips (like chill your dough, roll from the center out, keep it moving so it doesn't stick) and encouragement (like "It's okay if it breaks, you can patch it in the pie dish and it will still bake up delicious!"). The tone of the AI is generally patient and positive (after all, it has infinite patience), which can make a big difference. Sometimes just hearing "You've got this!" or "This part is tricky for many people, take your time," even from an AI, is the little boost you need to keep going.

Another great use of ChatGPT for confidence is practicing mentally before doing it physically. For example, *"What should I expect when I'm making caramel? How do I not burn it?"* The AI can walk you through the sensory cues: caramel starts as sugar and water, it will bubble, then turn golden – "when you see an amber color and smell a nutty aroma, take it off the heat." Knowing that ahead of time keeps you calmer during the real thing. It's like being briefed by a coach before you perform.

By continuously asking questions and getting answers, you'll find that over time you're learning a ton. Eventually, things like creaming butter or knowing how to measure flour correctly (ChatGPT will tell you: spoon and level, don't scoop and pack it tightly, to avoid using too much) become second nature. And the next time someone asks *you* how to do something, you might just know the answer – thanks to your AI baking mentor.

At this point, we've covered everything from spontaneous dessert ideas to advanced baking help. You've gathered a wealth of tips, prompts, and recipes throughout this chapter. To make it even easier, our final section is a "dessert prompt bank" – a collection of sample prompts ready for you to use whenever you need inspiration based on common pantry ingredients. Consider it your cheat sheet for sweet success. Let's dive in and wrap up this chapter with a handy dessert prompt bank to put everything we've learned into practice.

PROMPT BANK: DESSERT EDITION

Sometimes you just need a little inspiration to get started. Below is a "prompt bank" of example questions you can ask ChatGPT, all centered around common ingredients that many of us have in the pantry or fridge. These are designed to spark ideas – feel free to use them exactly or tweak them based on what you have. By now, you've seen how ChatGPT responds, so you know you can always follow up with more details or constraints. Think of these prompts as templates for turning whatever ingredients you have into a delicious dessert.

Oats: If you have a tub of oats sitting around, there's so much more than just oatmeal cookies or porridge. For example, you could ask ChatGPT: *"I have a lot of oats and want a dessert that isn't just oatmeal cookies. What creative dessert can I make with oats?"* This might prompt the AI to suggest something like homemade granola bars, oat-and-fruit crumble bars, or even a no-bake oatmeal chocolate fudge square, using oats as the base for a sweet treat. Another great oats-based query could be: *"I only have oats, peanut butter, and honey—no flour or eggs. Any simple dessert I can make with these?"* With that, ChatGPT would likely outline a no-bake peanut butter oat ball recipe or no-bake cookies where you stir together those ingredients (maybe with a touch of cocoa if you have it) and let them set. In short, oats can become everything from a crust to a candy-like bite, and a good prompt will get those ideas flowing.

Bananas: Overripe bananas are practically begging to be turned into dessert. You can try a prompt like: *"I have a couple of overripe bananas but I'm tired of banana bread. What else can I make for dessert?"* ChatGPT might inspire you with banana ice cream (blending frozen bananas into "nice cream"), banana-oat cookies (perhaps with just banana, oats, and a bit of cocoa or nuts, baked until set), or even a banana fritter or caramelized banana topping to serve over yogurt or ice cream. Another handy prompt: *"I have one ripe banana and a sweet tooth. What single-serving dessert can I make in 10 minutes?"* Expect an idea like a quick banana mug cake (mix mashed banana with a few spoonfuls of flour, sugar, and baking powder and microwave it) or sautéed banana slices with a drizzle of honey and cinnamon (instant banana dessert!). Bananas bring natural sweetness and moisture, so ChatGPT often leverages them as a sugar substitute or binder in desserts.

Chocolate: Who doesn't have some form of chocolate around?

For those times when a chocolate craving strikes, you can ask: *"All I have is a bar of chocolate (or some cocoa powder). What dessert can I make with minimal other ingredients?"* The AI might suggest melting your chocolate and mixing it with whatever you have—say, stirring in crushed nuts or cereal to make chocolate bark or clusters. If you specify cocoa powder, you might get a simple chocolate pudding recipe (cocoa, milk, a bit of cornstarch, sugar) or the ever-popular microwave chocolate mug cake which only needs basic staples. Another prompt could be: *"I want a creative chocolate dessert with a twist. Any ideas using a common spice or ingredient from the pantry?"* Here, ChatGPT might introduce you to ideas like chili chocolate brownies (a pinch of cayenne in the batter) or chocolate-covered pretzels (combining that sweet and salty we discussed). Even if it's just a plain chocolate bar, the AI might tell you how to make a quick ganache (by mixing chocolate with heated cream or even coconut milk) and use it to dress up fruit or cookies. Chocolate is a versatile star, and a quick prompt can unleash many indulgent possibilities.

Peanut Butter: A jar of peanut butter can be the starting point for countless easy desserts. Try asking something like: *"What dessert can I make with peanut butter that doesn't require an oven?"* ChatGPT might return with suggestions like peanut butter freezer fudge (mix PB with a touch of coconut oil and honey, freeze it), or no-bake peanut butter cookies (often oats, peanut butter, and sugar or honey mixed and chilled), or even a peanut butter banana smoothie you can call dessert. Another prompt angle: *"I love peanut butter and chocolate. What's a quick dessert I can make with those and maybe some cereal or oats?"* This could lead to ideas such as chocolate peanut butter cereal bars (think homemade "Rice Krispie treats" but with peanut butter and chocolate in the mix), or peanut butter chocolate popcorn (drizzling a melted PB-chocolate mixture over popcorn and letting it harden for a sweet-salty snack). Peanut butter is great for binding ingredients, so ChatGPT often uses it in no-bake recipes or as a flavor booster in simple baked goods.

Yogurt: You might not think of plain yogurt as dessert, but it can be a secret weapon for light, tangy sweets. Consider prompting: *"I* *have plain Greek yogurt. How can I turn it into a dessert?"* The AI might suggest a yogurt parfait layered with fruit and a bit of granola or crushed cookies, transforming breakfast ingredients into dessert. Or it might give you a recipe for yogurt panna cotta or frozen yogurt bark (spread yogurt on a tray, swirl in honey and fruits, then freeze and break into pieces). If you mention you want something healthy, ChatGPT could propose mixing the yogurt with a spoonful of peanut butter and cocoa to make a protein-rich "chocolate mousse," or simply sweetening it with honey and topping with cinnamon for a faux cheesecake flavor. Another example prompt: *"Can I bake with yogurt? I have vanilla yogurt—any simple dessert recipe for that?"* You might receive a suggestion for yogurt cake (there's a classic French yogurt cake recipe where the yogurt does wonders for moisture), or muffins that use yogurt in the batter. Yogurt adds moisture and a slight tang, and the AI knows lots of tricks to use it in everything from frozen treats to baked goods.

These sample prompts are just a starting point. Feel free to mix and match ingredients in your queries, or add more details like dietary needs (*"What dessert can I make with oats and peanut butter that's vegan?"*) or time constraints (*"...in under 15 minutes"*). The power of ChatGPT is that it can handle multiple elements: *"I have oats and yogurt – can those go together in a dessert?"* (Maybe overnight-oats turned into a parfait or oat-yogurt pancakes with syrup as a dessert). Or *"I have chocolate and bananas but I need it to be low-sugar."* (Perhaps chocolate-dipped frozen banana bites?).

The prompt bank above is meant to inspire confidence that no matter what you have on hand, you can formulate a question to unlock dessert ideas. Use these examples as templates: swap in the ingredients you actually have, and don't hesitate to specify what you're craving ("crunchy," "cold," "comforting," etc.). ChatGPT will tailor its answers to your situation, just as we've seen throughout this chapter.

Now, armed with all these examples and ideas, you're ready to put ChatGPT to work for your sweet creations. Experiment with these prompts, and let the AI surprise you. You might find yourself inventing a new family-favorite dessert out of the simplest ingredients, thanks to a little prompting magic.

In this chapter, we've seen how an AI like ChatGPT can become an indispensable helper for all things sweet. From turning pantry scraps into "dessert on demand," to finding clever substitutions when ingredients are missing, to whipping up instant treats and reimagining classic sweets with less sugar – you've learned strategies to prompt your AI assistant for just about every dessert dilemma. We explored how to get creative with flavors and textures, and how even a novice baker can feel supported through step-by-step guidance. The kitchen is often called the heart of the home, and now you have a new heart-to-heart friend in ChatGPT, ready to coach and inspire you anytime you have a craving or a question.

By now, you've built up a prompt toolkit that puts dessert creativity at your fingertips. The examples and prompt templates we covered can be your springboard. Don't be afraid to experiment – as you try these ideas, you'll become more confident not only in using ChatGPT, but in your own ability to improvise and adapt in the kitchen. The more you collaborate with this AI kitchen companion, the more you'll find cooking and baking to be an adventurous, low-stress, and rewarding experience.

Your journey with ChatGPT in the kitchen doesn't end here. As you continue through this book, you'll keep expanding your AI-assisted culinary skills, tackling new challenges and opportunities to make your cooking smarter and even more fun. With each dish – sweet or savory – you'll further discover that having an AI by your side is like having a knowledgeable friend in the kitchen. So keep that curiosity alive, keep experimenting with prompts, and get ready for the next step in our AI-first kitchen adventure. The skills and confidence you've gained in the dessert realm will serve you well as we move forward to the next delicious chapter.

11

LEARN BY COOKING

Cooking isn't just about getting dinner on the table – it can also be a journey of learning and discovery. Every time you step into the kitchen, you have a chance to pick up new skills, understand ingredients better, and build your intuition as a cook. In this chapter, we're going to show you how to learn by cooking with the help of ChatGPT. Instead of simply following recipes, you'll turn each cooking experience into a mini-lesson. With an AI kitchen companion by your side, even everyday meals become opportunities to grow your culinary know-how.

Throughout this chapter, you'll discover ways to ask not just *what* to do, but *why*. We'll start by looking at how you can turn recipes into lessons. That means asking ChatGPT for explanations behind each step so you grasp the reasoning, not just the instructions. You'll learn how to prompt the AI to explain techniques and the science behind your favorite dishes. And when things don't go as planned – maybe a cake sinks or a stew tastes bland – we'll cover how to ask the right "why" questions to figure out what happened and how to improve. Every success and every mishap in the kitchen can teach you something, and ChatGPT will help you decipher those lessons.

We'll also dive into the world of cooking techniques and make them feel simple. Have you ever been intimidated by terms like *braising*, *emulsifying*, or *tempering*? With ChatGPT, you can break down these complex methods into plain-language steps. This chapter will show you how to use AI to demystify sophisticated techniques – turning daunting culinary tasks into something you understand and can actually do. By learning the how and the why of methods like roasting a chicken or emulsifying a salad dressing, you'll cook with more confidence and skill.

Another powerful way to learn is by comparing different approaches side by side. So we'll explore prompts for having ChatGPT compare cooking methods. What's the difference between roasting vegetables in the oven and air-frying them? Is sautéing the same as stir-frying? By prompting ChatGPT to explain the pros, cons, and effects of each method, you'll get a clearer picture of which techniques suit your needs and what results to expect. These comparisons can sharpen your intuition about when to use one method over another, making you a more adaptable cook.

Understanding ingredients is just as important as mastering techniques. In this chapter, you'll see how to use ChatGPT as a friendly food science guide. You can ask why certain ingredients behave the way they do – like why adding salt can make a steak juicier or why egg whites turn fluffy when whipped. You'll learn how to prompt for flavor pairing ideas and find out what ingredients harmonize well together. And if you need to substitute one ingredient for another, ChatGPT can explain how that swap might change your dish. This ingredient science and flavor logic will help you cook more intuitively, because you'll know the *logic* behind the flavors.

We'll also encourage you to roll up your sleeves and do some kitchen experiments. Don't worry – these are fun, simple experiments you can try at home to see cooking principles in action. Think of it like a little science project in your kitchen: maybe searing one piece of meat but not another to compare, or baking cookie dough after chilling it versus right away. We'll show how you can ask ChatGPT for experiment ideas and step-by-step guidance. By tasting the differences for yourself, you'll reinforce what you've learned and remember it far better. It's hands-on learning, with ChatGPT as your guide to set up and interpret the results.

By the end of this chapter, you'll have a toolkit of strategies to make every meal a learning experience. We'll even walk through some real "teach me" style prompts and ChatGPT's educational responses. These examples will tie everything together, showing you exactly how an interactive chat with AI can build your skills with every dish you make. Cooking will feel less like following orders and more like a collaborative, enjoyable learning process. So, let's get started on turning your kitchen into a classroom – one where dinner and a lesson come as a package deal.

TURNING RECIPES INTO LESSONS

Have you ever followed a recipe to the letter and still felt unsure *why* you were doing all those steps? Turning recipes into lessons is all about asking questions and digging into the reasoning behind the instructions. With ChatGPT, you can transform any recipe into a mini cooking class. Instead of just doing step 1, step 2, step 3, you can ask at each stage: *Why am I doing this?* By getting explanations for the techniques and steps, you'll start to recognize cooking patterns and build intuition for future meals.

For instance, imagine you're making a simple stir-fry that instructs you to "marinate the chicken for 30 minutes before cooking." You might wonder what difference marinating actually makes. If you ask ChatGPT, you could say something like, *"Why does this recipe ask me to marinate the chicken, and what happens if I skip that step?"* In response, ChatGPT would explain that marinating helps flavor penetrate and can tenderize the meat slightly, and it might warn that skipping it could result in chicken that's less tasty or a bit tougher. Suddenly, that once-mysterious waiting time makes sense – you've learned the purpose behind the marinade.

Every step in a recipe exists for a reason. By asking about those reasons, you turn instructions into insights. Say a stew recipe tells you to sear the meat before simmering it. Instead of just doing it blindly, you can ask, *"Why should I sear the meat first?"* ChatGPT might reveal that the goal isn't to "lock in juices" (that's actually a cooking myth), but to develop deeper flavor through browning. In fact, high-heat searing triggers the Maillard reaction – a series of chemical reactions that create rich, savory flavors and aromas on the surface of the meat. Knowing this, you understand that this one extra step isn't about sealing moisture at all, but about building taste. The next time you see "sear before stewing" in any recipe, you'll remember exactly why it's worth doing.

You can do this with any part of a recipe. Perhaps the instructions say to sauté onions until golden before adding other ingredients. If you ask *"Why do I need to cook the onions first?"* you'll learn that this step draws out the onions' natural sweetness and creates a flavor base for the whole dish. Or maybe a curry recipe says to add garlic and spices toward the end of sautéing – you can ask why, and ChatGPT will explain that garlic can burn and turn bitter if cooked too long, so it's added later to preserve its flavor. With each answer, you're piecing together the logic of cooking. It's like having a coach by your side, ready to explain the reason behind every stir, every simmer, every pinch of salt.

This approach works wonders for baking as well. Baking recipes often have steps that seem fussy or trivial – but they usually have a purpose. Imagine your cookie recipe says to chill the dough for an hour before baking. It might be tempting to skip straight to baking, but if you ask ChatGPT why the chill time matters, you'll get some kitchen science insight. The AI could tell you that chilling the dough solidifies the fats (like butter), so the cookies won't spread too quickly in the oven. It also gives the flour time to absorb moisture, which leads to a better texture. Armed with that knowledge, you'll wait patiently, knowing your cookies will turn out chewier and more evenly baked. In short, you didn't just follow the recipe – you learned *why* that step makes a difference.

One effective strategy is to have ChatGPT walk you through a recipe with explanations at each step. For example, you might prompt: *"Give me a pancake recipe, but also explain what each step does and why it's important."* ChatGPT would then not only list the ingredients and instructions, but also add notes like, "Mixing dry ingredients separately keeps the baking powder from reacting too soon," or "Letting the batter rest for a few minutes helps the gluten relax so the pancakes turn out tender." Reading through such an AI-guided recipe feels like a knowledgeable chef is cooking alongside you, pointing out the little secrets that recipes don't always spell out. You start to see the big picture – how each action affects the final result.

By turning recipes into lessons, you'll find that you're not just *making* dinner – you're training yourself to be a better cook each time. You begin to predict why a new recipe calls for a certain step because you've seen it before and learned the reason. Over time, patterns emerge: you notice that many recipes start by sautéing aromatics for flavor, or that resting dough is a common theme in baking. These patterns are the building blocks of intuition. And when you have intuition, you can start cooking more freely, even without a recipe. But intuition also comes from understanding mistakes. Next, we'll see how asking "why" when things go wrong can turn kitchen frustrations into some of your best learning moments.

ASKING THE RIGHT "WHY" QUESTIONS

Not every cooking adventure goes perfectly – and that's okay. In fact, the mistakes and misfires often teach us the most. The key is to stay curious and not get discouraged. When a dish doesn't turn out as expected, it's time to ask "why?" in a constructive way. ChatGPT can be your kitchen confidant here, helping you troubleshoot what went wrong. Instead of just feeling frustrated that your bread didn't rise or your soup turned out bland, you can describe what happened and prompt ChatGPT to analyze it. This turns a disappointing outcome into a learning opportunity. Remember, every great chef has burned a dish or two on the way to mastery; the difference is, they reflect on it – and now you can too, with a little AI help.

The trick to getting a useful answer is to be specific when you ask your "why" question. The more details you give ChatGPT, the better it can pinpoint the cause. Instead of just saying, *"Why was my cake bad?"*, you'd get more insight with a question like: *"I baked a chocolate cake and it sank in the middle. I followed the recipe closely – I creamed the butter and sugar, used fresh baking powder, and didn't open the oven early. It was cooking at 350°F for 30 minutes as directed. Why would it collapse in the center?"* By laying out the scenario, you're helping ChatGPT act like a detective, considering all the clues. It might come back with targeted suggestions – maybe the cake needed a bit longer to fully set in the middle, or perhaps the batter was overmixed and too much air was knocked out. In any case, you'll get a clearer answer than a generic one.

Let's consider a common baking woe: a cake that collapses or comes out dense. If you pose the problem to ChatGPT with context, you might hear explanations you hadn't thought of. For example, it could explain that using too much leavening (baking powder or soda) can cause a cake to rise fast and then crash, or that under-baking leaves the center structure too weak to hold up once cooled. It might even ask if you checked your baking powder's expiration date – an old leavening agent could be the sneaky culprit. With each possible reason, ChatGPT can usually offer a fix: next time, measure leavening carefully, or give the cake a few extra minutes in the oven, or make sure ingredients are fresh. What started as a frustrating "failure" is now a checklist of lessons for your next bake.

This approach isn't just for baking. Maybe your stir-fry vegetables turned out soggy instead of crisp, or your beef stew tastes kind of flat even after simmering for hours. Bring these puzzles to ChatGPT. If your stew is bland, for instance, ChatGPT might run through a mental list: Did you salt it enough? Stews often need more salt than quick-cooked dishes, since potatoes and other ingredients soak it up. Did you add any acid or fresh herbs at the end to brighten the flavor? A squeeze of lemon or splash of vinegar at the finish can wake up a dull stew. Did you brown the meat and onions well at the start? That caramelization adds depth that no amount of simmering later can achieve. By asking these "why" questions about flavor, you're essentially learning how to season and layer tastes like a pro. And with each explanation, you can almost imagine how to improve the dish next time – maybe a pinch more salt early on, or remembering to deglaze the pan for those browned bits of flavor.

Sometimes the answers ChatGPT provides will point out factors beyond your recipe steps – things like your equipment or technique. Suppose you complain, *"My lasagna's edges always burn by the time the center is cooked. Why?"* Along with suggestions like covering the dish with foil if it's browning too fast, ChatGPT might prompt you to consider your oven or bakeware. Perhaps you're using a dark-colored metal pan. A dark pan absorbs heat more quickly, causing the edges of baked goods to cook (and brown) faster than the middle. The AI might explain that one solution is to lower your oven temperature by 25°F when using dark pans, or switch to a light-colored or glass pan which heats more evenly. It could also mention checking your oven's calibration – some ovens run hotter than their dial says, creating hot spots. These are insights even intermediate cooks don't always know, especially if no one told them. But by asking "why," you've uncovered them and can adjust accordingly.

To see how this works in practice, imagine this exchange with ChatGPT while troubleshooting:

User: I cooked a steak on the grill, but it came out really dry and tough. I seasoned it and cooked 5 minutes per side on high heat. Why did it turn out so dry, and how can I do better?

ChatGPT: There are a few possible reasons your steak ended up dry and tough:

- **Overcooking:** Five minutes per side on high heat, depending on the steak's thickness, could have overcooked it. A thinner cut might have gone past medium into well-done, which dries out the meat.
- **Cut of meat:** Some cuts (like flank or round) are leaner and can be tougher if not cooked or sliced properly. If you used a lean cut, it might need a different approach (for example, marinating or cooking to a lower temperature).

- **Lack of resting:** If you didn't let the steak rest after grilling, the juices inside didn't get a chance to redistribute. Cutting in immediately can make those juices spill out, leaving the steak drier.

To improve next time, try using a meat thermometer to cook to your desired doneness (for example, pull it off the grill at around 130–135°F for medium-rare). Then let the steak rest for about 5 minutes before slicing, so it stays nice and juicy. And if it was a very lean cut, marinating beforehand or cooking it a bit less can also help keep it tender.

In this example, a simple "why" question led to multiple insights – about cooking time, meat type, and resting. The advice is practical (use a thermometer, let it rest) and educational. You're not just fixing one steak; you're learning principles that apply to any time you grill meat.

As you can see, asking "why did this go wrong?" transforms kitchen flops into fuel for growth. Instead of a vague sense that "I'm just bad at this dish," you get concrete reasons and solutions. Over time, you'll start predicting issues before they happen – you'll remember to check the oven temperature, or not overcrowd the pan, or to add that dash of vinegar. Each troubleshooting session with ChatGPT makes you a more resilient and knowledgeable cook. Now that we've seen how to learn from missteps, let's shift to learning before things go wrong. In the next section, we'll use ChatGPT to break down complex cooking techniques so they're easy to grasp from the start.

TECHNIQUE DEEP DIVES MADE SIMPLE

Cooking can sometimes feel like a world of jargon and fancy techniques. You read a recipe that says "braise the pork" or "emulsify the dressing" or "temper the eggs," and it might leave you scratching your head. This is where ChatGPT really shines as a teacher. Instead of glossing over those terms and hoping for the best, you can ask the AI to break them down for you. A complex cooking method can be explained in plain English, step by step. With ChatGPT, you don't have to go to culinary school to understand techniques – you can get a clear, simple explanation tailored to your level of knowledge. That means no more intimidation when you encounter a new method; instead, you'll think, *"I can handle this – let's have ChatGPT explain how."*

Take *braising*, for example. If you've never braised anything before, it might sound complicated, but it's actually a straightforward method. You could ask ChatGPT, *"What does it mean to braise meat, and how do I do it?"* and get a friendly walk-through. ChatGPT would explain that braising is a way of cooking with both dry heat and moist heat. In practice, that means first searing the food in a hot pan (the dry heat browning step that adds flavor), then adding some liquid and cooking it slowly in a covered pot (the moist, steamy environment). The magic of braising is that it transforms tougher cuts of meat or hardy vegetables into tender, flavorful dishes. By searing, you develop flavor; by simmering in liquid, you gently break down fibers and infuse the food with moisture and seasoning. So in one answer, you've learned not just the definition of braising, but why each part of the process matters.

Now consider a term like *emulsifying*. Say you're making salad dressing and the recipe says "emulsify the olive oil into the vinegar." If you're unsure, you can prompt ChatGPT: *"What does emulsify mean in cooking?"* It will clarify that to emulsify is to force two liquids to combine that normally don't mix (like oil and water). In our dressing example, whisking or blending vigorously while slowly drizzling oil into vinegar lets tiny droplets of oil suspend throughout the vinegar, creating a smooth, unified dressing instead of a separated mess. ChatGPT might compare it to making mayonnaise or hollandaise, which are also emulsions – blending fat into liquid so well that they stay together. You could even follow up and ask, *"How do I keep an emulsion from breaking?"* and learn tips like adding an emulsifier (mustard or egg yolk in a dressing helps bind the oil and vinegar) or controlling temperature. Suddenly, a concept that sounded like chemistry class makes sense in your kitchen. You'll not only do it right, but also understand what's happening on a scientific level.

Another technique that benefits from a ChatGPT explanation is *tempering*. This term can refer to a few things in cooking, but let's say your recipe asks you to temper eggs. If you ask ChatGPT what that means, you'll learn that tempering eggs involves slowly combining them with a hot liquid so they warm up without curdling. For instance, when making pudding or custard, instead of just dumping egg yolks into hot milk (which would scramble them), you add a little hot milk to the yolks gradually while stirring, then a little more, effectively *easing* the eggs into the heat. This way, the eggs blend in smoothly and thicken the mixture without lumps. With ChatGPT's step-by-step guidance, you'll know to whisk constantly and pour the hot liquid in a thin stream – and you'll know *why* you're doing it that way. Tempering can also refer to chocolate (carefully melting and cooling chocolate to give it a glossy snap), and if you're curious, you can get an explanation for that too. The point is, no technique is too daunting to learn when you have a patient, knowledgeable explainer at your fingertips.

This approach can demystify any culinary term or method. Maybe you encounter an instruction to "deglaze the pan" and you're not certain how to do it – ChatGPT would tell you it means pouring in liquid (like wine or stock) to dissolve the brown bits stuck to the pan, creating a quick sauce. Or you see "julienne the carrots" in a recipe – ChatGPT can explain that it's a fancy word for cutting carrots into thin matchstick-like strips, and even give you tips on how to do it safely. Because you can ask follow-up questions, you might go from *"What is sautéing?"* to *"How much oil should I use to sauté these vegetables?"* to *"How do I know when to stop sautéing?"* all in one learning thread. Each answer builds your confidence to try the technique yourself. You're essentially getting a mini-lesson on demand, which means fewer worries about messing up and more focus on doing things right.

To illustrate, here's a brief example dialog breaking down a technique:

User: I'm not sure how to roast a whole chicken properly. Can you teach me the steps and why each step matters?

ChatGPT: Absolutely! Roasting a whole chicken is easier than it looks. Here's a simple process:

- **Preheat your oven to 375°F (190°C):** A hot oven ensures the chicken cooks evenly from the start and helps the skin get crispy.
- **Pat the chicken dry and season it generously:** Dry skin will crisp up better, and seasoning (with salt, pepper, and maybe herbs or lemon inside) infuses flavor throughout the meat.
- **Place the chicken on a roasting pan (or tray) breast-side up:** This positioning helps the breast meat (which cooks faster) not overcook since it's a bit further from the heat source if your heat comes from below. If using a roasting rack, it also allows heat to circulate and fats to drip away.
- **Roast until golden and cooked through (about 1.5 hours for a 4-pound chicken):** You'll know it's done when the juices run clear or a thermometer in the thickest part reads around 165°F (75°C). The steady heat cooks the meat through while browning the outside.
- **Let it rest before carving (about 10-15 minutes):** Resting allows the juices inside the chicken to redistribute, so they won't all spill out when you cut. This means juicier meat.

As you can see, each step has a purpose – from getting the skin crisp to ensuring the meat is juicy and flavorful. Once you understand these reasons, you'll roast with more confidence.

With ChatGPT's help, complex techniques turn into something you can tackle on a weeknight. Instead of skipping a recipe because "I've never done that before," you'll feel empowered to try, knowing you have clear guidance. Over time, you'll accumulate a whole arsenal of methods – braising, roasting, emulsifying, tempering, and beyond – and truly understand how they work. The next step in building your cooking savvy is to put that knowledge into context. It's one thing to know how to roast or braise; it's another to decide *which* one to use for a given dish. In the following section, we'll see how you can have ChatGPT compare different cooking methods side by side, so you can choose the best approach and appreciate the nuances of each.

COMPARING METHODS AND APPROACHES

As you get comfortable with individual techniques, you might start wondering how they stack up against each other. In cooking, there's often more than one way to achieve a similar result – say, baking versus air frying, or simmering on the stove versus using a slow cooker. Each method has its pros and cons. ChatGPT can help you compare different approaches side by side, so you can make informed decisions about which to use or simply satisfy your curiosity about how they differ. This kind of comparative insight is like having a knowledgeable cooking friend explain, "If you cook it this way, you'll get X, but if you do it that way, you'll get Y." It's great for understanding trade-offs in terms of flavor, texture, time, and even nutrition.

Let's look at an example: roasting vegetables in a conventional oven versus air frying them. At a glance, both methods are actually quite similar – air frying is essentially high-speed roasting in a small convection oven. But there are differences a home cook might care about. If you asked ChatGPT, *"What's the difference between roasting potatoes in the oven and air frying them?"*, it would break it down for you. It might explain that roasting usually involves a larger space (your oven) and can handle big batches, while an air fryer's smaller chamber circulates heat more intensely around the food. This means an air fryer often cooks faster (no long preheat needed, and more concentrated heat) and can give you very crispy results with less oil. In fact, many people find that an air fryer makes things *crispier* but at the same time *less dried out* compared to the oven. However, the trade-off is capacity – you might have to cook in batches if your air fryer is small, whereas you could roast a whole tray of vegetables at once. ChatGPT would likely note that flavor-wise, both give delicious browning (thanks to the Maillard reaction again) but the oven might develop a bit more deep caramelization if you roast long enough. In short, neither is "better" universally; each has situations where it shines. And now you'd know when to use one or the other.

Now consider **sautéing** versus **stir-frying.** These terms are sometimes used interchangeably because both involve cooking food quickly in a pan with a little oil, but there are classic differences. If you prompt ChatGPT with, *"Is stir-frying the same as sautéing?"*, you'll get a nuanced answer. It might start by saying both are quick, stovetop methods, but stir-frying typically means cooking over very high heat in a wok, with the food constantly in motion, whereas sautéing is usually done in a flat pan over medium-high heat with frequent but not continuous stirring. Stir-frying often calls for cutting ingredients into small, uniform pieces so they cook in just a few minutes, and it's a hallmark of many Asian cuisines. Sautéing, a term from French cooking, might handle slightly larger pieces and allows for a bit more browning time on each side. The AI could point out practical implications: for example, a stir-fry might require higher heat oil and constant attention to toss the food (to prevent burning), resulting in a bit of smoky char and crisper veggies, while sautéing might be more forgiving and develop a fond (those browned bits) you can deglaze for a sauce. Knowing this, you can see why a recipe might choose one word or the other – and you'll feel prepared to execute either technique properly.

You can compare just about any methods you're curious about. Ask about grilling versus broiling (one has flames from below, the other intense heat from above), or poaching versus boiling (gentle vs. vigorous heat), or using a pressure cooker versus slow cooking. ChatGPT will lay out the differences clearly, often listing factors like cooking time, flavor development, texture, ease, and equipment needed. If you want, you can even request the answer in a table format or a bullet list for clarity. For instance, you could say, *"Compare pan-frying and deep-frying in terms of oil needed, cook time, and texture, in bullet points."* The AI might respond with a neat list, making it easy to scan and understand. This way, you get a quick reference guide generated on the fly, tailored to your question.

Here's a sample exchange to demonstrate a comparison in action:

User: Which is better for crispy chicken wings, baking them in the oven or using an air fryer? What's the difference in how they turn out?

ChatGPT: Both methods can yield delicious crispy chicken wings, but there are some differences:

- **Cooking Time:** An air fryer usually cooks wings faster than an oven. You might air fry wings in about 20 minutes, whereas baking could take around 40 minutes (plus preheat time) because the oven has to heat a larger space.
- **Crispiness:** Air fryers circulate very hot air around the wings rapidly, which can make the skin extremely crispy. Oven-baked wings can also get crispy, especially if you use a high temperature or a convection setting, but it may take longer. You might need to flip the wings in the oven to crisp all sides, while the air fryer's fan does that work for you.
- **Oil Usage:** Both methods are healthier than deep-frying, but an air fryer typically requires just a light brush or spray of oil on the wings. Oven baking might also only need a little oil, but if you're using a wire rack, you'd grease it to prevent sticking. Either way, the oil amount is small, just enough to help with browning.
- **Capacity:** If you're making wings for a crowd, an oven can cook more at once on a big baking sheet. An air fryer has a more limited capacity (depending on the model), so you might have to cook in batches if making a lot.
- **Summary:** For a few servings, an air fryer is quick and great at making wings super crispy. For a large batch, the oven lets you cook more at once, though you might sacrifice a bit of that ultra-crisp texture for convenience.

Both methods can produce tasty, crispy wings – it's mostly about quantity and time.

Using ChatGPT to compare methods like this not only answers your immediate question but also gives you a deeper feel for how cooking works. You'll start to anticipate the effects of different techniques: you'll know that high heat and moving air mean faster, crispier cooking, or that gentle heat over time means tender, infused flavors. These insights make you adaptable – you could take a recipe and say, "What if I grilled this instead of baking it?" and have a good sense of the outcome. Now that we've compared the *how* of cooking, let's dive into the *what* – understanding the ingredients and flavors that you're cooking with. In the next section, we'll see how ChatGPT can teach you about ingredient science and flavor pairings, so you can make sense of why certain foods and spices work the way they do.

INGREDIENT SCIENCE AND FLAVOR LOGIC

Great cooking isn't just about techniques – it's also about understanding your ingredients and how they interact. Think of it as the "why" on a molecular level and a sensory level. Every ingredient brings certain properties to a dish: some provide structure, some add flavor, some trigger chemical reactions. And then there's the art of flavor itself – knowing which ingredients taste good together. In this section, we'll see how ChatGPT can act as your personal food scientist and flavor guru. You can ask about the science (why does adding salt make a difference? what exactly does an egg do in a batter?) and about the logic of flavors (what herbs go well with chicken? can I swap cinnamon for nutmeg?). With AI, you have a quick way to get the "whys and hows" behind the ingredients in your kitchen.

For example, have you ever been confused about the difference between baking soda and baking powder? They're both white powders that make things rise, but they're not the same. If you ask ChatGPT, *"Why do some recipes use both baking soda and baking powder?*", it will break it down: baking soda is a single ingredient (a base) that needs an acid to activate, while baking powder contains both a base and an acid in dry form. In other words, baking soda will only produce leavening gas (carbon dioxide bubbles) if there's something acidic in the batter (like buttermilk or lemon juice) to react with, whereas baking powder has its own built-in acid and just needs liquid (and heat) to work. Many recipes use both to get just the right rise and flavor balance. With that explanation, the mystery is gone – you won't accidentally swap them one-for-one, and you'll understand why a cookie recipe might call for a pinch of baking soda even when it already has baking powder. This is ingredient science made simple.

ChatGPT can also enlighten you on subtle differences that affect texture and taste. Suppose you notice your cookie recipe uses a mix of white sugar and brown sugar, and you wonder why. A quick question to ChatGPT – *"What's the point of using both brown and white sugar in cookies?"* – would teach you that brown sugar contains molasses, which adds extra moisture and a deeper flavor. Using more brown sugar tends to make cookies softer and chewier, while white sugar leads to more spread and a crisper edge. That's why many recipes blend the two: to get the best of both worlds in terms of texture and taste. Understanding this means you can tweak cookie recipes on your own – if you want it chewier, use more brown sugar next time, or if you prefer it crisper, lean on the white sugar. These kinds of insights turn a recipe from a rigid formula into a flexible guideline you can play with.

One extremely handy use of ChatGPT's ingredient knowledge is figuring out substitutions. We've all been there: you're in the middle of cooking and realize you're missing an ingredient. Instead of stopping everything to go to the store, you can ask, *"What can I use instead of buttermilk?"* ChatGPT will give you options. The most common substitution – which the AI would certainly mention – is to make "sour milk" by adding an acid to regular milk. For instance, you can mix about a tablespoon of vinegar or lemon juice into a cup of milk, let it sit for a few minutes, and boom: homemade buttermilk. The science here is that the acid curdles the milk slightly and brings the pH down, similar to real buttermilk, so your recipe will still rise properly and have that tangy tenderness. ChatGPT might also suggest yogurt thinned with milk, or even sour cream thinned with water, as other alternatives. Not only do you get the swap, you often get an explanation of how to do it and why it works, so you feel confident the substitute will behave in the recipe.

Beyond the chemistry, there's the creative side of ingredient knowledge: flavors and pairings. ChatGPT has a wealth of information on classic flavor combinations. You can ask something like, *"What herbs and spices go well with roasted potatoes?"* and get a list of ideas (perhaps rosemary, thyme, garlic, paprika – along with reasons like rosemary's piney warmth complementing the potato's earthiness). If you're cooking fish and curious about seasoning, you might ask, *"What flavors pair best with salmon?"* and learn that dill and lemon are traditional because they enhance the freshness, or that a soy-ginger glaze would give an Asian-inspired twist. The AI can draw on many cuisines, so it might tell you cumin and coriander give a warm, smoky note to vegetables, or that chocolate and coffee share flavor compounds which is why they often appear together in desserts. It's like having instant access to a gigantic flavor encyclopedia – you can quickly find out why basil and tomato are a perfect match, or discover new pairings to try.

To see this in action, imagine you're making a stir-fry and want to improvise a sauce. You could ask ChatGPT a targeted question: *"How will adding a bit of vinegar vs. sugar affect my stir-fry sauce?"* A thoughtful answer might come back explaining that vinegar will add acidity, giving the sauce a tangy brightness that can balance rich or salty flavors, whereas sugar will add sweetness and help the sauce caramelize and thicken into a glaze. In essence, you'd learn that acids (like vinegar or citrus) tend to brighten or sharpen a dish, while sugars sweeten and can create a sticky texture when heated. With that understanding, you can taste your sauce and decide if it needs one or the other. In another scenario, say you're curious why a stew recipe calls for a bay leaf – ChatGPT would tell you that bay leaf adds a subtle depth and aroma (some say it's vaguely herbal, like thyme and pine) that you'd miss if it weren't there. These little lessons, ingredient by ingredient, spice by spice, accumulate into a big picture understanding of flavor logic.

The more you ask ChatGPT about ingredients, the more you start cooking with intention. Instead of blindly following a recipe's ingredient list, you'll know *why* each item is there and how it contributes. This empowers you to tweak recipes confidently – to reduce sugar if you want it less sweet, or add an extra herb to punch up the aroma, understanding the likely outcome. It also helps you fix issues on the fly (too bland? maybe it needs salt or acid) because you understand what's missing. Now that we've got the science and flavor foundations, it's time to put them to the test. In the next section, we'll explore how you can set up simple kitchen experiments (with ChatGPT's guidance) to see these principles in action – learning by actually tasting and observing the differences.

KITCHEN EXPERIMENTS YOU CAN TRY

At this point, you've gained a lot of knowledge by asking questions and listening to explanations. The next step is to really cement that knowledge through experience. Nothing makes a lesson stick quite like seeing (and tasting) the results for yourself. That's where kitchen experiments come in. Think of it like a fun science project, except you can eat the outcome! With ChatGPT's help, you can design simple experiments during your normal cooking routine that illustrate how changing one thing changes the result. You don't need fancy lab equipment – just your regular ingredients and a willingness to try a couple of variations. By comparing outcomes, you'll get a crystal-clear understanding of cooking principles that might otherwise seem abstract.

For instance, let's say you're curious about whether marinating truly makes meat more tender or flavorful. You could run a little test: take two similar pieces of chicken breast or tofu. Marinate one of them in a flavorful sauce or seasoning for a few hours, and leave the other one plain (or just lightly season it right before cooking). Then cook both side by side under the same conditions. With ChatGPT, you can fine-tune the plan: you might ask, *"How should I cook them to fairly compare a marinated vs. non-marinated piece of chicken?"* and get advice to maybe grill or bake them identically. When you taste them, pay attention – is the marinated piece noticeably juicier or more flavorful inside, or just more seasoned on the surface? ChatGPT can help interpret the results too. If the difference is subtle, the AI might explain that some marinades don't penetrate deeply, or if the marinated one is much juicier, it might credit the oil or acids in the marinade for improving texture. Either way, you've learned something firsthand about what a marinade can and can't do.

Here's another experiment idea: the effect of heat and pan crowding on browning. Suppose you often hear "don't overcrowd the pan" but want to see why. You can try sautéing mushrooms in two batches – one where the pan is full of mushrooms crammed edge to edge, and another where the mushrooms have plenty of space between them. Cook both batches exactly the same way (same stove setting, same time). You'll likely observe that the crowded pan's mushrooms release a lot of water and end up steaming pale brown or gray, while the spaced-out batch browns nicely with a richer color and flavor. If you ask ChatGPT *why* afterward, it would clarify that when a pan is overcrowded, the moisture from the mushrooms has nowhere to escape, so it stays in the pan and the food essentially boils/steams instead of frying. In the uncrowded pan, excess moisture evaporates quickly, so the mushrooms can actually fry and caramelize. By doing this experiment, you won't just take it on faith next time a recipe says not to crowd the pan – you'll remember the visual and tasted difference.

You can come up with endless little experiments like this. Try cooking scrambled eggs on low heat vs. high heat to see how the texture changes (slow-cooked eggs come out creamy, while high-heat ones can turn out firm and dryer). Bake one tray of cookies with dough that's been chilled overnight and another tray with dough you bake immediately – observe how much they spread and how the texture differs. Make two pots of the same soup, but finish one with a squeeze of lemon juice and leave the other as-is, then compare the flavor (you'll likely notice the one with lemon tastes brighter and more lively). These tests don't have to be big production; even just separating a dish into two small pans to try a different technique on each can teach you a lot. And because you'll eat the results, it's never a waste – it's dinner and a lesson, all in one.

If you're not sure what to test, you can literally ask ChatGPT for experiment ideas. For example, *"Can you suggest a simple experiment to learn about how sugar affects cake moisture?"* might prompt the AI to suggest baking two mini cakes, one with the full amount of sugar and one with less, and then comparing their texture and freshness the next day. Or you could ask, *"What's a good experiment to understand what resting meat does?"* and ChatGPT would outline a plan: cook two small steaks or chops, let one rest after cooking but cut into the other immediately, and see which one loses more juice on the plate. The AI can guide you on how to set it up fairly – keeping other variables the same so the test is "controlled" – and even what to look out for when tasting or observing.

Imagine you ask for a few experiment ideas. The conversation might look like this:

User: I want to learn more about cooking through experiments. Can you give me some easy experiment ideas I can try in my kitchen?

ChatGPT: Sure! Here are three fun and easy kitchen experiments to try:

- **Salt Pasta Water vs. No Salt:** Cook pasta in two separate pots of water – one with a good amount of salt, and one with no salt. Taste the pasta from each pot. You'll discover how much seasoning the pasta absorbs (the salted-water pasta will taste better on its own). This shows why chefs always say to salt your pasta water.
- **Butter Temperature in Baking:** Bake two small batches of biscuits or scones. In one batch, use very cold butter, and in the other, use melted (or room-temperature) butter. Compare the texture. The cold butter batch should be

flakier, while the warm butter batch turns out flatter and denser. This illustrates how solid fat creates little air pockets for flakiness.

- **Rested Dough vs. Straight to Oven:** Mix up a pancake or crepe batter and cook some immediately, then let the rest of the batter sit for 30 minutes and cook another round. Notice any differences in texture or how much the batter spread. Often, a rested batter gives thicker, more tender results, because the flour has hydrated and gluten has relaxed.
- Feel free to try these and see the results firsthand. Each experiment is quick and uses basic ingredients, but you'll learn a lot about seasoning, baking chemistry, and batter science by doing them!

By engaging in these little trials, you turn cooking into an interactive learning lab. It's one thing to read or hear that "cold butter makes flaky biscuits," but when you actually see the difference in your own oven, the lesson sticks with you. Plus, it's pretty empowering to see that you can figure out the 'why' on your own terms – almost like debugging a recipe through testing. ChatGPT is there to spark ideas and explain outcomes, but you'll be building your own intuitive knowledge through observation. After a few experiments, you'll start instinctively knowing how to get the results you want. In the final section, we'll shift from these theory-focused exercises to real, everyday cooking scenarios where learning is happening. We'll look at some actual "teach me" style prompts in action, showing how ChatGPT's guidance and your kitchen curiosity combine to build skill with every meal.

REAL LEARNING PROMPTS IN ACTION

We've talked about all the ways you can use ChatGPT to learn while cooking. Now let's put it all together and see what those conversations actually look like. In this section, we'll walk through a few realistic examples of "learning in action" – real prompts a home cook might use, and the kind of helpful, educational responses ChatGPT would give. These examples illustrate how, no matter the scenario, you can turn to your AI kitchen companion not just for *what to do*, but for a deeper understanding of *why* and *how*. Consider these sample exchanges:

Example 1: Guided Recipe – Making an Omelette You want to make a simple omelette for breakfast, but also learn technique along the way.

User: I know how to make an omelette, but could you walk me through it step by step and teach me some tips while we do it?

ChatGPT: Sure! Let's make a classic cheese omelette together. I'll explain each step:

- **Crack and Beat Eggs:** Crack 2 or 3 eggs into a bowl. Beat them with a fork until the whites and yolks are fully mixed and a bit frothy. (Beating adds a little air, which makes the omelette fluffier.)
- **Preheat Your Pan:** Place a non-stick pan on medium heat and add a pat of butter. (Medium heat prevents the eggs from burning; the butter should melt and just start to bubble, coating the pan so the eggs won't stick and will develop a nice flavor.)
- **Pour and Swirl:** Pour the beaten eggs into the center of the pan. Tilt the pan to spread the egg evenly. (This ensures a thin, even layer so your omelette cooks uniformly.)
- **Cook Gently:** As the eggs begin to set, use a spatula to gently lift the edges and let uncooked egg run underneath. (This is a key technique – it lets the liquid egg reach the hot pan, so everything cooks without over-browning the bottom. It keeps the omelette tender.)
- **Add Filling and Fold:** When the eggs are mostly set (no big liquid puddles on top), sprinkle your cheese (like grated cheddar) on one half. Turn off the heat, and use the spatula to fold the omelette in half over the filling.

(Turning off heat now uses the pan's residual warmth to melt the cheese without overcooking the eggs.)

- **Serve:** Slide the omelette onto a plate. The inside should be soft and moist, and the cheese melted. Enjoy! (Resting just a minute on the plate can also finish cooking the eggs through with residual heat.)

There you go – a perfect omelette! The main tips were moderate heat, moving the egg around to cook it evenly, and folding at the right time. Those ensure your omelette is fluffy and tender rather than rubbery. Good job!

Example 2: On-the-Spot Fix – Thickening a Gravy You're making a gravy and notice it's too thin, so you ask for help with an explanation.

User: My gravy is a bit watery. What can I do to thicken it up quickly? And why does that work?

ChatGPT: To thicken a gravy at the last minute, you have two reliable options:

Option 1: Mix a teaspoon or two of cornstarch (or flour) with cold water to make a slurry, and then stir that into your simmering gravy. Within a minute or so, you'll see it thicken up. (This works because the starch granules swell and gel when heated, which adds body to the liquid.)

Option 2: Let the gravy simmer uncovered for a bit longer to reduce. As water evaporates, the gravy naturally thickens and the flavors concentrate. (This is slower than the starch method, but it's purely reducing the water content – less liquid means a thicker sauce.)

You can choose either method, or even combine them if needed. If you use starch, just be sure to fully boil the gravy for a minute after adding to cook out any raw starch taste. And remember, add the thickener gradually – you can always add more, but it's hard to fix an overly thick gravy. Good luck, your gravy should be nicely velvety in no time!

Example 3: Learning from a Cooking Issue – Fluffy Mashed Potatoes Your mashed potatoes turned out gluey last time, so you ask how to improve and learn why it happened.

User: My mashed potatoes sometimes come out kind of gluey or gummy. How can I make them fluffier and what am I doing wrong?

ChatGPT: Gummy mashed potatoes usually mean the potatoes were overworked, which released too much starch. Here are some tips to get fluffy mashed potatoes:

- **Choose the Right Potato:** Use starchy potatoes like Russets or Yukon Golds. (Waxy potatoes can turn gluey more easily because of their type of starch.)
- **Don't Overmix:** After boiling the potatoes until they're soft, drain them well and mash them just until smooth. If you use an electric mixer or food processor, it can break the potato cells too much and make it gummy. (Mashing by hand or using a ricer keeps the texture fluffy by not agitating too much starch.)
- **Add Butter First:** When the potatoes are hot and dry (right after draining), mix in the butter before any milk or cream. (Butterfat coats the starch and proteins, which helps keep the texture creamy and separates the granules. This prevents some glueyness.) Then add warm milk or cream a bit at a time while gently stirring.
- **Season and Serve:** Once everything is combined and smooth, stop mixing. Add salt and any extras (like roasted garlic or herbs), and serve. (Overworking at this stage can still make them pasty, so handle gently.)

By following these steps, your mashed potatoes should come out light and fluffy. The key is really to avoid excessive mixing – as soon as they're creamy with no lumps, you're done. That way you won't activate too much starch. Enjoy those cloud-like mashed potatoes!

Each of these scenarios shows how a simple prompt can turn cooking into a learning session. Whether you're getting a step-by-step lesson on a recipe, fixing a problem in the moment, or analyzing how to improve a dish, ChatGPT is there to not just tell you *what* to do, but to help you understand *why*. By now, you've seen how versatile this approach can be – it's like having a chef instructor, a food scientist, and a supportive friend all in one, available whenever you need advice in the kitchen.

From here on out, every meal can be a chance to grow your skills. You might start predicting ChatGPT's advice because you've learned so much: remembering those past explanations about heat, or salt, or technique. And when you encounter something new, you know exactly how to learn about it. With the strategies and examples from this chapter, you're well-equipped to continue your cooking journey with curiosity and confidence. The journey isn't over – ahead we'll build on this foundation and explore even more ways to make your kitchen an AI-powered creative space, taking your cooking to new heights.

12

FIX MY DISH! TROUBLESHOOTING IN REAL TIME

Mistakes and surprises are a natural part of cooking. One moment you're sailing along with a recipe, and the next you realize something's not right—the sauce is separating, the soup is too salty, or the chicken is still pink inside. Every home cook, no matter how experienced, faces these little kitchen crises. The difference between a kitchen disaster and a saved meal often comes down to how you react in that moment. This chapter is all about staying calm and **fixing your dish** in real time, with a little help from your AI kitchen companion.

Picture having a friendly, knowledgeable chef by your side every time something goes awry—a *virtual kitchen medic* on call. That's exactly what ChatGPT can be for you. Instead of scrambling for a cookbook or frantically searching the web with messy hands, you can simply ask ChatGPT for immediate advice. In the heat of the moment (sometimes literally), ChatGPT can guide you through a fix step-by-step, helping you recover from common cooking issues quickly and calmly. It's like having a seasoned sous-chef who never panics, right in your smartphone or smart speaker.

In this chapter, you'll learn how to effectively prompt ChatGPT when you encounter mid-cooking dilemmas. We'll cover a range of scenarios that can happen to anyone: over-seasoning a dish until it's nearly inedible, ending up with sauces that are too thin or completely broken, dealing with food that's burnt or undercooked, and rescuing meals that turned out bland or poorly timed. For each type of problem, you'll see how to describe the situation to ChatGPT and get useful, practical solutions in seconds.

The key to real-time troubleshooting is staying composed and being specific about the problem. It's all too easy to let frustration take over—*"My dinner is ruined!"*—but as you'll see, most cooking mistakes can be fixed or at least improved. ChatGPT excels at turning a panicked *"What do I do?!"* into a clear plan of action. The tone of its guidance will be calm and reassuring, which in turn helps you, the cook, stay calm too. By the end of this chapter, you'll have the confidence to tackle any kitchen mishap, knowing that a quick prompt to ChatGPT can rescue your dish or suggest a creative plan B.

We'll start by exploring how to engage ChatGPT as your on-the-spot problem solver, including tips on what details to include in your question. Then, we'll dive into specific common issues one by one—like oversalted soups, broken sauces, and timing snafus—to see exactly how an AI assistant can help. Throughout the chapter, you'll find plenty of example prompts and ChatGPT responses drawn from real-world cooking slip-ups. These examples will help you imagine how to use ChatGPT in your own kitchen, so when an "uh-oh" moment strikes, you'll know just what to ask.

So take a deep breath and don't worry—help is at hand. Whether your soup is too spicy, your sauce is lumpy, or dinner is ready an hour before your guests arrive, you can *cook smarter* with ChatGPT by your side. Let's jump in and see how your virtual kitchen medic can turn things around when a dish isn't going as planned.

YOUR VIRTUAL KITCHEN MEDIC

When you're in the middle of cooking and something goes wrong, think of ChatGPT as your *on-call kitchen medic*. It's there to talk you through the "injury" your dish has sustained and suggest a cure.

The first step is to stay calm and assess the situation. Take a quick breath, step away from the stove for a moment if you need to, and then tell ChatGPT exactly what's happening. The more clearly you can describe the issue, the more targeted and useful the advice will be. Remember, ChatGPT isn't a mind reader (or a taste tester), so it relies on the details you provide about what went wrong and what you have on hand.

How to Ask for Help: When prompting ChatGPT in the middle of a kitchen crisis, include key information so it can diagnose the problem effectively. Here are some tips for what to mention in your prompt:

Name the Dish: Start by stating what you're making (e.g., "tomato soup," "stir-fry with chicken," "chocolate cake"). This gives context.

Describe the Problem: Clearly explain what went wrong or what's worrying you. Is the flavor off (too salty, too spicy, bland)? Is the texture problematic (sauce separated, soup too thin, dough not rising)? Did something burn, or is it undercooked?

Mention What You've Done So Far: Briefly note the stage of cooking or how the issue came about ("I added salt twice by accident," or "I left the pot on high heat and now it's scorched.").

List Available Fixes: Let ChatGPT know what ingredients or tools you have at your disposal to fix the issue. This is crucial. For example, if your dish is too spicy and you have yogurt in the fridge, or if your sauce is thin and you have cornstarch, mention those. Also mention if you're low on time (e.g., guests arriving in 10 minutes).

Stay Calm and Specific: Instead of saying *"My dinner is ruined!"* try *"My curry turned out way too spicy for us to eat. I have coconut milk and sugar on hand. How can I fix it?"* A focused question will get a focused answer.

By providing these details, you enable ChatGPT to act like a seasoned chef who has walked into your kitchen and quickly sized up the situation. It will respond with a calm, practical tone—exactly what you need when you're flustered. For example, let's say you accidentally shook in far too much chili powder into your pot of chili con carne. Here's how you might prompt ChatGPT and what it might reply:

Home Cook: "Help! I'm making chili con carne and I made it *way* too spicy. It's been simmering for an hour and I just tasted it—my mouth is on fire. I still have 20 minutes before dinner. I have sour cream, a can of beans, and a bit of sugar in the kitchen. What can I do to save this dish?"

ChatGPT: "No worries, you can tone down that heat. First, add that can of beans (drained and rinsed) to increase the volume of the chili—this will dilute the spiciness. You could also chop up a potato or another mild vegetable if you have one, but beans will do the trick. Next, stir in a spoonful of sugar; a little sweetness can balance out the heat. Let the chili simmer a bit longer. Just before serving, mellow the spice by stirring in some sour cream (or serve a dollop on top of each bowl). Taste as you go, and you should find the chili becomes much milder and more enjoyable."

In this example, the prompt gave ChatGPT a clear picture: an overly spicy chili, what's already been done (simmered for an hour), how much time is left, and exactly which "rescue ingredients" are on hand (sour cream, beans, sugar). The response is calm and actionable, offering multiple steps: dilution (add beans), sweetness (sugar), and richness (sour cream) to fix the flavor. Notice how the tone is reassuring ("No worries, you can tone down that heat.") — this helps you feel guided rather than judged.

As you get comfortable talking to ChatGPT, you'll see that it's not just about the fix, but also about moral support. A chat assistant won't scold you for burning the onions; it will focus on the solution. This positive, can-do attitude is contagious. Soon you'll find yourself approaching kitchen problems with the same calm mindset, thinking, *"Okay, what can I do next to save this?"* — just like ChatGPT would.

When you have your virtual kitchen medic on standby, even a potential disaster becomes just a detour. You'll be back to cooking in no time, confident that a solution is at your fingertips.

Now that we've covered how to ask for help, let's get specific. One of the most common mid-cooking crises is realizing you've added too much of something—usually salt, spice, or sugar. Next, we'll see how ChatGPT helps balance a dish that's gone off the deep end flavor-wise.

OOPS, TOO MUCH SALT (OR SPICE, OR SUGAR)

Over-seasoning is one of the most common cooking mishaps. Maybe the saltshaker slipped, the chili powder was hotter than expected, or that stew got *way* too sweet after an overzealous honey drizzle. The good news is that adding "too much" of something doesn't have to spell doom for your dish. ChatGPT can quickly suggest flavor-balancing strategies to rescue the meal, often using everyday ingredients you already have. The key is to counteract the overpowering taste by adding other flavors or more volume. In other words, balance it out.

Too Salty? When your dish turns out saltier than the ocean, the general fix is to dilute or distract. ChatGPT might advise you to increase the volume of the dish or add ingredients that temper the saltiness. For instance, adding water, unsalted broth, or more of the main ingredients can spread out the saltiness. A bit of acid can also help: a squeeze of lemon juice or splash of vinegar can make a dish *perceive* less salty by brightening other flavors. Another trick is adding a touch of sweetness (sugar, honey, etc.) to counterbalance the salt. Dairy can mellow salt too – a swirl of cream in a soup or a dollop of yogurt in a sauce can smooth harsh saltiness.

And yes, you might have heard of the old "add a potato" trick: putting a raw potato into a salty soup to absorb salt. ChatGPT knows this advice, though it might explain that while a potato does soak up some salt, it also soaks up liquid, so it's not a magic bullet. Still, it won't hurt to try if you have one! The bottom line is, don't throw out the dish until you've tried to save it.

Let's see this in action. Imagine you've made a big pot of vegetable soup and accidentally doubled the salt. You quickly tell ChatGPT what happened and what you have on hand:

Home Cook: "I'm in the middle of making vegetable soup and it's *way* too salty. I was eyeballing salt and definitely overdid it. I still have some unsalted vegetable broth, a potato, and a lemon. What should I do to fix the soup?"

ChatGPT: "Too salty? Don't worry, it's fixable. First, pour in some of that unsalted vegetable broth (start with a cup or two) to dilute the soup. This spreads the salt out over a larger volume. Next, peel that potato and cut it into a few large chunks, then toss them in and let the soup simmer for another 15 minutes or so. The potato will absorb some salt (and you can discard it later). After diluting, give the soup a taste. If it's still very salty, squeeze in some lemon juice — a tablespoon or so to start. The acidity will brighten the flavor and counteract the saltiness. Finally, if you have any cream or unsalted tomato puree, you could stir a bit in to mellow things out, but it might not even be necessary. Keep adjusting gradually and tasting. Your soup will become balanced and tasty!"

In this exchange, ChatGPT offered several complementary fixes: dilution (adding broth), absorption (the potato), and acid (lemon). You might not end up needing every step, but having options means you can try one, taste, and then try the next if needed. The assistant's advice is encouraging and methodical, which helps you feel in control. A soup that seemed ruined can turn out just fine after these adjustments.

Too Spicy? Perhaps your hand slipped with the cayenne pepper, or those jalapeños turned out spicier than you thought. An overly spicy (hot) dish can actually cause panic—nobody wants to serve a meal that sets mouths on fire unexpectedly. ChatGPT's advice will focus on calming that heat. Common suggestions include adding dairy or coconut milk (capsaicin, the spicy compound, is fat-soluble, so creamy things help), adding sweetness, or simply increasing volume.

If it's a stew or curry, adding more broth or vegetables can dilute the heat. A bit of sugar or honey can take the edge off a fiery sauce. Acidic ingredients like vinegar or lime juice also help balance spiciness, much like they do with salt. And serving the dish with bland starches (rice, bread, noodles) can make each bite less intense.

Let's say you're whipping up a Thai green curry and tasted it to find it's unbearably spicy. You have an extra can of coconut milk in the pantry and some lime on the counter. Here's how that conversation with ChatGPT might look:

Home Cook: "My Thai green curry is delicious but *extremely* spicy – it's practically burning our tongues. I still have a can of coconut milk and a lime. What can I do to reduce the heat without ruining the flavor?"

ChatGPT: "To tame the heat in your Thai curry, definitely use that extra can of coconut milk. Pour in half the can first and stir well – coconut milk will mellow the spiciness and make the curry creamier. You can add more if needed. Next, squeeze in some lime juice (about half a lime to start). The acidity will balance the flavors and slightly cut the perception of heat. If you have a bit of sugar or palm sugar, add a teaspoon of that as well; a touch of sweetness can counteract the spice. Also, double-check that you've added enough salt, as proper seasoning can actually round out excessive heat. Let the curry simmer a few more minutes and then taste again. Serve it with plenty of rice, which will help absorb some heat too. It should be much milder and still delicious."

By combining a dairy (coconut milk) with an acid (lime) and a hint of sweetness, the curry's fire is brought under control. ChatGPT also slipped in a reminder about serving with rice – an example of how it thinks holistically about your meal. You might not have thought of that in a panic. This kind of comprehensive fix is where an AI assistant shines: it remembers all the little tricks so you don't have to.

Too Sweet? On the opposite end, maybe you added double sugar in your tomato sauce or your stir-fry sauce turned candy-sweet. When a savory dish is too sweet, the fixes involve adding sour, salty, or bitter notes to counteract the sugar. ChatGPT might recommend stirring in some vinegar or lemon juice to introduce acidity. A bit of salt can also help balance out sweetness (salt intensifies other flavors and can reduce perceived sweetness).

In some cases, adding more of a non-sweet ingredient will dilute the sugariness – for example, more tomatoes into an overly sweet pasta sauce, or more broth into a sweet stew. Spices like chili flakes or black pepper can add a hint of heat to distract from sweetness as well.

Imagine you're simmering a homemade barbecue sauce and realize it's far too sweet (perhaps the recipe had a heavy hand with brown sugar). You mention what you have available to fix it:

Home Cook: "Help, my barbecue sauce came out overly sweet – it tastes like candy! I have cider vinegar, Worcestershire sauce, and some canned tomato puree. How can I save this sauce?"

ChatGPT: "You can definitely rescue that barbecue sauce. Start by adding a good splash of cider vinegar — try two tablespoons and stir, then taste. The vinegar's acidity will cut through the sweetness. Next, add a few dashes of Worcestershire sauce; it brings tangy, savory notes that balance sugar (plus some umami depth). If it's still too sweet, stir in some of that tomato puree to bulk up the sauce without more sugar. Let it simmer for a few minutes to meld the flavors. Lastly, consider a pinch of salt if needed, as a little salt can help counter sweetness. Keep tweaking with small additions and tasting. Soon you'll have a tangy, balanced barbecue sauce that's no longer dessert-sweet."

After following this advice, your barbecue sauce would likely regain its smoky-savory character, and you've learned a handy lesson: most flavor bombs can be defused with the right counter-flavors. ChatGPT's real-time suggestions mean you can adjust the sauce on the fly, no lengthy web searches required.

Whether it's salt, spice, or sugar that's gone overboard, the theme is balance. By asking ChatGPT for help and mentioning what ingredients you have, you get tailor-made tips to swing the flavor pendulum back to center. Overshooting the seasoning is scary in the moment, but you now know it's usually fixable. With a few tweaks — and the calm guidance of your AI kitchen companion — that "ruined" dish can be pulled back from the brink.

Flavor issues are just one side of the coin. Sometimes the taste is fine, but the *texture* of a dish is off: sauces split, soups turn out too thick or thin, doughs misbehave. Next, we'll stir our way out of those predicaments with ChatGPT's help.

THICK, THIN, OR TOTALLY BROKEN

Not every kitchen mishap is about flavor; sometimes it's the consistency that goes astray. You lift the lid on a soup and find it as thin as water, or stir a sauce that ends up thicker than pudding. Worse, you might see a once-smooth sauce separate into oily and clumpy parts, which can send any cook into a frenzy. Texture troubles are incredibly common, but they're often fixable with a few tweaks. By describing the issue to ChatGPT, you can get step-by-step guidance to bring your dish back to the right consistency.

Let's tackle the simple ones first: too thick or too thin. If your soup or sauce is too thick (say, a stew turned stodgy or a curry that's more paste than sauce), the fix is usually straightforward: add liquid. ChatGPT will usually suggest stirring in some water, stock, or milk (depending on the dish) a little at a time until the consistency looks right. It might remind you to adjust seasoning after thinning out, since adding liquid can dilute flavor.

On the flip side, if that soup or gravy is too thin and runny, the solution is to remove water or add a thickener. ChatGPT could tell you to simmer the pot longer with the lid off to let excess liquid evaporate (essentially reducing the sauce). Or, if time is short, you can thicken quickly by mixing a teaspoon or two of cornstarch or flour with cold water (a "slurry") and stirring it into the boiling liquid. Other thickeners might be mashed potatoes, breadcrumbs, or a puree of some ingredients already in the dish (for example, blending a portion of a vegetable soup and pouring it back can thicken it naturally).

For example, imagine you've made a pan gravy to go with roasted chicken, but it's looking disappointingly thin and watery. You can ask ChatGPT how to rescue it:

Home Cook: "My chicken pan gravy is too thin and not coating the back of a spoon. I have flour and butter on hand (no cornstarch). How can I thicken the gravy quickly?"

ChatGPT: "To thicken a thin gravy, you can make a quick flour slurry. In a small bowl, mix about 1 tablespoon of flour with 2 tablespoons of cold water until it's smooth (no lumps). Bring your gravy back to a simmer and slowly whisk in the flour slurry. Keep stirring as it bubbles; within a minute or two, the gravy should start to thicken. If it's still thinner than you'd like, make a little more slurry and add it in gradually. Alternatively, since you have butter and flour, you could make a quick roux: melt a tablespoon of butter in a pan, stir in a tablespoon of flour to form a paste, and cook it for a minute. Then gradually whisk your gravy into that roux. But if the gravy is already made, the slurry method is faster. Don't forget to let it simmer for a bit to cook out any raw flour taste. Soon you'll have a nice, velvety gravy that coats the spoon."

ChatGPT gave two options here: the slurry (quick and easy, made right in the gravy pot) and a classic roux method (a couple extra steps, but useful if you don't mind an extra pan). Notice the answer also included a pro-tip about cooking out the raw flour taste, which is exactly the kind of detail an experienced cook or good recipe would mention. With this guidance, your gravy can go from watery to just right in minutes, and dinner is saved.

Now, what about a sauce that's **totally broken**? By "broken," we mean it has separated into parts – for example, a creamy sauce where the oil or butter has pooled and the solids are clumping, or a hollandaise that's curdled. This can happen if a sauce gets too hot, or if ingredients were added too quickly. It looks like a disaster, but ChatGPT can walk you through a rescue. Often, the advice is to create a new emulsion and slowly whisk the broken sauce into it. For a butter-based sauce like hollandaise or a broken mayonnaise, ChatGPT might say to whisk a fresh egg yolk in a bowl and then gradually drizzle the broken sauce into it while whisking vigorously, essentially "restarting" the sauce. For a dairy sauce that has curdled (say, a cream soup or cheese sauce), common fixes include removing it from heat immediately, adding a splash of something cold (like cold milk or even ice water) and whisking until it comes together, or thickening it with a starch to help bind it back. In some cases, blending the sauce can smooth it out if the break isn't too severe.

Suppose you're making a cheese sauce for macaroni and cheese, and suddenly it turns into a gritty, separated mess – the cheese has clumped and there's an oily layer on top. You send an SOS to ChatGPT:

Home Cook: "Oh no, my cheddar cheese sauce for mac and cheese **broke.** It's grainy and oily instead of smooth. I have more milk and an extra egg. Is there a way to fix it at this point?"

ChatGPT: "Don't panic—broken cheese sauce can sometimes be saved! First, take the sauce off the heat right away so it doesn't curdle further. Since you have an egg, let's use the egg yolk to re-emulsify the sauce. In a clean bowl, whisk the egg yolk with a tablespoon of warm milk. Now, slowly pour the broken cheese sauce into the bowl with the yolk mixture, whisking constantly. This will gradually bring the sauce back together as a smooth emulsion. Once it's looking creamy again, return it to low heat and gently warm it, stirring the whole time (do not let it boil). If you don't want to use the egg, another trick is to whisk in a teaspoon of cornstarch or flour into the sauce and heat gently; the starch can help pull it back together. And if all else fails, you can strain the sauce through a sieve to remove grainy bits – you'll lose a little cheese and thickness, but the remaining sauce will be smoother. Go slow and you should have a velvety cheese sauce again for your mac and cheese."

By laying out a clear plan (using an egg yolk to form a new emulsion), ChatGPT gives you a fighting chance to save a sauce that you might otherwise toss in frustration. It also offers a backup plan (using starch, or straining) which shows that even when the first fix doesn't fully work, there are additional measures to try. These are advanced techniques, yet the AI explains them in a calm, can-do manner that can give a novice cook the confidence to attempt them.

Texture problems aren't limited to liquids; doughs and batters can misbehave too. Maybe your bread dough is refusing to rise, or your cookie dough is so sticky you can't shape it. These issues can often be remedied if caught in time. If bread or pizza dough isn't rising, ChatGPT might ask you about your yeast (Is it old? Was the water too hot or cold?) and suggest moving the dough to a warmer spot to give the yeast a boost. It could recommend adding a pinch of sugar or a bit more yeast if you have it, to feed a sluggish dough. In a pinch, if time is nearly up and the dough is still a flat dud, the AI might get creative: for example, suggesting you roll it out thin and make a quick flatbread or pizza crust instead of a fluffy loaf, or even knead in some baking powder as a last resort to create a makeshift leavening.

Let's say you were expecting a nice puffy pizza crust, but the dough has barely risen after an hour and dinner time is near. You ask ChatGPT for advice:

Home Cook: "My pizza dough isn't rising, and it's been over an hour. I used active dry yeast but the dough is still pretty flat. I have more yeast and baking powder on hand. How can I salvage this for dinner?"

ChatGPT: "If your pizza dough isn't rising, first make sure it's in a warm, cozy spot — yeast can be slow in a cool kitchen. You could even put the bowl in a slightly warm (but turned-off) oven to help it along. Since time is short, let's try two things: First, dissolve a teaspoon of new yeast in warm water with a pinch of sugar, let it foam for 5 minutes, and then knead that into your dough. This can introduce some fresh yeast power. Cover the dough and give it another 20 minutes in a warm place. If it still doesn't puff up much, don't worry. You can roll the dough out thinner than usual and make a flatbread-style pizza. Another trick: mix in 1/2 teaspoon of baking powder into the dough — it's not traditional, but it will create some bubbles and lightness as it bakes. In short, either boost the yeast and wait a bit more, or pivot to a thinner crust. Either way, you'll get a tasty pizza for dinner!"

In this response, ChatGPT combined troubleshooting (warming the dough, testing the yeast) with a pragmatic backup plan (flatbread pizza with a chemical leavener). It's the kind of adaptive thinking that can turn a potential pizza failure into merely a slightly different style of pizza. Instead of no dinner, you've got a crispy flatbread pizza ready to go. The AI's suggestions remind you that in cooking there's often a plan B or C — you just need to know what to try.

By consulting ChatGPT for texture troubles, you gain insight into both the science and the craft of fixing a dish. Whether it's loosening up a thick paste, thickening a thin soup, or coaxing a stubborn dough, you'll get a calm voice guiding you through the solution. Texture issues can be nerve-wracking, but they're usually not final. A few adjustments, and you're back on track.

Even if flavor and texture are perfect, the *timing* of a meal can make or break the experience. Many home cooks have faced the scenario of a dish that's ready too early or too late. Next, we'll see how ChatGPT helps you juggle time itself in the kitchen when things aren't all coming together at once.

BURNT, UNDERCOOKED, OR OVERDONE

Sometimes the issue isn't flavor or consistency, but how far (or not far enough) the cooking has gone. You meant to sauté those veggies, not torch them to charcoal. Or maybe the casserole needed 10 more minutes, and now half of it is underdone. Overcooking and undercooking mishaps happen to everyone. The trick is figuring out if what's left is salvageable, and often it is. ChatGPT can help you determine the best course of action to save a scorched or dry dish, or safely finish cooking something that came out underdone. It's all about making the best of what you have.

Scorched but Salvageable: Let's start with burnt food. The golden rule: if something is burnt on the bottom of a pot, don't stir it! The uncharred portion above might still be okay. ChatGPT will likely walk you through the process of rescuing what's not burnt and leaving the rest. For example, it might advise you to carefully transfer the stew or sauce to a new pot, ladling it out and stopping before you reach the burnt layer. This way, you're removing the good parts without scraping up burnt bits. Next, you might need to combat any smoky or bitter taste that has seeped in. A common trick is to add a bit of something acidic (like vinegar or tomato) or a pinch of sugar to balance bitterness. Some cooks even drop in a spoonful of peanut butter or a piece of bread to absorb the burnt flavor – tricks ChatGPT might suggest if appropriate for the dish. The AI could also recommend adding aromatic spices or herbs to re-layer the flavor and distract from any remaining smokiness. The goal is to mask or offset the burnt notes so the dish is still enjoyable.

For instance, imagine you left a pot of chili on the stove a bit too long, and the bottom got scorched. The whole kitchen has that burnt smell now. You ask ChatGPT for help:

Home Cook: "I think I burnt the bottom of my chili con carne. It smells a bit smoky and burnt. I haven't stirred it yet. How can I save as much of it as possible?"

ChatGPT: "Good job not stirring! You can definitely salvage the chili above the burnt bottom. First, carefully spoon or ladle out the chili into a new pot or bowl, leaving behind any stuck-on bits at the bottom. Don't scrape the bottom of the pot – we don't want those charred pieces mixing in. Once you've moved the chili, taste it to see how much of a burnt flavor remains. If you detect a mild burnt taste, add a teaspoon of sugar or a tablespoon of tomato paste and stir well — a little sweetness and tomato can help neutralize bitterness and smoke. You could also add a splash of vinegar or lemon juice to brighten the flavors and cover up the burnt note. Another trick: if you have peanut butter and the flavor would mesh with your chili, stir in a small spoonful (it sounds odd, but peanut butter's richness can mask burnt flavors). Let the chili simmer on low in the new pot for a short while and taste again. You might find it's now perfectly fine. And hey, if there's still a slight smokiness, just call it "smoky chili" and serve it with a smile!"

By following these steps, you've rescued the majority of your chili. ChatGPT's suggestions — from the careful transfer to clever flavor fixes — can turn a near-disaster into a dish that's at least 90% of what you intended. The playful reassurance at the end ("call it 'smoky chili'") is a reminder that a bit of creativity and confidence can make even an imperfect dish enjoyable.

Dry or Overcooked? Overcooking usually results in dry or tough food. Chicken breasts, pork chops, steaks, fish fillets – if left too long, they lose moisture and joy. While you can't *uncook* something, you can often improve its texture or find a new way to serve it so it's not a total loss. ChatGPT might suggest adding moisture back into the food, like drizzling stock or sauce over sliced meat, or simmering overcooked vegetables in a little butter to give them softness and fat. Sometimes the advice is to repurpose: an over roasted chicken that's Sahara-dry could be shredded and mixed with mayo and herbs to become a chicken salad, or chopped and cooked with a flavorful sauce to become a new dish (like enchiladas or curry). The AI can offer these creative pivots when a straight resurrection isn't possible.

Let's say you grilled some chicken breasts and they turned out chalky and dry. You still want to serve them for dinner somehow, without your family reaching for water after each bite. You consult ChatGPT:

Home Cook: "Help! I overcooked these chicken breasts – they're so dry and tough. Dinner is in 10 minutes. What can I do to make them taste good or at least not so dry?"

ChatGPT: "Overcooked chicken happens, but we can definitely make it better. One quick fix: slice the chicken breasts thinly against the grain (this will make the pieces feel more tender). Warm up some chicken broth (even water with a bit of salt and butter if you don't have broth) and toss the sliced chicken in it for a minute or two. The meat will absorb a little moisture and reheat gently, helping with the dryness. Then, serve the chicken with a sauce or topping. Do you have barbecue sauce, teriyaki sauce, or even just some olive oil and lemon? A generous drizzle will add flavor and moisture. You could also chop the chicken and mix it into a quick pasta dish or a salad with a creamy dressing, so the dryness is less apparent. But if time is short, slicing and serving with a tasty sauce or gravy is your best bet. Garnish with something fresh (herbs or a squeeze of lemon) to give it a bright finish. Your chicken will be much more palatable, I promise!"

In this response, ChatGPT gave immediate triage (slice and soak in broth) followed by serving suggestions (add sauce, integrate into another dish). This two-pronged approach – fix what you can and then cleverly disguise or compensate for the rest – is exactly how professional chefs salvage overcooked meat. By following the advice, your dry chicken becomes a decent meal: thinner slices moistened with broth and perked up with a flavorful sauce. No one at the table needs to know the meat was overdone; they'll just taste a flavorful dish.

Undercooked and Running Out of Time: The flip side is pulling something out of the oven or off the stove only to find it's not cooked through. Perhaps the roast needs more time, or the brownies are gooey in the center (and not in a good way). If you catch it in time, the obvious answer is to cook it longer.

But if you only discover the undercooking at the moment of serving, you'll need a quick remedy. ChatGPT can help assess whether it's safe to quickly finish cooking and how. For meats, the AI might suggest cutting the protein into smaller pieces, which cook faster. For example, if a roast is underdone, slice it and quickly sear the slices or braise them in a pan of hot broth to bring them to doneness. If poultry is undercooked near the bone, you could carve off the cooked parts to serve, and return the underdone pieces to the oven or microwave to finish. In the case of underbaked goods like bread or cake, if it's just slightly underdone in the middle, you can often put it back in the oven for a few more minutes (covering the edges if they're already browned). Or you might embrace the "gooey" nature – underbaked brownies can be served as warm chocolate pudding with ice cream, for example, by leaning into the soft texture.

Consider you've roasted a beef tenderloin, sliced it open at the table, and found the center to be much rarer than your guests prefer. They're hungry now. You discreetly step into the kitchen and ask ChatGPT for a game plan:

Home Cook: "I have a roast beef that's undercooked in the middle (too rare for my guests). I've sliced it and I have a skillet and some beef broth on hand. What's the fastest way to finish cooking these slices without drying them out?"

ChatGPT: "For undercooked roast beef slices, a quick sear or braise will do the trick. Since you have a skillet and broth, try this: heat the skillet over medium-high heat and add a splash of that beef broth (just enough to cover the bottom). Once it's hot and steaming, lay the rare slices in the broth in a single layer. Cook them for a minute or two on each side – the hot broth will both cook the meat and keep it moist. Flip the slices and check doneness; they'll quickly turn from deep red to pink or brown depending on how well-done you need them. This basically gently poaches the beef in its own juices. Remove the slices as soon as they are cooked to your liking. You can then use the remaining broth in the pan as a light jus to spoon over the meat when serving. This method will get your beef up to temperature in just a few minutes without drying it out. Take a deep breath – your dinner is saved and your guests will be none the wiser!"

Here, ChatGPT combined speed with gentleness: using a bit of broth in a hot pan to rapidly cook the slices while preventing them from drying. It's essentially speeding up what the oven would do slowly, but with added moisture. The suggestion to use the leftover juices as a sauce is a bonus touch. With this quick fix, that underdone roast transforms into perfectly cooked slices by the time you return to the dining room.

By now you've seen that even burnt bits, bone-dry meat, or pink-in-the-middle roasts can often be rescued. The solutions usually involve removing what's ruined (or not quite done), adding moisture or flavor, and being unafraid to serve things a little differently than originally planned. ChatGPT, with its wealth of kitchen know-how, can guide you through these recovery missions calmly, helping you turn "uh-oh" into "it's okay!"

So far we've focused on taste, texture, and doneness, but there's another tricky aspect of cooking to consider: timing. Often, one part of a meal is done before the others, or guests arrive late and throw off your schedule. Next, we'll see how ChatGPT helps you juggle time itself in the kitchen when things aren't all coming together perfectly at once.

TIMING TROUBLE: IT'S NOT ALL READY AT ONCE

One of the hardest parts of cooking a full meal is getting every dish to finish at the same time. Perhaps the roast is done way before the vegetables, or the pasta is ready but the sauce still needs simmering. Maybe your dinner guests are running 30 minutes late, and you're worried your perfect meal will overcook or get cold. Timing issues can turn a calm cook into a bundle of nerves. Here, too, ChatGPT can be your coach, offering tips to adjust on the fly so that everything (and everyone) stays hot and happy.

If a dish is done too early, the key is to keep it warm without drying it out or overcooking it. ChatGPT might suggest using your oven's "warm" setting (around 200°F/90°C) or the lowest heat, covered with foil, to hold a dish. For example, resting a roast or steaks in a warm oven not only keeps them hot but can actually improve juiciness. If the sauce is ready but the rice isn't, the AI could remind you to turn the sauce to the lowest heat (or off) and cover it; most sauces can sit for a bit and be gently reheated if needed. Sometimes wrapping something in foil and towels and placing it in an insulated container (even a cooler with no ice) can keep it piping hot for quite a while. ChatGPT will have these tricks at the ready, tailored to what you're cooking.

On the other hand, what if something is behind schedule? You can ask ChatGPT for ways to speed it up or for quick alternatives. Say your side dish is taking longer than expected – the assistant might recommend cutting whatever you're cooking into smaller pieces to finish faster, or increasing the heat briefly (with caution to avoid burning). If the delay is irredeemable (for instance, you realize you don't have time to bake that side dish at all), ChatGPT can propose a fast substitute. Perhaps you can whip up a simple salad with ingredients on hand, or microwave some vegetables as a quick side. If you have bread, maybe toast it with garlic butter for instant garlic bread. The AI can get creative: turning that uncooked side into tomorrow's project and suggesting something you can do in five or ten minutes right now.

Plate-by-plate adaptation is another clever approach. Not everything must hit the table at once. ChatGPT might encourage you to serve in courses or a staggered fashion. For example, if the appetizer or salad is ready but the main needs more time, serve the salad first rather than letting it wilt. If one person's steak is perfect but another piece is underdone, start serving the properly cooked portions so they don't get cold, while you briefly return the underdone one to the pan. The chatbot can reassure you that it's okay to improvise the order of serving – dinner doesn't have to be a perfectly synchronized orchestra every time.

Let's look at a common scenario. You've roasted a chicken and it's finished faster than you anticipated, but your side dishes need another 15 minutes on the stove. What do you do to keep that chicken hot and juicy? You turn to ChatGPT:

Home Cook: "My roast chicken is done way too early – the sides won't be ready for 15-20 minutes. How can I keep the chicken warm without drying it out?"

ChatGPT: "Congrats on the chicken being done! To keep it hot and moist for the next 15-20 minutes, do this: tent the roast chicken loosely with foil (shiny side in) – that will retain heat but not trap steam so the skin stays a bit crisp. If you have an oven free, put the chicken in there on the lowest setting (around 175°F-200°F). If the oven is occupied with sides, no worries: wrapping the foil-covered chicken in a clean towel can act as insulation. Also, the resting time will actually make it juicier when you carve it. About 5 minutes before serving, you can pop it back into a hotter oven for just a couple of minutes to re-crisp the skin if needed. Your chicken will be nice and warm when the sides are finally ready."

In this advice, ChatGPT combined several tactics: foil tenting, using residual heat or a low oven, and even a trick to re-crisp the skin. It's a step-by-step game plan to navigate an awkward timing gap. Instead of panicking that the star of the meal will get cold, you've kept it in great shape until everyone is ready to eat.

Now consider the opposite problem: your main is almost done, but your planned side dish went up in smoke (oops!). Time is short and you need a replacement side *now*. You ask ChatGPT for a quick save:

Home Cook: "Uh oh, I burned the side dish I was making. Dinner is in 10 minutes. What's a super quick side I can make with basic ingredients?"

ChatGPT: "Don't worry, you've got options. If you have any fresh veggies or salad greens, that's the easiest route: throw together a quick salad. Even just sliced tomatoes drizzled with olive oil, vinegar, salt, and pepper can work as a simple salad. No fresh veg? Check your freezer – do you have frozen peas, corn, or mixed veggies? You can microwave or sauté those with a bit of butter and garlic, and they'll be ready in minutes. Another idea: whip up some quick couscous if you have it (it only takes about 5 minutes to fluff up with hot water or broth). Or even toast some bread and spread it with garlic butter for impromptu garlic bread. Basically, think simple: something that adds a bit of color and texture to the plate. It doesn't have to be fancy, just speedy and tasty. Your main dish will still shine, and no one will miss the original side."

In this response, ChatGPT rattled off a bunch of rapid side-dish ideas – salad, microwaved veggies, quick couscous, garlic bread – using items many kitchens have on hand. The tone is reassuring ("don't worry, you've got options") which is exactly the calm voice you need in a pinch. You pick one suggestion (say, the frozen peas sautéed with butter), and within 10 minutes you have a decent side on the table after all. Crisis averted, creativity to the rescue.

These time-management fixes highlight another strength of ChatGPT: it thinks of things we might overlook when we're stressed about timing. Whether it's reminding you about that packet of couscous in the pantry or giving you permission to serve the meal in shifts, it ensures that the *timing* of dinner doesn't derail the *enjoyment* of dinner.

We've now handled just about every kind of mid-cooking crisis, including the clock itself. Now, to cap it off, let's look at a medley of rapid-fire ChatGPT rescues across various scenarios – our trusty AI assistant in action, swooping in to save the day one prompt at a time.

PROMPT TO THE RESCUE: REAL-TIME EXAMPLES

To demonstrate how swiftly ChatGPT can come to your aid, here are several mini case-studies of kitchen crises and how you (the Home Cook) might phrase the prompt, followed by ChatGPT's concise advice. These examples cover a range of problems, showing the versatility of our AI kitchen companion's knowledge.

Home Cook: "My gravy tastes fine but it's full of lumps. How do I fix lumpy gravy?"

ChatGPT: "No worries. If your gravy has lumps, the fastest fix is to strain it: pour the gravy through a fine-mesh sieve into another pot, pressing the liquid through and leaving the lumps behind. Alternatively, you can use an immersion blender (or a regular blender carefully) to puree the gravy until it's smooth. Heat it back up and it'll be nice and lump-free."

Home Cook: "I made a stew, but there's a thick layer of grease on top. The whole thing looks oily. What can I do?"

ChatGPT: "An oily stew is common, especially with rich meats. First, skim off as much of the fat as you can with a spoon. To get the smaller droplets, try dropping an ice cube into the stew and stirring it around for 10-15 seconds – it will attract fat, which you can then scoop out (remove the ice before it melts). You can also float a piece of bread or a few lettuce leaves on the surface; they'll soak up oil quickly – just take them out before they disintegrate. After skimming, give the stew a good stir and it should look and taste less greasy."

Home Cook: "I'm about to make pancakes, but I just realized I have no eggs. What can I use instead of an egg in the batter?"

ChatGPT: "In pancakes, you have a few egg substitutes. If you have a ripe banana, mash about half of it to replace one egg – it'll bind the batter and add a little sweetness. No banana? Mix 1 tablespoon of flaxseed meal with 3 tablespoons of water and let it sit a few minutes; it becomes gel-like, similar to an egg (chia seeds work too). Even a quarter-cup of applesauce or yogurt can replace an egg in pancakes. Use whatever you have: whisk it into the batter as you would an egg, and you'll get fluffy pancakes just fine."

Home Cook: "I was whipping cream for dessert and I went too far – now it's clumpy and looks like butter. Did I ruin it?"

ChatGPT: "Sounds like you're halfway to making butter! Over-whipped cream separates into butter and buttermilk. Unfortunately, you can't turn it back into light whipped cream. But it's not ruined: drain off the liquid (buttermilk) and you'll have unsalted butter. Rinse it in cold water and squeeze it in a spoon to solidify if you plan to keep it. You can use this homemade butter on toast or in baking. If you still need whipped cream and have more heavy cream, start a new batch – and stop whipping as soon as it holds soft peaks next time."

Home Cook: "I have a pot of chili that was supposed to feed four, but now six people are coming over. How can I stretch it to serve more?"

ChatGPT: "To stretch your chili, add bulk and liquid. If you have a can or two of beans (or corn, or even diced tomatoes), throw them in – they'll increase the volume. You can also add some broth or water to thin it slightly (turn up the seasoning if you dilute the flavor). Another trick: serve the chili over rice or alongside plenty of bread. That way each person's bowl has more hearty filler and less need for extra chili. Top each serving with cheese or sour cream, which makes portions feel lavish. With these add-ins, your pot should comfortably satisfy six."

Home Cook: "My cookie dough turned out too runny, it's more like batter and I can't scoop it into cookies. How do I fix it?"

ChatGPT: "If cookie dough is too runny, it likely needs more structure. First, try chilling it in the fridge for 20-30 minutes; colder dough is firmer and easier to scoop. If it's still too soft, mix in a bit more flour – start with 2 tablespoons and see if it comes together into a thicker dough. Alternatively, if the recipe forgot a binding ingredient (like an egg) or too much liquid went in, you could add a spoonful of oats or breadcrumbs to absorb moisture. Once the dough holds its shape, scoop and bake. The cookies might come out a tad softer or cakier, but they'll be tasty!"

Home Cook: "Disaster! My cake broke into pieces when I took it out of the pan. It's for a party – how can I present it now?"

ChatGPT: "Don't panic. If your cake broke, you have a few creative serving options. Easiest: turn it into a trifle. Grab a big bowl or individual glasses, layer chunks of cake with whipped cream and maybe fruit or pudding. It becomes a delicious 'layered dessert' – no one will guess it was accidental. Or make cake pops: crumble the cake further, mix with a bit of frosting, roll into balls and chill, then dip in melted chocolate on sticks. If time is short, you can also "glue" the cake back together with frosting and then cut it into rustic squares, calling it a 'deconstructed cake.' Embrace the crumble! It'll still taste great."

Home Cook: "I added too much vinegar to my salad dressing – it's way too sour. How do I fix an overly acidic vinaigrette?"

ChatGPT: "That's an easy fix. Whisk in a bit more olive oil to mellow out the vinegar. Also, add something sweet: a teaspoon of honey or a pinch of sugar will balance the acidity. A little salt can help round it out too. Adjusting those ingredients will turn your dressing from puckering sour to pleasantly tangy. Finally, toss in an extra pinch of herbs or garlic to further mask any sharpness. Now you have a balanced vinaigrette ready to coat your salad."

You've now seen just how much of a safety net ChatGPT can be in the kitchen. In this chapter, we covered a gamut of kitchen nightmares and watched as our AI kitchen companion turned them back into mere speed bumps. From fixing flavors that were out of balance to rescuing the texture of sauces and saving dishes that were too burnt, too dry, or not done enough – you've learned there's almost always a solution at hand. The takeaway is empowering: **no kitchen mistake has to be final.** With a calm question to ChatGPT and a willingness to adapt, you can recover from just about any mishap and even learn something in the process.

Armed with these troubleshooting strategies, you can approach cooking with more confidence and less fear. Maybe you'll even take on that challenging recipe or cook for a crowd, knowing that if things go sideways, you have a clever helper on call. Every slip-up becomes an opportunity to improvise and improve, rather than a reason to panic or give up. Importantly, you've also built up your own intuition by seeing how ChatGPT diagnoses and fixes problems – over time, you'll start anticipating solutions even before asking.

As we move forward, we'll shift our focus from solving problems to making your cooking experiences even richer and more creative. You've mastered the art of kitchen damage control; now it's time to explore new horizons in the AI-assisted kitchen. With ChatGPT by your side, there's no limit to what you can cook up next!

13

KITCHEN SCIENCE, SIMPLIFIED

Cooking is often called an art, but behind every amazing dish is a bit of science. In this chapter, "Kitchen Science, Simplified," you'll learn how understanding the **why** behind cooking can make you a more confident and creative cook. We're diving into the science that explains textures, flavors, and all those little kitchen mysteries – and we'll show how ChatGPT can be your friendly guide through it all. By the end, you'll see that you don't need a lab or a PhD to grasp kitchen science; you just need a pinch of curiosity and the right questions.

Have you ever followed a recipe and wondered why you were doing a particular step? Maybe you've asked yourself, "Why do I need to sear the meat first?" or "What makes bread dough rise so much?" Home cooks naturally bump into these questions. This chapter encourages you to embrace that curiosity. Each section will highlight common cooking phenomena – like why heat changes food, how proteins behave, or what role acids play – and show you how to ask ChatGPT for clear, simple explanations. Think of ChatGPT as the teacher you always wish you had in the kitchen: patient, knowledgeable, and ready to break down any concept into plain language.

Throughout the chapter, we'll keep it practical. You'll find plenty of real-world examples from everyday cooking. Whether it's the secret behind a crispy roast potato or the science of a perfect vinaigrette, we'll illustrate how to use ChatGPT to uncover the answers. We'll also include lots of example prompts you can try. For instance, if you're curious about why your homemade soup tastes richer the next day, you'll see how to frame that question to get a satisfying answer. These examples make the learning interactive – almost like you're having a conversation with a chef or a food scientist, right in your kitchen.

Importantly, everything here is geared toward **home cooks of all skill levels.** You might be a beginner who's just starting to experiment, or you could be a seasoned home chef wanting to refine your techniques. No matter where you're at, the tone will stay warm and supportive. We know science can feel intimidating or overly technical. But "Kitchen Science, Simplified" is exactly that – a friendly simplification. We'll avoid jargon when possible, and when scientific terms do pop up (like "Maillard reaction" or "pH level"), we'll explain them in a down-to-earth way, often using analogies you can relate to.

By exploring these seven sections, you'll gain insights into: *why food behaves the way it does*, how *heat and time transform your ingredients*, what happens when *proteins break down and create flavor*, the magic of *emulsions and reductions*, the influence of *acids and bases* on your cooking, applying *kitchen chemistry in practice* for better recipes, and finally, *smart prompts* to keep the learning going as you cook. It's a journey from the basic to the applied – always with the help of ChatGPT to answer your questions on the spot.

So let's get ready to demystify your kitchen. Science isn't something apart from cooking – it's simmering in every pot and baking in every oven. With ChatGPT by your side, you'll find that understanding the science can be fun, empowering, and immediately useful. Grab your apron and your curiosity, and let's explore how to cook smarter through a bit of kitchen science!

WHY FOOD BEHAVES THE WAY IT DOES

Cooking can sometimes feel like a series of magic tricks. Dough doubles in size, meat turns brown and savory, onions go from sharp to sweet. **Why** do these transformations happen? In this section, we'll explore how to prompt ChatGPT to reveal the science behind such kitchen mysteries – the reasons for different textures, flavors, and outcomes in your cooking. It's all about asking "why" and getting a clear, helpful answer. When you start understanding the science, you'll not only satisfy your curiosity but also become a better cook, because you'll know what's really happening in your pots and pans.

One of the best ways to learn in the kitchen is to ask questions about everyday scenarios. For example, imagine you've just sautéed onions for a soup and they turned golden-brown and sweet. You might wonder, *"Why do onions get sweet when I cook them?"* This is a perfect question for ChatGPT. By phrasing it simply – *"Why do onions become sweet when caramelized on the stove?"* – you invite an explanation of the process. ChatGPT might explain that onions are full of natural sugars, and slow cooking lets those sugars break down and caramelize. In fact, as food science tells us (and as your AI assistant can confirm), caramelization is the process where heat causes sugar molecules to break apart and form new, sweeter-tasting compounds. That's why those browned onions have a rich, sweet flavor with no sugar added – their own sugars did the work.

Now think about texture. Maybe you've baked chicken and the skin didn't turn out crispy, or you fried potatoes and they came out soggy. You could ask ChatGPT, *"What makes foods like chicken skin or fries crispy or soggy?"* A good answer will mention factors like **moisture** and **heat**. Don't be surprised if ChatGPT's explanation touches on the idea that removing surface moisture is key to crispness. In the case of a roast chicken, patting the skin dry and cooking it at high heat helps water evaporate, allowing the skin to crackle. For French fries, the potato's starch and water content play a role: to get a fry crispy, you first cook it to soften the inside and gelatinize starch, then cook it again at higher heat to drive off water and crisp up the exterior. The AI might not give you the full double-frying lesson immediately, but it will point out that **dryness equals crispness.** If it doesn't, you can follow up: *"Why does removing moisture make foods crispier?"* – and it will dig into how water turning to steam leaves behind a crunchy structure.

Flavor is another area where "why" comes up often. Ever notice how a piece of meat or toast that's nicely browned tastes more complex and delicious? You could ask, *"Why does browning food make it taste better?"* This will likely lead ChatGPT to talk about the Maillard reaction – a fancy term for a bundle of chemical reactions that happen when proteins and sugars in food are exposed to heat. ChatGPT might say something like: *"Browning creates hundreds of new flavor compounds, which is why a grilled steak or toasted bread has such a deep, savory flavor compared to when they're raw."* Even if you don't remember the term "Maillard reaction," you'll understand that heat transforms the basic building blocks of food (amino acids and sugars) into new flavors and aromas. In short, brown = flavor, and that's the scientific truth. If you want to know more, you can always prompt, *"Explain the Maillard reaction in simple terms."* You'll get a friendly rundown about how heat drives this flavor-making process.

When asking ChatGPT for the "why" behind cooking outcomes, try to be specific about what you observed. Instead of a broad question like "Why did this happen?", frame it around the food and the method. For instance, *"Why did my bread dough rise so much overnight?"* will cue an explanation about yeast fermentation. The assistant might explain that yeast is a living organism that feeds on sugars in the dough and releases carbon dioxide gas, which gets trapped by the stretchy gluten network in the flour, causing the dough to expand. Essentially, your dough is full of tiny bubbles – like a balloon net – which is why it's puffed up in the morning. This kind of answer not only solves the mystery but also teaches you about yeast and gluten in a down-to-earth way (maybe even with a fun analogy, like comparing it to blowing bubbles into a soap solution).

The great thing is that no question is too simple or silly. If you wonder *"Why do I add salt to boiling water for pasta?"*, ChatGPT will happily tell you that it's mainly to season the pasta as it cooks, because noodles absorb salt from the water (making them taste better than if you add salt at the table). It might also mention that salted water boils at a slightly higher temperature, which can help the pasta cook a touch faster or more evenly – though the flavor impact is the big one.

By continuously asking these "why" questions, you turn cooking into a learning experience. ChatGPT can act like a knowledgeable friend who's always on hand to explain things. Over time, you'll start to see patterns: many answers relate to heat, time, and the inherent properties of ingredients. For so many kitchen questions, the answers boil down to how we use heat and time. These two elements are like the engines of transformation in cooking, affecting everything from texture to flavor. Let's explore them next, and see exactly how temperature and cooking duration change your food on a molecular level.

HEAT, TIME, AND TRANSFORMATION

If the kitchen had a master key, it would be **heat**. Apply heat for the right amount of **time**, and you transform raw ingredients into something entirely different. Much of cooking science boils down to how food changes with temperature over minutes or hours. ChatGPT can help you understand these transformations on a molecular level – but first, let's think about what's happening in our pots, ovens, and grills.

When you cook, you're essentially playing with energy. Heat causes molecules in food to move faster and collide more. A simple example is water turning into steam: at 212°F (100°C), water molecules move so fast they break free as gas (steam). If you've ever asked, *"Why does my steak sizzle and brown in a hot pan?"*, ChatGPT would explain that the high heat evaporates water on the steak's surface and triggers browning reactions. The sizzle is water rapidly turning to steam. Without enough heat, that steak would simply gray and release its juices instead of searing. This is why recipes often tell you to preheat a pan or oven – starting hot means food immediately begins the proper transformations rather than stewing or steaming slowly.

Different cooking methods are really different ways of managing heat and time. For instance, if you prompt ChatGPT with *"What's the difference between boiling and simmering a soup?"*, you'll learn that both involve cooking in water, but at different temperatures. Boiling is hotter and more agitated – great for pasta, but too rough for a delicate broth. Simmering, a gentler heat just below boiling, gives ingredients time to cook through evenly. A simmer is often key for stews because it allows **time** for flavors to develop without overcooking the solids. If you toss vegetables into furiously boiling water, they might cook on the outside faster than the inside. Ask ChatGPT *"Why do recipes say to simmer and not boil vigorously?"* and it might talk about heat distribution: at a simmer, heat penetrates food uniformly, whereas a rolling boil can lead to uneven cooking.

Heat and time work together in interesting ways. Sometimes high heat for a short time is what you need; other times, low heat for a long time does the trick. Consider asking *"Why do tough cuts of meat become tender with long, slow cooking?"* The answer lies in connective tissues like collagen. In a tough piece of beef or pork (think brisket or shoulder), collagen is a protein that's very chewy when undercooked. But given enough time at a moderate heat, collagen will gradually turn into gelatin, which is soft and jiggly. ChatGPT might explain: *"Above about 160°F (70°C), the collagen in meat begins to break down into gelatin. If you keep the meat at that temperature for a few hours, the tough fibers literally melt into tender gel, making the meat fall-apart soft."* That's why recipes for pulled pork or beef stew say to cook "low and slow." They keep the meat in the 160–180°F range for a long period. During that time, the dried-out muscle fibers get surrounded by gelatin, which makes them taste moist and succulent even though they're well-done. It's a perfect example of heat and time working magic together: too low a temperature and collagen wouldn't transform; too short a time and the process wouldn't complete.

On the flip side, consider a tender piece of fish or a lean chicken breast. Why do recipes insist you **not** overcook those? You could ask,

"What happens if I cook chicken breast too long?" The AI would explain that lean meats with little collagen simply dry out because their muscle proteins contract and squeeze out moisture when exposed to heat for too long. There's no connective tissue to melt and baste the meat. So for chicken breast, high heat for a shorter period – just until it's safely done – is ideal to keep it juicy. In other words, **time** is critical: even at the same oven temperature, a piece of food can go from perfect to overcooked if left too long. If you asked how to know when a roast chicken is done, ChatGPT might advise using a thermometer to check it's about 165°F (74°C) in the thickest part. After that, any extra time can start to dry it out.

Heat doesn't just cook food, it also moves through food. A thick roast or a loaf of bread cooks from the outside in. Heat travels inward by **conduction** – the outer parts heat up and pass that energy inward. That's why a roast needs resting (time again!) after you take it out of the oven: the outside may be much hotter than the center. Given a bit of time, the heat evens out internally, and juices also redistribute. If you slice too soon, the center might be a bit underdone or the juices might spill out and leave the meat drier. If you ask *"How does heat travel inside a roast?"*, you'd hear about how the surface gets hot first, and the importance of letting that heat redistribute (which is part of why resting meat is beneficial, as we'll soon cover in depth).

Different appliances apply heat differently. An oven surrounds food with hot air (even heating), a grill provides intense direct heat from below, and a pan on the stove gives direct contact heat. If you're unsure why a recipe picks one method, ask! For example, *"Why bake cookies at 350°F instead of 450°F?"* might lead to: at 350°F, the cookies have time to cook through evenly. At 450°F, they'd brown or burn on the edges before the middle set. The oven's moderate heat ensures the sugar and flour can caramelize and the cookie can dehydrate to the right texture without scorching. ChatGPT could also mention that many sugars and proteins develop the best flavors around that temperature range, aligning with the Maillard reaction's optimal zone.

One fascinating idea is "trading time for temperature." Many cooking reactions happen faster at higher temperatures, but given enough time, they can occur at lower temperatures too. That's the basis of sous-vide cooking. If you cook a steak sous-vide at 135°F (57°C) for a couple of hours, it will reach a perfect medium-rare throughout and become reasonably tender, even though 135°F is too low for boiling or baking. Time makes up for the lower heat. Prompt ChatGPT with *"How does sous-vide tenderize meat at low temperatures?"* and you'd learn that even at ~130°F, over a long time, some enzymes in the meat remain active and help tenderize it, and slow heating avoids squeezing out moisture. It's like a gentle coaxing instead of a forceful blast of heat.

By playing with questions about heat and time, you become better at judging how to cook things. You'll know why a stew isn't done in 30 minutes (collagen still tough), or why that quick-cook pancake batter shouldn't be at too low a heat (it'll dry out before browning). And in any situation where you're unsure – say you want to roast vegetables faster without burning them – ChatGPT can help you find that sweet spot of heat and time (maybe cut them smaller for faster cooking or use a higher heat initially then lower it).

Now that we've set the stage with heat and time, and seen a hint of proteins in action, let's zoom in on those proteins. They're at the heart of how textures form and flavors develop (especially that golden crust!). In the next section, we'll break down what happens to proteins when we cook – from meat fibers contracting to eggs solidifying – and how that builds up the flavors we love.

BREAKING DOWN PROTEINS, BUILDING UP FLAVOR

Proteins are the heavy lifters of texture in our foods. They make up the muscle fibers in meat, the albumin in egg whites, the casein in dairy, and even the gluten in dough. When we cook, we **denature** proteins – essentially unwinding their tight coils – and this leads to big changes in texture and flavor. In this section, we'll see how to prompt ChatGPT for explanations about things like why meat firms up, what creates that delicious brown crust, and why letting your steak "rest" really does make it juicier.

Let's start with a simple example: the humble egg. If you've ever fried or boiled an egg, you've watched a translucent, runny egg white turn solid and opaque. You might ask ChatGPT, *"Why do egg whites turn white and firm when cooked?"* The answer: protein denaturation. Egg whites are mostly proteins (like albumin) in water. Heat causes those protein molecules to unfold and then bond to each other, forming a new network. In plain terms, the egg white goes from a liquid to a delicate solid because its proteins have changed shape and locked together. This is why a cooked egg white is firm enough to pick up with a fork, whereas a raw egg white would slip right through. ChatGPT can break down that concept further if you like – perhaps using an analogy that it's like strands of yarn (proteins) tangling and clumping when heated, turning a fluid into a soft solid.

Now, consider meat. When you cook a piece of meat, several protein-related things happen. One is similar to the egg: the proteins in the muscle fibers denature and coagulate, which is why raw meat turns from translucent (or red) to opaque and firm when fully cooked. If you've ever wondered, *"Why does my chicken breast turn white and firm when I grill it?"*, it's that protein chemistry at work. But meat has another protein trick up its sleeve: the Maillard reaction, which we touched on earlier. This reaction involves proteins (more specifically, amino acids, the building blocks of proteins) and sugars on the surface of the food. When they react under high heat, they create entirely new flavor compounds. If you prompt ChatGPT with *"Why does a grilled steak have more flavor than a boiled steak?"*, it will likely explain that grilling causes browning via the Maillard reaction, which produces a host of savory, complex flavors. Those brown, crusty bits on a steak or the golden crust on a roast are literally flavor factories. By contrast, boiling a steak would cook it through without browning, yielding meat that might be tender but is comparatively bland.

To get practical, you could ask, *"How do I maximize flavor when searing meat?"* ChatGPT might advise patting the meat dry (to remove surface water) and heating the pan well before adding the meat. That's because dry, high-heat conditions favor the Maillard reaction, leading to a delicious crust. It could also mention not to overcrowd the pan – too much meat can lower the pan's temperature and cause steaming instead of searing. These are science-backed tips: moisture cools things down and prevents browning, and a hot surface ensures those proteins and sugars really "seize the moment" to create flavor.

Another common protein question is about tenderness. Let's say you tried a new marinade on a steak and it came out more tender. You might ask, *"How do acidic marinades tenderize meat?"* ChatGPT would tell you that acids (like vinegar or citrus) can help break down proteins on the meat's surface. Essentially, the acid starts to denature some of those proteins (like how heat does, but more gently), which can slightly soften the texture. If you've made ceviche (fish "cooked" in lime juice), you've seen how fish firms up and turns opaque in acid – that's proteins denaturing without heat. But the AI might also warn that too much acid for too long can make meat mushy; it "pre-cooks" the outer layer so much that it loses structure.

Enzymatic tenderizers are another angle. For example, *"Why does pineapple juice tenderize meat?"* Pineapple (and papaya) contain enzymes like bromelain that actively break down protein molecules. These enzymes can make a tough steak more tender by literally digesting some of the proteins. ChatGPT would likely caution that if left too long, these enzymes can make the texture overly soft and pasty – there's such thing as too tender.

Salt has a powerful effect on proteins as well. If you ask, *"What does brining do to meat?"*, you'll learn that soaking meat in a salt solution not only seasons it but changes the protein structure so the meat can hold more water. Salt causes some muscle proteins to unwind and gel, which improves their water-holding capacity. That's why a brined turkey can be juicier – it actually gains water weight during the brine, and its proteins then lock in that extra moisture during cooking. Also, as those proteins denature with heat, they form a matrix that's a bit more tender and less prone to squeezing juices out, thanks to the salt pre-treatment. The result is meat that's both well-seasoned throughout and plump.

One of the most misunderstood bits of cooking advice is to rest meat after cooking. Many folks wonder if it's truly necessary. Try asking ChatGPT, *"Why should I rest meat after cooking?"* and you'll get a juicy explanation. When meat cooks, its proteins tighten and push moisture towards the center (imagine squeezing a sponge – water moves away from the pressure). If you cut it immediately, those juices pour out onto the plate. But if you let the meat rest off the heat for a few minutes, those muscle fibers gradually relax and can reabsorb some of the liquid. So when you cut in after resting, far less juice escapes – it stays in each slice, making it taste juicier. Resting also evens out the temperature, finishing the cooking gently. ChatGPT might describe it like: *"Resting is letting the meat cool slightly so the juices redistribute and the meat finishes cooking evenly. It's the difference between a dry steak and a succulent one."* This is especially important for large cuts like roasts, but even a small steak benefits from a brief rest.

While meat and eggs are obvious protein stories, remember that proteins play a role in baking too – gluten, a protein in wheat, is key to bread structure. If you overmix muffin batter, gluten can make the muffins tough. If you use cake flour (lower protein) vs. bread flour (higher protein), you get a different texture. A curious baker might ask, *"Why does cake flour make a cake softer?"* The answer: cake flour has less protein, so it forms less gluten, leading to a more tender crumb. ChatGPT could also mention that things like adding a bit of acid (like buttermilk) to a cake can weaken gluten and tenderize the cake further – a protein adjustment again! On the flip side, kneading bread dough is all about encouraging protein (gluten) networks to form. It's fascinating how sometimes we want to develop proteins (chewy bread) and sometimes we want to limit them (tender cake).

By understanding proteins, you gain control over texture. You'll know why a slow-cooked pulled pork falls apart (collagen to gelatin) and why a quick-sautéed pork chop can turn tough (muscle fibers tightening without enough collagen to soften it). You'll see why scrambled eggs can go from creamy to rubbery if you cook them too hot (egg proteins tightening up too much). And whenever you face a kitchen puzzle involving texture – like "Why did my yogurt separate when I heated it?" or "How can I make my roast chicken more tender?" – you can turn to ChatGPT for a protein-centric explanation or solution.

We've covered a lot about structure and flavor through proteins. Now, let's venture into the realm of mixtures and chemistry – emulsions, reductions, caramelization – the science behind sauces, dressings, and sweets. It's time to stir up some kitchen chemistry and see how to ask ChatGPT about making and fixing these concoctions.

EMULSIONS, REDUCTIONS, AND REACTIONS

Some of the most intriguing kitchen questions arise when we're dealing with mixtures and transformations of liquids and sugars. How do oil and vinegar come together in a dressing without separating? Why does a sauce thicken and intensify after simmering? And what exactly is happening when sugar melts into caramel? In this section, we'll see how to prompt ChatGPT to explain the chemistry behind silky sauces, stable dressings, and perfectly browned sugars.

Emulsions are a great starting point. If you've made mayonnaise or vinaigrette, you know that oil and water normally don't mix – yet with the right technique (and a little magic from an emulsifier), they can form a stable blend. Suppose you ask ChatGPT, *"How do I keep my salad dressing from separating?"* You'll get an explanation of emulsions. An emulsion is a mixture of two liquids that usually repel each other (like oil and water), but one is broken into tiny droplets and dispersed in the other. For instance, mayonnaise is an emulsion of oil in water (vinegar or lemon juice) stabilized by egg yolk. The key is to add the oil slowly while whisking hard, so tiny oil droplets form and stay suspended. But they won't stay that way without an **emulsifier** – a molecule that can bond with both oil and water and keep them unified. ChatGPT might highlight that egg yolk contains lecithin, a natural emulsifier with a water-loving end and a fat-loving end. Lecithin molecules coat the oil droplets and prevent them from merging back together. In a vinaigrette, mustard can act as an emulsifier (mustard has compounds that help stabilize emulsions).

The advice you'd get: use an emulsifier (egg yolk for mayo, a dab of mustard for dressings), and incorporate one liquid into the other slowly while mixing vigorously. Temperature matters too – ingredients emulsify best when not too cold. You might follow up with, *"Why did my homemade mayo separate?"* and learn that adding oil too fast or not whisking enough can overwhelm the emulsifiers, causing the sauce to "break." ChatGPT would likely offer a fix: start with a fresh egg yolk and slowly whisk the broken sauce into it, re-establishing the emulsion.

Moving on to **reductions** – a fundamental technique for sauce-making. If you simmer a pot of tomato sauce or boil down pan drippings with wine for a gravy, you're reducing. You could ask, *"What does it mean to reduce a sauce?"* ChatGPT will explain that reducing means simmering or boiling a liquid so that water evaporates, thereby thickening the sauce and concentrating its flavors. Essentially, as steam leaves, what's left behind has the same amount of flavor compounds in less volume, so it tastes stronger. That's why a reduced soup or sauce often has a richer taste and thicker body. For example, if you start with 2 cups of broth and reduce to 1 cup, the salt, savory compounds, and any sugars present become twice as concentrated.

A good prompt might be, *"How can I thicken a sauce without flour?"* and an answer could be: by reduction. The AI might give practical tips, like using a wide pan for faster evaporation (more surface area for the liquid to evaporate from) and keeping the heat at a steady simmer (raging boil can cause splatters or even unwanted bitter flavors if things scorch). It could also note that reduction not only thickens but also deepens color and flavor – a wine reduction sauce takes on a glossy, intense character that raw wine plus broth wouldn't have. There's slight caramelization and Maillard reaction happening even in a reducing sauce, especially around the edges of the pan, which contributes complexity.

An interesting question is, *"Why do recipes say to skim fat but then reduce the juices?"* Removing excess fat makes the sauce less greasy and prevents an oil slick on top, while reducing the remaining watery portion intensifies the true flavor. ChatGPT might also mention defatting and then reducing ensures the sauce doesn't break (too much fat can sometimes separate when water content gets very low).

Now, **reactions** – especially caramelization, which is pure magic for sweets and more. You might ask, *"What is caramelization and how is it different from Maillard browning?"* Caramelization is the browning of sugar itself, which typically happens at higher temperatures (around 338°F for table sugar) and without needing any protein. Maillard, by contrast, involves both amino acids and sugars and can start at lower temperatures (around 300°F, even 280°F in some foods). So, caramelization gives you that nutty, toffee, burnt-sugar flavor and is responsible for the golden color of caramel, toffee, and even the natural sugars on roasted veggies or onions (though onions get both Maillard and caramelization).

If you're making caramel and it seizes or crystallizes, you can ask *"Why did my caramel turn grainy?"* and ChatGPT will explain that sugar recrystallized – maybe a few sugar crystals on the pan's side triggered a chain reaction. To avoid this, one often uses techniques like not stirring once sugar melts, or adding a bit of corn syrup or lemon juice to interfere with crystal formation. The AI would walk you through those solutions. It might say: *"Sugar is finicky. One crystal can seed many. Next time, wash down the sides of the pan with a wet brush while cooking, or add a spoonful of corn syrup to stabilize the molten sugar."*

Caramelization isn't just for desserts. Ever roasted carrots or onions until they're brown and sweet? That's caramelization of their natural sugars adding flavor. You could ask, *"Why do caramelized vegetables taste so sweet?"* and hear that the heat has broken down complex carbohydrates into simpler sugars and created new sweet compounds, much like making caramel. It's why slow-roasted onions become almost candy-like – their larger sugar molecules (and some Maillard, thanks to amino acids in them too) are transformed into a spectrum of flavorful substances.

Let's also touch on other chemical reactions: for example, **fermentation** as a reaction (like yeast making CO_2 for bread, or bacteria producing acid in yogurt). A curious prompt: *"How does yeast make bread rise and add flavor?"* ChatGPT could explain that yeast ferments sugars into carbon dioxide gas (for leavening) and alcohol plus other compounds (which contribute flavor). It might also mention that the alcohol mostly bakes off, but it leaves behind a wonderful aroma in bread. And enzymatic reactions in dough convert starches to sugars (food for yeast and flavor for us).

Or consider pickling: *"Why do we add vinegar (or let lactic acid form) to pickle vegetables?"* The AI would say acidity preserves the veggies by preventing harmful bacteria and also changes the texture slightly (making pickles crisp yet tender by breaking some pectins). That's more acid talk, which ties into the next section.

From mixing liquids smoothly to intensifying flavors and creating new ones through heat, emulsions and reductions and caramelization show that cooking is chemistry in action. Each of these can sometimes go wrong – a sauce can break, a reduction can burn, sugar can scorch – but knowing the underlying science helps you troubleshoot. And with ChatGPT, you can get quick advice: *"My sauce is too thin even after reducing; now what?"* (Maybe add a slurry or some butter to emulsify and thicken). *"My caramel is burnt; can I save it?"* (Burnt sugar is sadly done for – better to start over and watch more closely).

Now that we've stirred, whisked, and simmered our way through some kitchen chemistry, let's review the world of **acids and bases** and how they dramatically affect cooking. Ever wonder how baking soda affects cookies versus buttermilk in pancakes, or why adding vinegar can fix a too-salty soup? The pH scale is about to become your kitchen friend, with ChatGPT guiding the way to balanced, delicious results.

ACIDS, BASES, AND BALANCE

Have you ever added a squeeze of lemon to a soup or sauce and marveled at how it suddenly "woke up" the flavor? Or noticed a cookie recipe calling for baking soda and wondered what it really does? Acids and bases are powerful players in cooking – they can change a dish's flavor, color, and texture. In this section, we'll use ChatGPT to understand the role of pH in cooking and how ingredients like vinegar, citrus, and baking soda can be game-changers in your kitchen.

Acids (think vinegar, lemon juice, wine, tomatoes, buttermilk) add a bright, tangy flavor. If you ask ChatGPT, *"Why add acid to a recipe?"*, it might explain that a touch of acidity can balance rich or sweet flavors and make a dish more lively. For example, a squeeze of lemon in a cream sauce cuts through the richness and enhances the other flavors. Acidity literally makes our taste buds perk up – sourness is a signal that can make food seem more flavorful overall.

Acids also affect **color** and **texture.** Consider green vegetables: ever notice they turn army-green when overcooked or cooked with something acidic? Broccoli or spinach in a vinegar-spiked water can go olive drab. That's because acids cause chlorophyll (the green pigment) to dull. On the flip side, a little **baking soda** (a base) in the cooking water can keep greens bright – but you have to be careful. If you asked, *"How can I keep vegetables bright green?"*, ChatGPT would mention blanching briefly and maybe adding a pinch of baking soda to raise the pH. However, too much baking soda makes them mushy! Why mushy? Because alkaline water breaks down hemicellulose in cell walls, softening the veggies dramatically. So there's a balance: just enough base to preserve color, not so much that texture suffers.

Now think red and purple veggies, like red cabbage or beets. If you add vinegar, red cabbage stays a vibrant red-purple. Add a base like baking soda, it turns blue-green. You might ask, *"Why did my red cabbage turn blue?"* The AI would explain that anthocyanins (the pigments) change color with pH – acidic keeps them red, basic pushes them toward blue/green. That's a fun kitchen experiment: you can even make homemade pH indicator from red cabbage juice.

In baked goods, acids and bases are crucial for leavening and flavor. Baking soda (a base) needs an acid to react with – when it does, it produces carbon dioxide gas that helps things rise. For instance, classic buttermilk pancakes use baking soda (base) and buttermilk (acid). If you asked, *"Why do some recipes use baking soda instead of baking powder?"*, ChatGPT might clarify that baking soda alone works when there's an acidic ingredient present (like buttermilk, yogurt, molasses, brown sugar, cocoa). Baking powder contains its own acid and base. In terms of taste, using baking soda can neutralize some of the acid's tang (which can be good – you don't want your pancake too sour). But adding a bit too much baking soda can make things taste soapy or bitter (and give extra browning, since alkaline batter browns more readily). So bakers carefully balance how much baking soda to use depending on the acids in the mix.

Ever wonder, *"Why do my cookies call for baking soda **and** baking powder?"* ChatGPT would say: baking powder for overall rise (it has acid inside, usually reacts in two stages), and a bit of baking soda to neutralize acidity and encourage browning/spread. For example, brown sugar is slightly acidic; baking soda keeps the cookies from being too acidic and also helps them spread out and brown nicely. The pH can influence whether a cookie is thin and crisp (more soda, higher pH, more spread) or tall and cakey (less soda, lower pH, less spread).

Acid is also a meat tenderizer as we discussed (marinades), and it's a preservative (pickling). Ask, *"How does vinegar preserve food?"* and you'll learn that most bacteria can't grow in low pH. That's why pickles and relishes, high in vinegar, last so long. Lactic acid fermentation (like in sauerkraut or kimchi) generates acid that preserves the veggies naturally.

Acidic ingredients can prevent or cause some reactions. For instance, adding vinegar to a poaching water for eggs helps the whites coagulate faster (poached eggs hold their shape better) because the acid encourages the egg proteins to denature. But acid can also prevent some things: if you try to cook dried beans in a tomato sauce, they'll stay firm longer – acid keeps their cell walls tougher, delaying softening. So typically, you cook beans until tender, then add acidic tomatoes or sauce ingredients.

How about **taste balance**? A common kitchen tip is: if your dish is too acidic (sour), add a pinch of sugar to balance it; if it's too rich or sweet, add a dash of acid to brighten it. If something is too salty, a bit of acid can sometimes mask that perception (though only to a point). ChatGPT could confirm these tricks if you asked, *"How can I fix a soup that tastes too salty?"* Often: add water (dilute), add a peeled potato (myth that it absorbs salt – it absorbs some liquid, possibly some salt), or distract the palate with acid and sugar. Not a perfect fix, but it can help.

And let's not forget baking soda's role in something like pretzels or bagels: they're boiled in alkaline water (baking soda or lye solution) before baking to give that distinctive brown and chewy crust. The high pH accelerates the Maillard reaction, giving pretzels their deep brown color and flavor.

When cooking with dairy, acid can make it curdle (as in cheese making or when milk goes into a sour soup). If you asked, *"How do I add cream to soup without curdling?"*, ChatGPT would recommend tempering (slowly mixing some hot soup into the cream to warm it, then adding back) and maybe using higher-fat dairy (heavy cream resists curdling better than skim milk). Why? Fat and proteins in cream help keep it emulsified; lower fat means more likely the milk's proteins will clump when acid or heat hits. Also, you generally add cream at the end of cooking, off the boil, to minimize curdling.

The big picture: *balance.* Great cooking often comes down to balancing flavors: sweet, salty, sour, bitter, umami. Acids mainly contribute sour, but they also interact with saltiness and sweetness in complex ways to create harmony. If a dish tastes flat, a drop of vinegar or lemon can often fix it more effectively than more salt. If it's too sour, a bit more salt or sugar can round it out. The concept of balancing pH in food for flavor is something ChatGPT can guide you on if you describe what you're tasting. For example, *"My stew tastes dull even after salt, what can I do?"* might yield: add a teaspoon of vinegar or lemon juice to brighten it. Or *"This sauce is too tangy, how do I mellow it?"* could suggest a pinch of sugar or a bit of butter/cream to smooth it out.

So, acids and bases aren't just lab concepts – they're daily tools in the kitchen. Armed with the knowledge of what they do, you can tweak recipes on the fly: a dash of lemon here, a sprinkle of baking soda there, until the taste and texture are just right. And whenever something odd happens – like your garlic turning blue when pickled (yes, that can happen with certain pH and minerals, and it's harmless) – you can ask ChatGPT to decode the chemistry.

We've covered a lot of ground: from why things taste and feel the way they do to how to manipulate cooking conditions to get better results. Now, let's get very practical. How do you **apply** this science day-to-day? In the next section, we'll explore some common kitchen scenarios and see how ChatGPT can help tweak recipes and techniques for even better outcomes. It's time for some hands-on improvements using kitchen chemistry know-how.

KITCHEN CHEMISTRY IN PRACTICE

Now that we've peeked behind the curtain of kitchen science – covering heat, proteins, emulsions, acids, and more – it's time to apply that knowledge to actual cooking tasks. In this section, we'll look at how you can use ChatGPT as a virtual kitchen assistant to solve problems and improve recipes. Want fluffier pancakes? Crispier roast potatoes? Creamier soup? We'll show how to ask the right questions and get answers rooted in food science. This is where theory turns into better dinner, right in your home kitchen.

Baking Better: Let's say you're baking a cake and it came out a bit dense or dry. You could ask, *"How can I make my cakes lighter and moister?"* ChatGPT might remind you of a few key tricks. First, don't overmix once you've added flour – overmixing develops gluten, which can make a cake tough. Mix just until combined. Second, make sure you're using the right leavening and that it's fresh. If the recipe calls for baking powder and you skimped or it's old, your cake won't rise well. Third, using room temperature ingredients (eggs, butter, milk) helps create a smoother batter that traps air better. For moisture, maybe add a spoonful of sour cream or yogurt – these cultured dairy products tenderize the crumb and add moisture (they carry both liquid and some fat). Also, careful not to overbake; even a few extra minutes can dry a cake. The AI might even drop a fact like: creaming butter and sugar properly (until fluffy) incorporates air, which leads to fluffier cakes. So, if you rushed that step, spending an extra minute or two could help next time.

Crispier Crusts and Coatings: Imagine your oven fries or roasted veggies aren't as crisp as you hoped. You could query, *"How do I make roasted potatoes crispier?"* Based on science, ChatGPT might say: after parboiling the potatoes, shake them to rough up the surface (creating starchy slurry that turns into a crispy coating in the oven). Make sure to roast in a hot oven (around 425°F/220°C) and preheat the baking sheet so when the potatoes hit, they sizzle. Also, don't overcrowd the pan – they need space for moisture to escape. The assistant might mention using a bit of baking soda in the boiling water for potatoes (an alkaline water helps break down the outside pectin, making it fuzzier and primed to crisp). This technique is actually used in some roast potato recipes: a pinch of baking soda in the boiling water makes the exteriors almost paste-like, which leads to an amazingly crunchy shell once roasted.

For fried foods, a prompt like *"How can I get my fried chicken more crispy in the oven?"* could lead to the baking powder trick. ChatGPT could explain that coating chicken wings or thighs in a mixture of baking powder and salt and letting them sit in the fridge dries out the skin and raises its pH, which helps it crisp and brown better when baked. It will probably caution **not** to use baking soda (which can leave a soapy taste) and to stick with baking powder for that trick.

Soup and Sauce Upgrades: Suppose you have a soup that's a bit thin and bland. *"How can I improve a basic vegetable soup?"* ChatGPT might suggest a few science-based tweaks: Add a parmesan rind or some mushrooms/tomatoes while simmering to boost umami (they release glutamates that make broth savory). If it's bland, maybe it needs more salt or a splash of acid at the end (lemon or vinegar) to brighten flavors. To thicken slightly without a roux, you could purée a portion of the soup (the vegetable starch will give body) or add a slurry of cornstarch. If the soup has an odd sweetness or bitterness, it might recommend balancing with acid or a pinch of sugar respectively.

For a **cream soup**, if curdling has been an issue in the past, you could ask, *"How do I add milk to soup without curdling?"* and as we discussed, ChatGPT would guide you: use higher-fat dairy if possible (cream over milk), avoid boiling after adding dairy, temper the dairy by gradually mixing in hot soup before combining, and consider adding the dairy at the very end of cooking and just gently heating through. It might also mention that a roux or starch in the soup can help stabilize milk (flour in a chowder, for instance, can keep it from breaking because the starch interferes with protein clumping).

Maximizing Flavor: Perhaps you've made a tomato sauce and it tastes okay but not amazing. You might ask, *"How can I deepen the flavor of my tomato sauce?"* Some science-backed suggestions: cook it longer (allows Maillard reactions and caramelization of sugars in the tomatoes as water evaporates), add a little tomato paste and really sauté that paste in oil first (tomato paste is concentrated and has some caramelized character which frying enhances further), make sure you've got enough salt and maybe a pinch of sugar (to balance acidity). Perhaps add a dash of fish sauce or soy sauce – not enough to taste like Asian cuisine, but enough to increase the glutamate content for umami (Italian grandmas have been known to add a tiny anchovy or parmesan for the same reason). ChatGPT might also remind you to sauté your onions/garlic well at the start (that browning is flavor) and finish with fresh herbs or a splash of olive oil for brightness.

Tender and Juicy Meat Tweaks: If your pork chops often turn out dry, you might inquire, *"How can I cook pork chops so they stay* *juicy?"* Expect advice about brining them first (even a quick brine of 30 minutes in salted water can help), using a meat thermometer to avoid overcooking (stop at ~145°F and let carryover bring it a bit higher), perhaps choosing thicker chops (thin ones cook too fast and can overcook easily), and letting them rest after cooking so juices redistribute. Also, maybe use a marinade with a little sugar – sugar can help with browning and forms a kind of moisture-retaining coating. Or start by searing and then finish in the oven gently – that way you get a crust without drying the whole chop.

For **stir-fries** where meat sometimes comes out tough, you could ask about velveting (coating meat in a cornstarch, egg white, and rice wine mixture before cooking – a Chinese technique – to keep it tender). ChatGPT would explain that the starch creates a protective layer that prevents overcooking and retains moisture, giving that silky texture to chicken in stir-fries.

Preventing Common Mishaps: You can also use ChatGPT in the moment to fix things. Say your sauce is too salty – as mentioned, it might recommend adding acid or sugar, or bulking it up with more unsalted ingredients. If your stew is too thin at serving time, maybe mash a few of the beans/potatoes in it to thicken, or make a quick beurre manié (knead flour and butter and whisk in). If you burnt the bottom of a soup, don't stir it – gently pour the good part into a new pot, leaving the burnt bits behind (AI will confirm this trick to save the day).

And how about using science to salvage ingredients? Like stale bread – ask *"What can I do with stale bread?"* and you'll get ideas like bread pudding, French toast (the staleness actually helps soak up custard), or panzanella salad. Or *"Why put a cookie in a container with hard brown sugar?"* Because the sugar will absorb moisture from the bread and soften – a neat diffusion/osmosis trick.

Experimentation: ChatGPT can also encourage experimentation by explaining low-risk science-backed tweaks. For example, *"What happens if I brown butter for my chocolate chip cookies?"* You'd learn that browning butter (heating it until the milk solids toast) adds nutty, toffee notes due to the Maillard reaction of lactose and proteins in the butter. This could yield a richer cookie flavor. It might also advise that browned butter has less water (since some evaporates), which could slightly change the cookie's texture – perhaps making it crisper – so maybe add a teaspoon of water back to the dough if needed.

In essence, **ChatGPT can help you diagnose issues and prescribe solutions.** It's like having a seasoned cook/scientist in your kitchen. Over time, you'll internalize these tips. You'll automatically know, *"Oh, next time I'll use cake flour for that muffin recipe, it should be more tender,"* or *"This stew could use a dash of vinegar."* But it's great to have a backup brain to confirm or suggest ideas when you're not sure.

Home cooking is an endless learning process. Recipes give you the basics, but understanding the science lets you improvise and improve. With each question you ask and each answer you apply, you're essentially building your own mental cookbook of kitchen tricks and wisdom. And the more you practice these tweaks, the more intuitive they become. Keep ChatGPT as your sous-chef for ideas and reassurance until you feel you've got the hang of it.

We're almost at the end of our chapter journey. Before we wrap up, let's highlight one more thing: actual examples of prompts you can use anytime you're cooking and curious. In the final section, "Smart Prompts for the Curious Cook," we'll list some go-to questions you can pose to ChatGPT to learn on the fly and make your kitchen time even more enlightening and fun.

SMART PROMPTS FOR THE CURIOUS COOK

One of the best habits you can develop as a cook is to stay curious. Instead of just following a recipe, ask questions about it. Why am I doing this step? What if I try something different? With ChatGPT, you have a knowledgeable companion to explore those questions. In this final section, let's look at some real examples of prompts that can teach you the science of cooking as you go. Think of these as conversation starters with your AI kitchen tutor. They'll help reinforce what we've covered and inspire you to keep learning every time you cook.

Prompt: "I'm cooking steak, should I marinate it or not? Why?"

– This can lead to a discussion on how marinades work. You'll learn that marinades mainly flavor the surface (unless it's a thin cut or the marinade is very salty/acidic to penetrate a bit). Acidic marinades tenderize slightly, but too long can mush it. For tough cuts, a marinade won't break down deep collagen – slow cooking would be better. So the answer helps you choose the right approach for the cut of steak you have.

Prompt: "What's the science behind resting dough overnight?" – Think pizza or bread dough (or even cookie dough). ChatGPT will explain that long rests or "fermentation" allow enzymes to break down flour (improving flavor and texture), and for yeast doughs, it develops flavor (some alcohol, acids) and alters protein structure for better elasticity. You'll realize why that 24-hour pizza dough has more chew and flavor than a quick 2-hour dough.

Prompt: "How do I fix a broken mayonnaise?" – You might actually be in the middle of making mayo and see it separate. The prompt would get you a quick fix: start with a fresh egg yolk in a clean bowl, and slowly whisk the broken mayo into it as if it were the oil. It works like a charm, and you get an explanation of why (the new emulsifier in the yolk brings it back together).

Prompt: "Why do my chocolate chip cookies spread too much?" – Maybe yours turn into one big puddle. The AI will walk through possible causes: too low a temperature (dough too warm going in, or oven cooler than it says), not enough flour (or too much sugar/fat), or using only butter (which melts quicker than shortening). It could suggest chilling the dough, adding a touch more flour, or using part butter, part shortening if you really want them to hold shape. Also, ensure proper measurements (if you scooped flour too loosely, there might be less than intended). This prompt turns cookie flops into a lesson on fat melting and flour protein.

Prompt: "What makes bread crust shiny and brown?" – Perhaps you noticed some breads have that glossy crust. ChatGPT might tell you about brushing with egg wash (for shine due to proteins and fat that brown on the surface) or steam in the oven (which delays crust formation so it can expand fully, then helps gelatinize the starch on the surface for a shiny, chewy crust). It could also mention sugar or milk in dough contributes to browning. This prompt ties together steam, starch, and Maillard reactions in bread baking.

Prompt: "Give me a step-by-step to caramelize onions and explain each step's purpose." – Here you're asking not just for instructions, but the why. The answer might be: Step 1 – Slice onions evenly (for even cooking); Step 2 – Use a wide pan on medium heat with oil or butter (wide surface for moisture evaporation; medium heat to slowly draw out sugars without burning); Step 3 – Add a pinch of salt (helps draw out water from onions); Step 4 – Stir occasionally over 30-40 minutes (ensures even browning; long time allows onions' sugars to caramelize gradually); Step 5 – If they start to dry out or stick, add a splash of water to deglaze browned bits (prevents burning, incorporates those flavors back in). By the end, you understand each decision in the process.

Prompt: "Why should I sift flour for a cake? Does it really matter?" – The answer will likely discuss removing lumps and aerating the flour, which helps it mix more evenly and produces a lighter texture. It prevents overmixing too, since a pre-sifted flour incorporates faster with wet ingredients. If you're in a hurry, you might skip sifting, but at least you know the potential trade-off (maybe a slightly denser cake or a pocket of flour).

Prompt: "Explain why ice cream base is cooked into a custard." – For making ice cream, many recipes have you cook eggs, sugar, and milk/cream into a custard first. ChatGPT would explain that cooking thickens the mixture (egg proteins form a custard that gives creaminess and body), it also makes it safer by pasteurizing eggs, and the cooked mixture will trap less air when churned, leading to a rich, smooth texture. Raw bases (Philadelphia style, no eggs) rely more on heavy cream and are a bit less creamy typically. So if you were deciding which method to use, now you know the science behind each.

Prompt: "How do I know when to use baking soda vs. baking powder?" – This is a classic question for bakers. The response: use baking soda if the recipe has a good amount of acid (yogurt, vinegar, citrus, etc.) that needs neutralizing and you want the leavening from that reaction. Use baking powder for general rise when there's not enough natural acid; it's balanced to rise on its own. Sometimes use both – powder for the main lift, soda to tweak pH and assist browning/spread as discussed. This helps you troubleshoot or adjust recipes (say you want to reduce sugar, which may reduce acidity in a recipe, you might then cut baking soda a tad, etc.).

Prompt: "What does 'temper chocolate' mean and why do it?" – If you're ever working with chocolate, tempering is key to get that snappy, shiny finish. ChatGPT would outline that tempering is controlled melting and cooling to encourage cocoa butter to form stable crystals. Without tempering, chocolate can look dull or melt too easily at room temp. With it, you get a crisp snap and glossy look. Not strictly cooking a meal, but great kitchen science to know for candy-making or chocolate-dipping.

The idea is, whatever you're curious about, frame a clear question to ChatGPT. You can be very specific ("Why exactly 350°F for this?") or more open-ended ("What are different ways to thicken a sauce, and how do they each work?"). The more you practice, the more you'll figure out how to word questions to get useful answers. And don't hesitate to have a back-and-forth. If something in the explanation isn't clear, ask a follow-up. *"You mentioned gluten development – can you explain that simply?"* and you'll get it broken down in simpler terms.

Remember, the goal of using these prompts isn't to turn every cooking session into a science lecture. It's to sprinkle in learning so that over time, you just **know** why things are done a certain way and how to make food turn out the way you want. It builds confidence. Soon you won't just be following recipes; you'll be **understanding** them, tweaking them, even creating your own, with the assurance that your decisions are grounded in solid science (and lots of tasting, of course!).

By keeping that curious mindset and leveraging ChatGPT as your on-demand culinary coach, you transform your kitchen into a learning lab (minus the intimidating lab coats and plus a lot more deliciousness). Cooking will feel more approachable because when something stumps you, you have a place to turn for insight.

Let's wrap up our chapter by summarizing what we've learned and looking ahead. You've gathered a basketful of kitchen science knowledge and some practical prompting skills. In the conclusion, we'll tie it all together and set the stage for what's coming next in your AI-assisted cooking journey.

In this chapter, we journeyed through the science that simmers behind the scenes in our kitchens. We started by asking "why" – unlocking the reasons behind common cooking techniques. We saw how heat and time partner to turn raw ingredients into roasts, stews, and bakes. We unraveled the mysteries of proteins, from egg whites firming up to steaks browning and getting juicy. We blended liquids into emulsions, simmered sauces to reduce and intensify them, and caramelized sugars for that golden sweetness. We balanced acids and bases to keep colors bright, textures just right, and flavors in harmony. Most importantly, we learned how to use ChatGPT as a helpful guide at each step: asking it for explanations, solutions, and tips to become smarter cooks.

So what does this mean for you, the home cook? It means you've gained not just facts, but a way of thinking. You can approach recipes and kitchen improvisations with confidence and curiosity. You know now that when a recipe says something like "rest the dough" or "sear the meat," there's a sensible reason – and if you forget why, you can always ask ChatGPT to remind you. You can troubleshoot: soggy pie crust, chewy cake, flat meringue – none of these are mysteries, just puzzles to solve with a bit of science. As you continue to cook, try using those smart prompts to keep learning. The kitchen will become your classroom, and each meal a tasty experiment (with mostly happy results, and the occasional failure that you'll learn from).

In the next chapter, we'll build on this foundation. You now have the "why" and "how" of kitchen science under your belt. Coming up, we'll venture into even more practical territory, focusing on advanced techniques and creative ways to use ChatGPT in meal planning and culinary exploration. The journey from a recipe-follower to an innovative, confident cook continues. For now, pat yourself on the back – you've demystified a lot of kitchen science. As you close this chapter and move to the next, carry that sense of confidence with you. Cooking is a craft you can master, and with your AI kitchen companion by your side and science in your toolkit, there's little you can't tackle. Onward to the next delicious lesson!

14

SMARTER THAN YOUR COOKBOOK: REIMAGINING FAMILY FAVORITES

Imagine flipping through a weathered recipe card from your grandmother. The edges are stained with vanilla and butter, the handwriting slightly faded. Instantly, you can almost smell the cookies baking and hear her laughter in the kitchen. Family recipes like these are more than instructions for food – they're capsules of memory and love passed down through generations.

Every dish tells a story. The act of cooking from a beloved family recipe connects you to those who stirred the same pot decades ago. In fact, passing down recipes is "an intimate form of storytelling, a way to preserve and share the flavors that have shaped our lives". A bite of a treasured dish can transport you to your childhood or to a culture halfway around the world. These heirloom recipes carry history and identity, binding us to our roots.

Yet as precious as these recipes are, sometimes they need a little refresh for today's kitchen. Perhaps Grandma's pie filling is a bit too sweet for modern tastes, or your uncle's stew recipe feeds twenty when you only need dinner for four. Maybe the recipe assumes you're cooking on a wood stove or uses ingredients hard to find now. How do you update a classic without losing its soul? How can you keep the heartwarming tradition alive while accommodating gluten-free guests, new appliances, or healthier habits?

This is where ChatGPT steps in as a 21st-century kitchen ally. Think of it as being *smarter than your cookbook* – not because it replaces family wisdom, but because it helps you augment it. ChatGPT can take those handwritten instructions and translate them into modern cooking guidelines, suggest ingredient swaps to suit a vegan or low-sugar diet, and even fill in the blanks of a half-remembered recipe. It's like having a culinary assistant who respects Grandma's legacy and also knows the latest cooking trends.

In this chapter, you'll learn practical ways to blend cherished traditions with cutting-edge AI assistance. We'll explore how to:

- Give your legacy recipes a **digital heirloom upgrade**, feeding old handwritten recipes into ChatGPT and modernizing them without losing their soul.
- **Adapt recipes for modern diets**, from gluten-free and vegetarian makeovers to low-sugar and allergy-friendly tweaks.
- **Preserve culture and memory** by using ChatGPT to uncover the origins and stories behind your family's favorite dishes.
- **Scale down and simplify** multi-generation recipes for smaller households or modern equipment, making them weeknight-friendly without sacrificing charm.
- Make **flavor tweaks without losing identity**, gently updating spices, salt, or proteins while keeping the dish's heart intact.
- **Cook from memories, not measurements**, leveraging ChatGPT to recreate beloved dishes when all you have is "grandma used to make something like this...".
- **Revive and reinvent** family favorites through real-world prompt examples – from casseroles to cookies – showing exactly how AI can help honor tradition in a modern kitchen.

By the end of this chapter, you'll be empowered to honor your culinary heritage while keeping it relevant. It's a friendly, supportive guide to help you modernize family favorites with confidence. Let's dive in – starting with how to bring those old recipe cards into the digital age and give them a new life in your kitchen.

THE DIGITAL HEIRLOOM UPGRADE

That cherished recipe on a stained index card or in grandma's cursive handwriting needs to make its way into the digital realm before we can work with it. To start your digital heirloom upgrade, you'll want to feed that legacy recipe into ChatGPT. If it's on paper, you can type it out word-for-word into the chat. Better yet, with the latest ChatGPT features, you can even snap a photo of the recipe card and show it to the AI – it's capable of reading images and extracting the text for you. Once ChatGPT has the recipe text, the real magic begins.

Begin by prompting ChatGPT to modernize the recipe. For example, you might write: *"Here is my grandmother's chocolate cake recipe: [paste text]. Please update it with modern measurements, standard temperatures, and clearer instructions, but don't change the original flavor."* With a prompt like this, ChatGPT will analyze the old instructions and rewrite them in a more contemporary, user-friendly way. It's careful to preserve the recipe's heart while making it easier to follow today.

One immediate benefit is that ChatGPT will clarify antiquated terms and measurements. Those old notes that say *"add a pinch of this, a smidgeon of that"* can leave modern cooks scratching their heads. ChatGPT comes to the rescue by translating such phrases into precise quantities (for example, "a pinch" becomes about 1/8 teaspoon). If a century-old recipe calls for baking in a "slow oven," you'll no longer be puzzled – ChatGPT will note that this means roughly 300°F. In other words, the AI turns Grandma's poetic instructions into concrete guidance without losing their folksy charm.

It will also convert units of measurement that might be unfamiliar or outdated. Perhaps your family recipe uses terms like *"butter the size of an egg"* – ChatGPT knows that means approximately 1/4 cup (half a stick) of butter. Or maybe it references a *gill* or a *peck*; the AI can explain that a gill is roughly half a cup and a peck is about two gallons. If the recipe was written in metric and you prefer US customary units (or vice versa), ChatGPT can seamlessly convert grams to ounces, Celsius to Fahrenheit, and so on. The result is a recipe that speaks your kitchen's language.

Another part of modernization is handling ingredients that have become rare or that you might not prefer to use. Classic recipes sometimes include things like lard, saltpeter, or hartshorn (an old-fashioned baking leaven). ChatGPT's vast knowledge shines here: it can suggest modern equivalents for such ingredients. For instance, one baker discovered that the old leavening *hartshorn* could be replaced by baking powder. ChatGPT would not only make that recommendation, but also adjust the quantity to ensure the same leavening strength – about 1 teaspoon of baking powder for 1/2 teaspoon of hartshorn in this case. Similarly, if your recipe calls for "oleo" (an old term for margarine) or other bygone products, ChatGPT will flag it and propose a suitable substitute like butter or a modern plant-based spread.

Crucially, ChatGPT can help fill in blanks or assumptions in the recipe. Our ancestors often wrote recipes with a lot of implicit knowledge – they might not mention how long to bake something or to preheat the oven, because it was understood. When modernizing, the AI will typically add these details. If Grandma's pie recipe forgot to say how long to bake, ChatGPT can suggest, for example, "bake for 45 minutes or until golden brown," based on its understanding of similar pies. It's like having an experienced cook proofreading the instructions to ensure nothing important is left unsaid. It may even gently alert you to steps that were probably just assumed (e.g. reminding you to preheat, or to let a roast rest before carving) so you don't miss a beat.

You remain in control of how much changes. You can instruct the AI to keep the recipe's original tone or phrasing if you want to preserve that nostalgic feel, or ask it to present the instructions in a standard format (ingredients list followed by step-by-step directions).

If you're concerned about a particular old technique (say the recipe uses raw eggs in a frosting), you can ask ChatGPT for a safer modern method – and it might suggest a workaround like using pasteurized eggs or an eggless frosting alternative. ChatGPT can even add helpful extras at your request, such as estimating the prep and cook time, the number of servings, or a brief note about the recipe's origin. These are things our grandmothers assumed everyone just knew, but having them written down makes life easier for the next generation of cooks.

After this digital makeover, you'll have a neatly typed recipe that reads like something from a modern cookbook – yet it still feels like Grandma's dish. You might see instructions like *"Preheat your oven to 350°F (moderate heat). Cream the butter and sugar until light and fluffy..."* instead of the terse *"make a moderate oven and beat butter and sugar"* that the old note had. The updated recipe is far easier to follow and less prone to misinterpretation, especially for family members who never had a chance to watch the original cook in action. It's quite exciting to watch a jumble of old notes transform into a clear, trustworthy recipe – like seeing a faded photograph restored to full color.

By feeding your legacy recipe to ChatGPT and getting this upgraded version, you've built a bridge between past and present. The recipe retains its soul, but now anyone in the family can recreate it with confidence. Plus, it's safely stored in digital form and easy to share with relatives, so you never have to worry about that old card getting lost or fading away. Now you can also easily share these recipes with your relatives or save them in a digital cookbook, ensuring the tradition lives on through technology. With the basic recipe modernized, you're ready for the next step: adapting these family favorites to today's dietary needs and preferences without losing what makes them special.

ADAPTING FOR MODERN DIETS

Cooking for family has changed a lot over the years. Where once everyone ate the same hearty stew, today one person might be gluten-intolerant, another is vegetarian, and someone else is watching their sugar intake. Adapting those beloved family recipes to these modern diets can be a puzzle. Fortunately, ChatGPT is like a culinary translator for dietary needs – ready to rework any recipe so that everyone can enjoy it.

The key is to clearly tell ChatGPT what adjustment you need. You can simply prompt: *"Make this recipe fit a _____ diet."* Fill in the blank with gluten-free, vegetarian, vegan, low-sugar, nut-free, dairy-free – whatever you require. ChatGPT will then thoughtfully modify ingredients and steps to meet that need while striving to keep the dish's original character. In many cases, it will present a revised ingredient list and instructions that omit or swap out the problematic items.

For example, imagine you want to convert Grandma's gravy into a gluten-free version for a relative with celiac disease. A prompt could be as straightforward as: *"Can you adjust this turkey gravy recipe to make it gluten-free?"*. ChatGPT would recognize that the usual culprit for gluten in gravy is flour (used as a thickener). It might suggest using cornstarch or arrowroot slurry instead of flour, or perhaps a gluten-free flour blend, to thicken the gravy. It will likely also double-check any broths or soy sauce in the recipe (since some contain wheat) and recommend gluten-free alternatives if needed. The result? A gravy that tastes just as rich and comforting, but is safe for everyone at the table.

Now let's say your cherished family lasagna recipe is full of meat and cheese, but you have a new vegetarian in the family. You could tell ChatGPT you need a vegetarian version of that dish. (In fact, the AI can even tackle big holiday challenges – people have asked for *"a vegetarian alternative to roast turkey for Christmas dinner"* and gotten creative suggestions.) For your lasagna, the AI might get creative – suggesting a layered vegetable lasagna with eggplant and zucchini in place of meat, or proposing a hearty lentil and mushroom filling that mimics the savory depth of the original meat sauce. It would replace chicken broth with vegetable broth, swap gelatin-based ingredients with plant-based ones, and ensure all components align with a vegetarian diet. Importantly, ChatGPT would aim to keep the spirit of the dish: for a lasagna, it might emphasize maintaining a rich tomato sauce and creamy cheese layers (perhaps using ricotta mixed with spinach) so that even without the meat, the dish still feels like your family's classic.

Low-sugar and lower-carb adaptations are another area where ChatGPT shines. If you hand it Grandpa's beloved cookie recipe and say, *"Please modify this for a lower sugar content,"* it will intelligently cut back on the sugar and suggest alternatives to keep flavor and texture. For instance, it might reduce the sugar by one-third and recommend adding a teaspoon of vanilla or cinnamon to enhance sweetness perception. It could propose using unsweetened applesauce or mashed banana to replace some of the sugar (and maybe some of the fat), since fruits bring natural sweetness and moisture. If artificial sweeteners or sugar alcohols (like erythritol) are an option for you, ChatGPT can incorporate those as well. The end result is a cookie that's not as cloyingly sweet but still hits the spot – all achieved without you having to do multiple test batches on your own.

Allergy-related substitutions are another common need. Perhaps your aunt's pecan pie needs to be nut-free for a cousin with allergies. Ask ChatGPT to help, and it might suggest using toasted oats or sunflower seeds in place of pecans to give a similar toasty crunch, or even recommend a "pretend pecan" pie using oatmeal filling. In one real instance, a cook was struggling to adapt a beloved family recipe to accommodate a visitor's nut allergy, and ChatGPT not only provided a perfect substitution but even suggested a simple tweak that improved the texture. That's the kind of bonus insight you get by brainstorming with an AI – it might think of using an ingredient in a new way that makes the dish even better.

What's impressive is how much culinary knowledge ChatGPT can draw on for these adjustments. It knows, for example, that flaxseed or chia seeds mixed with water can act as an egg substitute (useful if you need an egg-free cake). It's aware that gluten-free baking often benefits from a bit of xanthan gum to mimic the elasticity of gluten, and it will bring that up if applicable. If you're making a dairy-free version of a creamy soup, ChatGPT might suggest coconut milk or cashew cream as a stand-in to maintain that silky mouthfeel. Concerned that your vegetarian stew won't have the depth of flavor of the original? The AI might recommend adding a splash of soy sauce or miso paste for umami, to replace the savory punch of meat. These are the kinds of tips even seasoned cooks might not think of right away, but ChatGPT has them ready in its repertoire.

Using ChatGPT to adapt recipes is also a huge time-saver. Rather than scouring dozens of blogs for "vegan brownies" or "keto casserole" tips, you can get a customized solution for your specific family recipe in one go. You can even give multiple requirements at once: *"Make this recipe gluten-free and vegan"* will lead the AI to tackle both challenges together – perhaps it will use almond milk and flax eggs for the vegan part and almond flour for the gluten-free part, all in one combined set of instructions. If the first draft of the adaptation isn't quite to your liking, you can ask follow-up questions: *"Can you also make it lower in salt?"* or *"Any suggestion to make the texture fluffier since it's gluten-free?"* ChatGPT will iterate on the recipe, fine-tuning it until you're satisfied.

The wonderful thing is that after these adjustments, the recipe still feels like the one you know and love. Your gluten-free gravy will have the same savory aroma, your vegan lasagna will still draw the family to the table, and those low-sugar cookies will disappear just as fast. By harnessing AI in this way, you ensure no one is left out due to dietary needs. And you've proven that it's possible to honor tradition while embracing change. With ingredients now adaptable to everyone's preferences and health, we can turn our attention to another aspect of family favorites – the stories and heritage that make them truly special.

PRESERVING CULTURE AND MEMORY

Family recipes aren't just about ingredients and steps – they carry the heritage of who we are. The dishes passed down in your family often have roots in specific cultures, regions, or personal histories. Using ChatGPT, you can dive into the stories and meanings behind those recipes, making sure that as you modernize them, you never lose sight of where they came from.

One way to use ChatGPT is as a culinary historian or storyteller. You might prompt it with something like, *"Tell me about the history of this dish and its significance in [our culture]."* For example, if your family always makes a particular bread for a holiday, you can ask ChatGPT about that tradition: *"What is the origin of Easter sweet bread in Italian culture?"* The AI can then share that Easter breads are common in many European countries, symbolizing renewal, and might even give specifics about Italian variations. It's like having a knowledgeable friend who can give context to the recipe your grandparents brought from the old country.

Because ChatGPT has been trained on recipes and food lore from around the world, it often has insight into cultural connections. The web is full of people sharing their family recipes and the stories behind them, and ChatGPT draws on that collective knowledge. *"The internet serves as a modern-day recipe box where families can document their culinary legacies and discover new traditions,"* as one article puts it. That communal spirit lives on in ChatGPT – it can tell you, for instance, how your Polish grandmother's pierogi recipe resembles and differs from dumplings in other cultures, or explain the significance of certain spices in Indian family cooking if that's your heritage. In short, it helps you appreciate the broader tapestry that your recipe is a part of.

You can also ask ChatGPT to help preserve personal memories alongside the cultural facts. Maybe you want to write a little blurb to go with the recipe in your family cookbook, something that explains why it's special. Try prompting: *"Write a short paragraph about what this dish means to my family, including how my dad learned it from his dad and how we serve it every New Year's."* ChatGPT will craft a heartfelt narration that you can then tweak to fit just right. It might say, *"This dish has been the centerpiece of our New Year's table for three generations, ever since Grandpa first made it after immigrating in 1970..."* etc. It gives you a beautiful starting point to express the sentiment and history, which you can refine with your own personal details and corrections.

Of course, while ChatGPT is a treasure trove of information, it's always good to approach cultural information with a bit of care. Sometimes, the AI might not get every detail exactly right – maybe it confuses two similar dishes, or gives a legend that your family doesn't relate to. Use it as a springboard for your own recollections or further research. Importantly, make sure the cultural context stays true: one food writer warns that removing a recipe from its cultural context can do harm to the communities it came from. In other words, if ChatGPT gives you a generic answer about your traditional dish, you might want to verify it or add the specific touch that you know from your family. The goal is to enrich the recipe's story, not rewrite it in a way that erases its roots. The good news is that by asking questions and feeding ChatGPT the details you remember ("My grandmother brought this recipe from southern China in the 1940s"), you help the AI give more tailored, accurate insights.

One really fun use of ChatGPT in this realm is exploring variations and meanings. You can ask, *"What does the name of this dish mean?"* or *"Why is this spice mix important in our culture's cooking?"* You might learn that the name of your dish translates to something poetic, or that the spice mix was a staple because it could preserve food in hot climates. You could also inquire if similar recipes exist elsewhere: *"Are there dishes in other cuisines similar to this one?"* Such questions might reveal, for instance, that your family's empanadas share common roots with various hand-pies globally, connecting your tradition to a larger human story about portable meals and celebrations.

ChatGPT can also act as a bridge to the past when human sources aren't available. If you never got to ask your great-grandparents about a recipe's origin, posing those questions to ChatGPT can at least give you some plausible stories or historical context. It's not the same as hearing it from an elder, but it can fill in some gaps or inspire you to dig deeper. Some users even use ChatGPT to generate interview questions: *"What should I ask my mom to learn more about her recipe?"* The AI might suggest questions about who first taught her to make it, what occasions she remembers cooking it for, and how it's changed over time. This can guide a family conversation that uncovers precious anecdotes you can then preserve.

In preserving culture and memory, ChatGPT is less a final authority and more a helpful assistant. It provides pieces of the puzzle – historical facts, cultural significance, eloquent wording – which you can combine with your personal knowledge. Together, you get a richer story to accompany the recipe. After all, the reason we treasure Grandma's recipe isn't just because it tastes good, but because of the love and heritage baked into it. By using AI to put that heritage into words, you ensure that future generations will know not just how to make the dish, but why it mattered.

Armed with this deeper understanding of your family favorite, you'll appreciate cooking it even more. And while cherishing that history, you can also adapt the practical side of the recipe to suit your life today. Next, we'll look at how to scale down those multi-generational feasts and simplify complex steps, so that honoring tradition can happen even on a busy weeknight.

SCALING AND SIMPLIFYING OLD RECIPES

When Grandma wrote down her stew recipe, she probably assumed a big family dinner with ten or more people. But what if you're cooking for two tonight? Or conversely, what if you want to make that beloved dish for a big family reunion? Scaling recipes up or down is another task where ChatGPT can lend a hand, sparing you from tricky math and potential kitchen mishaps.

To scale a recipe, you can literally tell ChatGPT how many servings you want to end up with. For instance: *"This recipe serves 12, but I only need it to serve 4. Adjust the ingredient amounts accordingly."* The AI will recalculate each ingredient quantity to fit the new serving size. No more guessing or ending up with way too much food (or too little). If the original called for 3 cups of rice to feed a dozen people,

ChatGPT will let you know you only need about 1 cup for four people, and it will do the same for each ingredient down the list.

But ChatGPT doesn't stop at just dividing or multiplying – it understands that not all ingredients scale equally. Seasonings and spices, for example, often need a proportionally smaller increase when scaling up, so the dish doesn't become too salty or overpowering. An experienced chef knows you might not double the hot chili powder even if you double a soup, and ChatGPT knows this kind of nuance too. It can adjust those "to taste" elements more gracefully. It might say something like, "Instead of doubling the salt, start with 1.5 times the amount and adjust as needed," which is exactly how a human cook would handle it. This intelligent scaling ensures the flavor balance stays on point, in addition to the quantities.

Another thing ChatGPT can do is update cooking times and equipment suggestions when you change batch size. Perhaps the original casserole was in a huge dish – if you quarter the recipe, ChatGPT might advise using a smaller pan so the food doesn't spread too thin and dry out. It may also warn that baking a smaller amount could take a bit less time, so you should start checking sooner. Conversely, if you're scaling up a cake recipe, it might mention that you'll need multiple pans or to increase the baking time for a larger volume. These are details that recipe books often leave you to figure out on your own, but ChatGPT spells them out if you ask for guidance.

Simplifying recipes is a related challenge. Some treasured recipes are, frankly, a bit complicated or time-consuming for today's busy schedules. You can ask ChatGPT to streamline the process or adapt it for modern appliances. For example: *"How can I simplify this recipe for coq au vin?"* ChatGPT might reply with suggestions like using pre-cut carrots and onions, or employing a slow cooker: *"Sear the chicken and sauté the veggies, then transfer everything to a slow cooker with the wine and broth and cook on low for 6 hours,"* thereby skipping the need to monitor it on the stove. It can also shorten marinating or resting times if possible, or suggest using a pressure cooker to achieve slow-cooked tenderness in a fraction of the time.

If a recipe calls for techniques that you find intimidating (say, making a pastry from scratch or using a candy thermometer), you can ask for easier alternatives. ChatGPT could suggest using a store-bought pie crust for that intricate tart, or provide a simplified "no thermometer needed" method for your grandfather's fudge. It will do so in a non-judgmental way – the goal is to help you actually make the dish rather than scare you off with strict rules. After all, the spirit of a family recipe isn't in laboring for hours; it's in the enjoyment and sharing of the result. So if using a food processor to chop what used to be hand-minced saves you time, ChatGPT will propose it.

Modernizing equipment is another huge win. Many old recipes assume tools that have since been upgraded. ChatGPT can convert cooking methods: *"Convert this stovetop stew into an Instant Pot recipe."* It might output something like, "Use the Sauté setting to brown the meat and onions, then add the rest of the ingredients, seal the lid and cook on High Pressure for 35 minutes, followed by a natural release." Suddenly, a stew that took all afternoon can be done after work on a Tuesday. Or maybe your recipe says to "grind spices with a mortar and pestle" – ChatGPT could suggest approximate times/pulses if you use a spice grinder or blender instead. It bridges the gap between yesterday's kitchen and today's gadgets.

Another way ChatGPT simplifies things is by providing clear, beginner-friendly instructions. Older family recipes might assume you know certain basics ("make a roux" or "cook until done"). If those phrases leave you uncertain, you can prompt: *"Explain this to me like I'm new to cooking."* The AI will happily break down the steps: *"To make a roux, melt the butter in a pan, then stir in the flour and cook them together for a few minutes, stirring constantly, until it looks like a smooth paste that's golden in color."* No more mystery jargon – you get plain guidance. You can even have ChatGPT rewrite the whole recipe in simple terms. It might turn a paragraph of Grandma's notes into a list of numbered steps with timings and visual cues ("simmer for about 20 minutes, until the sauce thickens and coats the back of a spoon").

Between resizing portions and simplifying steps, you'll find that no recipe is too daunting to tackle. Maybe you don't have a crowd to feed or a whole day to spend in the kitchen – that's okay. ChatGPT helps mold the recipe to fit your reality, whether that means making a smaller batch, using a one-pot method, or explaining techniques you haven't tried before. By adjusting the recipe to your needs and tools, you keep it alive and practical. Now that you know how to tailor the process and quantity, you might want to tweak the flavors as well. In our next section, we'll explore how to update the taste of a dish while keeping its soul intact.

FLAVOR TWEAKS WITHOUT LOSING IDENTITY

Once you have the right portions and process for a recipe, you may still want to adjust the flavors to better suit your family's preferences or health needs. Maybe you wish Grandma's soup had a little more kick, or you need to cut back on salt for Dad's blood pressure. With ChatGPT, you can make these flavor tweaks carefully, so that the dish still tastes like the one you remember – just tweaked to be a perfect fit.

To start, be specific about what you want to change. You can say, *"I'd like this chili to be spicier,"* or *"I love this pickle recipe, but it's too salty for me – how can I reduce the salt?"* ChatGPT will respond with targeted suggestions. Importantly, it tends to suggest moderate changes, not overhauls. For adding heat to a mild dish, for example, it might recommend adding a small amount of cayenne pepper or a chopped jalapeño, and perhaps provide an option to serve additional hot sauce on the side for those who want even more. The idea is to layer in a bit of extra flavor without overwhelming the original balance.

When reducing ingredients like salt or sugar, ChatGPT knows how to compensate so you don't end up with something bland. If you ask to make a recipe less salty, it may suggest using herbs, spices, or acids to boost flavor in place of the missing salt. (As nutrition experts often note, using a squeeze of citrus or a splash of vinegar can brighten up flavors when you cut down on salt.) So if you tell ChatGPT, "My grandmother's stew is delicious but a bit high in sodium; how can I reduce that without losing taste?" it might advise you to use low-sodium broth, increase aromatic herbs like bay leaf and thyme, and finish the stew with a dash of lemon juice to enhance flavor. You'll get a stew that still tastes hearty and comforting, just with less salt.

Perhaps you want to swap one main ingredient for another, but keep the dish's character. Say your recipe traditionally uses pork, but you'd prefer to use chicken or turkey. ChatGPT will outline how to do that while preserving the essence. It might note that chicken is leaner and cooks faster, so you should shorten the cooking time and possibly add a bit of oil or butter for richness. It will keep the same spice rub or sauce so the flavor profile remains familiar. If you're replacing a strong-flavored meat like beef with a milder protein, the AI might suggest adding an extra umami element (like a bit of soy sauce or mushroom powder) to make up for it. Foodies often use mushrooms or even walnuts to give vegetarian dishes a "meaty" depth – don't be surprised if ChatGPT recommends something like that to ensure the dish remains satisfying.

Even small adjustments for personal taste are on the table. Imagine your family chili recipe is almost perfect, but you think a touch of smokiness would make it even better. You could ask, *"How can I add a smoky flavor without changing the chili too much?"* ChatGPT might suggest adding a teaspoon of smoked paprika or a bit of chipotle chili, noting that these will introduce smokiness that complements the chili's beans and tomatoes. Crucially, it would likely advise to start with a small amount so as not to overpower everything. You can always add more, it might remind you, echoing the wisdom of cooks everywhere.

Another scenario: you love a casserole but find it a bit one-note, maybe needing brightness. ChatGPT could propose stirring in a tablespoon of fresh lemon juice or some chopped fresh herbs at the end to liven it up. These kinds of tweaks can lift the flavor while keeping the core identity intact. The casserole will still taste like the traditional comfort food you expect, just with a slightly more dynamic flavor.

What if there's an ingredient someone simply doesn't like?

Suppose your recipe calls for cilantro, but half your family can't stand it. You can ask for a flavor-preserving substitute. ChatGPT might recommend using fresh parsley or a mix of mint and basil in place of cilantro – herbs that give a fresh green note without that cilantro taste. The dish remains essentially the same, just minus the polarizing herb.

Throughout this process, ChatGPT acts like a gentle cooking coach. It often explains the reasoning behind a suggestion ("Add rosemary because it will enhance the savoriness but still fits the profile of a roast lamb"). Understanding the why helps you trust that the change won't sabotage the beloved recipe. And if you're unsure, you can tell ChatGPT your concerns: *"I'm afraid if I remove the butter, it won't taste as good. Any tips?"* It might then suggest a smaller amount of butter or a healthy substitute like olive oil plus a touch of garlic for flavor, ensuring you keep that satisfying taste with a bit less fat.

The beauty of these small edits is that you can apply them gradually. Try one change at a time, and because ChatGPT has given you a heads-up on the expected effect, you can judge the result. Over a few cooking sessions, you might achieve your perfect version of the recipe – spicier, less salty, more herbaceous, or however you envision – all without ever losing the dish's soul. It still feels like the family favorite you grew up with, just tuned to the present moment. In this way, you can truly make the recipe your own while honoring its origins – a satisfying balance of old and new.

By now, we've updated ingredients and flavors to our liking. But what if you don't have a written recipe to update in the first place? Many of us carry the memory of a dish in our minds without any recipe card at all. In our next section, we'll explore how ChatGPT can help recreate those treasured dishes from nothing more than fond recollections and a craving.

COOKING FROM MEMORIES, NOT MEASUREMENTS

Not every cherished dish comes with a recipe card. Sometimes all you have is a fond memory: a flavor, an aroma, a description passed down in stories. Recreating a dish from memory alone can feel like chasing a ghost. Yet it isn't impossible. ChatGPT can act as a culinary detective, helping you piece together the clues of taste and aroma that you provide, and turning them into a workable recipe.

The first step is to tell ChatGPT everything you remember about the dish. Think of it like describing the dish to a skilled chef. You might say, *"I want to make a dish my grandma used to cook. I don't have the recipe, but I recall it was a creamy chicken casserole with a crunchy topping, maybe breadcrumbs, and it had peas and carrots in it. It was savory, a little tangy, and she always made it for holidays."* With details like that, ChatGPT can piece together a likely recipe. It might respond with something like, "It sounds like a classic chicken divan or pot pie-style casserole. Here's a possible recipe: [lists ingredients and steps]." The first draft might call for chicken, a cream sauce with a bit of sour cream (for tang), peas, carrots, and a buttered bread-crumb topping – essentially aligning with your memories.

Now, this initial recipe might not be perfect, but it gives you a concrete starting point. You can then think about what seems right or wrong. Maybe you remember that Grandma's version had a hint of sherry wine flavor, and the AI recipe didn't include that. You can tell ChatGPT, *"It looks close, but please add a bit of sherry to the sauce, that was in her version."* Or perhaps the AI suggested cheddar cheese but you're pretty sure the flavor was more like Parmesan – you can correct that. ChatGPT will update the recipe accordingly. This back-and-forth is like having a conversation with the past: you provide memories, the AI provides structure, and together you iterate towards the lost recipe.

In some cases, you might not even know what the dish was, just what it was like. For instance, *"My mother-in-law used to make a cold cucumber soup with dill – no idea how, but it was very refreshing."* ChatGPT can recognize this description and say, "That sounds like a variation of tzatziki or a cold cucumber yogurt soup. Here's a recipe that might match." Suddenly, you have a tangible set of instructions to try out. Or you might recall a dessert by its nickname, like "Nana's 'surprise cake' had walnuts and a caramel glaze." The AI could respond with a recipe for something like a walnut spice cake with caramel sauce, reasoning that those elements fit your clues.

It's important to remember that while ChatGPT is incredibly helpful, it isn't psychic – it doesn't know your grandma's secret touch. Even the developers of these models note that personalized nostalgia is hard to perfectly replicate. But the magic here is getting as close as possible. By testing the AI's proposed recipe and then tweaking, you can hone in on the flavor of memory. After you cook the first attempt, you might tell ChatGPT, *"It's close, but the sauce isn't as thick as I remember."* The AI might suggest adding a bit more flour or cooking it down longer. Or you realize the color was more yellow – ChatGPT might guess, *"Perhaps she used a dash of turmeric for color,"* and add that.

Through a few iterations, you can often arrive at a recipe that family members say *"tastes just like how she used to make it!"* This process can be really meaningful. One person might finally recreate their late father's special barbecue rub by describing the smell and tang it had, and ChatGPT could output a rub recipe with paprika, brown sugar, mustard powder, and a hint of chili – and upon trying it on ribs, it turns out to unlock that familiar flavor almost exactly. Maybe they then remember a subtle aroma of clove or cumin was present; they mention it to ChatGPT, which revises the rub. The next batch of ribs comes out so close to Dad's that it moves the family to smiles and maybe a few happy tears. Such moments can be profound – it's like retrieving a piece of family history with the help of an algorithm.

A handy tip is to involve any relatives or friends who also remember the dish. You can combine your recollections – and even feed those into ChatGPT together. For example, *"My sister says she recalls a bit of ginger in the recipe too."* The AI can incorporate that. This collaborative approach, with family memories and AI guidance, can be a wonderful way to preserve something that almost slipped away.

In the end, you might not get a 100% perfect clone of the original – but you'll likely get very close, close enough that it brings back warm memories with each bite. And crucially, you'll have captured a recipe that was on the verge of being lost. It can now be written down and passed along – ensuring this piece of family culinary heritage is preserved. Future generations won't have to rely on memory alone; they can taste and experience that beloved dish for themselves.

Recreating recipes from memory shows just how far we've come in bridging past and present. It's both a culinary adventure and a way to honor those who cooked before us. Now that we've seen how ChatGPT can assist with every aspect of reviving family favorites – from modernizing and adapting written recipes to resurrecting unwritten ones – let's look at some real-world examples that put all these capabilities together. In the next section, we'll walk through a few sample scenarios where AI helps modernize and reinvent classic family dishes, so you can see how it all comes to life.

REVIVE AND REINVENT: PROMPT EXAMPLES

Example 1: Lightening a Classic Casserole

Scenario: A beloved tuna noodle casserole from the 1950s is deliciously nostalgic but loaded with canned soup and sodium. The goal is to make it fresher and healthier while keeping its cozy character.

User Prompt: "How can I modernize my grandma's tuna casserole? It uses a can of cream of mushroom soup and lots of salt, but I want a healthier version that still tastes comforting."

ChatGPT's Suggestions: ChatGPT might recommend making a simple homemade mushroom sauce instead of using the canned soup (using fresh mushrooms, low-fat milk, and a bit of flour for thickness). It could suggest adding fresh peas and carrots for more veggies and flavor, and using whole-grain noodles for extra nutrition. To reduce salt, it might advise using low-sodium broth and boosting herbs like thyme and parsley. For that crunchy topping, it could propose panko breadcrumbs mixed with a little olive oil as a lighter swap for fried onions. Overall, the casserole would come out with the same creamy, savory goodness – just less processed and salty. The family still recognizes it as the old favorite, and no one misses the canned soup.

Example 2: Updating a Hearty Stew

Scenario: A family beef stew recipe makes enough to feed an army and assumes you'll be simmering it on the stove all day. Today, you want to make a smaller batch for a weeknight dinner, using modern tools.

User Prompt: "I have a traditional beef stew recipe for 10 people, cooked for hours. How can I scale it down for 4 people and maybe use my Instant Pot to save time?"

ChatGPT's Suggestions: The AI would first scale down ingredient quantities – e.g., suggesting 1 pound of beef instead of 3, and adjusting the veggies and broth accordingly. It knows to slightly reduce the amount of spices so the flavor stays balanced. It might then provide Instant Pot instructions: for example, sauté the beef and onions right in the pot, add the other ingredients, then pressure cook for, say, 30 minutes instead of simmering 2 hours. It would likely mention that you should use the Quick Release or Natural Release appropriately to avoid overcooking the veggies. Additionally, ChatGPT could advise cutting the stew meat into smaller pieces (since pressure cooking favors uniform pieces) and maybe using a bit less liquid (because Instant Pot doesn't allow much evaporation). The result is a rich, tender stew that tastes like it's been on the stove all day, but it's ready in under an hour and perfectly portioned for a family of four.

Example 3: Adapting a Family Cookie Recipe

Scenario: Grandma's famous chocolate chip cookies are a family treasure, but now one of the grandchildren has developed a gluten intolerance. We want to make the same cookies gluten-free (and maybe cut down the sugar a tad) without losing the chewy, chocolatey joy.

User Prompt: "Can you help adapt our traditional chocolate chip cookie recipe to be gluten-free and a bit less sweet? I still want it chewy and delicious."

ChatGPT's Suggestions: ChatGPT would likely suggest a 1:1 gluten-free flour blend as a direct substitute for regular flour, and might recommend adding a pinch of xanthan gum if the blend doesn't already have it (to help the cookies bind and stay chewy). It could propose reducing the sugar by maybe 1/4 and adding a teaspoon of vanilla or a touch of cinnamon to enhance sweetness perception without more sugar. The AI might remind to let the dough rest (common for gluten-free batter to improve texture) before baking. It could also suggest checking the cookies a minute or two earlier, since gluten-free dough can sometimes bake faster. In the end, the cookies come out golden and chewy. The flavor is still full of butter and chocolate, and most eaters wouldn't guess they're reduced-sugar and gluten-free. The grandchild with intolerance gets to join the fun, and the tradition of Grandma's cookies continues with a modern twist.

Example 4: Streamlining a Celebration Dish

Scenario: Every year, Uncle Joe makes a traditional holiday plum pudding that requires hours of steaming and some hard-to-find ingredients like suet. This year, we want to simplify the process and maybe lighten it up, while keeping the signature flavors (spiced cake with dried fruits and brandy).

User Prompt: "I'd like to simplify our family's Christmas plum pudding recipe. It usually uses suet and takes 6 hours to steam. How can I make it easier (maybe using butter instead of suet and a quicker cooking method) but still have it taste like our plum pudding?"

ChatGPT's Suggestions: ChatGPT might jump in with a variety of modern tricks. First, it would confirm that cold butter or even vegetable shortening can replace suet one-for-one in the pudding batter, preserving the rich moisture without the fuss of suet. It could then suggest using an Instant Pot or slow cooker for steaming – for instance, pouring the batter into a pudding mold or metal bowl, covering it, and pressure cooking it for maybe 1 hour instead of 6 hours of gentle steaming. To ensure the flavor remains authentic, the AI would keep all the warm spices (cinnamon, nutmeg, cloves) and the mix of dried fruits, perhaps even suggesting soaking the fruits in brandy overnight for extra depth. It might also propose a smaller pudding size if you don't need to feed as many people, noting that a smaller pudding will cook faster and can be eaten sooner (no month-long maturation needed unless you want!). The final pudding would emerge moist and fragrant with spices and fruit. You can flame it with brandy and serve it with the usual hard sauce, and it delivers that nostalgic holiday taste – but you managed to pull it off with far less hassle.

Each of these examples shows how ChatGPT can assist with very specific recipe goals. Whether it's making a dish healthier, faster, allergy-friendly, or just more convenient, the AI offers practical suggestions that respect the original dish. By following its prompts and advice, home cooks are able to reinvent their family favorites in a way that honors tradition and satisfies current needs. It's like having a wise kitchen helper who knows your family's food history and also has one foot in the future. With these real-world cases in mind, you can confidently apply ChatGPT to your own recipe challenges and enjoy the process of bringing old dishes into a new era.

In this chapter, we've learned how to breathe new life into family favorites with a little help from AI. We saw how to feed old recipes into ChatGPT and get modernized versions, tailor dishes to new dietary needs, enjoy the cultural stories that make each recipe special, scale big recipes down (or up) to suit our tables, tweak flavors gently to match today's tastes, and even resurrect treasured dishes from just memories. At each step, the essence of our family recipes remained at the heart of the process. With ChatGPT's friendly guidance, you've discovered that it's entirely possible to honor tradition while embracing innovation in your kitchen.

Equipped with these new skills and examples, you are ready to keep your culinary heritage alive in a way that suits your life today.

The comfort of the past and the conveniences of the present can coexist beautifully on your plate. As we move forward to the next chapter, we'll continue this journey of empowering your home cooking with AI. The adventure isn't over – there's always more to explore in blending old wisdom with new technology to make your kitchen more creative, efficient, and fun.

15

VOICE, VISION, AND THE SMART KITCHEN AHEAD

The kitchen is rapidly evolving into a high-tech hub where **AI assistants** like ChatGPT become your sous-chef. In this chapter, you'll learn how voice commands, visual recognition, and smart devices are transforming home cooking. We'll explore cutting-edge appliances that **adapt in real time** to what you're doing, from fridges that suggest recipes to ovens that know when your meal is done. You'll see how speaking to your kitchen gadgets can make cooking truly **hands-free** and how augmented reality (AR) might one day overlay recipe guidance right onto your countertop. We'll also dive into the world of **wearable tech and wellness**, showing how your smartwatch and kitchen could team up to keep you healthy. Sustainability is a theme too – discover how AI can help you reduce food waste and make climate-smart cooking choices. Finally, we'll discuss how you can stay ahead of the curve, embracing these innovations with confidence. By the end of this chapter, you'll be inspired and prepared for a future where **AI enhances your everyday kitchen life** in practical, caring ways.

What will you learn in this chapter? In the first section, The Rise of the Smart Kitchen, we'll see how AI is making appliances smarter than ever – think ovens, fridges, and even mixers with built-in intelligence that assist you as you cook. Next, Voice-Activated Cooking will show how voice interfaces (like ChatGPT's voice mode or Alexa's new AI upgrades) enable you to cook without touching a screen or cookbook – you can set timers, get cooking tips, and adjust recipes all by speaking. Then, in Cooking with Cameras and AR, we look ahead to AI that can actually see your food: cameras and augmented reality that guide you with visual cues, from identifying ingredients to showing you where to chop or when to flip a steak. After that, Wearables and Wellness in the Kitchen connects the dots between your kitchen and your fitness trackers – how AI might use data from smartwatches or health apps to suggest meals that meet your nutritional goals, remind you to hydrate, or even count cooking as exercise! In AI-Powered Food Sustainability, we'll explore how intelligent systems help you waste less food and save energy, like planning meals around what you have and optimizing appliance use for the environment. The section Getting Future-Ready in Your Own Kitchen will give you friendly advice on staying curious and adaptable as these new tools emerge – practical tips to gradually introduce AI into your routine and make the most of it. Lastly, A Note of Thanks and What's Next wraps up our journey with a heartfelt thank-you and an invitation to continue the conversation beyond these pages.

Get ready for a chapter that is both **visionary and down-to-earth.** We'll paint a picture of the smart kitchen of tomorrow, but with plenty of examples you can try **today** using ChatGPT. Whether you're asking a voice assistant to walk you through a recipe, snapping a photo for cooking advice, or syncing your meal plan with your health goals, this chapter will empower you to embrace the future of cooking. By learning about voice, vision, and the smart kitchen ahead, you're not just keeping up with technology – you're discovering new ways to make home cooking easier, healthier, and more fun. Let's step into the kitchen of the future and see what's cooking!

THE RISE OF THE SMART KITCHEN

The concept of a "smart kitchen" has moved far beyond having a fancy fridge with a touchscreen or a wifi-enabled oven. Today, **artificial intelligence is taking smart tech and making it smarter.** We're entering an age where your kitchen appliances don't just obey commands – they *learn*, *adapt*, and even *anticipate* your needs in real time. In this section, we'll explore how ChatGPT-style intelligence is being integrated into ovens, fridges, and kitchen tools, turning them into collaborative helpers in your culinary adventures.

Not long ago, a "smart" oven simply meant one you could preheat with an app. Now, the latest **AI-powered ovens** can monitor your food and predict exactly when it will be perfectly cooked. For example, Bosch's Series 8 smart ovens use sensors and algorithms to gauge a dish's doneness. You no longer need to poke a thermometer into your roast or guess if the cake is baked through – the oven can notify you the moment your meal is ready. It learns how you cook over time, getting more accurate with each use. **Smart ovens** today often come with built-in cameras and connectivity. You can peek at your food via a smartphone app and get alerts if anything needs attention. The AI goes a step further by adjusting temperature and cook time on the fly, so that nothing burns or undercooks. It's like having a vigilant sous-chef who never takes its eyes off the stove.

Smart refrigerators are also evolving from passive storage to active assistants. Modern smart fridges (such as Samsung's Family Hub models) can **identify the food inside and suggest recipes** based on what you have. They use interior cameras and image recognition to keep track of your groceries. One AI-powered fridge can even detect when an item is starting to spoil and warn you in advance. Imagine your fridge alerting you, "Your strawberries will go bad in two days – why not make a smoothie now?" – and even providing the smoothie recipe! These fridges can display recipe steps on a screen, tell you the weather while you cook, or stream your favorite music to set the mood. The goal is to make cooking more convenient and to help you use what you have (so that forgotten spinach at the back of the drawer doesn't end up in the trash). Some smart fridges can sync with your calendar and grocery list, or even **order items online** when you run low. We're not far from a future where "running out of milk" is a thing of the past because your fridge already took care of it.

It's not just the big appliances – even countertop gadgets are getting smart. Take the example of the **GE Profile Smart Mixer**, a stand mixer with AI features. It has a built-in scale and can **connect to voice assistants** for hands-free operation. This mixer can detect the texture of your dough or batter and adjust its speed to avoid over-mixing. It will automatically shut off once your whipped cream reaches the perfect stiff peaks or your bread dough is fully kneaded. For anyone who's walked away only to have batter splatter everywhere, a mixer that *thinks* is a game-changer. There are also multi-cookers and pressure cookers with AI programs that learn how you like your food. In fact, a startup in India introduced a device called **DelishUp**, essentially an all-in-one cooking assistant with ChatGPT built in. It has an 8-inch touch screen and a "smart jar" that can **chop, stir, and cook**; you just add ingredients and it guides you step by step. If you're curious about a new recipe, you can even ask its AI (nicknamed "UpBot") for tips or for variations to suit your taste. This shows how AI can be embedded directly into kitchen tools to make them more capable and interactive.

One of the most exciting developments is how **generative AI** (like the tech behind ChatGPT) is being used in kitchen apps and appliances. For instance, GE's SmartHQ app features *Flavorly™ AI*, which can create custom recipes based on the ingredients you have on hand. Instead of searching a recipe website and manually tweaking what you find, you can enter "chicken, broccoli, cheddar" and get a tailored recipe that uses all three – perhaps a cozy chicken broccoli casserole – complete with cooking instructions. This AI doesn't just pull from a static database; it actually invents a recipe that fits your request. Miele, a high-end appliance brand, has even experimented with an oven that uses its internal camera to analyze your dish and suggest changes to the cooking settings as it goes. Think about that: you put a lasagna in the oven, and halfway through cooking the oven's AI might recommend lowering the temperature because it sees the edges browning too fast. It's like having a seasoned chef peek into your oven and make adjustments in real time.

All these advancements contribute to a kitchen that **works in tandem with you.** You get real-time assistance and peace of mind. If you're multitasking (and who isn't, these days?), your smart kitchen can keep an eye on the roast while you help the kids with homework in the next room. If you're unsure how to use a particular appliance feature, you can simply ask a connected AI assistant instead of thumbing through a manual. Many appliances now come with their own apps or integrate with smart home systems, so they can **talk to each other.** Your oven can send a notification to your phone or smartwatch when the food is ready, or your fridge can communicate with your grocery app to check items off your shopping list. The kitchen is becoming an ecosystem of devices + AI + you, all collaborating.

Let's look at a scenario that illustrates the **smart kitchen in action.** It's 6 pm, and you're not sure what to cook. You check your fridge (or its app) and see you have some ground beef and veggies that need to be used. You ask ChatGPT (via your phone or smart speaker), "What can I make for dinner with ground beef, tomatoes, and a bell pepper?" Within seconds, it suggests a hearty stuffed pepper recipe, using the beef, the pepper, and a can of tomatoes from your pantry. You like the idea – so you press a button to send the recipe to your smart oven and smart display. The oven preheats itself to the right temperature, and your kitchen display (say, a tablet or an Alexa Show) starts reading out the first step. As you follow the instructions, the smart oven's camera keeps track of the peppers as they bake. It knows the usual time, but because yours are extra-large, the oven's AI extends the cooking by a few minutes and lowers the heat slightly to cook them evenly. You wouldn't have known to do that, but the oven handles it. Meanwhile, your smart fridge notices this recipe used up the last of the cheese, and quietly adds "cheddar cheese" to the shared grocery list on your phone. In the end, you've made a great dinner with minimal stress – the AI orchestrated the timing and helped you use what you had efficiently.

Such a seamless experience is increasingly possible thanks to the rise of the smart kitchen. The key takeaway is that **your kitchen is becoming a partner.** It's moving from being a collection of tools you operate to a set of tools that also *operate with you.* And underpinning many of these innovations is AI – often the conversational kind exemplified by ChatGPT – which enables more natural interactions. Instead of pressing a dozen buttons, you might just say, "preheat the oven to 375°F," or instead of guessing what to do with leftovers, you might ask, "ChatGPT, give me a quick recipe idea." The learning capability of AI means the more you use these features, the better they get at helping you. It's an exciting virtuous cycle for home cooks.

Here are a few examples of how you might use ChatGPT or an AI assistant in a smart kitchen today:

Example Prompt: "What recipe can I make with the ingredients in my fridge?" – You could provide a list of odds and ends (e.g., *"I have half an eggplant, some feta cheese, and leftover roasted chicken"*) and the AI would create a recipe that combines them in a tasty way. It's like having a personal recipe developer on call, ensuring nothing goes to waste.

Example Prompt: "My smart oven says 'Food will be ready in 5 minutes.' What should I do next?" – You might ask this if you're unsure about resting time or how to plate the dish. ChatGPT could answer: *"Once it's done, let the chicken rest for 5 minutes before slicing. Use that time to toss your salad."* This way, the AI assistant coordinates your tasks around the appliance's timing.

Example Prompt: "How do I clean the filter on my smart dishwasher?" – Rather than flipping through a manual, you can ask an AI assistant this maintenance question. It can pull up the specific steps (e.g., *"Twist the filter at the bottom counter-clockwise and lift it out, rinse under running water..."*) and even link to a short video if available. Your appliances' smart features become easier to manage with AI guidance.

Through these examples, you can see the practical side of a smart kitchen powered by AI. It's not about tech for tech's sake – it's about making your life simpler, meals better, and cooking more enjoyable. With appliances handling the tedious or tricky parts, you get to focus on the creative and fun aspects of cooking.

As our kitchens become smarter, a natural question arises: how do we best interact with all this intelligence? The answer is increasingly **with our voice**. Talking to your kitchen – whether it's to set a timer or to ask for a recipe – is becoming as normal as using our hands. In the next section, we'll explore how voice-activated AI is taking center stage in the smart kitchen, enabling truly hands-free, conversational cooking assistance.

VOICE-ACTIVATED COOKING

One of the most convenient ways to harness AI in the kitchen is by using your **voice**. Cooking is a messy, hands-on activity – you might be covered in dough or juggling hot pans – so the ability to *speak* commands or questions and have an AI respond is a game changer. Voice-activated cooking means you can interact with recipe assistants, timers, and appliances **without ever touching a screen or button**. In this section, we'll see how AI voice interfaces (from ChatGPT's voice mode to smart speakers like Alexa and Google Assistant) are evolving to support hands-free help, step-by-step guidance, and even dynamic recipe adjustments on the fly.

If you've used a voice assistant like Siri, Alexa, or Google in the kitchen, you know how handy it is for simple tasks: "Hey Google, set a timer for 10 minutes," or "Alexa, how many tablespoons in a quarter cup?" We've all enjoyed not having to wash and dry our hands just to check a measurement. Now, with advances in AI, these voice assistants are becoming far more *capable and conversational*. The latest generation of voice AIs – powered by large language models similar to ChatGPT – can handle complex questions and multi-step interactions. Instead of just giving one-off answers, they can engage in a dialogue. For example, you could say, "I want to cook pasta tonight," and your assistant might ask, "Sure. Do you want a vegetarian recipe or something with meat?" – leading you through a decision process as a human would.

Hands-free recipe guidance is one of the killer features of voice-activated AI in the kitchen. Imagine you're following a brownie recipe with your hands full of flour and chocolate. You can ask, "What's the next step?" and the AI will read it out to you. Good voice assistants can pause, repeat, or even rephrase instructions on request. If you're confused, you might ask, "Wait, how do I fold in egg whites?" – and a smart assistant can explain that technique verbally, maybe even with a short audio cue or reference to a video. This kind of natural back-and-forth makes cooking *so much easier* than trying to swipe through a recipe with gunky fingers. We're moving towards a world where you can have a continuous conversation with your cooking assistant: "Add two eggs... (you say: already added) ...Okay, now stir in the flour until just combined... (you: done, what next?) ...Now pour the batter into a pan and set it in the oven." It's like cooking alongside a patient friend who's reading the recipe for you.

Modern voice AIs are also getting better at handling **context and adjustments**. Let's say you're in the middle of a recipe and something changes – you realize you're out of an ingredient or you want to halve the recipe. With older voice systems, that would be hard to communicate. But with AI like ChatGPT, you could simply say, "I don't have sour cream, what can I use instead?" and it will understand you're asking for a substitution *in the context of the current recipe*. It might reply, "You can substitute plain yogurt for sour cream in this recipe, using the same amount." Similarly, you could say, "Actually, I'm cooking for 8 people, not 4 – how do I adjust?" and a savvy voice assistant could do the math and even warn you if your pot might not be big enough. This ability to **handle follow-up questions and remember what you're doing** is where AI voice interfaces shine. It transforms voice assistants from simple command executors into true conversational partners in the kitchen.

Another benefit of voice-activated cooking is managing **timing and multitasking**. Skilled cooks often have several things going at once – sauce simmering, oven preheating, veggies chopping. A voice assistant can act like a coordinator. You can say, "Remind me to check the stew in 15 minutes," without stopping your chopping. If you set multiple timers (e.g., one for the stew, one for the bread in the oven, one for steeping tea), you can ask at any point, "How much time is left on my timers?" and get a quick rundown. Advanced systems will even know which timer is which: "Your stew has 5 minutes remaining, and the bread has 12 minutes." This might seem simple, but when you're in the thick of cooking, these verbal check-ins and reminders feel like having an extra set of eyes on the clock.

Voice interfaces also make the kitchen more **accessible and inclusive.** Not everyone can easily read small recipe text or stand by the stove thumbing through a cookbook. With voice guidance, visually impaired cooks, elderly folks, or anyone who finds it easier to listen can enjoy cooking with more independence. The AI doesn't get impatient if you ask it to repeat the temperature for the third time – it's happy to help. This supportive, judgment-free assistance is very much in line with the friendly tone we want in our kitchens.

So how do you actually use voice-activated AI while cooking? You might use a dedicated device like a smart speaker, or a smartphone with a voice assistant, or even newer appliances that have voice control built-in. For instance, some new microwaves and ovens are Alexa-enabled – you can literally say "Alexa, microwave for 2 minutes on high" and it will. But you don't need special appliances to start using voice help. The ChatGPT mobile app, for example, now has a voice mode where you can speak to it and it talks back. You could prop up your phone and have a full conversation: "ChatGPT, I'm making curry – what's the first step?" It might reply, "Sure! First, chop your onions, garlic, and ginger. Let me know when you're done." After you say you've done that, it continues to the next step. This is already possible with current AI technology and will only get smoother over time.

Let's consider a real-life use case to see voice AI in action. Suppose you're trying a new recipe for the first time – say, a complicated soufflé. You can start by saying, "Start recipe for chocolate soufflé." The assistant might fetch a well-reviewed recipe and begin:

"Preheat your oven to 375°F. Step 1: Butter the ramekins and dust them with sugar." You go ahead and do that. Instead of coming back to a device to scroll, you simply say "Next," and it says: "Step 2: Melt the chocolate and butter together. You can use a double boiler or microwave in short bursts. Let me know when it's melted." As you melt the chocolate, you realize you're not sure about using a double boiler. So you ask, "How do I make a double boiler?" The assistant pauses the recipe and explains, "To make a double boiler, set a heat-proof bowl over a pot of simmering water, making sure the bowl doesn't touch the water. Put the chocolate and butter in the bowl to melt gently." You follow the guidance. Once done, you say "Chocolate is melted." The assistant knows where you left off and continues: "Great. Step 3: In a separate bowl, whisk egg yolks..." and so on. During a critical moment, you might ask, "Can you repeat that?" or "What should the texture look like?" and a smart voice AI could answer, e.g., "It should be smooth and glossy with no lumps." By the time you get the soufflé in the oven, you haven't had to touch a single device – all interactions were voice-based, and the AI adapted to your questions and pace. It's easy to see how this can boost a home cook's confidence with tough recipes.

Dynamic adjustments mid-cooking are another powerful feature. Suppose you're following a voice-guided recipe and you say, "Actually, I'd like to add vanilla extract – the recipe didn't mention it. Can I do that now?" A traditional voice assistant might be stumped, but an AI like ChatGPT could integrate that on the fly: *"Sure! Go ahead and stir in a teaspoon of vanilla extract into the mixture now. It won't affect the cooking time. I'll incorporate that into the remaining steps."* It figuratively "edits" the recipe for you in real time. This flexibility makes the AI feel more like a human collaborator than a rigid program. And if you make a mistake – say you added salt twice because you missed a cue – you can tell the AI, and it can help you troubleshoot ("Hmm, it might be a bit salty. Maybe add a pinch of sugar and a squeeze of lemon to balance it."). Old-school voice assistants wouldn't know how to handle that; new AI ones can try to rescue your dish.

Of course, voice cooking isn't perfect. Kitchens can be noisy (sizzling, blenders, etc.), so the assistant might mishear occasionally. It helps to speak clearly and perhaps pause noisy appliances when asking a question. The technology for voice recognition (like OpenAI's Whisper system) has gotten remarkably good at parsing speech even with background sounds, so this is improving. And yes, there's the occasional funny misunderstanding – you say "basil," it hears "bagel" – but AI is learning context to avoid most of those hiccups. In a friendly kitchen atmosphere, a misheard command can be a source of laughter rather than frustration, especially as errors become rarer.

Let's highlight a few *practical voice commands* or prompts that showcase what voice-activated cooking can do:

Conversational Recipe Guidance: *"ChatGPT, let's make lasagna together."* – This would initiate a step-by-step dialogue for a lasagna recipe. You can respond with "next," "repeat that," or "I only have gluten-free noodles, is that okay?" and it will adjust and guide you through it all in conversation form. It's very much like having a patient teacher in the kitchen.

On-the-fly Help: *"Alexa, ask ChatGPT: I spilled some egg yolk into my egg whites. What do I do?"* – In a voice-enabled ChatGPT scenario, the AI could advise how to salvage a meringue if a bit of yolk got in (usually, you might need to start over, but it could suggest trying a bit of vinegar to clean the bowl and starting fresh). This shows how voice AI can assist with *kitchen emergencies* or unexpected situations, hands-free.

Multitasking and Timers: *"Hey Google, read my recipe while I chop the vegetables."* – This ensures Google Assistant keeps talking through the steps so you can keep working. If you need to pause, you can say "Pause recipe" or ask a question about the current step. Additionally, *"Set a pasta timer for 8 minutes and a bread timer for 20 minutes."* – This sets two timers by voice. Later you can ask, "How much time on the pasta?" without having to recall which timer was which – the assistant will know.

Shopping and Planning via Voice: *"Siri, add all the ingredients* *from this recipe to my shopping list."* – If you decided on a recipe, a voice command like this could extract the list of ingredients (minus what you already have, if it knows from your smart fridge or your input) and add them to a grocery list. This blends cooking assistance with meal planning, all done by simple speech.

Voice-activated cooking is all about **convenience and empowerment.** It lets you keep your focus on the food, not on the device or the book. As AI voice assistants get more knowledgeable, you'll find you can ask them *why* a step is needed, or *what if I do this instead*, and get meaningful answers. This turns cooking into more of a two-way interaction – you're learning and creating with the AI, not just being led by the nose.

With voice interfaces making it easy to *talk* to our kitchen, the next frontier is giving AI the ability to *see* into our kitchen. After all, cooking is highly visual: we check if something is brown, we gauge amounts by eye, we recognize ingredients by look. Wouldn't it be amazing if our AI assistant could watch the process and give feedback? In the following section, we'll explore just that – how computer vision and AR are poised to bring **eyes** into the smart kitchen, guiding us in new, visual ways.

COOKING WITH CAMERAS AND AR

We've given our kitchen a voice – now let's talk about giving it **vision.** The idea of an AI that can see what's happening on your cutting board or stove opens up thrilling possibilities. In this section, we look ahead to cooking with the help of **cameras and augmented reality (AR).** This means your AI assistant could literally observe your ingredients or your technique and provide guidance as if a chef were standing beside you. We'll explore current examples of kitchen devices with cameras, and the emerging trend of AR apps and smart glasses that overlay helpful information onto your real kitchen environment. It's a peek into the not-so-distant future where your cooking assistant isn't just a voice in a speaker – it has "eyes" on the action, making the assistance even more interactive and tailored to you.

Computer vision (the ability of AI to interpret images and video) has advanced tremendously. You may have already used it in simple ways, like an app that identifies a plant from a photo or counts your daily steps from camera footage. In the kitchen, vision-enabled AI can identify foods, track cooking progress, and even gauge technique. One practical example available today is the smart oven with an internal camera: some AI ovens can recognize the food you put in (say, it knows a pizza from a pie) and automatically set the optimal cooking program. The June oven (a popular smart countertop oven) can visually identify common foods and cook them with a tap. Miele's experimental oven, as mentioned, uses a camera to watch the food browning and can suggest adjustments. These are early steps, but very useful – they take some uncertainty out of cooking. If an oven can tell that your cookies are golden at the edges, it could ping you or turn itself off, even if the timer hasn't gone off yet.

Augmented reality in cooking is an exciting frontier. **Augmented reality** means layering computer-generated information onto your view of the real world. In a kitchen context, imagine holding up your phone or wearing AR glasses that display helpful tips as you cook. For instance, you look at a piece of meat on your cutting board through your phone's AR camera, and it shows a line where you should cut, or a label that says "2 cm thick slices". Or you point your phone at a pot, and it shows a virtual thermometer reading or a timer floating above it. AR can guide your movements visually, which is incredibly intuitive – after all, cooking is largely about *looking* at things (Is it boiling? Is it finely chopped? Is it the right color?).

Researchers have been playing with AR cooking guides. One prototype at a university developed an AR headset app that recognizes ingredients and cookware, then displays the next step right in your field of view. For example, step 1 might highlight the saltshaker and the bowl, signaling "add salt to the bowl." After you do it (the system can tell by seeing the action or the result), step 2 might put an arrow on the frying pan indicating "put the pan on the stove and turn on heat." This might sound futuristic, but the underlying tech exists – it's a matter of refining it for home use. Tech companies have also demoed **smart glasses for cooking**: you put on glasses that can overlay recipes and even detect what you're doing. One vision is that the glasses could notice if you skipped a step or if something doesn't look right and then alert you ("Your sauce looks a bit dry, consider adding a splash of water").

Even without fancy glasses, our existing devices can offer some AR-like help. **Smartphone cooking apps** are beginning to include camera features. You might see apps where you can snap a photo of an ingredient and get suggestions (point your camera at an eggplant, it recognizes it, then shows recipe ideas for eggplant on screen). Or you could use a generic tool like Google Lens to identify an unusual vegetable or find info on an ingredient by sight. We can expect specialized cooking AR apps to become more common. For instance, an app might let you scan your pantry shelf and then automatically compile a list of what you have, using image recognition on the labels – essentially a quicker way to inventory your kitchen.

One very cool potential of AI vision is **feedback on technique**. Think about when you learn from a cooking video or in a class: the teacher might say "that's too thick, slice thinner like this." In the future, an AI could play a similar role. You could hold up your phone to your diced onions, and the AI (either on the device or via cloud like ChatGPT's vision models) could analyze the pieces and say, "Try to cut the onions more evenly – some pieces are much larger than others, which could affect even cooking. Aim for a consistent size." It might even highlight the big chunks on your screen so you can recut them. This kind of personalized feedback at home would be revolutionary for improving cooking skills. It's like having a chef mentor looking over your shoulder, gently correcting you – except it's an AI that's available anytime.

Another scenario: You're frying a steak and not sure if it's the right moment to flip. With an AI camera setup, you could literally ask, "Does this look ready to turn over?" and show the camera the steak. An AI that's been trained on thousands of images of steaks at various doneness could analyze the browning and say, "Yes, the edges are brown – go ahead and flip now for a medium-rare." In fact, companies are training AIs to recognize food states (like how a "perfectly golden" pancake looks versus burned or underdone). This could be integrated into smart stovetops or camera attachments. We already see something like this in smart coffee makers that can detect milk foam quality, or rice cookers that adjust based on how the grains look during cooking.

Augmented reality recipe instructions could take many forms. With AR glasses, you might see a floating to-do list in the corner of your vision with checkboxes you can "air click" when done. Or your glasses might project a virtual measuring cup onto a bowl, showing you how high to pour the flour. If glasses aren't your thing, a tablet on a stand can do a basic version: as you cook, you can point the tablet's camera at your work area whenever you want a check, and the app could draw guidance on the live video feed. Some experimental apps have a mode where as you move through the recipe, they visually monitor – for example, using the camera to ensure you actually added the two eggs the recipe called for (counting them as they appear in the bowl). If it doesn't see the eggs, it might gently remind you before you move on. This reduces human error in a friendly way.

Let's not forget **ingredient recognition** – a simpler but very handy aspect of AI vision. Suppose you have a mystery spice jar that lost its label, or some leftover food in a container and you can't recall what it is. An AI vision model could identify it for you: *"That looks like ground cumin,"* or *"This is a type of curry paste, possibly Thai red curry paste."* It might not be 100% right all the time, but even a good guess can jog your memory or at least prevent you from mistaking sugar for salt. Some apps already let you scan the ingredients you have, then the AI suggests recipes (taking the idea of "what's in my fridge" to a visual level). OpenAI's own vision-capable ChatGPT demo showed snapping a picture of your fridge contents to figure out dinner – for example, a photo with eggs, green onions, and butter might lead the AI to suggest an omelet. This feels almost magical: you show the AI your reality, and it responds with ideas tailored to exactly what it *sees*.

The AR future might also include **virtual chef avatars or overlays.** You could have a cute virtual character on your kitchen counter (visible through your device) that walks you through a recipe and points at things: "Now pick up *this* (highlighting the spoon) and stir the pot." Companies are exploring these sorts of interfaces to make the cooking experience more engaging and less intimidating, almost like a game. Gamifying cooking with AR could even encourage kids to participate, following along with a friendly animated guide.

While much of this is still emerging, we're already partway there. Newer smartphone apps with **multimodal AI** (which means they handle text, voice, and images together) can do things like: you send a photo of the open fridge and type "What can I make?", and they'll answer with a recipe, understanding the image and the question together. As AI like Google's Gemini and others come out, we'll see more robust systems that can parse a whole scene: *"I see carrots, celery, and onion – those are the makings of a mirepoix. Perhaps you could start a soup."*

It's worth noting some current gadgets as precursors: The Amazon Echo Show (the Alexa device with a screen) can use its camera to do limited things like recognizing food packages or triggering cooking classes where you're on camera (sort of like a Zoom cooking class with AI hints). And some smart cooktops have built-in cameras above them – initially for safety (to detect smoke or boil-overs) – but those could double as vision for cooking assistance soon. Even your kitchen hood or a clamp-on camera could provide the video feed needed for an AI to watch the stovetop.

Let's illustrate how cooking with vision might work in a near-future kitchen scenario: You're making a stir-fry and have a bunch of vegetables. You put on a pair of AR glasses or set up your tablet. As you start chopping a carrot, the system outlines the carrot on your screen and shows segments, suggesting, "Cut here for equal pieces." You follow along and end up with nicely uniform slices. Next, you hold up a bottle of sauce to the camera (because the recipe calls for something and you wonder if your bottle is a good substitute). The AI reads the label and says, "That's oyster sauce, which is a bit saltier than soy sauce. Use half the amount the recipe calls for, and add a little water." Great, disaster averted. Now as you stir-fry, you ask aloud, "Is my pan hot enough?" The system notices the level of sizzle and maybe the little plume of smoke, and through your earbud it says, "It's very hot – reduce to medium to avoid burning the garlic." A virtual thermometer reading could even appear showing ~400°F pan surface. Throughout this process, you feel like the kitchen itself is *responsive*: visual cues and gentle audio alerts keep you on track. By the end, you've cooked with more confidence and precision than ever, thanks to that extra set of "eyes."

To get a bit more concrete, here are some **examples of prompts or uses** for vision and AR in the kitchen:

Using ChatGPT with an image prompt: "(Image of an open fridge) ChatGPT, what meals can I make with these items?" – You snap a picture of your fridge's interior. ChatGPT (with vision enabled) analyzes it: it sees maybe a carton of eggs, some spinach, a block of cheese, and leftover rice. It replies with a few suggestions: *"How about a spinach and cheese omelette with a side of fried rice? You have eggs, cheese, spinach for the omelette, and you can use that leftover rice to make a quick fried rice. Need a recipe for either?"* This is AI vision doing inventory and meal planning in one go.

Augmented Step Verification: "(Image of chopped vegetables) Are these chopped finely enough for the recipe?" – You take a quick photo of your cutting board and ask the AI. It might respond, *"They're a bit rough – try to cut the onions a little smaller for a smoother soup. The carrots look good though!"* This kind of feedback is super helpful, almost like having a chef tutor giving you tips.

Identifying something: "(Image of a spice) What is this spice and what can I use it for?" – Suppose you found a spice jar in the back of the cupboard. The AI looks and says, *"This is garam masala (based on the color and texture). It's a blend of spices used in Indian cuisine, great for curries and roasted veggies."* Not only do you identify it, you also learn how to use it.

AR Guided Cooking: (This is more of a use-case than a text prompt) **Following on-screen AR cues while cooking.** For example, the app might display text like *"Now pour about 2 tablespoons of oil – I'll tell you when to stop."* As you pour oil into the pan visible on camera, the AI gauges the amount (by the area it spreads or just by time) and a checkmark pops up when you've hit roughly the right amount. Then it might show a blinking icon on the pan indicating "add onions here." This reduces guesswork especially for visual learners.

Cooking with cameras and AR brings a **whole new dimension** to kitchen assistance. It moves us beyond the realm of just words (reading or hearing) into the realm of sight – which is how we humans predominantly interact with the world. When AI can see, it can guide us in ways that feel very natural. You don't have to describe what you see; the AI sees it too and can cut to the chase. While fully integrated AR cooking is still developing, each incremental feature (be it a smart oven camera or a grocery-scanning app) adds to our toolbox. It won't be long before checking if your onions are caramelized enough could be as simple as asking your kitchen to take a look.

Now that we've talked about AI that can listen and even watch in the kitchen, there's another aspect of cooking that tech can enhance: *you*, the cook! What if your kitchen could also pay attention to your well-being as you cook? In the next section, we'll explore how wearables and health tracking devices can integrate with AI to make sure you're not just making a delicious meal, but a healthy one too – aligning cooking with your wellness goals in smart, subtle ways.

WEARABLES AND WELLNESS IN THE KITCHEN

Your kitchen and your health are deeply connected – after all, it's where most of your nutrition comes from. In this section, we'll discuss how AI might soon bridge the gap between cooking and personal wellness. **Wearables** like smartwatches, fitness trackers, or health monitors can provide real-time data about your body (heart rate, activity level, sleep quality, etc.), and when that data is combined with an AI assistant in the kitchen, the possibilities are exciting. Imagine your kitchen suggesting meals that perfectly fit your fitness goals or dietary needs, or reminding you to hydrate and stretch while cooking. We'll explore how AI can use information from wearables to make your cooking experience healthier and more personalized, effectively turning the kitchen into a partner in your wellness journey.

Consider what many of us have now: maybe an Apple Watch, Fitbit, or Oura ring that tracks steps, calories burned, heart rate, and sometimes even things like blood oxygen or stress levels. These devices create a picture of our daily health habits. On the other side, we have apps for logging food or planning meals. **AI is the link** that can connect these two – using your health data to influence your eating in a positive way, and vice versa.

For example, suppose your smartwatch knows you *slept poorly* last night (it recorded you tossing and turning). A clever kitchen AI might then recommend a breakfast that gives you an energy boost – perhaps suggesting a smoothie with extra protein and B-vitamins or a fiber-rich meal to keep you going. If it knows you usually drink coffee but your heart rate is already elevated from lack of sleep, it might gently suggest *decaf or herbal tea* to avoid adding jitters on top of fatigue. This kind of **adaptive recommendation** treats you as a whole person: linking how you feel and function to what you eat and drink.

Another scenario: your fitness tracker shows you haven't been very active today, only a couple thousand steps. It's nearing dinner time. The AI in your kitchen might consider that information when helping you plan dinner. Perhaps it will suggest a lighter, low-carb meal since you didn't burn many calories today, or even encourage you to take a short walk while something is baking. The AI could say, "Your casserole will be in the oven for 30 minutes – how about a quick walk around the block? I'll remind you to come back in 25 minutes." Suddenly, your kitchen assistant is also a mini fitness coach, but in a friendly, integrated way. You might actually do it, because it feels like a helpful suggestion rather than a nag.

Wearables can also detect **health metrics** like heart rate or even hydration levels (some advanced devices and smart water bottles do this). If you're cooking and your heart rate is unusually high (maybe you're stressed or maybe chopping veggies is more of a workout than you thought!), an AI might notice and advise a short break: "It seems like you're working hard. Take a minute to breathe – cooking should be fun!" Or if you've been standing for a long time, your smartwatch's "time to stand" reminder might coincide with the AI saying, "While we let the dough rest for 10 minutes, how about you sit down or do a quick stretch?" In this way, the kitchen of the future cares about *the cook's comfort* too.

Nutrition tracking is a big area where AI, wearables, and kitchen life converge. There are already apps where you can snap a photo of your meal and an AI tries to estimate the calories and nutrients. If that becomes more accurate, your kitchen AI could automatically log what you cook and eat, creating a food diary without you manually entering data. Over time, it learns your patterns and can highlight trends: "You've had red meat three times this week; how about fish or a plant-based protein tonight for balance?" Or "Your fiber intake has been low today – consider a side of steamed veggies or a salad with dinner." These suggestions would be informed by dietary guidelines and your personal history, aiming to keep you on track with any goals you have (be it weight management, muscle gain, blood sugar control, etc.).

There's talk of **"digital health coaches"** that companies like Apple are developing. These would use AI to synthesize data from wearables and give tailored health advice. In a kitchen context, that might appear as your smart display saying in the morning, "Good morning! Based on your 7-hour sleep and today's workout plan, I recommend a higher-carb breakfast for energy. How about oatmeal with fruit? I can walk you through a quick recipe." It's easy to see how that would get your day started on the right foot, nutritionally speaking.

Hydration is another seemingly small thing that AI could help with. Many of us forget to drink water, especially while busy cooking or doing chores. A smartwatch can detect signs of dehydration (e.g., elevated heart rate, or simply by tracking that you haven't logged any water intake). The kitchen assistant might chime in, "Drink alert: Don't forget to have a glass of water." Or if you have a smart water bottle that knows how much you drank, it could integrate with the system to remind you if you're behind your goal. When you're simmering soup for an hour, a little nudge to sip some water yourself is a caring touch the AI can provide.

Let's consider how this might look for someone with specific health goals or conditions. If you're managing diabetes, for example, a wearable glucose monitor could inform the AI that your blood sugar is a bit high right now. The kitchen assistant could adjust dinner plans accordingly: *"Maybe skip the starchy side dish tonight and do a salad instead, your blood sugar is above target. And take a 10-minute walk after dinner to help bring it down."* This is very personalized advice that normally a doctor or nutritionist would give – but an AI could give it in real time, every day, making disease management much easier. Importantly, it would do so with sensitivity and evidence-based recommendations.

For those on specific diets (say, training for a marathon, trying keto, or needing low-sodium meals for blood pressure), AI can be a vigilant helper. Your wearable and health apps provide the targets – like a daily calorie goal, macronutrient ratios, or sodium limits – and the kitchen AI can intervene in the moment to keep you on track. *"This recipe uses a lot of salt and cheese. Given your blood pressure goal, shall I help you modify it? We can cut the salt in half and add extra herbs for flavor."* It might even remember to use a low-sodium broth you have in the pantry instead of regular. Over time, you learn healthier habits because the AI has been modeling them for you.

Another interesting angle is counting **cooking as exercise or activity.** Ever notice you might be on your feet and moving quite a bit during a big cooking session? Your smartwatch does. Perhaps the AI could give you credit for that: "You were active for 45 minutes cooking dinner – that's roughly 150 calories burned. Nice! Cooking can be a workout too." Such positive reinforcement could encourage people who love cooking that it's also beneficial physically (aside from the result of yummy food). And for people who need to be more active, it shows that doing something like home cooking, which involves chopping, stirring, cleaning up, is better than sitting on the couch waiting for takeout. It subtly promotes a healthier lifestyle overall.

Wearables could also contribute safety data. If you have certain medical conditions (like a risk of fainting, or if you are an older adult with a fall detector watch), the kitchen could respond to emergencies. An extreme but life-saving example: your smartwatch detects an irregular heartbeat or a fall in the kitchen, the AI could turn off the stove (if it's connected) and call for help. While we hope such events are rare, designing a smart kitchen with awareness of the cook's well-being means incorporating those safety nets. Some smart stoves already have automatic shut-off if no motion is detected for a while (to prevent accidents). Tying that to wearable data (like noticing you haven't moved *and* your heart rate dropped) could distinguish between you taking a quiet phone call in the other room vs. you potentially needing assistance.

A lighter safety example: If your fitness tracker senses a high stress level (maybe your heart rate jumps when the oil catches fire in the pan!), the AI can react calmly: "It looks like things got a bit heated – don't worry, just remove the pan from heat and cover it. You've got this." It sounds a bit sci-fi, but the tech pieces for stress detection and response do exist; it's about integrating them smoothly.

There is also the angle of **posture and ergonomics.** Some wearables or smart devices (even cameras) could detect if you're hunched over the counter for a long time. The AI might then suggest adjusting your setup: "Try raising your cutting board or take a stretch break – your back will thank you." It's akin to how office workers get reminders to adjust posture or look away from the screen to rest eyes, but tailored to kitchen tasks.

Let's put this into a narrative to see it in action. Imagine it's midday and you've been super busy (your smartwatch shows high stress, few steps, and maybe slightly elevated blood pressure from a hectic morning). You step into the kitchen thinking about lunch. The AI in your kitchen, through your phone or a speaker, gently says: "How about a heart-healthy lunch today? A nice mixed salad with grilled chicken would be easy. I noticed you haven't moved much today – we could do a quick set of squats or countertop push-ups while the chicken is grilling, if you're up for it." Maybe you chuckle, but you do a few squats – why not, no one's watching except an AI that won't judge! You make the salad following the voice assistant's instructions, and at the end it says, "Great job! By the way, this meal has lots of veggies – that's fantastic for your fiber and vitamin intake, hitting about 50% of your daily needs. Enjoy your meal, and remember to drink some water. I'll check in later to plan something light for dinner since this was a substantial lunch." This scenario shows the AI interweaving cooking guidance with wellness coaching in a very natural, supportive manner.

It's important that all this is done in a **supportive tone** – like a knowledgeable friend or a kindly coach, not a drill sergeant or a scold. The tone we aim for (and which we maintain throughout this book) is friendly and empowering. The AI might celebrate your improvements: "You've cooked at home 5 nights this week – amazing! Your body is getting great nutrition." Or if you have a goal to reduce sugar, it can congratulate you when you choose fruit for dessert instead of ice cream, possibly by noting, "That fruit salad looked delicious and it's a much smarter choice for your blood sugar than cake – well done!" Positive reinforcement goes a long way in building healthy habits.

Let's highlight some concrete ways to use ChatGPT (or similar AI) with wearables and wellness info:

Meal Suggestions from Fitness Data: "ChatGPT, my Fitbit says I burned 500 extra calories today from a long run. What should I eat to refuel?" – The AI could suggest a meal rich in protein and carbs to help recovery, like *"How about a chicken burrito bowl with brown rice and veggies to replenish energy and protein? And maybe a banana or some yogurt for extra potassium and carbs."* It's using your fitness data (500 cals, long run) to tailor nutrition advice.

Hydration Reminder: You might not even have to prompt this. If your smart water bottle logs only 2 cups of water by 4pm, the AI could pipe up, "You've only had about 16 ounces of water so far. For optimal hydration, try to drink another 2-3 glasses this evening. Maybe start with one now while you prep dinner." It's proactive assistance, which you can always ignore, but often such reminders are welcome.

Dietary Restriction Checks: "ChatGPT, based on my health data, is this recipe good for me?" – You could provide a recipe (by linking or listing ingredients) and mention your health focus (like lowering cholesterol). The AI can analyze it: *"This recipe is quite high in saturated fat (from butter and cream). For your cholesterol goals, you might swap butter for olive oil and use Greek yogurt instead of cream. Shall I give you an adjusted recipe? "* This merges nutritional expertise with personal health priorities.

Mindful Cooking Breaks: If your wearable detects stress or prolonged inactivity, you could even have a prompt: **"I've been stressed today – any cooking suggestions to help me relax and still eat healthy?"** The AI might answer, *"Consider a simple, calming recipe like a vegetable stir-fry or a one-pot soup. The chopping can be therapeutic. Play some music you love while at it. I'll guide you through a quick stir-fry with ginger and greens – that can actually help lower cortisol (stress hormone) levels. Ready to start?"* It addresses both the mental state and the nutritional aspect, giving you a plan that soothes and nourishes.

The integration of wearables with kitchen AI underscores a larger point: **the kitchen isn't an isolated part of our lives** – it's connected to our daily routines, our bodies, and our well-being. By tapping into that, AI can ensure that what we cook aligns with how we feel and what we need. It can act as the friendly bridge between *health advice* and *home cooking*, which traditionally might have been hard to follow consistently.

In a way, this also makes technology a guardian of those intangible "old-school" values: caring for oneself and one's family. Grandma used to say "eat your veggies" or "drink water" – now AI, informed by actual data, can echo that caring voice in a personalized way.

As we embrace these wearable-driven insights, one thing becomes clear: **the future kitchen is not just about making cooking high-tech, but making it healthier and more attuned to you.** You won't need to consult a dozen sources for diet tips – your kitchen assistant will seamlessly incorporate them as you go about cooking.

Taking care of ourselves is one side of the coin; taking care of our planet is the other. As we have AI helping to track our personal wellness in the kitchen, we can also enlist AI's help in keeping our cooking sustainable and eco-friendly. In the next section, we'll explore how AI is contributing to smarter use of food and resources – from reducing waste to making climate-conscious meal choices – so that our home cooking can be healthy for the Earth, too.

AI-POWERED FOOD SUSTAINABILITY

Cooking isn't just about feeding ourselves – it's also connected to how we treat the world around us. Think about food waste, energy usage, and sourcing of ingredients: our kitchen habits have a real impact on the planet. The good news is that **AI can be a powerful ally in making our cooking more sustainable.** In this section, we'll look at how smart kitchen systems and ChatGPT-like assistants can help reduce waste, optimize the food we buy, and guide us toward more climate-friendly choices. This is about being a savvy, eco-conscious home cook without added hassle – letting technology help us do the right thing for the environment while we cook great meals.

Food waste is a huge issue globally (households throw away a significant chunk of the groceries they buy, unfortunately). One of the simplest ways AI aids sustainability is by **helping us use up what we have instead of letting it go bad.** We touched on this with smart fridges suggesting recipes for soon-to-expire items. With an AI assistant, you could routinely ask, "What needs to be used up in my kitchen?" If your fridge has tracking (via barcodes, RFID tags, or the AI "remembering" what you told it you bought), it can answer, *"Your yogurt and spinach will expire in two days. Here are two recipes this week that use them."* By following those suggestions, you prevent waste and save money. Even without a fancy fridge, you can tell ChatGPT what leftovers or aging produce you have, and it will give you ideas to transform them. A simple prompt like, "I have leftover rice from two days ago and some wilting carrots and peppers – what can I do?" might yield a fried rice or stir-fry recommendation that ensures those bits get eaten, not binned.

AI can also assist in **meal planning with efficiency in mind.** For example, it might plan multiple meals that share ingredients so you can buy in bulk and use everything. It could suggest, "Buy a whole chicken for Monday. Roast it, then on Tuesday use the leftover meat in tacos, and on Wednesday make soup from the bones." This way, one ingredient stretches across meals with zero waste. It's like having a meal planner who always remembers to incorporate the extras. Traditionally, doing that kind of planning is tedious for a person, but an AI can juggle it easily – ensuring that Thursday's recipe uses the other half of the cilantro bunch you bought on Monday, for instance.

Another aspect is **portion planning.** AI can help you cook just the right amount. If you often find yourself with too much leftover (or conversely, not enough and then you have to cook again), you can lean on AI to calculate portions. "ChatGPT, I have 3 adults and 2 kids – how much pasta should I cook so we don't waste any?" It can give a pretty good estimate (e.g. "Cook about 12 ounces of dry pasta"). Over time, as it learns your family's appetite, it might fine-tune those suggestions. Cooking the right quantity means you're not scraping plates into the trash or overstuffing yourself just to avoid waste.

Let's talk about **energy efficiency.** Kitchen appliances can use a lot of energy – ovens, stoves, dishwashers, etc. An AI might schedule or suggest cooking methods that save energy. For example, if you're roasting vegetables, it could advise, "Roast multiple things at once since the oven is already on – perhaps roast tomorrow's potatoes alongside tonight's veggies and just reheat tomorrow, to save energy." Or it might prompt you to use a toaster oven or microwave for a small dish instead of a big oven, if that would be more efficient. If your utility has variable rates (cheaper electricity at certain times), a smart kitchen could even nudge you to bake during the off-peak hours or use a slow cooker in the afternoon rather than the electric oven at dinnertime. These are subtle optimizations that reduce energy consumption (and your bills) without you having to think about it.

Sustainability also means thinking about the source of our food. AI can help us make more **climate-friendly ingredient choices**. For instance, it knows that certain ingredients have a higher carbon footprint (red meat, especially beef, tends to have a large environmental impact, whereas legumes or chicken have less). So if you ask for a "climate-smart dinner", it might steer you toward a vegetarian option or a chicken dish over beef, with an explanation if you're curious. It can also factor seasonality and local availability: *"It's summer and local farmers have a lot of zucchini and tomatoes (low carbon footprint right now), how about a ratatouille?"* Or *"Avocados are not in season and shipping from far away – maybe try a local eggplant spread instead of guacamole this time."* By following these nudges, you end up cooking with ingredients that are fresher, often cheaper, and better for the planet.

There are already tools aiming to **measure the carbon footprint of recipes**, and AI can consolidate that info for you. You could literally ask, "Which of these two recipes is more eco-friendly?" and if the AI has knowledge (or data) on it, it might respond, *"Recipe A uses beef and imported out-of-season veggies, estimated carbon footprint ~10 kg CO_2, while Recipe B is vegetarian with seasonal produce, ~2 kg CO_2. So Recipe B is much more eco-friendly."* Even if you don't get exact numbers, it can qualitatively guide you: *"The lentil soup is a greener choice than the steak."* This empowers you to make informed decisions in line with your values.

Now consider **smart shopping** with AI: By planning intelligently, it prevents the common scenario of buying something, using a bit, and forgetting the rest. It might generate a shopping list for you that's lean and mean – only what you truly will use. And if you allow it to coordinate with others (like maybe a neighbor or community), one day we might see AI helping to **share excess**. For example, if it knows you won't finish a big bunch of bananas before they go bad, it might suggest, "Why not make banana bread and maybe share a loaf with your neighbor?" – turning potential waste into a generous act. There are already community apps for sharing surplus food; AI could dovetail with those, alerting you when you have too much and even helping find takers.

Another sustainable practice is composting. AI could encourage that too: "You're peeling a lot of potatoes – consider composting the peels. I can show you how to start a simple compost bin if you're interested." Or if you have city compost services, "Put those scraps in the green bin for compost pickup." It basically keeps you mindful of not just how you consume food, but how you dispose of waste.

Speaking of disposal, AI can assist in **smart recycling**. Packaging from our kitchen often ends up in landfill because we're not sure what's recyclable. You could ask, "What do I do with this empty oil bottle or this styrofoam tray from the meat?" and it can advise the proper recycling or disposal method (even location-based if it knows your city's rules). That's sustainability beyond food – but part of kitchen eco-consciousness.

There's also water conservation. Some AI-enabled dishwashers already optimize water usage by sensing load and soil level. A general AI assistant could advise you on when to run them (full loads only) or even suggest repurposing water (e.g., *"The water you used to rinse vegetables can be used to water your plants, if you like."*). These little tips might seem small, but together they foster a resource-conscious mindset.

Consider a day with an **AI sustainability coach in the kitchen**: In the morning, it notices a few sad-looking apples in your fruit bowl. It suggests, "Those apples are a bit soft – perfect for applesauce or baking. How about making apple muffins? I'll halve the sugar since the apples are sweet, and we'll use the rest of the apples so they don't go to waste." Great, you make muffins. At lunch, you're about to toss leftover rice from yesterday. The assistant chimes in, "Leftover rice works well for fried rice. You have some carrots and peas; shall we do a quick veggie fried rice? It prevents waste and gives you a nice meal." You do that. By dinner, your fridge is pretty cleared out, and you plan to cook a fresh meal. The AI suggests a menu that uses mostly what you have, just adding a couple fresh items. It also says, "I noticed the oven will be on at 375°F for your chicken – you could roast the broccoli at the same time on another rack, it will save energy and time." After dinner, as you clean up, you ask how to handle the used oil from frying – and it reminds you not to pour it down the drain (bad for environment and plumbing) but to collect it in a jar and dispose of it properly. This day showcases continuous, gentle guidance that results in almost no waste, efficient cooking, and eco-friendly actions, *without* you having to constantly think about it – the AI keeps an eye on those details.

Here are some example prompts and interactions focusing on sustainability:

Zero-waste recipe ideas: "ChatGPT, I have a bunch of vegetable scraps (onion ends, celery tops, etc.). Can I use them for something instead of throwing them out?" – The AI might suggest making a vegetable stock: *"Yes! Keep those scraps and simmer them in water to make a homemade vegetable broth. You can freeze it and use it as soup stock. It's a great way to use scraps and adds flavor to future dishes."*

Eco-friendly swaps: "What's a climate-friendly substitute for beef in this stew?" – The AI could answer, "Try using lentils or mushrooms instead of beef. They provide a hearty texture and flavor with a fraction of the carbon footprint. I can adjust the recipe for lentil stew if you'd like." It educates you on the impact and offers a solution.

Energy-saving tips: "I want to bake cookies and a casserole. How can I save energy doing both?" – "You can bake them together! The casserole at 350°F and cookies at 375°F are close enough; you could bake the cookies towards the end as the oven heats a bit more, or bake everything at 360°F as a compromise (just watch the time). Also, consider using a convection setting if available – it can cook more evenly with slightly lower temp." This way, one oven run handles two tasks.

Food waste audit: "Help me plan next week's meals so I use all the leftovers from this week." – The AI might look at what you have (you tell it or it knows from tracking): *"You have cooked rice, roasted vegetables, and some chicken left. Let's do a stir-fry on Monday using the rice and veggies. The leftover chicken can become tacos on Tuesday. You also mentioned extra herbs – we'll make a pesto or sauce on Wednesday to* *use those up with pasta."* It systematically plans so little remains unused.

AI can even tap into broader food systems. For example, if integrated with a grocery service that sources local produce, it might highlight those choices: *"The app shows local organic zucchini is abundant (and on sale) – shall we incorporate that into the meal plan?"* This supports local farmers and reduces transport emissions.

By following AI's sustainable guidance, you're essentially implementing a lot of the best practices environmental experts recommend, but without needing to be an expert yourself. It lowers the barrier to eco-friendly living. You don't have to remember all the tips – the assistant does, and it mentions them at the right times.

Perhaps one of the nicest outcomes of this is **feeling good about your cooking beyond the plate.** There's a special satisfaction in knowing you made a fantastic soup *and* you used up leftovers *and* you didn't waste water *and* you saved some cash. It makes the cooking experience more holistically rewarding. AI's role is to make those wins easier and more frequent.

As home cooks, by embracing these AI tools, we turn our kitchens into models of sustainability. We become part of the solution to big issues (like food waste and climate change) through the small actions we take each day. And importantly, we do so while still enjoying delicious, satisfying meals – proving that eco-friendly doesn't mean compromising on flavor or fun.

Embracing smart, sustainable, and health-conscious practices with AI might seem like a lot of change. But as we've seen, the technology is here to help make it seamless. How do we as home cooks stay open to these changes and make the most of them? In the next section, **Getting Future-Ready in Your Own Kitchen**, we'll discuss how to cultivate curiosity and adaptability. We'll share practical tips on experimenting with new tools and maintaining a balance between tech and tradition. The future is bright (and green!) for kitchen innovators – and that means you, getting ready to lead the way in your own home.

GETTING FUTURE-READY IN YOUR OWN KITCHEN

We've journeyed through voice assistants, visual AIs, health integrations, and sustainability – all the exciting ways AI is transforming the kitchen. Now the question is: how do *you* prepare and adapt to all this in your everyday life? This section is all about being **future-ready** in your own kitchen. It's less about any one technology and more about mindset and practical steps. We want you to feel *curious* and *confident* about trying new AI tools and integrations as they emerge, rather than overwhelmed. Think of it as cultivating a new set of "digital kitchen skills" alongside your cooking skills. We'll offer tips for staying up-to-date, experimenting with tech in a low-stress way, and blending these innovations into your routine in a manner that suits *you*. The tone remains friendly and supportive – we're in this together, learning and adapting.

Embrace curiosity: The first ingredient in being future-ready is a pinch of curiosity. The fact that you're reading this book means you're already interested in what AI can do for your cooking. Keep that inquisitive spirit alive. When you hear about a new kitchen gadget or app, allow yourself to explore it a bit. You don't have to buy every new device, but read reviews, watch demos, or try a free app version. Maybe your friend gets a smart toaster that perfectly browns bread via an app – ask them about it, or give it a test run next time you visit. The more you familiarize yourself with what's out there, the less intimidating it becomes. Think of new tech like new recipes: at first it might seem complicated, but once you try it, you often find it's not so hard and can even be fun.

Start small and build confidence: You don't need to transform your kitchen overnight. Incorporate one new thing at a time. Perhaps you'll start by using ChatGPT on your phone to plan next week's dinners. Once you're comfortable with that, you might get a smart speaker for the kitchen so you can use voice while cooking. After that, maybe you'll experiment with a smart thermometer that alerts your phone when meat reaches the right temperature. Each small addition will feel less radical as you go, because you're layering it onto a base of experience. It's like learning cooking techniques one by one – first you sauté, then you braise, then you try baking bread, and so on.

Integrate with what you already do: The best tech enhancements will slide into your existing routines. If you always write a grocery list on Sundays, you can involve AI by saying "Hey ChatGPT, here are the meals I'm thinking of – what's my shopping list?" and then use that output. If you normally meal prep on Mondays, perhaps use that time to also explore a new recipe suggested by your AI assistant, or have the AI optimize your prep order (e.g., chop all veggies first, then do the sauces, etc.). By tying new tools to habits you already have, you ensure they actually get used and provide value. Your kitchen shouldn't feel like a tech showroom, it should feel like *your* kitchen – these tools are just new utensils in the drawer.

Stay updated (in an enjoyable way): Technology changes fast. To stay future-ready, it helps to keep a finger on the pulse of new developments – but this doesn't mean drowning in technical journals. Find sources of info that match your style. Maybe it's subscribing to a favorite cooking blog that occasionally features smart kitchen tips, or a YouTube channel where someone reviews kitchen gadgets. Perhaps join a community (online forum or a Facebook group) of foodies who like tech; you'll hear real stories of what works and what doesn't. Even following appliance brands or AI cooking startups on social media can give you tidbits of what's coming. The idea is to make learning continuous and fun. You could treat it like continuing education in your hobby of cooking: each month, discover one new thing, however small – like a new Alexa cooking skill or a nifty hack with your existing appliances. Over time, you'll find you have a rich knowledge base to draw from.

Don't be afraid to ask for help – ironically, often from the AI itself! If you get a new device and aren't sure how to use it fully, you can literally ask ChatGPT or your voice assistant, "How do I best use my [smart blender] for cooking?" It might give you tips and even recipes tailored to that gadget. Many AI-enabled products come with community forums or FAQ chatbots. Take advantage of those.

Remember, part of being future-ready is knowing how to learn. It's completely fine if you don't know how to calibrate your smart oven's settings initially – you learn it, either from the manual, a quick web search, or asking an AI. In the old days we might ask a neighbor or relative about a recipe; now we might ask an online community or an AI about a feature. The spirit of seeking and sharing knowledge remains the same.

Maintain a balance: As you integrate more tech, it's okay (and important) to decide what *not* to use or when to put the tech aside. Future-readiness doesn't mean you must use AI every single time or for everything. It means you have the *option* and the comfort to use it when it helps, and the wisdom to know when you prefer the old-school way. Love your grandmother's way of eyeballing measurements? You can keep doing that, and maybe just use AI to scale the recipe up for a big family gathering. Enjoy the meditative chopping of vegetables in silence? You don't have to have an AI chime in – just because it's there doesn't mean it must talk. You are in control of your kitchen experience. The technology should amplify your enjoyment and creativity, not detract from it. So feel free to use it on your terms. Being future-ready also means setting boundaries with tech – for example, disabling voice assistants during family dinner time so that human conversation prevails. Empowerment means *you* decide how AI joins your kitchen life.

Privacy and security: A practical aspect of embracing connected tech is making sure your setup is secure and your privacy is respected. As you adopt new devices or apps, take a moment to review settings. Use strong passwords for your Wi-Fi and any accounts. Check if your smart fridge or oven has firmware updates (many will update automatically if connected to the internet). All these devices collect data to function – mostly harmless stuff like temperature logs or what recipes you looked at – but be aware of what's shared. Stick to reputable brands or services that have clear privacy policies. For instance, if you use an AI camera for cooking guidance, ensure it isn't inadvertently streaming video to the cloud unless you want it to. Most of this is just following setup guides and using common sense, but it's worth mentioning: being future-ready means being savvy about tech responsibilities too. Think of it as kitchen safety in the digital age – just like you wouldn't leave the stove on unattended, don't leave your IoT devices on default passwords or outdated software. It's all part of good kitchen hygiene.

Teaching and involving others: As you become comfortable with AI in the kitchen, you can actually lead the way for your family and friends. Show your kids how to use the voice assistant to convert measurements (they might find it cool and it reinforces math skills). Or involve your partner by saying, "Hey, let's plan the menu together with this new app – it even finds recipes that match our diet." If you have older relatives who are less tech-inclined but love cooking, maybe demonstrate one helpful tool at a time (like dictating a recipe to an assistant so they don't have to squint at a book). The key is to share the benefits without forcing it. When others see you effortlessly asking "Jarvis" (or whatever you name your AI) to stir the pot (some smart induction cooktops actually stir automatically on command!), they might be intrigued and want to try too. By empowering others around you, you create a supportive mini-community that embraces these advancements. You can swap notes on what works or troubleshoot together – "Did the AI also give you a weird salt measurement? Oh, we should report that bug or adjust how we ask."

Mindset of adaptability: Technology will keep evolving. Five years from now, there may be new tools we haven't even imagined. Being future-ready isn't about predicting exactly what will come – it's about being adaptable so you can smoothly ride the wave of change. This means keeping an open mind. Maybe one day you'll 3D-print your dinner or use a kitchen robot arm – who knows! If so, you'll approach it the same way we've done everything in this chapter: with curiosity, a sense of fun, and a focus on practical benefit. And if something doesn't catch on (remember those one-purpose gimmicky appliances that end up in the yard sale), that's okay too. You'll try things, keep what works, and politely pass on what doesn't. Every cook's kitchen will look a bit different based on personal preference, and AI can cater to that.

One helpful practice is to occasionally reflect: *how is this new tech helping me?* If the answer is, it saves me time, reduces stress, teaches me something, or makes cooking more enjoyable, great! If not, maybe it's not the right tool for you, or not yet mature enough. For example, if you find that a recipe AI keeps giving you recipes that don't quite suit your taste, you might decide to use it just for inspiration but still rely on your own tweaks or trusted cookbooks. That's perfectly fine. The goal of being future-ready isn't to replace everything that came before, but to *enhance* and *expand* your capabilities.

Celebrate your progress: Don't forget to pat yourself on the back for learning new tricks. The kitchen is traditionally a place of continuous learning (we're always picking up a new recipe or technique). Adding digital skills is just an extension of that. The first time you successfully have ChatGPT generate a family meal plan that everyone loves, cheer for yourself! Or when you fix an appliance issue by asking your SmartHQ assistant rather than calling a repair person, enjoy that empowerment (and perhaps the money saved on a service call). Each step you take makes you a more resilient and versatile home cook.

Let's consider some **practical prompts or exercises** to become more future-ready:

Explore a Feature: *"ChatGPT, what's one kitchen technology I might enjoy learning about?"* – If you ask this, the AI might suggest something like smart sous-vide cookers or a particular cooking app, explaining its benefits. You could then decide to explore that suggestion further, just to keep expanding your horizons.

Troubleshoot with AI: Next time you have a kitchen problem (burnt sauce, oven not heating properly, etc.), try asking an AI for help before searching randomly online. For instance: *"My cake collapsed in the middle. Why might that be?"* The AI might explain common reasons (like under-baking or too much leavening) and how to fix it next time. This builds your trust in using AI as a resource.

Mix Tradition with Tech: Take a beloved family recipe and see how AI might modernize it. *"Here's my grandma's stew recipe [you list it]. Can you make it quicker or suggest a pressure cooker version?"* – The AI could maintain the essence but give you a 30-minute Instant Pot adaptation. Try it side by side with the original sometime and compare – it can be a fun experiment that also teaches you about different cooking methods.

Keep Learning: Maybe set a small goal, like *"Every month, try one new AI-assisted cooking tool or feature."* It could be using the grocery app's new AR scanner in January, trying a voice recipe skill in February, maybe linking your fitness app to a meal planner in March, and so on. By the end of the year, you'll have a repertoire of tech skills added to your cooking arsenal.

Being future-ready is ultimately about **confidence and adaptability**. Remember how you felt when you first learned to cook something complicated, like a Thanksgiving turkey or baking bread? At first, it might have been daunting, but after doing it (maybe a couple of times), you likely felt accomplished and no longer intimidated by it. It becomes part of what you can do. The same goes for integrating AI and new tech. The first few times you talk to a stove or have an AI critique your chopping, it might feel odd. But soon it will just be another part of the experience, and you'll take it in stride.

One final element: **stay human-centric**. The heart of cooking is love, creativity, and sharing. Future-ready means using AI to amplify those human elements, not to overshadow them. Use these tools to free up time so you can enjoy dinner with your family a bit longer, or to give you confidence to invite friends over because you know your smart kitchen has your back in delivering a great meal. The technology is impressive, but *you* are still the chef and the decision-maker. AI provides options and support; you provide the heart and soul in the food. Keep that partnership in mind, and you'll navigate the future of cooking with grace.

As we wrap up this section, reflect on how far you've come – not just in reading this chapter, but as a cook over the years. Adapting to new things is something you've done all along (new ingredients, new appliances, new diets, etc.). AI is just another new thing – a very powerful, sometimes surprising thing – but one that ultimately bends to your needs. Be bold in trying it, be wise in how you use it, and stay grounded in the joy of cooking. With that mindset, you're more than ready for whatever the smart kitchen of tomorrow brings.

You've now equipped yourself with knowledge and a forward-looking attitude that will serve you well. As we move to the final part of this chapter, we want to express our gratitude for joining us on this exploration. In the next section, **A Note of Thanks and What's Next**, we'll share a heartfelt thank-you and talk about how the conversation can continue beyond this book – including ways you can connect with us and a community of like-minded home cooks as we all journey into this exciting future together.

A NOTE OF THANKS AND WHAT'S NEXT

As we come to the end of this chapter – and indeed, to the culmination of *How to Use ChatGPT in the Kitchen* – we want to take a moment to say **thank you.** Thank you for sticking with us through this exploration of the smart kitchen ahead. Your willingness to dive into new ideas, to imagine possibilities, and to try out the examples means the world to us. We wrote this book to empower and inspire home cooks, and you've been exactly the curious, open-hearted cook we hoped to reach. By embracing topics like voice assistants, AI vision, wellness tech, and sustainability, you're not only improving your own kitchen life – you're also helping shape the future of cooking for everyone. **Home cooks like you are the true pioneers** of the smart kitchen era, because your feedback and creativity will guide how these technologies evolve.

Over the course of this chapter, you've learned how ChatGPT and AI can become your kitchen companions – assisting with everything from real-time recipe help to managing your grocery list in planet-friendly ways. Let's quickly recap what we've covered: We started by looking at the **Rise of the Smart Kitchen**, seeing how appliances are getting brainier and how ChatGPT-style intelligence is integrating into ovens, fridges, and more to help in real time. Then we explored **Voice-Activated Cooking**, discovering the ease of hands-free assistance and conversational recipe guidance. In **Cooking with**

Cameras and AR, we peered into the future where AI can actually see and provide visual cues, making cooking even more intuitive. We connected our kitchen to our bodies in **Wearables and Wellness**, learning how our health data can tailor our meal choices and routines for better living. We tackled the planet-conscious side in **AI-Powered Food Sustainability**, finding out how AI can help us waste less and choose more eco-friendly ways to cook. And just now in **Getting Future-Ready in Your Own Kitchen**, we talked about mindset and practical steps for adapting to all this with confidence and balance.

That's a lot of ground covered! If it feels a bit overwhelming, remember that you don't have to implement everything at once (or at all). The goal is to give you insight into what's possible and coming, so you can pick and choose what resonates with you. Even if you take away just one or two ideas that make your cooking easier or more enjoyable, that's a win. Maybe you're excited to try using your voice assistant more often for recipes, or perhaps you're intrigued by the idea of reducing food waste with the help of AI meal plans. Whatever it is, we encourage you to **experiment and have fun**. Treat the kitchen as your playground, with AI as a helpful playmate.

Looking ahead, the world of AI and cooking will continue to grow. New gadgets will hit the market, AI models will get smarter (and faster), and integration between devices will become more seamless. You, as a forward-thinking home cook, will always have new frontiers to explore. But we hope that after this chapter, you feel *prepared and even excited* for that journey. The kitchen has always been a place of innovation – from fire, to stoves, to microwaves, and now to AI assistants – yet it remains a place of comfort, creativity, and connection. That essence won't change. You'll still pour love into your dishes; you'll just have some high-tech sous-chefs to help when you want them.

We also want to extend an invitation: **let's continue the conversation.** The end of this book is not the end of your learning (nor ours!). We, the authors, would love to hear about your experiences as you start using ChatGPT or any AI in your kitchen. Did you come up with a particularly clever prompt that made your life easier? Did you encounter challenges or funny moments with a voice assistant? What tech are you excited about, or what would you love to see invented? Your insights can help fellow readers and even guide future editions of this work.

We encourage you to reach out and connect with us on LinkedIn (or your preferred platform). We're building a community of AI-empowered home cooks, and your voice is important in it. Share your successes, your recipes, your questions – and even your failures (we all burn things now and then, even with AI, and that's okay!). By connecting, we can learn from each other and push this field forward in a way that truly serves users. Consider this an open invitation to message us or tag us in your posts about smart cooking adventures. We are genuinely excited to hear from you and continue learning together. Who knows – perhaps your idea or feedback will spark the next chapter (pun intended) in this ever-evolving story of AI in the kitchen.

Finally, a heartfelt thanks for allowing us to be part of your kitchen for these chapters. Writing this book and imagining these scenarios has been a joy for us, but the real reward is knowing it's in the hands of passionate cooks like you. Your time and attention are precious, and we're honored that you spent them with us. We hope you feel the **friendly, supportive spirit** we aimed to convey, and that you carry that positivity forward. As you cook your next meal – whether it's with high-tech help or just a wooden spoon and your grandma's recipe – know that you have a whole community (and some smart AIs) rooting for your success.

The smart kitchen ahead is bright. It's full of innovation, yes, but more importantly, it's full of opportunities for richer cooking experiences and more meaningful connections – to our food, our health, our environment, and each other. You are now equipped to stride into that future, spatula in one hand and smartphone (or smart-whatever) in the other, ready to whip up magic. We can't wait to see what you'll do.

Happy cooking, and welcome to the future!

ABOUT THE AUTHORS

Marc Champagne (https://www.linkedin.com/in/marc-champagne-a573b417/) brings more than twenty-five years of experience in the restaurant and hospitality world, working behind the scenes to help new locations open smoothly, existing kitchens operate efficiently, and teams deliver great guest experiences. Throughout his career, he has collaborated closely with culinary leaders, operations teams, and foodservice professionals - giving him a front-row seat to how restaurants think about ingredients, workflow, menu design, and the craft of serving great food.

That background shaped his approach to home cooking. Marc has always appreciated the blend of creativity and discipline that makes a kitchen run well, and he brings that same mindset into his own. He's spent years helping restaurants turn concepts into reality, and he's learned that the right tools, used the right way, can make all the difference.

That's why AI caught his attention. As he began experimenting with ChatGPT, Marc found that it could bring many of the same advantages he saw in professional kitchens: better planning, clearer instructions, smarter substitutions, and the confidence to try new things without the stress. It didn't take long for him to see how AI could help everyday cooks enjoy the process more and get consistently better results.

In Cook Smarter with ChatGPT, Marc shares that practical, hospitality-driven perspective. He understands what makes a meal work, what makes a process efficient, and what makes cooking enjoyable—even for people who don't consider themselves "naturals" in the kitchen. His goal is simple: help readers bring a little restaurant-level clarity and creativity to their home cooking, powered by the ease and flexibility of AI.

When he's not supporting hospitality teams or fine-tuning AI-assisted recipes, Marc enjoys exploring new restaurants, traveling, and spending time with his family.

Andy Forbes (https://www.linkedin.com/in/andyforbes/) has spent years helping organizations harness the power of Salesforce and more recently of artificial intelligence. By day, he works guiding companies through the shift to CRM+AI driven operations. By night, he applies the same curiosity and problem-solving mindset to his own kitchen.

While his wife is the true culinary talent in the family, Andy has used AI to elevate his cooking well beyond where he ever expected it to go. From learning new techniques to designing meals around whatever ingredients happen to be in the fridge, he discovered that tools like ChatGPT can make everyday cooking simpler, more creative, and far more accessible for anyone—especially people who don't consider themselves natural cooks.

That journey inspired this book. Andy believes that if AI can help him become a more confident, capable home cook, it can help anyone. His goal is to show readers how to use AI not just as a recipe generator, but as a flexible, supportive kitchen companion that meets them exactly where they are, whether they're experimenting with a new dish, planning meals for the week, or just trying to get a decent dinner on the table after a long day.

When he's not writing or building AI-powered solutions, Andy can be found testing new dishes, traveling with his wife, refining his collection of cooking prompts, and exploring all the ways AI can enrich everyday life.

Made in the USA
Monee, IL
05 November 2026

67914382R10243